The Many Dimensions of Poverty

The Many Dimensions of Poverty

Edited by

Nanak Kakwani
University of Sydney
Former Director, International Poverty Centre, Brazil

and

Jacques Silber
Bar-Ilan University, Israel

UNDP financial support to the International Poverty Centre for holding the International Conference on 'The Many Dimensions of Poverty' and the preparation of the papers in this volume is gratefully acknowledged.

First published 2007 by
PALGRAVE MACMILLAN
Houndmills, Basingstoke, Hampshire RG21 6XS and
175 Fifth Avenue, New York, N.Y. 10010
Companies and representatives throughout the world

PALGRAVE MACMILLAN is the global academic imprint of the Palgrave Macmillan division of St. Martin's Press, LLC and of Palgrave Macmillan Ltd. Macmillan® is a registered trademark in the United States, United Kingdom and other countries. Palgrave is a registered trademark in the European Union and other countries.

ISBN-13: 978-0-230-00490-0   hardback
ISBN-10: 0-230-00490-3   hardback

This book is printed on paper suitable for recycling and made from fully managed and sustained forest sources. Logging, pulping and manufacturing processes are expected to conform to the environmental regulations of the country of origin.

A catalogue record for this book is available from the British Library.

Library of Congress Cataloging-in-Publication Data
The many dimensions of poverty / edited by Nanak Kakwani and Jacques

  Silber.
    p. cm.
  Papers originally presented at an international conference in
    Brasilia on August 29–31, 2005.
  Includes bibliographical references and index.
  ISBN 0-230-00490-3 (alk. paper)
    1. Poverty – Congresses.   2. Public welfare – Congresses.   I. Kakwani,
Nanak. II. Silber, Jacques.
  HC79.P6M355 2007
  339.4'6 — dc22   2007022328

10   9   8   7   6   5   4   3   2   1
16   15   14   13   12   11   10   09   08   07

Printed and bound in Great Britain by
Antony Rowe Ltd, Chippenham and Eastbourne

Contents

List of Tables and Figures

Tables

Figures

Foreword

The International Poverty Centre (IPC) is one of the three global thematic facilities established by the United Nations Development Program (UNDP) to bring knowledge-based development services closer to country partners around the world. The IPC has been built on a partnership between UNDP and the Government of Brazil's Institute of Applied Economic Research (IPEA). Its main goals are to expand the knowledge and capacity of developing countries to design and implement effective human development policies, to facilitate knowledge sharing through South – South cooperation for the reduction of poverty and to promote global debates to improve our understanding of development and the achievements of the Millennium Development Goals.

The IPC, which is almost three years old, is fully immersed in a global agenda aiming at reducing poverty. It took a major initiative in organizing an international conference on 'The Many Dimensions of Poverty', which took place in Brasilia on 29–31 August 2005. More than forty papers were presented by participants from all parts of the world. Although the majority of papers were of very high quality and often reported on very original research, the IPC could only publish 26 selected papers in two books. The present book, entitled *Many Dimensions of Poverty*, is mainly focused on conceptual issues relating to the multidimensional nature of poverty, while the second book, which is more applied, presents various quantitative approaches to the measurement of multidimensional poverty. The topics covered in the two books are not entirely mutually exclusive and, as expected, some overlap of issues could not be avoided.

The last three decades have indeed witnessed a blossoming of research on poverty. The serious and also rigorous research on poverty began to take place in the 1970s following Amartya Sen's 1976 seminal paper on poverty measurement. Most of this research has been focusing on income or consumption-based poverty measures. With the publication of the UNDP's Human Development Index in 1990, there has, however, been a clear shift towards a multidimensional approach to poverty analysis. Poverty is now viewed as multifaceted, reflecting deprivation suffered by people in many aspects of life such as unemployment, ill-health, malnutrition, inadequate shelter, lack of education, vulnerability, powerlessness, social exclusion and so on.

Yet again Amartya Sen's (1985, 1992) seminal work on functionings and capabilities has been the most influential in defining poverty in a multidimensional framework. The capability approach provides the most logical and comprehensive framework to understand multidimensional poverty. A functioning is an achievement, and a capability is the ability to achieve. Thus, functionings are directly related to what life people actually lead, whereas capabilities are connected with the freedom people have in choice of life or functionings. According to this approach, poverty is viewed in terms of capability deprivation. An individual is defined as poor if he or she lacks basic capabilities. To reduce poverty, the capability approach advocates the expansion of people's basic capabilities. The income approach on the other hand advocates increasing the incomes of those who are below the poverty line. Thus, policies aimed at reducing multidimensional poverty have to be holistic, looking at several kinds of deprivations simultaneously.

It must be emphasized that implementing a multidimensional approach to poverty is a complex undertaking. In this volume, Thorbecke has argued that 'most of the remaining unresolved issues in poverty analysis are related directly or indirectly to the multidimensional nature and dynamics of poverty'. In order to achieve Millennium Development Goals, it is necessary to better identify and understand the various dimensions of poverty, which interact over time and space. This book is the first one to provide the reader with the most updated research on multidimensional poverty.

The shift of emphasis from a unidimensional to a multidimensional approach to poverty offered also the opportunity to conceptualize poverty from different perspectives. Poverty is now increasingly viewed as multidisciplinary. Part I of the book, 'Different Disciplines, Diverse Perspectives', presents five perspectives on the many dimensions of poverty, giving the viewpoint of five disciplines – namely, economics, sociology, anthropology, psychology and institutional economics. Part II 'On Poverty and Freedom', brings out the linkage between poverty and the concept of freedom, as articulated by Amartya Sen, in terms of capabilities that are valuable to people. Part III of the book, 'Extending the Concept of Multidimensional Poverty', looks at two topics on which important work has appeared in recent years: chronic poverty and vulnerability. Finally Part IV, 'Critical Policy Issues', examines several critical issues which policy makers dealing with poverty have been facing: the political economy of poverty alleviation and the pro-poorness of government programs.

In my view, this book on 'The Many Dimensions of Poverty' provides one of the most comprehensive reviews of current thinking on multidimensional poverty. It is a joint contribution of many scholars with international reputation. It should have an impact on how we view poverty and will certainly encourage additional multidisciplinary research on poverty.

NORA LUSTIG
SHAPIRO VISITING PROFESSOR
ELLIOTT SCHOOL OF
INTERNATIONAL AFFAIRS
GEORGE WASHINGTON UNIVERSITY
FORMER DIRECTOR, POVERTY GROUP
BUREAU OF DEVELOPMENT POLICY
UNITED NATIONS DEVELOPMENT PROGRAM

Preface

In recent decades, Poverty reduction has become an overriding goal of development policy. To inform policy, research on poverty has focused on income- or consumption-based poverty measures. But the most important development of poverty research in recent years is certainly the shift of emphasis from a uni- to a multidimensional approach to poverty. Poverty is now defined as a human condition that reflects failures in many dimensions of human life such as hunger, ill health, malnutrition, unemployment, inadequate shelter, lack of education, vulnerability, powerlessness, social exclusion and so on. Poverty is not only multidimensional but also multidisciplinary.

Recognising the importance of multidimensional and multidisciplinary nature of poverty, the International Poverty Centre took a major initiative in organizing an international conference on 'The Many Dimensions of Poverty', which took place in Brasilia on 29–31 August 2005. The initial idea of holding such a conference came from Professor Jacques Silber and I, as the Director of the International Poverty Centre, implemented the idea.

I wish to express my gratitude to Jacques, who put enormous efforts in bringing together a group of about fifty internationally renowned scholars in the field. More than forty papers were presented by participants from all parts of the world. Although the majority of papers were of very high quality and often reported on very original research, we could only publish 26 selected papers in two books. The present book, entitled 'The Many Dimensions of Poverty', is focused mainly on conceptual issues relating to the multidimensional nature of poverty, while the second book, which is more applied, presents various quantitative approaches to the measurement of multidimensional poverty.

The UNDP requires that all its publications be peer reviewed. I am grateful to Professor Stephan Klasen for providing an excellent overall review of this book. He made very thoughtful comments on every paper. The earlier versions of the papers presented at the conference have been revised in the light of comments made by the reviewer.

In his review, Professor Klasen writes that the strength of the book is that it can really become one of the central reference works on poverty research in developing countries from a multidisciplinary but always policy-oriented perspective. So he warmly welcomed this book and supported its publication.

The organization of an international conference is a major undertaking. I am indeed grateful to many people, who put wholehearted efforts in the organization of the conference on 'Many Dimensions of Poverty'. I owe particular thanks to Eduardo Zepeda, Sandra Viergever, Marcelo Medeiros, Hyun Son, Fabiane Florencio, Fabio Veras, Rafael Osorio, Andre Lyra, Francisco Filho, Joana Costa, Alexandre Chaves and Dimitri Silva. I am particularly grateful to Roberto Astorino who provided excellent expert assistance in taking care of the technical aspects of the book.

Finally, I express my gratitude to Nora Lustig and Terry McKinley for supporting the publication of this book.

NANAK KAKWANI

List of Contributors

Sabina Alkire, University of Oxford, Oxford, UK.

Ruth Alsop, The World Bank, Washington DC, USA.

Sara Berry, Johns Hopkins University, Baltimore, MD, USA.

Cesar Calvo, Universidad de Piura, Peru.

Robert Chambers, University of Sussex, Brighton, UK.

Stefan Dercon, University of Oxford, Oxford, UK.

David B. Grusky, Stanford University, Stanford, CA, USA.

David Hulme, University of Manchester, Manchester, UK.

Andrew McKay, University of Sussex, Falmer, Brighton, UK.

Marcelo Côrtes Neri, Getúlio Vargas Foundation (FGV) and Brazilian Institute of Economics, Rio de Janeiro, Brazil.

Joaquina Palomar Lever, Iberoamerican University, Mexico, DF, Mexico.

Linda Jansen Van Rensburg, North-West University, South Africa.

Alice Sindzingre, National Centre for Scientific Research (CNRS), Paris, and School of Oriental and African Studies, University of London, London, UK.

Hyun Son, Asian Development Bank, Manila, The Philippines.

Erik Thorbecke, Cornell University, Ithaca, NY, USA.

Marcelo Casal Xerez, Getúlio Vargas Foundation (FGV) and Brazilian Ministry of Finance, Rio de Janeiro, Brazil.

Kim A. Weeden, Cornell University, Ithaca, NY, USA.

Introduction

Nanak Kakwani and Jacques Silber

On 29–31 August 2005 an international Conference on *The Many Dimensions of Poverty* took place in Brasilia. This conference was organized by the International Poverty Centre (IPC), one of the three global thematic facilities created by the United Nations Development Programme (UNDP) to bring knowledge-based development services closer to country partners around the world. The present book brings together updated versions of 13 of the papers that were presented at this conference.

Although there had been studies of poverty for more than 100 years, starting eventually with the work of Charles Booth on *Life and Labour of the People in London*, which appeared in 1889 and that of Seebohm Rowntree on *Poverty, A Study of Town Life*, published in 1901, the systematic analysis of poverty, and especially of the ways to measure it, became an important topic of research among economists only in the late 1970s, following the publication of Amartya Sen's (1976) famous article. In this study Sen stressed that poverty analysis requires two stages –, that of identifying the poor and that of aggregating the information into a unique measure of poverty. Most of the numerous works that followed Sen's path-breaking study took a unidimensional approach to poverty measurement, whether based on income or consumption data.

Identifying the poor requires determining a poverty line so that those individuals or households who are below the poverty line are 'labelled' as poor. But as is well-known, there is no unique way of defining a poverty line. One can take an 'absolute approach' where the poverty line implies mainly defining a basket of goods and services assumed to fulfil the basic needs of people in terms of food, clothing, shelter, etc... Such an approach is evidently relevant in poor countries where basic needs are not met by many people. One can, however, also take a 'relative approach' to poverty measurement by deciding that the poverty line will be some fraction of the mean or median income and such a point of view is clearly more adapted to developed countries because it assumes that poverty exists when one is far from being able to have the standard of living of the average citizen in the population. Some economists have even suggested defining the poverty line on the basis of subjective questions on the level of satisfaction of individuals or households with their income or standard of living, and techniques have been proposed to translate such questions into an actual poverty line. There is thus no unique way of determining a poverty line and the choice of the poverty line depends on the objective that one wants to achieve.

The second stage of unidimensional poverty analysis implies, as mentioned before, aggregating the information on each household or individual into an overall measure of poverty. But actually this is a very difficult task because aggregate measures can look at different aspects of poverty. Economists Stephen Jenkins and

Peter Lambert have in fact launched the expression 'The Three I's of Poverty' that refer to three different aspects of unidimensional poverty measurement:

- the 'Incidence' of poverty which is really the proportion of poor in the population and is measured by what is called the headcount ratio
- the 'Intensity' of poverty, a concept which asks the question 'how far on average is the income of the poor from the poverty line?' and this intensity is generally measured by what is known as the income-gap ratio
- the 'Inequality' (or 'Severity') of poverty, a notion that concerns the degree of the inequality of a truncated distribution of income (expenditures) that is limited to those considered as poor and hence whose income (or expenditures) is below the poverty line.

Proposals have been made to combine these three aspects of poverty into a unique indicator and this is really the idea that lies behind Sen's famous poverty index or the well-known FGT poverty index (FGT referring to its inventors, Foster, Greer and Thorbecke). It should, however, be clear that by ending up with a unique measure one loses information.

Identifying the poor and aggregating information on them is, however, not the end of the story. In recent years attention has been drawn to other important aspects of unidimensional poverty analysis, as will be mentioned later. But the most important development of poverty research in recent years is certainly the shift of emphasis from a uni- to a multidimensional approach to poverty. Conceptualizing the multiple facets of poverty is however not an easy task.

The first part of the present book presents five different perspectives on the many dimensions of poverty, taken by five different disciplines. Thorbecke's contribution (Chapter 1) gives the point of view of economists. For the author, implementing a multidimensional approach to poverty is a complex undertaking because, among other reasons, one has to define a list of relevant attributes to be taken into account and decide how much weight to give to each of these dimensions. For Thorbecke, the most comprehensive starting point in an attempt to capture the concept of multidimensional poverty is Sen's 'capabilities and functionings' framework. In order to function, an individual requires a minimum level of well-being contributed by a set of attributes and the standard way to determine whether an individual is above or below the poverty threshold is income. The drawback of the income approach is that some (non-monetary) attributes cannot be purchased because markets do not exist or operate imperfectly so that prices do not reflect the utility weights households assign to these attributes. Using Income as the sole indicator of well-being is limited as it does not incorporate such key dimensions of poverty as life expectancy (longevity), literacy, the provision of public goods, freedom and security.

The multidimensional approach also suffers from several difficulties, among which the most serious is the estimation of the interactions between attributes. Attributes can be either substitutes or complements. If the dimensions of poverty are substitutes it implies that an individual can trade off one attribute for another (say more food for less shelter) and remain at the same level of well-being. In contrast, if attributes are complements, an increase in the amount of one raises the marginal utility of the other (more education increases the present discounted value of the future stream of income).

This difficult combination of attributes into the utility space explains, says Thorbecke, why the empirical applications attempting to measure multidimensional poverty have limited themselves until now to dealing with usually two dimensions. He stressed also the fact that dimensions of well-being can be substitutes in the short run while being complementary and re-enforcing in the long run because of a path-dependence between the form poverty takes today and future poverty outcomes.

The author concludes by stating his belief that although the economic literature on multidimensional poverty measures has made considerable progress in clarifying the concept of functioning and in identifying many of the related theoretical issues there are still too many unresolved questions left to consider seriously using multidimensional measures in any truly operational sense.

Chapter 2 takes a different approach. Written by sociologists David Grusky and Kim Weeden, it argues that recent years have seen some convergence between economists and sociologists working in the field of inequality and poverty. On the one hand economists have come to doubt the traditional 'income paradigm' that equates inequality and poverty with income inequality and poverty whereas, on the other, sociologists have grown more and more sceptical of the usefulness of the so-called 'class paradigm' to study inequality and poverty. The authors suggest that progress in the field depends on converting such disciplinary priors into testable hypotheses about the structure and form of poverty. They contend that such tests are best conducted within the multidimensional poverty space, but such an approach still lacks a compelling methodological platform. Latent class modelling, which has now been generalized to accommodate mixed-mode data, provides precisely the platform needed to test disciplinary assumptions about the structure of poverty and to monitor changes in the shape and form of poverty. Although much is known about trends in the degree of poverty, knowledge is scarcer about trends in its form; and the form of poverty may be just as consequential as the amount in understanding how it is experienced and how it may develop. For Grusky and Weeden, it is necessary to move beyond simplistic measurements of headcounts and treat distributional issues of inequality and poverty with the same seriousness that is accorded measurements of total economic activity and output.

Sara Berry, an anthropologist, is the author of the third chapter of this book. She argues that anthropologists have contributed to the study of poverty in a variety of ways, although usually as a corollary of ethnographic research, rather than a primary focus of inquiry. Ethnographic inquiry is in fact relevant both for questions of method – what to count, what (and what not) to measure and how – and for professional and popular debates about how poverty occurs, whom it affects, and what ought to be done about it. For Berry, quantitative measurement and ethnographic observation are both complementary and conflicting modes of representing social reality and, together, they provide insights into multidimensional aspects of poverty that neither method yields alone. To illustrate, the chapter emphasizes a few themes like time and temporality, institutions, and social relationships, using examples from ethnographic writings on Africa. It thus suggests ways in which ethnographic inquiry can qualify or expand understandings of poverty based on quantitative analysis.

The author of Chapter 4, Alice Sindzingre, analyses multidimensional poverty through the prism of the new institutional economics and evolutionary perspectives. She argues that institutions and norms are constitutive of the various dimensions of poverty and of the relationship between them. First, institutions may determine achievements and access to income, health and other dimensions. Secondly, institutions and norms are cognitive mechanisms. They both determine individual perceptions and result from them. They therefore determine mental models and behaviour regarding the capacity to escape poverty. Sindzingre stresses that poverty is maintained by mental representations that perpetuate poverty because these perpetuate powerlessness. The poor may not even consider institutions that could help them to escape poverty. The poor lack incentives to claim their rights because of lack of bargaining power and asymmetries of information. They lack incentives to participate in the market institutions and in the political institutions that could help them escape poverty, and they also lack the incentive to save, which in turn generates poverty traps and polarized societies. These mechanisms work intergenerationally because the poor not only lack incentives to escape poverty but also transmit this lack of incentives to their children (their main assets), who will themselves lack the incentives, education or health that could incite them to participate in institutions or claim their rights. One should not forget that trust is based on expectations that the others are worthy of trust or are altruistic: trust in institutions is a condition for the functioning of institutions, while in an endogenous way well-functioning institutions create trust in others and reinforce other-regarding behaviour. In her chapter Sindzingre borrowed concepts from development economics, evolutionary institutionalism and psychology. She justly contends that the bridging of these disciplines is an increasingly promising field of research and that such a cross-conceptualization should contribute to a better understanding of the multidimensionality of poverty.

In Chapter 5 Joaquina Palomar Lever adopts a psychological viewpoint. For her the psychological dimension cannot be ignored when considering the multidimensional nature of poverty. Psychological research has thus shown that stress derived from economic hardship affects marital relations, making it less likely that couples will express love, warmth, support and respect to each other. As a consequence they are less able to solve their problems in common and this increases the level of hostility and stress between them. They then tend to less socialize with their children and often to show hostility toward their children's needs, leading to a decline in parent–child relationships Poverty has also been associated with numerous psychological variables such as depression, anxiety, self-esteem, strategies for coping with stress, achievement motivation, perception of social support, and locus of control, among others. For Palomar Lever, it is therefore imperative that psychosocial elements be considered in the designing of public policies oriented toward providing support to the most vulnerable groups in the population.

The second part of the book is devoted mainly to the link between poverty and the concept of freedom. This connection in fact underlies Sen's capability theory. The capability approach proposes that social arrangements should be primarily evaluated according to the extent of freedom people have to promote or achieve 'functionings' they value. Whereas resources refer to the material goods and services which confer capability on individuals –, that is, provide them with the capacity to do things – the concept of 'functionings' captures the notion of how well individuals are functioning as human beings. Economists have traditionally identified well-being with market command over goods, thus, confounding the 'state' of a person – well-being – with the extent of his or her possessions – being well off. A functioning, on the contrary, is an achievement of a person – what she manages to do or to be – and reflects a part of the 'state' of that person. In other words, according to Sen, the mere command over commodities cannot determine the valuation of the goodness of the life that one can lead for 'the need of commodities for any specified achievement of living conditions may vary greatly with various physiological, social, cultural and other contingent features'. Commodity command is simply a means to the end of well-being.

It should be stressed that the capability approach does not assume that one set of domains of poverty is relevant for all evaluative exercises. Sen himself has refused to give a list of such domains but others, such as Martha Nussbaum, have done so. One should also emphasize that the capability approach does not focus only on 'functionings' and stresses also the idea of process freedom or agency. It may not be necessary to measure freedoms, but it is necessary to consider them.

Sen's capability approach is not, however, the only possible framework for analysing the dimensions of poverty. In a recent survey, Sabina Alkire, the author of Chapter 6, reviewed many other approaches. This chapter is devoted, however, to the capability approach. Alkire first locates the topic of multidimensional poverty with respect to the capability approach and then addresses two central issues. First, if multidimensional poverty measures are used to represent capability poverty directly, how can one identify the relevant domains for a particular exercise? Further, how can direct multidimensional poverty measures give adequate consideration to people's freedoms, which form a constitutive component of the capability approach? In examining these questions, the chapter draws upon some multidimensional studies which have advanced the measurement of capability.

The importance in the field of development of the idea of freedom is examined in more details in Chapter 7, which is devoted to the concept of empowerment. For Ruth Alsop, the author of this chapter, empowerment is to be considered as both a goal and driver of development. But what is empowerment? For Alsop empowerment is 'enhancing an individual's or group's capacity to make purposive choice and transform that choice into desired actions and outcomes'. Using the concepts of asset-based agency and institution-based opportunity structure, she suggests that investments in both can increase people's capacity to make effective choices and contribute to poverty reduction. This chapter draws on evidence of the relationship between empowerment and poverty outcomes from five country case studies. Thus in Brazil participatory budgeting increased the flow of information about municipal governance and seemed to lead to a reduction of extreme poverty. In Ethiopia, participation to the Women's Development Initiatives Project (WDIP) improved economic outcomes and power for women to make decisions in their household and break restrictive norms. Similar results were obtained in Nepal in so far as a greater empowerment of women reduced domestic violence and improved, for example, health seeking behaviour. In fact, increases in agency through the accumulation of assets such as education, information, psychological assets and income or consumption assets, are often (but not always) associated with changes in gender-based inequalities as well as with influencing other traditional norms such as 'untouchability' in India and Nepal.

Related to this concept of empowerment is the need to pay more attention to incorporating poor people's views about poverty when formulating public policies. This is in fact the topic of Chapter 8 which is devoted to the ideas of participation, pluralism and perceptions of poverty. The author, Robert Chambers, starts by stressing how in the past decade and a half we have come a long way in the invention, evolution and spread of participatory approaches and methods and their contributions to understanding poverty. He then argues that participation goes with changing power relations and behaviours, and sharing, while pluralism goes with openness, mutual learning, eclectic improvisation and creativity. Perceptions of poverty are both those of professionals and of people living in poverty. The primary role of professionals is hence to convene, facilitate, learn and later communicate. The chapter ends by noting that it is only then that the diversity of deprivations becomes more evident as well as the many forms that multidimensional poverty can take. The potentials for combining these to enhance the well-being of those who suffer multiple deprivations have thus scarcely begun to be tapped. As stressed by Caroline Robb (2002) in her review of participatory poverty assessments 'the moral imperative of giving the poor a voice in the poverty debate is self-evident. The bonus is that engaging with the poor also leads to better technical diagnosis of problems and implementation of solutions... The poor deepen our understanding of poverty and can influence policymaking...'

Another aspect of the link between poverty and freedom is the emerging emphasis on human rights. As stressed by Peter Townsend in the keynote lecture he gave at the conference which is at the origin of the present book, the idea is that

> rights that free individuals from multiple forms of deprivation and meet their needs for basic social services can be distinguished from fundamental rights to income... Methods of measuring human rights are still in their infancy. The operational definition of rights demands imaginative and sustained quantitative, but also qualitative, methods of investigation. The violations are not those only that end life, or involve extreme abuse, the scales of which have to be assembled in statistical handbooks, but those that represent affronts to human dignity and identity...

A similar point of view was stressed by UNICEF in its 2000 report *Poverty Reduction Begins with Children*:

> Poverty is a denial of human rights and human dignity. It means not having a good primary school or health centre to go to and not having access to safe drinking and adequate sanitation. It means insecurity, powerlessness, exposure to violence and discrimination and exclusion from the mainstream of society. It also means not having a voice to influence decision-making, living at the margin of society and being stigmatized. Obviously poverty reduction involves more than crossing an income threshold.

This notion of human rights is precisely the topic of Chapter 9, authored by Linda Jansen van Rensburg. She starts from the idea that poverty constitutes a denial of human rights and human dignity. Such a human rights-based approach implies therefore protection by law of the fundamental freedoms and entitlements needed for a decent standard of living. In other words, when the fundamental rights relating to poverty are infringed, the persons concerned need social protection. Van Rensburg then explains the importance of the rights-based approach followed by the South African Constitutional Court in the protection of the rights of the poor. Thus, for example, the Court concluded that the real question in terms of the South African Constitution is whether the measures taken by the state to realize social rights are reasonable. It also stated that those whose needs are the most urgent and whose ability to enjoy all rights therefore is most in peril must not be ignored by the measures aimed at achieving realization of the right. There is thus a concept of 'progressive realization' that admits that rights cannot be realized immediately but emphasizes that the Courts must keep in mind that the material needs of those persons who are most vulnerable ought to enjoy priority.

The third part of this book is entitled 'Extending the Concept of Multidimensional Poverty'. This part covers two important issues, that of chronic poverty and that of vulnerability. In Chapter 10, David Hulme and Andy McKay attempt to identify and understand the concept of chronic poverty. They argue that the duration aspect of time merits particular attention because priority should be given to individuals having, *ceteris paribus*, experienced longer spells of poverty. There is a distinction in eighteenth-century France between the 'pauvres' and the 'indigents', the former experiencing seasonal poverty (because, for example, of bad crops), the latter being permanently poor because, say, of illness. There have in fact been many studies in recent years of what is now called 'chronic poverty', but most of them looked at developed rather than developing countries. Moreover this research on chronic poverty remains focused excessively on narrow monetary measures of poverty and on panel datasets. The latter issue should be a particular concern given the weaknesses of income/consumption measures for tracking poverty duration. In this chapter the authors examine, in particular, asset-based and needs/human development measures and comment on their suitability for identifying and measuring chronic poverty.

Chapter 11, written by Cesar Calvo and Stefan Dercon, is devoted to the concept of vulnerability, which is another aspect of poverty that has been ignored until very recently. For Calvo and Dercon vulnerability refers to the fact that people are exposed to risk, and in particular, to the threat of failing to meet minimum standards in any particular dimension of well-being. The authors argue that such a threat causes a form of distress which is a kind of hardship on its own right. More specifically, they define vulnerability as an assessment of the magnitude of the threat of poverty, measured *ex-ante*, before uncertainty is resolved. They show how this difficult concept can be made operational and propose families of vulnerability measures both at the individual and aggregate level.

The final part of the book deals with 'Critical Policy Issues'. Chapter 12, written by Marcelo Côrtes Neri and Marcelo Casal Xerez, is an original examination of the political economy of poverty alleviation. The authors discuss the economic rationality and practical problems related to a system of social targets and credit, such as those defined by the Millennium Development Goals (MDGs), as a way for some federal government to increase efficiency in the use of the social budget it transfers to local governments (states, municipalities, etc....). As the fight against poverty transcends mandates and boundaries, the first proposal made by the authors is that specific locations, in particular those at the sub-national level, announce a commitment with the global targets specified. In practice, this would involve that states and municipalities, other than nations, challenge their respective population to reach the proposed targets. Since the deadline for the global goals outlasts the time frame of a single government, it inhibits discontinuity of actions between political mandates. In other words, international MDGs enjoy the attributes of being exogenously given, which allows not only time consistency in decisions, but also a better integration of social efforts across different government levels. The second proposal studied is that the distribution of resources transferred from higher to lower government levels be linked to social performance indicators through a social credit contract.

Neri and Xerez present, in fact, an extension of the standard principal–agent model and demonstrate that the use of the focalization criteria, whereby the poorest municipalities get more resources, may lead to adverse incentives to poverty eradication. Unconditional transfers from the federal government are also shown to crowd out social expenditures. The authors argue, on the contrary, in favour of the use of contracts where the greater the improvement in relevant social indicators, the more resources each municipality would receive. With the establishment of social targets it thus becomes possible to generate proper incentives so that social spending is distributed more equitably between groups.

The book ends with an attempt by Nanak Kakwani and Hyun H. Son to assess the pro-poorness of government programmes. In this chapter the authors propose a new 'Pro-Poor Policy (PPP)' index, which measures the pro-poorness of government programmes, as well as basic service delivery in education, health and infrastructure. The index provides a means to assess the targeting efficiency of government programmes compared to perfect targeting. The chapter also deals with the policy issue of how the targeting efficiency of government programmes varies across socioeconomic groups. To this effect, Kakwani and Son develop two types of PPP indices by socioeconomic groups – within-group and total-group PPP indices. The within-group PPP index captures how well targeted a programme is within a group. If, however, the objective is to maximize poverty reduction at the national level, the targeting efficiency of particular groups should be judged on the basis of the total-group PPP index. Using micro unit-record data from household surveys from Thailand, Russia and Vietnam, and 15 African countries, the chapter evaluates a wide range of government programmes and basic services.

To conclude, this book on *The Many Dimensions of Poverty* attempts to present a panorama, hopefully as wide as possible, of the many facets of poverty. In inviting contributions representatives from various disciplines, stressing the central importance of freedom in analysing poverty and emphasizing some important policy issues we hope that the broad view of poverty that this book has attempted to offer will not only orient the research on poverty in directions that may have been neglected hitherto, but will also eventually help those whose daily task it is to implement poverty reduction policies.

Part I
Different Disciplines, Different Perceptions

Part I

1
Multidimensional Poverty: Conceptual and Measurement Issues

Erik Thorbecke

1.1 Introduction

Our understanding of the concept of poverty has improved and deepened considerably in the last three decades or so following Amartya Sen's seminal work. Presently we possess the analytical tools to identify and locate the poor, to describe their characteristics and to measure the extent of poverty at different levels of aggregation. Yet, in spite of spectacular methodological advances in the analysis of poverty a number of conceptual and measurement issues remains to be addressed or further clarified. Ravi Kanbur (2002) has argued that the research on distributional issues in economics and development economics in the last thirty years can be divided roughly into two periods: (i) the 1970s to the mid-1980s and (ii) the mid-1980s to the end of the last century. The first 15 years were a 'period of great conceptual leaps and ferment' while the second period was marked by 'consolidation, application and fierce policy debate'. Very recent methodological contributions suggest that we are entering a period of resurgence in research attempting to sharpen and broaden our view of poverty.

The objective of this chapter is to review a number of issues related to poverty, while taking stock of the ongoing research. Most of the remaining unresolved issues in poverty analysis are related directly or indirectly to the multidimensional nature and dynamics of poverty. Before the Development Community can become more successful in designing and implementing poverty alleviation strategies, within the context of growth, we need to identify and understand better the various dimensions of poverty and how the latter interact over time and across space. Some households are endowed with portfolios of attributes that keep them in a poverty trap under which they remain permanently (chronically) poor, while others with somewhat different portfolios move in and out of poverty or can escape altogether falling into a state of poverty. Section 1.2 discusses issues related to the concept of multidimensional poverty; section 1.3 reviews a number of multidimensional poverty measures; section 1.4 is devoted to an analysis of multidimensional poverty and vulnerability over time; section 1.5 addresses further issues related to the measurement of multidimensional poverty; and section 6 concludes.

1.2   Issues related to the concept of multidimensional poverty

Poverty has to be defined, or at least grasped conceptually, before it can be measured. The broader the definition of poverty, the more difficult is its measurement. In fact, as will be shown subsequently, the difficulties inherent in measuring a broadly-based, multidimensional concept of poverty impose severe restrictions on the number and the type of attributes that constitute poverty. The most comprehensive and therefore logical starting point in an attempt to capture the concept of poverty is Sen's 'capabilities and functionings' theoretical framework.

According to this framework, what ultimately matters is the freedom of a person to choose her functionings. In order to function, an individual requires a minimum level of well-being brought about by a set of attributes. The standard way of assessing whether an individual is above or below the poverty threshold is income. The logic and rationale behind the money-metric approach to poverty is that, in principle, an individual above the monetary poverty line is thought to possess the potential purchasing power to acquire the bundle of attributes yielding a level of well-being sufficient to function.

The standard procedure in real income comparisons is to use market prices to aggregate different goods and services consumed or enjoyed by a given individual, these weights (prices) being anonymous. (Atkinson and Bourguignon, 1982). This procedure replaces the actual (unknown) individual welfare function by an indirect utility function defined over the income of the person and the price vector (Atkinson and Bourguignon, 1982). The drawback of the income approach is that some (non-monetary) attributes cannot be purchased because markets do not exist, for example, with some public goods. It is also clear that in many settings – particularly in developing countries – markets operate very imperfectly as in the case of formal rural credit markets from which many small farmers are sealed off because of inadequate collaterals. The use of income to pinpoint poverty presupposes that a market exists for all attributes and that prices reflect the utility weights all households within a specific setting assign to these attributes. Therefore, income as the sole indicator of well-being is limited, if not inappropriate, as it typically does not (or cannot) incorporate and reflect such key dimensions of poverty as life expectancy (longevity), literacy, the provision of public goods and even, at the limit, freedom and security. The state of well-being is strongly correlated with the quality of life but less so with income. Note that the conventional definition of household or individual income according to the national income accounts and household surveys does not usually even include the imputed value of social benefits (for example, health and education).

Another drawback of using the income approach to capture poverty is that even if it were possible to specify the minimum thresholds of each and every basic need and put a price tag on them and aggregate across minimum thresholds to derive the monetary poverty line, there is no guarantee that individuals with incomes at – or even above – the poverty line would actually allocate their incomes so as to purchase the minimum basic needs bundle. For instance, there are examples of household heads who receive an income above the poverty line and allocate it to satisfy wants for alcohol and tobacco at the expense of satisfying the minimum caloric requirements of their children. In the money-metric approach, such households would be classified as non-poor whereas in reality at least some of their members are deprived of some basic needs and therefore should be considered poor. This illustrates the difference between basic needs and wants. The welfare functions of such households – at least as reflected by that of a dictatorial head – yield perverse outcomes in the sense that high enough incomes to potentially escape poverty are allocated instead to yield deprivations and poverty.

According to Sen, capability measures the freedom to achieve alternative functionings. If an individual possesses a large enough endowment or portfolio of capabilities, she can, in principle, choose a specific functioning to escape poverty. As Tsui (2002: 72) noted, 'the capability of a person is an opportunity set of bundles of functionings and not the functionings achieved'. The concept of capability presumes that individuals are well enough endowed that they have the freedom to choose an appropriate non-poor functioning. The inherent difficulty with this approach to poverty is that it is in practice very cumbersome, if not impossible, to measure the capability endowment *ex ante*. Within limits, as will be discussed subsequently, an achieved functioning can be measured *ex post*. If only outcomes can be measured, it would imply that in some instances individuals might have had the capability of selecting a non-poor functioning, yet – as in the case of a selfish household head mentioned above – chose poverty functionings. The distinction between *ex ante* capability and *ex post* achieved functioning raises an immediate question: should an individual or household endowed with the potential capability of choosing a functioning satisfying all basic needs and yet opting for an alternative bundle within which at least some minimum thresholds of attributes are not met (for example, some of the children in that household could be malnourished) be considered poor? A pragmatic, as opposed to a philosophical, approach would argue that it is the actual outcome that matters and that, in any case, *ex ante* capability cannot be ascertained. Poverty analysts can only judge the state of poverty from observing the actual functioning. The fact that a person or a household had the means to avoid deprivation does not alter an outcome marked by malnutrition and ill-health. If the actual state of living is one of poverty in at least some of its dimensions, the fact that it could have been avoided by the choice of a different allocation of income and other attributes by a given individual does not affect the prevailing state of poverty.

The key issue is how to define the configuration of relevant attributes, including their minimum thresholds, that constitute an acceptable – that is, non-poor – level of functioning. It would be that configuration that would allow individuals to 'manage and to be' outside of poverty. Most analysts would start with the set of basic needs developed in the 1970s and early 1980s (see Streeten, 1981). Clearly in addition to income, such tangible basic needs as nutrition, health, education, shelter, clothing and access to information would be high on the list of crucial attributes used to judge whether a person was or was not poor. There are other possible dimensions of poverty that are not as clear-cut and for which a minimum threshold is almost impossible to determine such as different kinds of freedoms (of oppression, of religion, of expression), security, and the degree of discrimination and social exclusion below which an individual is thought to be deprived.

Except perhaps for nutrition, it is hard enough to set minimum levels for such basic needs as shelter (number of square metres per person, quality of roof and floor), let alone agreeing on the minimum acceptable level of human rights below which an individual should be considered deprived. It is doubtful that we can agree and rely on robust indicators of such intangible yet essential dimensions of well-being as freedom, security and discrimination. To compound the difficulty, norms as to what is acceptable to function with dignity tend to be highly context-specific and vary widely from one society to another and from one setting to another. The measurement of these attributes faces almost insurmountable practical and operational problems, yet they cannot be ignored as their deprivation could push individuals into a state of poverty. A person who lives under an oppressive regime or who is discriminated against or socially excluded is constrained in its function-ing and in that sense can be conceived as poor.

There are currently two main methods of setting the poverty line in the conven-tional money-metric procedure – the Cost of Basic Needs (CBN) and the Food–Energy–Intake (FEI) methods. The CBN approach has the advantage of ensuring *consistency* (treating individuals with the same living standards equally) while the FEI approach has the advantage of *specificity*, offering a better reflection of the actual food consumption behaviour of individuals around the caloric threshold given their tastes, preferences and relative prices.

It has been cogently argued by Ravallion and Bidani (1994) and Ravallion (1998) that in order to make valid welfare comparisons the reference basket (bundle) yield-ing the caloric threshold should remain constant. The monetary poverty line (z) at any point in time is then obtained by multiplying the constant quantitative reference basket by the variable price vector to obtain z at current (nominal) prices and then deflating it by an appropriate price index (often the consumer price index) to express z in real terms. The conflict between the two criteria becomes apparent when it is realized that the main (if not the only) reason for adopting one, and only one, national basket is to allow welfare comparisons when, in fact, tastes, preferences, prices and diets may differ considerably from one region to another. The selected national CBN basket might only be consumed by a small minority of the house-holds around the poverty line and is often significantly different from the actual basket consumed by individuals whose income is near z. Hence for the sake of wel-fare comparisons the actual behaviour of the poor is ignored, if not altogether dis-missed. It is as if realism was sacrificed on the altar of welfare consistency.

This clash between these two criteria is even more pronounced in multidimen-sional poverty analysis than in the simpler income approach because of: (i) the broader set of attributes (in particular the non-monetary ones) taken on board in the former; (ii) the enormous difficulties of establishing objective standards for such elusive concepts as freedom and social exclusion; and (iii) the likely greater inter-regional and inter-community variability of non-monetary attributes.

The determination of threshold levels for the myriad of dimensions of poverty, besides being context-specific, is very much in the eyes of the beholders. Should these levels be set at the local community level by community leaders or at the regional or even national levels by political leaders? Or, alternatively, should analysts ask individuals directly (say, through participatory poverty assessments and focus groups) what they perceive subjectively to be minimum thresholds of attributes below which they would feel deprived? The poverty estimates are very sensitive to the method used to establish these standards. If national standards are set in terms of one bundle of basic needs applying to all residents of a given country then, in principle, *consistent* inter-regional welfare comparisons can be made (making the unrealistic assumption that basic needs and preferences for meeting them are identical across regions). On the other hand, reliance on local bundles, while much more realistic in respect of the actual consumption pattern of these local households, precludes, according to welfare theorists, such inter-regional welfare comparisons. The conflict between the *consistency* criterion and the *specificity* criterion that plagues the conventional income-metric approach to poverty analysis applies equally well to a multidimensional approach to poverty analysis.

Now let us assume that, notwithstanding all the difficulties discussed above, agreement has been reached on a list of attributes related to poverty and their threshold levels. How can such information be used to derive measures of multidimensional poverty and make poverty comparisons? Start with the simplest case, for example, that of an individual who is below each and every attribute threshold level. Such a person would be classified as unambiguously poor. Analogously, comparing two individual poverty profiles (A and B) where the attribute scores for all of the n dimensions in the profile of A are above that of the profile of B, it can be inferred unambiguously that A is better off in terms of well-being (less poor) than B. This last example reflects first order stochastic dominance to which we return shortly.

Absent first order stochastic dominance, where an individual is deprived in terms of some attributes (is unemployed and receives an income below the monetary poverty line) but not for others (possesses an educational status above the threshold), how can we determine whether or not this person is poor?

Similarly, if the profiles of individuals A and B intersect so that A scores better on some dimensions and vice versa, how are we to judge who is less poor? A utility (welfare) function is needed to answer these questions. Such a utility function would include the relative weights to be assigned to the various attributes and the individual and joint welfare contributions of the set of attributes. In the income approach the weights are anonymous and given by the market prices. As pointed out earlier, this approach is flawed as (1) it does not provide price signals in the cases of goods and services for which there are missing markets (can one conceive of a market for freedom?); (2) the prevalence of imperfect markets and government intervention in much of the developing world results in artificial prices that do not reflect scarcity value; (3) market prices are essentially efficiency prices and do not reflect distributional considerations (the marginal utility of a good satisfying a basic need below the deprivation level could actually rise rather than fall with income).

Hence to ascertain poverty and make poverty comparisons within a multidimensional framework requires the approximation of a welfare function that includes the specification of the relative welfare weights and conveys information about the direct marginal benefits of each attribute and about the interaction among these attributes. In particular, this last requirement represents a tall order. It is difficult enough estimating the direct (individual) benefits, let alone the multiple and often complex interactions among sets of attributes. The latter can be substitutes or complements. On the one hand, if dimensions are substitutes, it means that a person can trade-off one attribute for another (say more food for less clothing) and remain on the same iso-utility curve. On the other hand, if attributes are complements, an increase in the amount of one raises the marginal utility of the other (more education increases the present discounted value of the future stream of income). It is also possible that some combinations of poverty dimensions are neither substitutes nor complements.

1.3   Multidimensional poverty measures

It is difficult enough to ascertain the degree of substitutability or complementarity on a pair-wise basis, let alone among combinations of n dimensions taken 3, 4, up to *n* at a time. Such a complete mapping of combinations of attributes into the utility space appears daunting, if not altogether utopian. This is the reason why efforts at measuring multidimensional poverty until now have limited themselves to dealing with at most four (and most typically only two) dimensions in their empirical applications – while showing that in theory their methods could be extended to cope with n dimensions. Let us now review some of these attempts and in the process highlight some related issues.

In one of the earliest attempts to analyse multidimensional welfare, Atkinson and Bourguignon (1982) focused on the case where the government is concerned both with monetary variables, such as income, and with non-monetary variables. More specifically, they tried to 'assess the extent of international inequality allowing for differences between countries both in incomes and in life expectancies, with the judgment depending on the distribution of each variable taken separately and on the way they vary together' (Atkinson and Bourguignon, 1982: 183). As they point out in the study of multiple deprivation, an essential issue is to determine how different forms of deprivation (such as low income, poor health and inadequate shelter) tend to be associated and to draw a contrast with what one would observe if they were independently distributed.

Bourguignon and Chakravarty (2003) take as their fundamental starting point in the development of multidimensional poverty measures that poverty consists of a shortfall from a threshold on each dimension of an individual's well-being. In other words, 'the issue of poverty arises because individuals, social observers or policy makers want to define a poverty limit on each individual attribute: income, health, education, etc.' (p. 28). They proceed to build a multidimensional measure of poverty assuming only two attributes. The first issue is whether a person should be considered poor if she falls short of the thresholds for all attributes, or only one. In the two-attribute case if $x_1 < z_1$, and $x_2 < z_2$, the person would be poor in both dimensions and therefore unambiguously poor. Alternatively, the shortfall might be in only one dimension, in which case the determination would depend on the nature of the relationship between the two attributes. If the attributes are substitutes and an individual has a sufficiently high level of the first attribute above the threshold to more than compensate, in terms of welfare, for the shortfall in the second attribute, then the person cannot be classified as poor.

In the literature the distinction between being poor in two (and at the limit all) dimensions and in only one dimension has been referred to as the *intersection* and *union* definitions of poverty. This can be illustrated using an example drawn from Duclos, Sahn and Younger (forthcoming): if well-being is measured in terms of income and height (as an indicator of health) then a person could be considered poor if her income falls below an income poverty line *or* if her height falls short of a height poverty threshold. This case would be defined as a *union* definition of poverty. In contrast, an *intersection* definition would consider an individual as poor only if she were to fall below both thresholds.

Bourguignon and Chakravarty (2003) analyse the implications of various degrees of substitutability and complementarity between attributes on the utility space. They build a class of multidimensional poverty measures which is a multidimensional extension of the FGT (Foster, Greer, and Thorbecke, 1984) measure that satisfies a number of desirable axioms and which is consistent with key properties of interacting attributes. Among others, they argue that in the case of substitutes the drop in poverty decreases less with an increase in attribute j for persons with larger quantities of the other attribute k. For example, the reduction in poverty caused by a unit increase in income is less important for people who possess educational levels close to the education poverty threshold than for individuals with very low levels of education. In contrast, the drop in poverty should be larger for individuals endowed with more education if these attributes are supposed to be complements.

The family of bi-dimensional poverty measures they derive is limited to the case where both attributes are below their poverty thresholds (for example, the *intersection* definition) and are substitutes – assuming different degrees of substitutability. The measure is simply the summation of the shortfalls appropriately weighted raised to the power α, where α can be interpreted as a poverty aversion parameter as in the uni-dimensional FGT measure. Although they argue that, in theory, these families of poverty indices could be generalized to any number of attributes, this would require assuming the same elasticity of substitution between attributes, which seems most unrealistic. To illustrate the applicability of the measures, the evolution of rural poverty in Brazil in the 1980s is analyzed. The two dimensions of poverty that are scrutinized are income and educational level. During the period, income poverty increased while educational poverty fell. As one would have expected, the poverty outcome in the B-C multi- (bidimensional) measure is very sensitive to the relative weights and degree of substitution assumed between income and educational level below their thresholds.

Duclos, Sahn and Younger (forthcoming) develop a dominance approach to multidimensional poverty. They extend the concept of a poverty line in one dimension to a poverty frontier in multiple dimensions. The question they raise and proceed to answer with the help of a few concrete examples is 'what is the area of poverty frontiers over which we can be sure that poverty is lower for A than for B?'

They show that it is possible for a set of univariate analysis done independently for each dimension of well-being to conclude that poverty in setting A is lower than poverty in setting B (say rural vs urban Vietnam), while a multivariate analysis concludes the opposite, and vice versa. The reason behind the above contention lies in the interaction among the various dimensions of well-being included in the poverty measure and their (multiple) correlations in the sampled populations. A reasonable poverty measure should allow the level of deprivation in one attribute to affect the assessment of how much poverty declines if there is an improvement in another attribute.

An increase in income for a severely deprived person in terms of health and education should cause a larger reduction in poverty than the same increase in income going to a less severely deprived individual. Clearly, 'one at a time' comparisons of poverty in terms of income, education, health, and so on, cannot capture these interdependencies. Populations that exhibit higher correlations among attributes of well-being will be poorer than those that do not, relative to what one would expect on the basis of univariate comparisons alone.

The dominance measure Duclos, Sahn and Younger (forthcoming) propose is essentially a two-dimensional generalization of the FGT index. An important feature of the D-S-Y measure is that it is influenced by the covariance between the two elements. Another interesting feature is that separate poverty aversion parameters can be selected for the two dimensions. Again, the measure is based on the assumption that the two attributes are substitutes. Three interesting empirical applications are presented to illustrate that their approach can cover wide ranges of poverty thresholds, yield two, three and even four-dimensional surfaces where one distribution dominates another – as in the case of urban vs rural people in Vietnam using incomes and nutritional status as the two elements.

The authors are aware of the limitations of the substitutability assumption and discuss the implications of having instead assumed complementarity. For instance, if the production complementarities between education and nutritional status are strong enough (through the close link, beyond a certain threshold, between maternal education and the quality of the diet leading to significant improvements in the health status of household members) 'it may overcome the usual ethical judgment that favors the multiply-deprived, so that overall poverty would decline by more if we were to transfer education from the poorly nourished to the better nourished.....Similarly, one might argue that human capital should be granted to those with a higher survival probability (because these assets would vanish following their death)' (p. 9). The issues of substitutability vs complementarity among attributes and budgetary rules in allocating funds to fight poverty are of crucial importance within a dynamic framework and are returned to subsequently.

1.4   Multidimensional poverty and vulnerability over time

The present state of well-being for any given individual will influence her future state. This is particularly true for the poorest members of the population. Each household, at any point in time, is endowed with a given portfolio of attributes allowing it to function more or less well. Some portfolios are so deficient, for example, members of the household are so deprived in key dimensions, that they are particularly vulnerable to shocks. In turn, even transitory shocks can have permanent and persistent effects on the future level of well-being. This means that certain configurations of attributes today can generate a condition akin to a continuing multi-dimensional poverty trap. It is precisely the interaction among (deprived) attributes that can bring about this condition.

Vulnerability can be defined as facing uninsurable risks. Christiaensen and Boisvert (2000) contrast poverty and vulnerability in the following way. Poverty is concerned with not *having* enough *now*, whereas vulnerability is about having a high probability now of suffering a future shortfall. Their notion of vulnerability is the risk of a future shortfall and is expressed as a probability statement regarding the failure to attain a certain threshold of well-being in the future. In the uni-dimensional income approach vulnerability is measured as the probability of falling below the poverty line z, multiplied by a conditional probability-weighted function of a shortfall below this poverty line. Consistent with the FGT poverty measure, they use a vulnerability-aversion parameter α such that by setting $\alpha > 1$, households with a higher probability of large shortfalls become more vulnerable.

Dercon (2005b) provides a useful conceptual framework to link present risk to future (poverty) outcomes. Households face a multitude of risks, and, given their options and characteristics (that, in turn, depend on their portfolios of attributes), they will make risk management decisions. This *ex ante* decision-making process has implications for outcomes in both the short and the long run. Next shocks may occur – effectively a new realization of the state of the world – and people's response or lack of response will have implications for outcomes in terms of the various levels of dimensions of well-being. The most prevalent source of risk within the Third World is that faced by rural households engaged in agriculture. The risk is related to the rainfall and climatic pattern and the typical form the risk takes is in terms of a drought. Other high-risk factors are family illness and deaths. In the urban areas important risk factors are the fear of unemployment and of social exclusion. There are, of course, a plethora of other risks, including the possible transitional negative impact of globalization on community social protection and solidarity networks.

A state of deprivation in some key attributes such as health, education and income can increase vulnerability and lead shocks to have cumulative and persistent effects over time. Whereas in a static framework (at one point in time) different dimensions of poverty can be thought of as substitutes using a consumption lens, where trade-offs are possible and iso-poverty maps can be drawn, in a dynamic production framework many of these attributes are complements. Dercon (2005a) provides numerous examples of how certain interactions among attributes affect future poverty, for example: (1) high infant and child mortality rates, for example, the risk that children will not survive beyond a certain age, increases the fertility rate and further impoverishes the household; (2) poor nutrition, particularly in a child's early life, leads to stunting and often persistent health effects and lower educational performance and cognitive ability (an erosion of human capital); (3) lack of insurance and credit markets implies that recovery of assets used in temporarily smoothing consumption after a crisis or destroyed by it may take a long time; (4) negative income shocks causing households to withdraw children from schools may result in a permanent loss of human capital even if these children return to school later. It can be argued that when levels of well-being are permanently affected by transitory shocks, a poverty trap ensues (Dercon, 2005a).

The fact that dimensions of well-being can be substitutes in the short run while being complementary and re-enforcing in the long run has fundamental implications for the measurement of poverty. First, assume that a well-designed household survey allows us to determine the various degrees of substitution among attributes based on a cross-sectional approach. One finding may be that the same level of multi-dimensional poverty can be achieved with different combinations of education and income. An individual (A) who has slightly more education and less income than B may be on the same iso-poverty curve as B. However, the existence of a static cross-sectional trade-off between these two attributes does not and should not imply that B can purchase (instantaneously) more education and trade places with A. Clearly over time B can use part of his income to acquire more human capital but in the short run such a trade is hypothetical at best. Trade-offs among other basic needs such as between food and housing are, of course, possible in the short run.

A first implication of the above is that different combinations of attributes yielding the same poverty level in the short run can have different impact (influence) on poverty outcomes in the future. For example, if A and B are on the same iso-poverty surface, and if A's household is relatively healthy and well educated but deprived income-wise, it may be less vulnerable and better able to withstand a shock than B's household that possesses a higher income, but is more deprived in terms of health and education. In other words, present measures of multidimensional poverty, in comparing individuals, tend to ignore the differential risk and vulnerability conditions of alternative portfolios of attributes yielding the same level of poverty today. Hence, there exists a path-dependence between the form poverty takes today and future poverty outcomes. B may be judged as less poor than A today, but given his endowment of attributes and his greater vulnerability to shocks B is likely to be poorer than A in the future.

A second implication is that a better understanding of the complex interactions of attributes over time is crucial in the design of effective programmes and budgetary allocations meant to relieve poverty within a growth and development context. If good health and education are a sine qua non to raising labour productivity and finding employment, they should be given a high priority in the budget. A more subtle point relates to social programmes and insurance schemes that could reduce households' vulnerability to shocks and thereby affect poor households' *ex ante* behaviour *vis à vis* crises. The risk-aversion displayed by the poor in their decision-making processes is a rational reaction to their perception of the distribution of the states of nature resulting from their decisions and actions.

The essence of vulnerability is the uncertainty of future income streams and the associated loss of welfare caused by this uncertainty. As Ligon and Schechter (2003) put it, the critical issue is that 'a household with very low expected consumption expenditures but with no chance of starving may well be poor, but it still might not wish to trade places with a household having a higher expected consumption but greater consumption risk'. A subsistence farmer facing the choice of alternative technologies will select an inferior technology in terms of expected yield *if* there is a non-zero probability of a catastrophic outcome (that would threaten the household's survival) with the superior, higher-yielding (on average) technology. Likewise, poor farmers tend to devote a larger proportion of land to safer, traditional varieties than to riskier varieties. Dercon (1996) shows that in the context of Tanzania the crop portfolio of the wealthiest quintile yields 25 per cent more per adult than that of the lowest quintile. Dercon (2005a) provides numerous additional examples and concludes that 'there is increasing evidence that uninsured risk increases poverty, through *ex ante* behavioral responses, affecting activities, assets and technology choices, as well as through persistent and possibly permanent effects from transitory shocks via the loss of different types of assets'.

The costs of social insurance schemes that would alter the *ex ante* behaviour of poor and vulnerable households could be a fraction of the additional benefits derived from overcoming their risk-averse strategies. Similarly, asset decapitalization to smooth consumption in response to shock can be undertaken on a scale that leads to dramatic loss in long-term well-being. According to de Janvry and Sadoulet (2005), these adverse consequences can be driven by three phenomena where: (1) decapitalization below a threshold leads to irreversible consequences (as in the case where the nutrition of a child under five is reduced and brings about irreversible physical development and even death); (2) decapitalization that leads to very high re-entry costs with irreversible consequences for those who are deterred from re-entry; and (3) decapitalization that results in critical loss of economies of scale such as reducing a herd below a minimum size. In a number of instances social programmes and safety nets can be designed that would alter the attitudes of the poor with respect to risk, for example reduce their anticipation of risk, and thereby change their *ex ante* behaviour.

A key question at this stage is whether vulnerability and consequent risk – aversion is part and parcel of multidimensional poverty in the sense that certain sets of shortfalls of attributes (deprivations) generate vulnerability or whether vulnerability is a separate dimension of poverty. In a major conceptual breakthrough, Ligon and Schechter (2003) break down vulnerability into two components reflecting poverty and risk, respectively. The first component is supposed to represent that part of vulnerability due to (chronic) poverty, while the second reflects risk and uncertainty and, presumably, transitory poverty. While this distinction is ingenious and useful in estimating the utility gain that could accrue to the poor if there were a means to decrease their anticipation of risk through some social insurance programme, it could mask the fact that certain types of current poverty (portfolios of deprivations) render those households more vulnerable. In turn, higher risk by altering the behaviour of the poor pushes some of them further into a poverty trap. In this sense vulnerability (risk) and poverty are inherently inter-related.

Elbers and Gunning (2003) show that vulnerability can change dramatically over time as a consequence of both sustained growth and adjustment to shocks. An important implication of their approach is that the usual identification of chronic poverty with structural determinants and transitory poverty with risk breaks down.

They show that 'a household can be chronically poor because its response to risk lowers consumption permanently' (p. 2). This feature of their approach is fundamental in that it incorporates the possibility of households deciding within an intertemporal framework to reduce their mean consumption to reduce consumption variability and risk. Wood (2003) referred to this trade-off as the 'Faustian Bargain'. The quest for household security can lock poor people into social structures that reduce vulnerability but which also keeps them poor. Based on ethnographies derived from qualitative research, Wood shows why many households 'stay poor' in an attempt to 'stay secure'. One of the important conclusions of the Elbers and Gunning exercise is that if measures of chronic poverty are based on mean consumption over time, then a large part of chronic poverty could in fact reflect risk.

1.5 Further issues related to the measurement of multidimensional poverty

The multidimensional poverty measures that have been discussed up to this point are quantitative in nature. Increasingly, sociologists and anthropologists are relying on essentially subjective Participatory Poverty Assessments (PPAs) to try to capture the multidimensional nature of poverty. As Amartya Sen's emphasis on capabilities and functionings is becoming the dominant paradigm in poverty analysis, a clear implication is that a definition of poverty based exclusively on the material welfare status of an individual at one point in time misses key features of poverty that can only be unveiled through PPAs.

The qualitative (PPA) approach to poverty assessment is more inductive and subjective than the quantitative approach. The 'hands on' iterative interviewing technique generates hypotheses that can be formally and quantitatively tested by the more deductive quantitative methodology that relies on econometric and statistical tools. These hypotheses might be either confirmed or rejected after having been subjected to quantitative testing. If the hypotheses are rejected or only weakly confirmed, this information can be conveyed to practitioners of the PPA approach who could then try to generate new (modified) hypotheses to be tested subsequently by quantitative researchers. This iterative process could lead to a productive dialogue between the two schools and the identification of a set of richer findings. (Thorbecke, 2003).[1]

The most subjective approach to the analysis of well-being is found in the literature on the 'economics of happiness'. The latter simply asks individuals to indicate their degree of happiness, usually on a scale of one to ten. Both the PPA and happiness approaches can obtain more accurate estimates of the extent of deprivation people feel with respect to such intangible potential dimensions of poverty as freedom, security, and social exclusion. An interesting feature of those subjective approaches, when they ask whether a person feels poor or unhappy, is that the answers given rely implicitly on the utility function of the subject in question. In other words, the individual stating that he does not feel poor uses an implicit set of individual weights and minimum thresholds for the various attributes of well-being and aggregates accordingly to obtain a scalar measure. This resolves the very thorny and essentially arbitrary issue of having to select a set of attributes' weights in the alternative quantitative multidimensional poverty measures and indicators. Here again a marriage between the quantitative and qualitative approaches could yield useful information on the relative weights individuals in a given setting assign to different dimensions of well-being.

In general, the qualitative approach tends to be highly context-specific. Researchers and interviewers focus on specific villages and communities and obtain a mass of useful and comprehensive information on the socioeconomic structure of each village studied. One revealing difference in the diagnosis of poverty between the two approaches is that some households who are clearly below the poverty line on objective money-metric grounds when interviewed by PPA analysts claim that they do not consider themselves poor and vice versa. One likely explanation can be found in the extent of income and wealth inequality within the neighbourhood and village of those households. On the one hand, within a multidimensional framework, a household surrounded by individuals at similar and lower levels of income (below z) and comparable levels of deprivations in terms of education, health, and shelter may not 'feel' poor. On the other hand, a household better off (for example, less poor in terms of quantitative multidimensional measures) living in a village with a much more unequal distribution of income and other attributes and surrounded by individuals with higher standards of living and less deprivation may 'feel' poor even though its consumption is above the multidimensional poverty thresholds' surface. This suggests that the perception of poverty is often relative to the living standards of neighbours rather than to an absolute level. Does this mean that a comprehensive and robust multidimensional measure should incorporate distributional information in addition to information on attributes' thresholds and shortfalls?

The design of a poverty measure sensitive to the extent of inequality around the poverty surface (including individuals just above it) could help in the identification of the perception of poverty. Also, given the crucial importance of context-specific conditions in shaping the perception of poverty, it can be argued that the setting of the poverty surface at a more location-specific level would lead to a more accurate appraisal of poverty. The use of a national or even provincial poverty surface in the light of major intra-regional and inter-village differences in socio economic conditions can distort the poverty diagnosis at the local level. Again, this illustrates the inherent conflict between the specificity and consistency criteria. It is not possible to satisfy both simultaneously.[2]

The validity and robustness of poverty comparisons over space and over time based on the unidimensional income approach is debatable on a number of grounds. Over an extended period of time, relative prices can change significantly leading to substitution by consumers among basic goods and services away from those whose relative prices rose and towards those with lower relative prices. It is not unreasonable to argue that the longer the time period over which poverty comparisons are attempted, the more weight should be assigned to the specificity criterion. With the market appearance of somewhat different goods, both qualitatively and quantitatively triggered by technological progress, consumers' tastes and preferences are likely to evolve as well. In this case, the maintenance of a historical reference bundle over a long period simply to satisfy the consistency criterion could fly in the face of a different contemporaneous basket actually consumed by the near-poor today.

The cost of a basket of goods satisfying food requirements grows with GDP per capita for several reasons such as: changes in the range of goods consumed as income increases, rising prices of basic foodstuffs compared to the prices of other goods, increasing proportion of the population in urban areas where foodstuffs may be more expensive than in rural areas, and gradual disappearance of subsistence farming. It can readily be observed that basic needs expand with development, particularly at an early stage of development. For example, as the rural to urban migration occurs, the new urban dwellers may have to use public transport and be charged for a variety of public services that were essentially either not available or free in the villages they left behind. For all these reasons it may be reasonable over an extended time horizon to update and re-compute the basic needs basket, and by extension in the multidimensional poverty framework, the bundle of non-monetary attributes.

This problem of inter-temporal comparisons applies even more forcefully to multidimensional poverty measures. Political and economic regimes can undergo major, even radical, changes affecting civil liberties, security, incentives structures and affect overall socioeconomic growth leading to major changes in relative prices (as would be the case of an economy in transition from central planning based on artificial prices to a free enterprise, market economy). Reforms and policy changes, such as structural adjustment programmes, are likely to entail large-scale changes in social programmes affecting health, educational and pension benefits. Services previously provided by the state may no longer be available. The changing environment may give rise to new norms and needs that if not met would cause deprivation in those new dimensions. In short, the new set of poverty thresholds for the attributes of well-being could differ significantly from the earlier one and therefore invalidate or, at least, render questionable a poverty comparison based on the historical poverty surface.

Some of the same arguments also hold relative to spatial poverty comparisons. For example, assuming a similar bundle of minimum thresholds of attributes in comparing a rural and urban setting is fraught with possible pitfalls. Not only are there different sets of basic needs (such as the need for transportation by a new migrant mentioned earlier) but, in addition, the social environments are likely to differ significantly. A rural household is likely to be able to rely more on social capital and a supportive community and solidarity network provided by neighbours, friends and the extended family than its urban counterpart. In this sense, it might be less vulnerable to certain types of shocks such as major financial crises affecting the whole country (the Asian Financial Crisis triggered a massive reverse urban-to-rural temporary migration in Indonesia in search of better safety nets). For all those reasons, inter-regional and, even more so, international poverty comparisons need to be carefully qualified.

1.6   Conclusions

The most comprehensive starting point in an attempt to capture the concept of multidimensional poverty is Sen's 'capabilities and functionings' framework. In order to function, an individual requires a minimum level of well-being brought about by a set of attributes and the standard way to determine whether an individual is above or below the poverty threshold is income. The drawback of the income approach is that some (non-monetary) attributes cannot be purchased because markets do not exist or operate imperfectly so that prices do not reflect the utility weights households assign to these attributes. Income as the sole indicator of well-being is limited as it does not incorporate key dimensions of poverty such as life expectancy (longevity), literacy, the provision of public goods, freedom and security.

In order to ascertain poverty and make poverty comparisons within a multidimensional framework, a welfare function has to be approximated that reflects the preferences of the households under scrutiny. This welfare function should include: (1) the relative welfare weights households assign to each and every attribute; (2) the poverty thresholds of all attributes; (3) information about the direct marginal benefits of each individual attribute; and (4) information about the benefits that result from the joint interaction among these attributes. In particular, this last requirement represents a tall order. It is difficult enough estimating the direct (individual) benefits, let alone the multiple and often complex interactions among sets of attributes. The latter can be substitutes or complements. If attributes (dimensions of poverty) are substitutes it means that a given individual can trade-off one attribute for another (say more food for less shelter) and remain at the same level of well-being. In contrast, if attributes are complements, an increase in the amount of one raises the marginal utility of the other (more education increases the present discounted value of the future stream of income).

It should be clear that a complete mapping of combinations of attributes into the utility space appears daunting, if not altogether utopian. This explains why the empirical applications attempting to measure multidimensional poverty – reviewed and discussed in Section 1.3 – have limited themselves until now to dealing with at most four (and more typically only two) dimensions while claiming that in theory their methods could be extended to cope with n dimensions.

Each household, at any point in time, is endowed with a given portfolio of attributes allowing it to function more or less well. Some portfolios are so deficient, for example, members of the household are so deprived in key basic needs (such as health and education), that they are particularly vulnerable to shocks. In turn, even transitory shocks can have permanent and persistent effects on their future level of well-being and result in poverty traps.

The fact that dimensions of well-being can be substitutes in the short run while being complementary and re-enforcing in the long run has fundamental implications for the measurement of poverty over time. There exists a path dependence between the form poverty takes today and future poverty outcomes. The quest for household security can lock poor people into social structures that reduce vulnerability but which also keeps them poor.

Qualitative and subjective approaches such as Participatory Poverty Assessments and the 'Economics of Happiness' can provide important complementary insights to the information generated by quantitative measures of multidimensional poverty. An interesting feature of those subjective approaches is that the answers that are given by the interviewees reveal implicitly their welfare (utility) functions. This could help resolve, or at least reduce the arbitrariness of, the thorny problem of the selection of attributes' relative weights in the quantitative multidimensional poverty measures.

In summary, it is clear that the economic literature on multidimensional poverty measures has made considerable progress in clarifying the concept of functioning and in identifying many of the related theoretical issues. Yet, as this chapter has tried to highlight, there are too many unresolved questions left over to consider seriously using multidimensional measures in any truly operational sense.

Notes

1. For an excellent discussion of the advantages and disadvantages of the two schools of thought and an attempt to reconcile them, see Kanbur (2003).
2. Tarp et al (2002) provide a good start to the exploration of this conflict within a money-metric approach in the context of Mozambique.

References

Atkinson, A.B. and F. Bourguignon (1982) 'The Comparison of MultiDimensional Distributions of Economic Status', *Review of Economic Studies*, 49, 183–201.
Bourguignon, F. and S.R. Chakravarty (2003) 'The Measurement of Multidimensional Poverty', *Journal of Economic Inequality*, 1, 25–49.
Christiaensen, L. and R.N. Boisvert (2000) 'Measuring Household Food Vulnerability: Case Evidence from Northern Mali'. Working Paper, Department of Agricultural, Resource, and Managerial Economics, Cornell University.
de Janvry, A. and E. Sadoulet (2005) 'Designing Social Safety Net Programs to Directly Protect from Shocks the Assets of the Vulnerable'. Paper prepared for the World Bank/DFID Workshop on Growth and Risk, Leuven, June.
Dercon, S. (1996) 'Risk, Crop Choice, and Savings: Evidence from Tanzania', *Economic Development and Cultural Change*, 44(3), 485–513.
Dercon, S. (2005a) 'Risk, Growth and Poverty: What Do We Know, What Do We Need to Know'. Paper prepared for the World Bank/DFID Workshop on Growth and Risk, Leuven, June.
Dercon, S. (2005b) 'Vulnerability: a Micro Perspective'. Paper presented at the ABCDE for Europe.
Duclos, J.-Y., D. Sahn and S. Younger (forthcoming) 'Robust Multidimensional Poverty Comparisons', *Economic Journal*.
Elbers, C. and J.W. Gunning (2003) 'Estimating Vulnerability', Department of Economics, Free University of Amsterdam.
Foster, J. J. Greer and E. Thorbecke (1984) 'A Class of Decomposable Poverty Measures', *Econometrica*, 52, 761–5.
Kanbur, R. (2002) 'Conceptual Challenges in Poverty and Inequality: One Development Economist's Perspective', Working Paper 2002–09, Department of Applied Economics and Management, Cornell University.
Kanbur, R. (ed.) (2003) *Q-Squared: Combining Qualitative and Quantitative Methods of Poverty Appraisal*. Delhi: Permanent Black.

Ligon, E. and L. Schechter (2003) 'Measuring Vulnerability', *Economic Journal*, 113, 95–102.

Ravallion, M. and B. Bidani (1994) 'How Robust is a Poverty Profile?', *World Bank Economic Review* 8(1), 75–102.

Ravallion, M. (1998) *Poverty Lines in Theory and Practice*, Living Standard Measurement Study Working Paper 133. Washington DC: World Bank.

Streeten, P. *First Things First: Meeting Basic Human Needs in Developing Countries*. New York: Oxford University Press.

Tarp, F., K. Simler, C. Matusse, R. Heltberg, and C. Dava (2002) 'The Robustness of Poverty Profiles Reconsidered', *Economic Development and Cultural Change*, 51(1) 77–106.

Thorbecke, E. (2003) 'Tensions, Complementarities and Possible Convergence Between the Qualitative and Quantitative Approaches to Poverty Assessment', In R. Kanbur (ed.), *Q-Squared: Combining Qualitative and Quantitative Methods in Poverty Appraisal*. Delhi: Permanent Black.

Tsui, K.-Y. 'Multidimensional Poverty Indices', *Social Choice and Welfare*, 19, 69–93.

Wood, G. 'Staying Secure, Staying Poor: the "Faustian Bargain"', *World Development*, 31, 3.

2
Measuring Poverty: The Case for a Sociological Approach[1]

David B. Grusky and Kim A. Weeden

2.1 Introduction

We could not fault our readers for approaching yet another treatise on the proper way to measure poverty with a healthy degree of scepticism and more than a little irritation. Haven't academics been debating issues of measurement endlessly? Isn't it high time to stop debating and get on with the tasks of measuring poverty, developing policy, and taking action? We too would have hoped that by now a framework for measuring poverty and inequality would be as well developed as our sprawling and influential social indicator system for measuring total economic output. The unfortunate fact of the matter, however, is that a comprehensive and consensual framework is not in place, and such tools as now exist are not fully adequate to the task of representing the structure of poverty. The purpose of this chapter is to expose some of the assumptions about poverty measurement with which the disciplines of sociology and economics have been burdened, to show that these assumptions have not always served scholars in these disciplines well, and to develop a framework for poverty measurement that provides a more rigorously empirical foundation for measurement.

We argue, in particular, that neither sociologists nor economists have appreciated that decisions about how to measure poverty are ultimately empirical decisions and should therefore be justified in empirical terms. Moreover, insofar as measurement models are understood to be empirical claims about the structure of poverty, the focus of such claims properly shifts from narrow judgements about how much poverty there is to more complicated judgements about the form and shape that it assumes. We therefore take on the task of developing an empirical framework for measuring poverty that makes it possible to monitor not just the amount of poverty but also its shape and form. We hope to show that much can be learned about poverty by converting assumptions about its shape and form into testable hypotheses.

When scholars measure and analyse poverty, they typically do so with whatever measurement approach happens to be preferred within their discipline or theoretical camp; and in this sense their preferred measurement approach becomes little more than a badge of affiliation. As shown in Table 2.1, economists have tended to default either to an income paradigm or to a multidimensional capabilities framework,

Table 2.1 Examples of preferred measurement models by discipline

	Measurement approach	
Discipline	*Gradational*	*Multidimensional*
Economics	Income (i.e., the 'income paradigm')	Capabilities approach
Sociology	Income (i.e., the 'income paradigm')	Social class (e.g., the 'underclass')

with the decision between these two approaches typically being made on the basis of the 'school' to which the scholar subscribes, not any empirical evidence. Similarly, when sociologists choose between an income paradigm or a social class formulation (featuring, for example, a postulated 'underclass'), the decision is again mainly a function of preexisting theoretical commitments rather than narrowly empirical considerations. As a result, relatively little effort has been made to choose or adjudicate among measurement approaches on scientific grounds, even though the decision is a fundamentally empirical one.

It is difficult to justify such an aggressively non-empirical approach to measurement. We seek to develop here a stronger empirical foundation for poverty measurement by describing a modelling framework that may be used to determine whether poverty takes a gradational, categorical, or disorganized form. This framework exploits recent developments in latent class modelling to describe the underlying structure of a multivariate space made up of endowments and investments (such as education), working conditions (such as autonomy and authority), and rewards (such as income and wealth). If a gradational form emerges, our framework will allow researchers to assess whether or not conventional income-based approaches adequately specify the relevant gradient. If instead a categorical or 'class' form emerges, our framework will allow researchers to determine how many poverty classes there are and whether those classes correspond to existing sociological models of social classes. Although our objective here is merely to describe this new framework, we will be applying it in subsequent research.

2.2 The poverty measurement literature in economics and sociology

The intellectual backdrop for our project is the quite striking disarray within the field of poverty measurement. Within economics, now-standard critiques of unidimensional, income-based measurement of poverty (the 'income paradigm') rest mainly on the argument that income fails to 'take cognizance of other aspects of the quality of life that are not well correlated with economic advantage' (Nussbaum, 2006, p. 47; Bourguignon, 2006; Sen, 2006). This line of criticism has led to calls for multidimensional strategies for measuring and analyzing inequality and poverty. The most famous multidimensional measure, the Human Development Index (HDI), is closely monitored throughout the world (UNDP, 2001), but has been widely criticized as simplistic and under-theorized (for example, Kanbur, 2001) and hence has spurred much revisionist work.[2]

The resulting industry of multidimensional index building is unsatisfying in two ways. First, any attempt to reduce the multidimensional space of poverty into a single scale, such as HDI or any other index, will be descriptively misleading insofar as the underlying space is not in fact unidimensional. This simple observation has sparked much fretting among economists about the difficulty of parsimoniously characterizing the structure of poverty once multiple dimensions are allowed (Sen, 1997). To be sure, the dominance approach may allow us to order two or more populations in terms of their overall amount of poverty (within the context of a multidimensional poverty space), but such methods treat the shape or form of poverty as relevant only insofar as they affect conclusions about the overall amount (see Duclos, Sahn, and Younger, 2005). We will be arguing, to the contrary, that the structure of poverty regimes cannot be fully understood without elevating issues of shape and form to center stage. That is, in addition to asking whether population A has more poor people than population B, we should additionally ask whether poverty in either population takes on a gradational form, a class form, or a 'postmodern' form in which advantage and disadvantage are partly compensating. It is striking that, even as multidimensionalism becomes ever more fashionable in development economics, there is a continuing fascination with reducing comparisons to a single graded dimension. The commitment to multidimensionalism within development economics is in this sense quite superficial.

The second main concern with conventional indices is that they are purely statistical summaries and fail, therefore, to capture in any obvious way the structure of institutionalized social groups. In indices such as HDI, no effort is made to measure the social organization of inequality, especially the emergence of social networks, norms, and 'adaptive preferences' (such as tastes or culture) among people who are in similar life situations and circumstances. It is simply assumed that the sum of three variables provides an adequate description of poverty. Because the social organization of poverty is wholly ignored, the policy recommendations coming out of analyses of HDI have almost invariably treated poverty as an individual-level phenomenon that can be addressed with individual-level policy, such as increasing the human capital of some subpopulations (Grusky and Kanbur, 2006).

Within sociology, the lure of unidimensional gradationalism has historically been strong as well, although it has played out principally in the form of socioeconomic scales of occupations. As with HDI, these scales are merely weighted combinations of analytically separable dimensions, namely education and income (applied, however, to occupations rather than countries or individuals). It was not so long ago that these scales were understood among sociologists as capturing the most fundamental features of the inequality space. The massive research literature on these scales, a literature that eerily foreshadows the contemporary HDI literature, focused principally on the complications that arise in reducing a multidimensional space into a unidimensional one (see Hauser and Warren, 1997). For our purposes, we can safely ignore this literature, not just because socioeconomic scales have largely fallen out of fashion within sociology, but also because they only index the social location of currently or recently employed workers and cannot, as a result, be readily applied to the study of poverty. Among sociologists who prefer a gradational model, poverty has therefore typically been studied in terms of an income paradigm, just as in economics.

This is not to suggest that the income paradigm is dominant within sociology. The distinctive contribution of sociology to the study of poverty is arguably a 'class model' that characterizes individuals in terms of (i) the extent of their attachment to the labour market (measured by, for example, age-adjusted amount of labour force experience), and (ii) the sector or class in which employment most frequently occurs (if it does at all). Although there are all manner of competing class models of poverty, perhaps a leading candidate for a standard model is a three-class formulation that includes an 'underclass' with virtually no attachment or commitment to the labour market, a 'formal-sector poor' with a precarious attachment to low-wage labouring and service employment, and an 'informal-sector poor' with a precarious attachment to self-employment in the labouring and service sector.[3] The informal-sector category is populated by self-employed street vendors, day labourers, taxicab drivers, and all manner of other labouring and service occupations that are frequently taken up when formal-employment opportunities are scarce. In more developed countries, the formal sector tends to be larger than the informal sector, yet pockets of substantial informal employment can still be found in immigrant enclaves and the inner city.

The class model of poverty is further complicated because these three poverty classes take on very different forms in urban and rural settings. Although an underclass is present in both settings, the inner-city underclass is often distinguished by extreme segregation into spatially demarcated poverty neighbourhoods, dense intra-class interactions, and a greater likelihood that a class culture will emerge within these neighbourhoods of dense interactions. The other poverty classes take different forms across these settings because the constituent occupations differ. In rural economies, primary sector activities tend to dominate (especially agricultural labour), and such activities imply a very distinct type of poverty experience (most notably highly cyclical employment). The full sociological model of poverty is obtained, then, by cross-classifying the setting (rural, urban) with the three categories outlined above (the underclass, formal-sector poor, informal-sector poor).

This formulation potentially solves each of the two problems with conventional multidimensionalism to which we referred earlier. The daunting complexity of the multidimensional poverty space is addressed by brazenly characterizing it in terms of a relatively small number of categories, and the purely nominal, statistical character of conventional scales (such as HDI) is overcome by making explicit reference to institutionalized groupings (such as the 'underclass'). It is not difficult to understand why many sociologists have found class models attractive. As sociologists ourselves, we must confess to no small sympathy for the class approach, but we also question our discipline's characteristic assumption that class models should be blithely adopted without any evidence in support of the strong assumptions they embody. On this matter the disciplines of economics and sociology are equally disappointing. That is, just as economists have not typically treated HDI or the income paradigm as testable claims about the structure of the poverty space, so too sociologists have not typically treated class formulations as testable claims about its structure. We turn below to the task of converting measurement models into hypotheses.

2.3   A multidimensional inequality space

The first step in building a multidimensional account is to develop a list of life conditions that, taken together, adequately characterize the inequality space. If the relevant literatures in economics, sociology, and philosophy are consulted (see, for example, Bourdieu, 1984; Nussbaum, 2006), one finds considerable agreement on the following three classes of variables: (1) *investments and endowments* (*I*) refer to formal schooling, vocational schooling, and literacy; (2) *working conditions* (*C*) refer to authority, autonomy, mobility prospects, union status, type of employment contract (for example, salaried or wage), and type of labor market (for example, firm size); and (3) *rewards* (*R*) refer to earnings, investment income, income from welfare, and wealth. This list omits variables that are typically unavailable in large-scale surveys (for example, IQ) or that are best viewed as the consequences of poverty or inequality rather than their constituents (for example, attitudes, health, or consumption practices). It is nonetheless comprehensive enough to shift the burden of proof to those sceptics who believe that adding more variables would lead to fundamental changes in our understanding of poverty and inequality.

The various measurement paradigms on offer can now be understood as making different simplifying assumptions about this space. The income paradigm, for example, is built on the assumption that inequality is gradational and can be parsimoniously captured by a single, master income variable. Under this formulation, inequality and poverty are 'all or nothing' affairs in which high-income individuals are advantaged on all dimensions and low-income individuals are disadvantaged on all dimensions. The gradationalism of the income paradigm also implies that there are no subpopulation clusters (that is, classes) in which the dimensions of interest are independent of one another.

By contrast, the class paradigm assumes that the poverty space resolves into distinct bundles of conditions, with the scores on the dimensions being independent *within* these bundles. The poverty space is not only lumpy and discontinuous but may additionally encompass at least some bundles in which advantages and disadvantages come together as 'compensating differentials'. The relatively low wages of the routine non-manual class are coupled, for example, with working conditions that are comparatively desirable. These types of inconsistencies underlie the insistence on the part of some class analysts (see, for example, Erikson and Goldthorpe, 1992) that class categories do not form any simple unidimensional gradation.

It is conventional to apply a class model to the entire inequality space rather than just the least desirable sectors of it. Indeed, many class models ignore the underclass altogether, simply defining it away by restricting attention to individuals in the formal labour force. There is much debate among sociologists about the structure of classes within these more desirable sectors of the inequality space (see Wright, 2005). Rather than attempting any summary of those debates, we simply note that many, but not all, class models are based on aggregate occupational categories (for example, professionals, managers, routine non-manuals, craft workers, and operatives). These classes are typically presumed to imply a relatively strong and reliable attachment to the labour market.

In all sectors of the inequality space, such classes can be understood as marking off deeply institutionalized bundles of conditions (investments, working conditions, and rewards), bundles that give structure to the inequality space and make it possible to characterize it parsimoniously. The underclass, for example, is defined by an exceedingly weak attachment to the labour force and is characterized by poorly developed human capital investments (such as limited schooling), inferior working conditions (whenever there is engagement with the formal or informal labour market), and a weak economic situation marked, in particular, by high reliance on programme income rather than earnings. The formal-sector poor, by contrast, have a stronger (but still precarious) attachment to labouring and service employment and are characterized by slightly more substantial human capital investments (such as vocational training), slightly better working conditions, and slightly more income, most of which now comes from earnings. Similarly, the informal-sector poor are also concentrated in low-level labouring and service jobs, but they are self-employed rather than employed. The various non-poverty classes are likewise defined by structural positions in the division of labour (that is, occupations) and are presumed to capture the most prominently institutionalized packages of life conditions. The class of craft workers, for example, has historically comprised individuals with moderate educational investments, substantial investments in vocational training, relatively desirable working conditions, and average income.

2.4 Latent class models

To this point we have argued that the income and class paradigms embody hypotheses about the structure of the multidimensional inequality space. How might these hypotheses be tested?

We will show that the answer lies with exploratory and confirmatory latent class models, both of which are tailor-made for the measurement approach that we are developing. Until recently, latent class models for continuous and categorical indicators developed along separate tracks, thus precluding any analyses that combined the two scale types. However, these two tracks have now joined, making it possible to apply latent class models to mixed-mode data with both continuous and categorical indicators (see Vermunt and Magidson, 2002; Magidson and Vermunt, 2002; Hagenaars and McCutcheon, 2002). The latent class model for such mixed mode data can be represented as follows:

$$f(\mathbf{y}_i/\theta) = \sum_{k=1}^{K} \pi_k \prod_{j=1}^{J} f_k(y_{ij}/\theta_{jk}).$$
(2.1)

Here, $\mathbf{y}_i$ denotes the respondent's scores on the manifest variables, K is the number of latent classes, π_k refers to the probability of belonging to the kth latent class (thus indexing latent class sizes), J denotes the total number of manifest variables, and j is a particular manifest variable. The distribution of $\mathbf{y}_i$ is a function of the model parameters of θ that takes the form of a mixture of class-specific densities (that is, $f_k(y_{ij}/\theta_{jk})$).

We need to specify the appropriate univariate distribution for each element y_{ij} of $\mathbf{y}_i$. For continuous y_{ij}, the natural choice is the univariate normal, whereas for discrete nominal or ordinal variables it is the (restricted) multinominal. It is typically assumed that the manifest variables are independent within latent classes and that all of the observed association between manifest variables is therefore attributable to the particular patterning of latent class membership. That is, whenever a class member has a score that deviates from the class mean, this deviation doesn't convey any information on the likelihood of deviating on any of the other variables. The so-called assumption of local independence can be relaxed, yet we insist on it because it captures a main constraint embodied in the class hypothesis.

This framework may be used, then, to define various measurement models and to assess the extent to which the structure of the inequality space is consistent with those models. In all cases, our measurement models are best regarded as ideal types, with the question at hand being whether the structure of poverty and inequality is becoming more or less consistent with that ideal type.

2.5   Ideal-typical poverty spaces

We illustrate this approach by considering a simplified case in which the poverty space is defined by only three variables. Although we leave these hypothetical variables unspecified in the following discussion, it may be useful to imagine that one variable has been arbitrarily selected from each of the three classes of life conditions that define the multidimensional space (investments and endowments, working conditions, rewards). We would of course use the full complement of variables in any actual analysis.

The graphs presented below will represent the 'poverty subspace' as it might appear in either the rural or urban setting. In an actual latent class analysis, one is well advised to fit models to the full inequality space, even if one mainly wishes to test hypotheses about the structure that emerges in the less desirable sectors of that space (hereafter, the 'poverty space'). If the full space is analysed, it becomes possible, for example, to examine how distant the poverty classes are from other, more desirable classes in the inequality space.

We use three symbols to signify manifest class membership: (i) squares index membership in the underclass; (ii) triangles index membership in the formal-sector poverty class; and (iii) circles index membership in the informal-sector poverty class. We also allow for the possibility of two sub-classes emerging within each of these three big classes. The formal-sector poverty class might, for example, be divided into two sub-classes, one pertaining to labourers (indexed by light triangles) and another to service workers (indexed by dark triangles). The other big classes are likewise populated by two shadings that will signal possible sub-class sectors.

We can now lay out some of the lines of questioning opened up by this new approach to poverty measurement. We begin by asking whether the poverty space

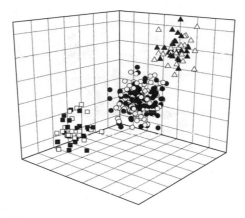

Figure 2.1   Big-class regime

takes on a form consistent with class models and then ask whether the space takes on a form consistent with the income paradigm and other non-class models. Throughout this presentation, it should be borne in mind that our particular three-class specification is purely illustrative, merely one of the many class models that might be examined.

Can standard big-class models capture the association in the poverty space? As we have argued, the implicit claim of class analysis is that the poverty space has a relatively low dimensionality, indeed a dimensionality no more or less than the number of postulated classes. This type of class model is conventionally treated as an assumption, but it may be tested by forcing the latent classes of Equation 2.1 to be perfectly defined by big-class membership, thus rendering latent classes manifest. The big-class solution, which is represented by Figure 2.1, implies that the individual-level variables are independent of one another within each big class and that sub-dividing into micro-classes or allowing for a gradational structure within big classes is accordingly unwarranted. If the observed data appear as in Figure 2.1, one would not be able to reject this big-class constraint.

Are there non-sociological big classes? The long-standing presumption among sociologists has been that poverty is generated at the 'site of production' and that our three manifest classes (or some other class model) will therefore account for the structure of poverty (see, for example, Parkin, 1979). Although the latent class model allows one to fit confirmatory models that test these 'sociological' class schemes, it can also be used to fit exploratory models that allow classes to freely emerge outside the site of production. As Figure 2.2 shows, the poverty space might resolve into big classes that are defined by characteristic packages of scores, without those classes also being consistent with conventional sociological categories defined at the site of production (the underclass, formal-sector poor, and informal-sector poor). This non-sociological solution is represented in Figure 2.2

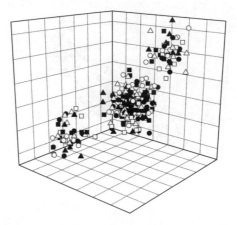

Figure 2.2   Big-classes forming outside site of production

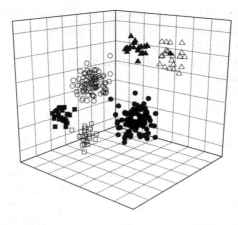

Figure 2.3   Micro-class regime

by populating each big class with an assortment of squares, triangles, and circles. If such a solution were secured, one would naturally wish to determine whether some other manifest variable, such as education, is defining these classes (see Meyer, 2001).

Are there micro-classes? The sociological big-class formulation might alternatively fall short because the three postulated classes are themselves amalgams of distinct subclasses. As shown in Figure 2.3, the independence constraint might be violated at the big-class level, but then hold once big classes are subdivided. We have else-where argued that the big-class categories of conventional class analysis are only weakly institutionalized in the labour market and that much of the structure at the site of production obtains at a lower occupational level (see Weeden and Grusky, 2005a; Grusky and Weeden 2006). It is possible, for example, that the 'formal-sector poor'

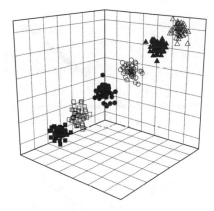

Figure 2.4   Gradational micro-class regime

is a wholly artificial amalgam and that the constituent occupations (construction labourers, gardeners, fast-food workers, and the like) differ substantially in the conditions they imply. If so, the poverty space will take on the more fissured form of Figure 2.3. We do not necessarily anticipate too many fissures of this sort. Although some micro-class distinctions will no doubt emerge, it has to borne in mind that occupationalization is less developed at the bottom of the class structure and that such distinctions may therefore be comparatively weak relative to what prevails in the professional sector and some of the other 'home grounds' of occupationalization (Weeden and Grusky, 2005b).

Is the poverty space gradational? In Figures 2.1–2.3, we have assumed that the class structure cannot be understood in simple gradational terms, meaning that at least some classes are formed by combining high values on one dimension with low values on another. The gradationalist challenge to conventional class models involves the claim that big classes or micro classes can be scaled on one or more dimensions (see Figure 2.4). We can test for such a structure by estimating scale values for the manifest classes or, less restrictively, by imposing ordinality constraints on them (see Rost, 1988; Croon, 2002). This test for gradationalism will be accepted insofar as classes are hierarchically ordered in terms of the extent to which they imply advantage or disadvantage. Although there is much research on how particular dimensions of inequality (especially income) are changing, we don't know whether late-industrialism has also brought on a form of crystallization in which the dimensions that make up the poverty and inequality space are coming together to form a more purely gradational structure.

Does inequality take on a fractal character? Although the regimes of Figures 2.2–2.4 are inconsistent with standard sociological class models, they nonetheless salvage the class concept in revised form by allowing for non-sociological classes (Figure 2.2), micro-classes (Figure 2.3), and gradational classes (Figure 2.4). By contrast, Figure 2.5 represents a case in which the class concept itself must be rejected because, no

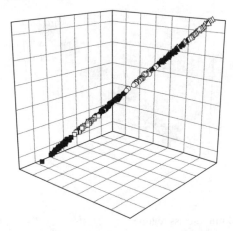

Figure 2.5   Fractal individualized inequality

matter the level of disaggregation, the underlying variables continue to covary with one another. This ideal type may be understood as an extreme micro-class solution in which the diagonal of Figure 2.4 thins out to the point where each individual becomes a class unto himself or herself. We refer to this solution as fractal because the same gradational solution is apparent at each and every level of disaggregation. The economist should recognize this solution as consistent with the claim that income is a master variable, that it perfectly signals all other individual-level measures of inequality, and that no higher-level class organization therefore appears. Obviously, this ideal type would never be empirically realized in such extreme form, but it is nonetheless important to ask whether the simple income paradigm comes closer to being realized in some societies or time periods than in others.

Is inequality becoming increasingly disorganized? The regime of Figure 2.6, in contrast to that of Figure 2.5, doesn't allow the underlying individual-level variables to covary. This may be understood as a 'one class' solution or, equivalently, a non-class regime. Although there is much inequality under this specification, it takes a uniquely structureless form in which the independence assumption holds throughout the poverty space, not just within a given latent class. This ideal type is again very extreme and not likely to hold in any known poverty space. We have presented it here simply because it is important to monitor the extent to which the poverty space is becoming more or less organized (see Pakulski, 2005).

We can't claim to have exhausted here the many ideal-typical forms that either class-based or classless poverty regimes might assume. Rather, we wish merely to stress the importance of developing a methodology for characterizing the form as well as extent of poverty, a task that takes on special importance once the multi-dimensionality of inequality is appreciated. This approach allows us to explicitly test long-standing disciplinary assumptions about the structure of poverty.

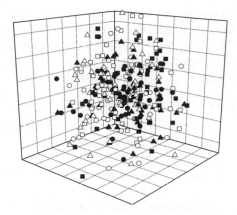

Figure 2.6   Disorganized inequality

2.6   Class effects

How might defenders of the income or class paradigm react insofar as it is shown that their approaches cannot well represent the poverty space? There are many possible reactions, but perhaps the main choices are to (i) simply concede that a more complicated representation of the poverty space is indeed required, (ii) argue that the poverty space was operationalized in an excessively encompassing way and therefore includes superfluous dimensions that fall outside the poverty concept, or (iii) argue that the preferred approach, while failing to represent the poverty space in its entirety, nonetheless captures those features of the space that are important in explaining outcomes or social behaviors of interest (for example, Goldthorpe and McKnight, 2006). As we see it, argument (ii) is entirely non-empirical and hence beyond our purview, whereas argument (iii) is an explicitly empirical claim and hence worth considering in some detail.

If the objective is indeed to measure poverty in terms of classes or variables (most obviously income) that have true causal effects, presumably much research effort should be devoted to establishing such effects. We haven't, however, seen much effort of this sort to date. The challenge here is to offer convincing evidence that inter-class differences in behaviour cannot be explained away as the effects of (i) investments and endowments that drive selection into particular classes, (ii) working conditions, including unionization or authority, that can affect how interests are gauged and behaviors selected, and (iii) job rewards (for example, income) that likewise may affect how interests are gauged and behaviours selected. If, for example, one finds that an apparent 'underclass effect' on political behavior disappears when income is controlled, then presumably one can refer only to an income effect on politics, not a true class effect. The case for a true class effect likewise requires controlling for all the other constituent dimensions of the poverty or inequality space.

Why might net effects of class be detected even with such rigorous controls? In addressing this question, what must be stressed is that classes are organic packages of conditions, and the constituents of these packages may combine and interact in ways that lead to an emergent logic of the situation. The underclass may be understood as a combination of negative conditions (limited education, limited experience, low income) that, taken together, engender a sense of futility, despondency, or learned helplessness that is more profound than what would be expected from a model that simply allows for independent effects of each constituent class condition (Wilson, 2006). To be sure, a committed reductionist might counter that, instead of allowing for class effects, one merely needs to include the appropriate set of interactions among the constituent variables. This reformulation is correct but unhelpful; that is, insofar as classes define the relevant packages of interacting conditions, it just becomes an unduly complicated way of sidestepping the reality of classes.

The foregoing may be understood, then, as a rational action interpretation of how class effects are generated as class members attempt to optimize, satisfice, or otherwise react to the emergent logic of their class situation. The second main argument for a net class effect rests on the claim that class-defined packages of conditions are associated with distinctive cultures that take on a life of their own and thus independently shape behaviour and attitudes. At minimum, class cultures may simply be 'rules of thumb' that encode optimizing behavioural responses to prevailing environmental conditions, rules that allow class members to forego optimizing calculations themselves and rely instead on cultural prescriptions that provide reliable short cuts to the right decision. The 'formal-sector poor' may disparage educational investments not because of some maladaptive oppositional culture but because such investments expose them to an especially high risk of downward mobility (see Goldthorpe, 2000). Typically, the children of the working poor lack insurance in the form of substantial family income or wealth, meaning that they cannot easily recover from an educational investment gone awry; and those who nonetheless undertake such an investment therefore face the real possibility of utter ruin. The emergence, then, of a poverty culture that regards educational investments as frivolous encodes this conclusion and thus allows poor children to undertake optimizing behaviors without explicitly engaging in decision-tree calculations.

If one allows for class cultures of this sort, it is not entirely clear that such cultures always develop at the national level. After all, an underclass culture is presumably generated and transmitted at the city or neighbourhood level, where members of the underclass interact with one another, develop shared interpretations of their situation and how best to react to it, and transmit those interpretations to one another (see Wilson, 2006). Given that inner cities differ in their industrial mix, employment opportunities, and welfare programmes, the environment that underclass members face may differ substantially by city, and so too will the rule-of-thumb cultures that emerge. The most important fissures within the underclass may therefore be defined by cities rather than detailed occupations.

Can these fissures be overcome? In some countries, the underlying environmental conditions will be much the same across all inner cities, thus breeding rule-of-thumb cultures that are likewise much the same. Because there is very little cross-city contact among underclass members, the rise of a national underclass culture must be understood as a patchwork of many local cultures that independently 'hit upon' the same rule-of-thumb interpretations, not the result of any cross-city diffusion of such interpretations. In some cases, political elites or other opinion leaders may also act as vanguard intellectuals who broadly instruct all underclass members on the proper interpretation of their situation, thereby creating cross-city homogeneity that is top-down in its origins rather than bottom-up. This top-down process takes place mainly within countries, such as Venezuela, in which the underclass is large enough to induce party elites to build a political platform tailored to its putative interests.

This line of reasoning suggests that defenders of class analysis need not shy away from an empirical test of class effects. It is altogether possible that real big-class or micro-class effects will surface and provide a further rationale for measuring poverty in terms of classes. We nonetheless see no great rush among class analysts to carry out such tests. In this sense, class analysts have behaved rather like stereotypical economists, the latter frequently being criticized (and parodied) for their willingness to assume almost anything provided that it leads to an elegant model.

2.7   Conclusions

It should by now be clear that sociologists operating within the class-analytic tradition have adopted very strong assumptions about how poverty is structured. The class concept may be motivated either by claiming that the inequality space has a (low) dimensionality that equals the number of social classes or by claiming that the class locations of individuals have a true causal effect on behaviors, attitudes, or practices. These claims, like those underlying the income paradigm, have long been unstated articles of faith. We have suggested that progress in the field depends on converting such disciplinary priors into testable hypotheses about the structure and form of poverty.

These tests are best conducted within the multidimensional poverty space. Although the turn to multidimensionalism is prominent in development economics and other fields, the approach has foundered to date for lack of a compelling methodological platform. We have argued that latent class modeling, which has now been generalized to accommodate mixed mode data, provides precisely the platform needed to test our disciplinary assumptions about the structure of poverty.

The further virtue of this platform is that it allows us to monitor changes in the shape and form of poverty. Although we know much about trends in the amount of poverty, we know rather less about trends in its form; and the form of poverty may be just as consequential as the amount in understanding how it is experienced and how it may develop. We don't know, for example, whether poverty is increasingly taking on a highly organized class form, whether new types of inconsistencies and disorganization are emerging within the poverty space, or whether poverty is increasingly assuming a simple gradational form of the sort that the income paradigm implies. These gaps in our knowledge can only be addressed by developing a multidimensional monitoring system that moves beyond simplistic measurements of headcounts and treats distributional issues of inequality with the same seriousness that is accorded measurements of total economic activity and output.

Notes

1. The research reported here was supported with discretionary funds from Stanford University and Cornell University. We are grateful for the comments of participants in the United Nations Development Programme International Conference on Multidimensional Poverty, 29–31 August 2005, Brasilia, Brazil.
2. Although HDI was initially treated as an aggregate index (measured at the country level), it has subsequently been recast as an individual-level index.
3. There is also a long tradition of class scholarship in which the underclass is simply defined away by virtue of restricting analysis to members of the labour force. We will be focusing here on more encompassing class models that treat the absence of a strong attachment to the labour force as the defining feature of membership in the 'underclass'. In operationalizing the underclass, the objective is to identify those who are at risk of being in the labour force, but who have not evinced much labour force activity in the past.

References

Bourdieu P., (1984) *Distinction: a Social Critique of the Judgement of Taste*, translated by R. Nice. (2006) New York: Cambridge University Press.

Bourguignon F., (2006) 'From Income to Endowments: The Difficult Task of Expanding the Income Poverty Paradigm', in *Poverty and Inequality*, edited by D. B. Grusky and R. Kanbur. Stanford: Stanford University Press, pp. 76–102.

Croon M., (2002) 'Ordering the Classes', in *Applied Latent Class Analysis*, edited by J. A. Hagenaars and A. L. McCutcheon. Cambridge: Cambridge University Press.

Duclos J., D. E. Sahn and S. D. Younger (2006) 'Robust Multidimensional Poverty Comparisons', *Economic Journal* 116 (514), 943–68.

Erikson R., and J. H. Goldthorpe, (1992) *The Constant Flux: A Study of Class Mobility in Industrial Societies*. New York: Clarendon Press.

Goldthorpe J. H., (2000) *On Sociology: Numbers, Narrative, and the Integration of Research and Theory*. New York: Oxford University Press.

Goldthorpe J. H., and A. McKnight (2006) 'The Economic Basis of Social Class', in *Mobility and Inequality: Frontiers of Research in Sociology and Economics,* edited by S. L. Morgan, D. B. Grusky, and G. S. Fields. Stanford: Stanford University Press, pp. 109–36.

Grusky D. B., and R. Kanbur (2006) 'Conceptual Ferment in Poverty and Inequality Measurement: The View from Economics and Sociology', in *Poverty and Inequality*, edited by D. B. Grusky and R. Kanbur. Stanford: Stanford University Press, pp. 1–29.

Grusky D. B., and K. A. Weeden (2006) 'Does the Sociological Approach to Studying Social Mobility Have a Future?' in *Mobility and Inequality: Frontiers of Research in Sociology and Economics,* edited by S. L. Morgan, D. B. Grusky, and G. S. Fields. Stanford: Stanford University Press, pp. 85–108.

Hagenaars J. A., and A. L. McCutcheon (eds) (2002) *Applied Latent Class Analysis*. Cambridge: Cambridge University Press.

Hauser R. M., and J. R. Warren (1997) 'Socioeconomic Indexes of Occupational Status: A Review, Update, and Critique', in *Sociological Methodology*, edited by A. Raftery. Cambridge: Blackwell Publishers, pp. 177–298.

Kanbur R., (2001) 'Economic Policy, Distribution and Poverty: The Nature of Disagreements', *World Development* 29, 1083–94.

Magidson J., and J. K. Vermunt (2002) *Latent Class Models*. Boston: Statistical Innovations, Inc.

Meyer J. W., (2001) 'The Evolution of Modern Stratification Systems', in *Social Stratification: Class, Race, and Gender in Sociological Perspective,* 2nd edn, edited by D. B. Grusky. Boulder: Westview Press, pp. 881–90.

Nussbaum M., (2006) 'Poverty and Human Functioning: Capabilities as Fundamental Entitlements', in *Poverty and Inequality*, edited by D. B. Grusky and R. Kanbur. Stanford: Stanford University Press, pp. 47–75.

Pakulski J., (2005) 'Foundations of a Post-Class Analysis', in *Approaches to Class Analysis*, edited by E. O. Wright. Cambridge: Cambridge University Press, pp. 152–79.

Parkin F., (1979) *Marxism and Class Theory: A Bourgeois Critique*. New York: Columbia University Press.

Rost J., (1988) 'Rating Scale Analysis with Latent Class Models', *Psychometrika*, 53, 327–48.

Sen A., (1997) *On Economic Inequality*. Oxford: Oxford University Press.

Sen A., (2006) 'Concepts and Measures', in *Poverty and Inequality*, edited by D. B. Grusky and R. Kanbur. Stanford: Stanford University Press, pp. 30–46.

UNDP (2001) *Human Development Report*. New York: Oxford University Press.

Vermunt, J. K. and J. Magidson (2002) 'Latent Class Cluster Analysis', in *Applied Latent Class Analysis*, edited by J. A. Hagenaars and A. L. McCutcheon. Cambridge: Cambridge University Press.

Weeden K. A., and D. B. Grusky (2005a) 'The Case for a New Class Map', *American Journal of Sociology* 111, 141–212.

Weeden K. A., and D. B. Grusky (2005b) 'Are There Any Big Classes at All?', in *The Shape of Social Inequality: Stratification and Ethnicity in Comparative Perspective,* edited by D. Bills. *Research in Social Stratification and Mobility, Volume 22*. Amsterdam: Elsevier, pp. 3–56.

Wilson W. J., (2006) 'Social Theory and the Concept "Underclass"', in *Poverty and Inequality*, edited by D. B. Grusky and R. Kanbur. Stanford: Stanford University Press, pp. 103–16.

Wright E. O., (ed.) (2005) *Approaches to Class Analysis*. Cambridge: Cambridge University Press.

3
Poverty Counts: Living with Poverty and Poverty Measures

Sara Berry

3.1 Introduction

Counting or measuring poverty is frequently meant to explain how poverty counts – how it affects people's lives and the conditions in which they live. Anthropologists have contributed to the study of poverty, although often as a corollary rather than as a central objective of ethnographic research. Partly because of their disciplinary tradition of studying remote, exotic social groups and places, many anthropologists write of people and places that are, or appear, disadvantaged relative to larger, richer, more powerful societies (see, for example, Ferguson, 1999) As a discipline, anthropology aspires to holism – inquiry into 'the study of man' in its entirety. Within the sub-field of social-cultural anthropology, many researchers aim for an integrated understanding of economic, political, social and cultural practices and relationships within a particular social, spatial and/or cognitive locality, which may or may not be culturally or territorially bounded. If poverty or 'relative deprivation is... a multi-dimensional concept, embracing "all the spheres of life"' (Lister, 2004: 22) then combining ethnographic insights with quantitative measures of poverty should enhance our understanding of its many dimensions.[1] The present essay seeks to amplify and illustrate this point, using examples from ethnographic literature on Africa.

For the student of poverty, anthropology is relevant both for questions of method – what (and what not) to measure and how – and for analysis – how poverty occurs, whom it affects, and what ought to be done about it. Ironically, given recent critiques of anthropology as a 'colonial science' (Hymes, 1972; Asad, 1973; Stocking, 1984), some of the first anthropologists to study modes of livelihood as a policy issue were British ethnographers commissioned by colonial authorities to investigate agricultural production, nutrition and food security in Africa, in order to assess the need for policy intervention. First published in 1939, Audrey Richards' classic study, *Land, Labour and Diet in Northern Rhodesia*, sought 'to show what anthropologists could contribute to the study of nutrition in African society, by an analysis of the social and economic factors affecting the intake of food in a particular tribe...' (Richards, 1939: vii. See also Moore and Vaughan, 1994: 1–10 and *passim*) Over the course of the next 15 years, anthropologists and others produced a number of quantitative as well as ethnographic inquiries, from farming surveys and household budget studies to national income accounts,[2] which both reflected and helped to promote officials' growing concern with government responsibility for social welfare. As the cost and complexity of extending the welfare state to the colonies became increasingly clear, colonial regimes began to rethink the sustainability of empire. In the early 1960s, they withdrew, leaving to their African 'successors the task of leading the transformation of a continent they themselves could not control...' (F. Cooper, 1996: 472).

Since the end of the colonial era, anthropologists have been increasingly critical of 'the development enterprise' in general, and what some have called 'the hegemony of the measurable' in particular (Lister, 2004: 38). James Ferguson's widely-cited critique of development research and policy in Lesotho as an 'an anti-politics machine', disguising its own political agenda under the rubric of 'technical assistance', or Peter Uvin's self-critical reflections on the complicity of the development enterprise in the Rwandan genocide are just two, Africa-focused examples (Ferguson, 1990; Uvin, 1998). Anthropologists have been particularly critical of quantitative analysis, arguing that it depicts poverty and development as 'technical' problems amenable to mechanistic 'solutions', and evades or covers up the political agendas of those who design poverty interventions and those who create the conditions they address (Mitchell, 1991, 2002. See also Escobar, 1995; Cooper & Packard, 1997; Gledhill, 2001). Others point out that the production of aggregate data is a complex and contentious political process in its own right. In the words of one former official of the IMF, 'the managing director makes the big decisions, and the staff then puts together the numbers to justify them' (quoted in Wade, 2004: p. 584; see also Harper, 2005).

While agreeing that many of these points are well-taken, the present chapter stops short of the view that quantitative methods are so inherently flawed as to be worse than useless, or that numbers should be dropped entirely from the lexicon of poverty studies. Compiling and examining quantitative indices can be a fruitful way of posing questions for further inquiry and reflection, not least because if honestly labelled and read, numbers help to clarify the limits of our knowledge. Quantification provides a powerful tool of aggregation, allowing analysts to discern social 'forests' among the profusion of 'trees' produced by close-grained ethnographic research, and assess their significance for social analysis and policy design. In the following pages, I discuss measurement and ethnographic observation as both complementary and conflicting modes of representing social reality that, together, provide insights into multidimensional aspects of poverty that neither method yields alone. Rather than propose new or modified techniques for measuring poverty, this chapter seeks to show how ethnographic insights can enhance understanding of the meaning and limitations of quantitative indicators as tools for describing and explaining both the causes of poverty, and its consequences for people's aspirations, actions and relations with one another and the conditions in which they live. To illustrate, I will focus on a few themes – time and temporality, institutions, and social relationships – using examples from ethnographic writings on Africa to suggest ways in which ethnographic inquiry can qualify or expand understandings of poverty based on quantitative analysis.

3.2   Time and temporality: Contexts, methods, resources

Rather than rehearse familiar debates about the measurement of trends and fluctuations, this section comments briefly on time and temporality as perspectives – ways of experiencing and understanding social and material conditions and processes – that shape social practices and frame analysts' interpretations of them.[3] Since Meyer Fortes introduced the question of multiple temporalities into anthropological notions of social structure, anthropologists have paid increasing attention to 'the problem of time... as an inescapable dimension of all aspects of social experience and practice' (Munn, 1992: 93; Fortes, 1970, 1975; Faubion, 1993). The following examples illustrate some of the ways in which ethnographic studies of temporality may enhance our readings of some common poverty measures.

In people's everyday pursuit of livelihood and a chance to get ahead, time figures as both a resource and a constraint. People who live in or close to poverty, without access to land, capital, infrastructure and/or marketable skills, are almost entirely dependent on their own time and effort and, for that reason, are also highly vulnerable to both natural and man-made temporalities – rhythms and contingencies, from weather to market fluctuations and bureaucratic delays – that they can neither escape nor control. Converging periodicities of seasonal and/or institutional routines create everyday dilemmas of time allocation and management, placing a premium on people's own time and energy, limiting their ability to secure a livelihood, and leaving them vulnerable to anticipated as well as unforeseen events. In some circumstances, people literally run out of time: in African villages, anthropologists found, children may go hungry during labour peaks in the farming cycle, even if their mothers have not run short of foodstuffs, because the women are too tired to cook (Richards, 1939: 104–5; Haswell, 1975: 99ff.). In Gambia a scheme to help rural women augment meagre household incomes by planting dry season vegetable gardens nearly foundered on conjugal struggles over the allocation of women's time between watering their gardens and preparing food and baths for their husbands and husbands' guests (Schroeder, 1999; compare Carney, 1988; Carney and Watts, 1990). Such constraints may operate in periods of prosperity as well as dearth. In Nigeria, motor mechanics were hard pressed to keep up with demand during the oil boom of the 1970s because time spent on necessary tasks such as buying spare parts and visiting 'regular customers' took them away from their shops, where unpaid apprentices accomplished little in the master's absence (Berry, 1985: 153ff.).

In recent years, as HIV/AIDS has claimed more and more young adult victims, most drastically in southern and parts of eastern Africa, children and elderly survivors confront additional burdens of caring for the sick and providing for siblings, grandchildren, and neighbours left helpless by the incapacity and death of their former providers. Often poor to begin with, many of these caretakers are entirely dependent on their own time to negotiate the daily burdens of living with poverty, illness and death.

With limited options for earning income, many also find that returns to their efforts are highly unpredictable. In rain-fed agriculture, the predominant form of small-scale farming across much of Africa, crop yields depend crucially on farmers' ability to time inputs and cultivation practices to coincide with variations in rainfall and temperature, pest and disease attack, or the rhythms of plant growth and maturation. For resource-poor farmers, the unpredictability of environmental factors can become unmanageable when someone falls ill, whether it is the farmer herself, one or more of her livestock, or a relative or neighbour who might have helped with farm work, but needs care instead (Haugerud, 1988: 170–1). Such hazards are compounded by seasonal fluctuations in market conditions, especially for farmers who cannot afford to store crops until prices recover from post-harvest lows, or for petty traders who may walk miles to market, only to return at the end of the day with goods unsold and proceeds too meagre to provide the evening meal. For those with little in reserve, an unlucky turn of events may make farming itself impossible. As a Russian peasant explained, 80 years ago, to a government enumerator, 'today I am a middle peasant, tomorrow I become a poor peasant. If the horse dies, I'll have to hire myself out' (quoted in Shanin, 1972: 114–15).

The burdens of self-reliance and the unpredictability of circumstance affect not only levels of income and vulnerability, but also practices of personal and social management. In a richly detailed study of rural women in Gambia, anthropologist Caroline Bledsoe found that, faced with a daily regimen of unremitting toil and uncertain food supplies, women were more concerned with their own and their children's welfare than with the total number of their offspring. A woman needs time, they explained, to establish the health of her infant and regain her own health and strength after the birth of one child before she incurs the physical costs of another. Without the strength to do physically demanding labor for long hours every day, she won't be able to provide for the children she already has. In Bledsoe's sample, the small but significant proportion of women who used Western contraceptives did so 'to ensure the production of *more* living children than they would have achieved' without contraception, rather than to limit their total fertility (Bledsoe, 2002: 137).

As Bledsoe's illuminating study shows, Gambian women's reproductive goals are multidimensional – balancing the desire for many children against the need to provide for them in the face of enduring poverty and constant uncertainty about the next day's demands. Questions about 'desired lifetime fertility', the index favoured by demographers as a predictor of reproductive practice, were likely to be met with non-committal piety: 'it's up to God' (ibid.: 140ff). Gambians, Bledsoe concludes, do not 'measure' reproductive potential in terms of linear temporality, dividing the time between menarche and menopause by the average length of a birth interval, as westerners do. Rather, they believe that a woman is born with an 'endowment... of potential fetuses that God has bestowed upon [her]... to spend on behalf of her husband and his family... Once this endowment is finished, reproduction is finished, regardless of her age' (ibid.: 165). Since the number of her foetuses is unknown until they are finished, a woman's reproductive 'budgeting' aims not to achieve a target number of live births, but to manage her own health and that of her babies so as to achieve as many live births as possible out of her potential total.[4] Reproduction and aging are not 'bound to a time clock' as westerners assume, but form 'a God-given endowment that must be realized within a life course of contingent physical tolls' (ibid.: 211–12).

Studies such as Bledsoe's, which elucidate basic intercultural differences in understandings of social temporality, can be as illuminating for the analysis of economic indicators as for demographic ones. Struggling with prolonged economic stagnation or decline and widening inequality, many Africans have grown pessimistic about their children's prospects for getting ahead in life, but this does not mean they don't think about the future or frame current options in terms of past experience. Comparing budget studies of Ghanaian households in the 1950s and the late 1980s, Guyer (2004) points out that, contrary to 'Engel's Law', the proportion of household income spent on food was roughly the same for all levels of income, both in the 1950s and in the 1980s, despite dramatic changes in Ghana's economic and political fortunes during the intervening years.[5] The contrast between household budget data for Ghana and those collected elsewhere, and the consistency of Ghanaian expenditure patterns over time, raise questions about widely accepted explanations of economic behavior. Reading the data against ethnographic literature on Akan communities in Ghana and Yoruba communities in Nigeria, Guyer suggests that many West Africans orient income generation and use towards anticipated 'career paths' rather than immediate household needs, adapting specific activities to current exigencies, while maintaining a sense of purpose and direction shaped by past experience (ibid.: 147ff.). As individuals' incomes rise, they strengthen social ties by spending more on feeding other people. In such contexts, respect for 'tradition' may be a source of resilience rather than inflexibility. Faced with prolonged hardship and shrinking opportunities in the stagnant economy of the 1990s, Asantes 'struggled hard to fulfill their still vigorous commitment to lineage connections', drawing strength from their pride in 'the very latest tradition' (Clark, 1999: 81–2).

Bringing temporal perspectives to bear on economic activities and conditions also helps to elucidate patterns of production and income use that are often dismissed as unproductive or irrational. Two classic examples in the anthropological literature on Africa are visiting and social payments – activities that contribute little or nothing to current income or productivity, but may play a crucial role in establishing and maintaining social relationships that, in turn, shape access to resources and opportunities over time. Yoruba car mechanics whom I interviewed in 1978/79, during the height of the Nigerian oil boom, described outlays on food, shelter, clothing, etc., for themselves and their dependents as 'expenses'. What remained from their earnings after these 'expenses' were covered was 'profit', to be used 'for myself' which meant investing in the business (Berry, 1985: 153). Observers have frequently commented on the prevalence of social expenditures – marriage payments, funeral donations, gifts – in African household budgets. Often classified by economists and statisticians as unproductive 'transfers' of goods and money, such transactions have been shown to play a key role in establishing a person's social identity and nurturing relationships that facilitate productive investment as well as providing economic security.[6]

In the decades since independence, economic crises and political turmoil have led to persistent economic stagnation, decline and spreading poverty in many African countries, undermining families' capacity to provide security, let alone

opportunity for their members, and some argue that the strength of family relations has declined as a result. 'The pressures that erode lineage families also erode
household relations.... Youth begin to fend for themselves at an early age' and 'different interests within the household begin to exert their own interests', leading to
'struggles between elders and youth and men and women' (Amanor, 2001: 118;
compare Sharp and Spiegel, 1985). Others point out that, while declining economic opportunities have eroded people's capacity to assist others, they have also
increased people's reliance on social networks as potential, albeit shrinking, safety
nets. In the mid-1990s, Clark writes, 'Asante [were] not degenerating into irre-
sponsible individualism but struggling hard to fulfil their still vigorous commitment
to lineage connections...' (Clark, 1999: 81). Similarly, Amanor notes a 'discourse
[that] builds upon the solidarity of relations between grandmothers, mothers and
daughters in farming and the transmission of women's farm property' to argue
'that women should have equal access to family property as men in their own
right' (Ibid.: 118. Compare B. Cooper, 1997; Brydon and Legge, 1996) In conversation, Ghanaians lament the 'decline' of family obligations and mutual assistance
in contemporary life, but expressions of anxiety do not always correspond to practice. What is striking is ordinary Africans' increasing reliance on, as well as vulnerability to, the global economy, and a corresponding incorporation of global
economic inequalities *within* families and communities in Ghana. In re-studying a
peri-urban community in 2002, I found the place transformed from the village
I visited in 1993, to a sprawling suburb filled with houses newly built with remittances
from Ghanaian emigrants in Europe and North America, that were occupied by
the emigrants' poorer relatives as well as (or instead of) rent-paying tenants.

As these examples suggest, bringing close ethnographic observations to bear on
measurements of income, expenditure and asset formation enhances and clarifies
our view of the multidimensionality of poverty, and the experience of living with
it on a daily basis. Understanding how people experience and interpret the daily
routines, 'normal' contingencies, crises and long-term changes that lie behind
numerical indices of income and wealth can help to explain how poverty deepens
and spreads. By drawing attention to the dynamism of everyday life, anthropological studies underscore the degree to which poverty analysts and policy makers
alike are trying to 'hit a moving target' (Maxwell, 1986, 2004).

3.3 Institutions in motion: Household, marriage, family

Most measurements of poverty use households as their basic unit of analysis.
Recent publications by UNDP and other organizations acknowledge that the
dynamism of African households complicates efforts to measure levels and inci-
dences of poverty, but many challenges remain.[7] Constructing a sociologically
meaningful definition of the household is a challenge in any context, but
nowhere more so than in African societies where one residential structure may
house dozens of people who relate to one another in many different ways, and
individuals move in and out continually, living their everyday lives, so to speak,
in motion. Accustomed to conventions of domestic stability in Europe, colonial

officials complained endlessly about the difficulties of governing African 'subjects', who seemed never to stay in one place long enough to be counted, instructed or taxed. African governments faced similar challenges after independence, as they attempted to exercise effective authority over the mobile, diverse, often-divided populations within their borders. Children often move among several domiciles as they grow up, learning new skills and building relationships with kin, teachers, friends, even strangers who help prepare them for adulthood and may serve as future patrons (Bledsoe, 1990; Berry, 1985; and many others). In southern Ghana, husbands and wives may reside in different houses, sending children to carry meals and messages between them, visiting each other when circumstances permit, and traveling separately to trade, work, or visit distant relatives, sometimes for extended periods of time. In a longitudinal study of a Nigerian village before and after the oil boom of the 1970s, I found that while the total population had remained constant between 1971 and 1978, 60 per cent of those resident in 1971 had moved away and been replaced, not by strangers but by other members of their extended families. This kind of residential independence and mobility is also paralleled in economic life. Siblings, parents and children, even husbands and wives manage their incomes and expenditures separately, and assets are often individually owned, even when they are combined in the process of production. Goheen's ethnography, *Men Own the Fields, Women Own the Crops* (1996) refers to one small polity in southwestern Cameroon, but the title is emblematic of practices that regularly confound efforts to count 'household assets' or construct meaningful measurements of 'household income'.

In societies where domestic arrangements are varied, complex and dynamic, policy makers would be better served by data that measure poverty for individuals rather than for imagined standardized 'households.' The cost and logistics of collecting individual data are high, especially in societies without reliable censuses or adequate administrative infrastructure, but policies that ignore social realities can be costly too.[8] Citing data that show a lower incidence of poverty among married couples than among single adults with children in the US, the present federal administration promotes marriage as a strategy for poverty alleviation. Among poor unmarried women, however, employment is viewed as a precondition rather than a corollary of marriage since, in their experience, economic security leads to stable marriages, rather than the other way around (Edin & Kefalas, 2005). Evidence from West Africa tends to support their position. Recent studies report increasing numbers of men and women who postpone marriage or avoid it altogether, explaining that they do not marry because they cannot afford to (Clark, 1999; Brydon, 1987). Declining marriage rates do not necessarily portend weakened or diminished family relations (see, for example, Brydon, 1987), but they do reflect declining opportunities for both personal and collective economic advance, and the increasing difficulty people have in rising out of poverty in the current era of market liberalization.

In short, numbers are both powerful tools of aggregation and limited in their ability to represent multiple and contradictory dimensions of living with poverty, or address the challenges of designing and carrying out effective policy interventions.

Ethnographic observations are hard to add up, but expand understanding in ways that numbers do not. Together, they illuminate not only the many dimensions of poverty, but also the way they change over time.

3.4   From assets to investment: Social relations as 'property' and process

In developing multidimensional approaches to measuring poverty, recent studies acknowledge that access to income-generating opportunities and/or ability to make productive use of them may be enhanced by the assistance of other people, as well as by access to markets and purchasing power.[9] '[S]ocial groups play an important role in protecting the needs of poor people and mediating against risk', declares a recent World Bank report, adding that '[s]ocial institutions refer to the kinship systems, local organizations, and networks of the poor and can be usefully discussed as different forms or dimensions of social capital'. (World Bank, 2001: 128) Recognizing the role that institutions and networks play in people's experiences with poverty is important, but equating them to 'social capital' tends to conceptualize them as things – stocks of objects, ideas and/or interpersonal connections that add to or diminish people's capacity to produce or earn income (Bourdieu, 1985; Dasgupta, 2000; Foley and Edwards, 1999; Manski, 2000). Building on Bourdieu's pioneering work in sociology, economists have drawn attention to the potential 'profitability' of interpersonal connections, and it has become commonplace to list 'social capital' among the assets that promote development and/or alleviate poverty (World Bank, 2001; Chen and Ravaillon, 2004).

In this vein, it is interesting to note that there is an implicit contradiction between theories of 'market liberalization' which argue that markets function best when market signals are not 'distorted' by social obligations or the exercise of power, and the concept of 'social capital' which emphasizes the productive potential of social relationships and institutions. This apparent conundrum reflects, in part, the language of economic analysis, which distinguishes between income, defined as a moving flow of goods and/or purchasing power, and assets that have the potential to generate income because they retain value over long periods of time. Such terminology tends to downplay the plasticity and instability of assets themselves, including social relationships or 'non-market' institutions. Unlike markets, for example, which are conventionally evaluated according to their 'openness' and flexibility, non-market institutions are often pictured as stable, unchanging, and/or rooted in a distant or imagined past. People 'fail to respond' to opportunities or new ideas, it is said, because they are wedded to immobile traditions.

A striking example is provided by a film, 'These Girls are Missing: the Gender Gap in Africa's Schools' (Robertson and Camerini, 1997), which seeks to dramatize the value of girls' education in Africa. Sponsored, in part, by the World Bank, 'These Girls...' sends a curiously mixed message about the obstacles to improving educational opportunities for African girls. The soundtrack is a series of conversations with adults – older men in a Guinean village who insist that sending girls to school will lead to immoral behaviour and undermine traditional authority, and staff and parents at an elite girl's school in Malawi who dwell on premarital pregnancy as a primary reason why girls leave school before completing their studies.[10] The auditory message of the film is clear: traditional male attitudes towards girls' sexuality impede African progress.

Visually, however, the film tells another story. While men talk in the Guinean village, the camera shows girls and women engaged in manual labour – fetching water and firewood, pounding grain, sweeping dirt floors, scrubbing clothes, hoeing fields – in an unending effort to keep up with daily household needs. In the Malawian section of the film, we see girls in school, bent over their books or leaving school, at the insistence of uncles or fathers, to give birth and devote themselves to child-care and housework, while we listen to parents and teachers bemoan the weak mores that distract young women from academic pursuits and compromise their futures. In short, while the soundtrack blames cultural intransigence for low rates of academic achievement among African girls, the camera suggests that, without their labor, many African households would not function.[11]

In the policy discourse that prompted 'These Girls are Missing', social processes such as education, tradition and culture are represented as things – social assets or liabilities that increase or reduce productive capacity in potentially measurable amounts. Conceptualizing social processes in this way belies the difficulty of measuring the interactive practices through which people generate and sustain them. What units should we use to calculate quantities or degrees of sisterhood or seniority? What numerical or ordinal scales capture the ambivalent dynamics of love, fear, respect, hope, suspicion and betrayal that play out through people's daily lives, or the dialogics of expectation and (mis)understanding that make and unmake attitudes and relationships? I am not suggesting that these are questions that anthropologists can answer, but statisticians cannot. The vividness with which skilled ethnographers bring people to life by weaving together detailed accounts of their words, deeds, performances and interactions testifies to the limitations as well as the strengths of anthropological methods for charting the multiple dimensions of poverty. By chronicling people's experiences with poverty through detailed accounts of practices, perspectives and patterns of experience in specific times and places, anthropological studies both illuminate dimensions of poverty that are in some sense un-measurable, and demonstrate their own inability to solve the problem of aggregation that is needed to apprehend, and therefore address, poverty as a social rather than an individual problem (compare Espeland and Mitchell, 1998).

In bringing these different methods to bear on each other, it may be useful to approach social relationships as micro-histories of social interaction that inform, reinforce or revise people's possibilities and perspectives, rather than as institutionalized networks of authority and obligation that persist through time. In this vein, fixed assets might be seen as vehicles or venues for social interactions that enhance people's sense of possibility and self-worth, as well as their material standards of living. Investments in housing are a case in point. As early as the 1940s, field studies commented on the physical transformation of rural communities in cocoa-farming regions of Ghana and southwestern Nigeria, or small-scale coffee-and dairy-producing areas in central Kenya, as farmers used a portion of their incomes to replace mud walls and thatched roofs with cement blocks and corrugated iron (Beckett, 1944; Fortes *et al.*, 1948; Hill, 1963; Brokensha, 1966; Okali, 1983; Peel, 1983; Berry, 1985, 1993). Housing remains a priority today among people in all walks of life, absorbing a significant amount of remittances sent home by African emigrants in Europe and North America, as well as earnings of those closer to home. (Osili, 2004; Ammassari, 2004)

As numerous anthropological studies have shown, in many African contexts, houses have a social and symbolic as well as a market value. Many provide sheltered spaces for commercial, artisanal, educational, religious and/or professional activities as well as residential use, and there is a long history of Africans using earnings from farming, trade, artisanry, or professional employment to build houses in areas where there is no rental market, but where they have ancestral or other social ties. West Africans have also channeled savings from farming, trade, wage employment and other sources into building houses in urban areas. Reinforced by widespread evidence that the value of land and landed property tends to appreciate over time, houses have gained a widespread reputation as physically and financially durable assets, that can be kept as a form of long-term insurance, and transferred to descendants and heirs, creating a legacy that outlives their builders and helps to reproduce family ties from one generation to another (Berry, 2001, 2002).

Houses also provide spaces where their owners may offer hospitality to kin, neighbours, colleagues and deserving strangers. Stable venues for multiple forms of social interaction, houses give concrete testimony to their builders' commitment to kin and community, enhancing their reputations for social responsibility as well as personal success, and strengthening people's claims to the loyalty and resources of others (Van der Geest, 1998). Houses are particularly important for the security, autonomy and dignity of African women, especially widows and divorcees whose children are unable or unwilling to support them. In the predominantly Muslim city of Maradi (Niger), for example, Hausa women make lifelong efforts to acquire 'houses of their own' (B. Cooper, 1997: 82ff). 'Property is crucial to women', Cooper writes 'not simply as a material asset, but because it creates, defines, and facilitates social relations' (ibid.: 87). Owning a house positions a woman 'as a *mai gida*, someone who is master of a house, like a man', with authority over potential dependents, from sons and daughters to clients and tenants (ibid.). Cooper's findings for Maradi are corroborated in other studies. Owning property, especially landed property such as a house, places Yoruba women 'in a position to form social relationships in the wider community that are politically significant... legitimat[ing their] entry into the public domain' (Barnes, 1990, p. 275).[12]

In another context, Paul Lubeck (1985) has suggested that the gentrification of northern Nigerian cities, where affluent elites used wealth from Nigeria's oil boom to build walled villas in the 1970s and 1980s, led to declining access to food and shelter for itinerant Koranic students who, for decades, had escaped seasonal hunger in the rural areas by following their teachers to the cities, where they lived on alms and slept in the open reception rooms at the entrance to the houses of the devout. The resulting experience of disruption and exclusion contributed directly, Lubeck argues, to a series of millenarian protests against 'modern' lifestyles and affluence in the 1980s and 1990s, in which followers of an iconoclastic prophet seized public latrines and market spaces in cities across northern Nigeria, in defiant repudiation of the privatization of urban space. Violently suppressed by Nigeria's armed forces, these uprisings left hundreds of people dead and wounded, most of them from the poorest strata of urban society (Lubeck, 1985).

Lubeck's argument came to mind during a recent survey of occupants in a peri-urban neighbourhood of Kumasi, when a Muslim informant reacted angrily to questions about how he had built his house. Home on a visit from the Netherlands, where he had lived for over ten years, he complained of commentators on Dutch TV who criticize African immigrants for squandering their earnings on houses and other 'luxuries' in their home countries rather than investing in 'development'. Such instances dramatize the contextuality of asset values, suggesting why – despite assurances from property rights enthusiasts that titling land and houses promotes investment by providing a source of collateral for loans – Africans have often proved reluctant to wager their land and houses against the vagaries of their unstable economies (Berry, 1993, 2001). Houses are simply too valuable to risk losing them to foreclosure – in part, because their value exceeds what the market measures.

As these examples illustrate, poverty is not a state of being, but a social process in which people's fortunes rise and fall through interactions with others, as well as through changes in circumstance and capacity. In recognizing that the precarious-ness of impoverishment and people's chances of improvement depend on their assets as well as their current income, it is important also to recognize that assets can and do change over time – not only because people gain and lose access to them, but also because the value of the assets themselves can appreciate, alter or decline even if the terms of access to them do not change.

3.5 Living with poverty measures: Implications for policy

To conclude this discussion, I offer a few examples to illustrate the way in which anthropological studies may contribute to strategies for poverty alleviation. The above-cited film on girls' education in Africa illustrates the value of direct obser-vation for qualifying explanations of poverty that are derived from quantitative analysis – in this case, the correlation between levels of per capita income and national average rates of school enrolment by girls (Odaga, 1995). The following examples illustrate further possibilities for going behind standard measurements of poverty levels and beyond some of the policy conclusions drawn from them, by bringing in anthropological accounts of temporality and social interaction.

Improving agricultural productivity. If scarcity of one's own time is a significant constraint on people's ability to gain income, time allocation becomes a crucial skill for managing livelihood struggles. Otherwise well-intentioned efforts to provide public assistance, or raise poor people's incomes by developing 'appropriate' tech-nologies, often overlook this point. Researchers working in the 1980s and 1990s to adapt 'Green Revolution' technologies to different agro-ecological conditions typ-ically measured the success of their experiments in terms of gains in yield – assuming, in effect, that land is the principal constraint on poor farmers' ability to expand production.[13] For many years, plant breeders, entomologists, agronomists and others measured the results of their experiments in terms of biomass per hectare, overlooking the possibility that many poor farmers stood to gain more from crops that took less time to mature – thus freeing farmers' time for other pressing activities *and* reducing their need to store or buy food for the hungry season – than from those that squeezed more from a given plot of land once a year, but left the farmer with a choice between post-harvest sales when prices were low, or watching stored supplies dwindle from mildew, pests, rodents and the threat of fire (Collinson and Haugerud, 1990).

Accessing government resources. While many African governments are themselves chronically starved of resources for public services and investments, for impoverished citizens, the state remains a key source of both economic and logistical support. As Villalon (1995) demonstrates in his study of everyday practices of state power in a rural town in Senegal, the Senegalese state has compensated for its lack of distributable resources by extending bureaucratic practices into every aspect of social life.

To an extent far greater than many of its neighbours on the continent, the state in Senegal has been able to both regulate societal activities and prescribe the degree of access to its own resources. 'This relative hegemony... creates for the state a realm of services which become essential, but which only it can provide... In a situation of severe scarcity the Senegalese state thus manages to maintain its appeal in large part by its monopoly over the satisfaction of needs which would not themselves exist without the state' (Villalon, 1995: 102–3).

While Villalon emphasizes the exceptional degree of bureaucratic self-reproduction that operates in Senegal, the process he describes is not unusual. In South Africa, poor people may spend weeks navigating bureaucratic procedures to obtain the very modest grants that government offers to caretakers of children who have been orphaned by HIV/AIDS (Baim-Lance, 2005). Here as in Senegal and elsewhere, proliferating administrative institutions and procedures place demands on citizens' time and effort that fall most heavily on those who are most in need of whatever meagre resources they can find to stave off complete destitution (Compare Juul & Lund, 2002).

Family planning for poor people. In the above-cited study of reproductive practices in rural Gambia, Bledsoe found that women 'were using high-technology contraceptives to construct through careful cultural strategies... what demographic analyses term "natural fertility"...', effectively 'subvert[ing] the intentions of family planning programs' (Bledsoe, 2002: 325). Such anomalous results call, she argues, not for replacing statistics with ethnography, but rather for closer integration of methods and theories from demographic, social and medical sciences in the description and analysis of human reproductive behaviour in different social contexts. Such collaborative efforts can also elucidate counterintuitive policy responses, like those of Gambian women who use contraceptives to increase their fertility, allowing analysts to rethink policy options accordingly.

3.6   Conclusion

Framing poverty and policy debates in terms of social context and process may not extend the scope for measuring multidimensionality, but it underscores the dynamics of the social outcomes we seek to understand, including the role of poverty as a cause, as well as an effect, of apparently disabling or wasteful practices, such as keeping girls home from school, or investing in houses rather than farms or factories. By drawing attention to temporalities, social interactions, and the conceptual and practical implications of anthropological methods for poverty analysis and policy design, this chapter seeks to stimulate further reflection and debate about these important and challenging issues.

Notes

1. Contributions from biological anthropologists, who have provided important evidence and analysis of the physiological dimensions and effects of economic and social deprivation, are beyond the scope of this Chapter.
2. See, for example, Haswell (1963); Galletti *et al.* (1956); Deane (1953).
3. Fabian's denunciation of anthropology's 'allochronic' epistemology as an imperialist project is a classic example of autocritical anthropological writings of the 1980s. Fabian (1983).
4. Gambian men are also concerned about their children's health and will accept a wife's sexual abstinence or even contraceptive use until the health of the last-born child is established. If she uses contraceptives past the point of weaning, however, her husband is likely to conclude that 'she is trying to end her marriage to him... by limiting fertility... [and] must be saving [her remaining fetuses] for someone else.' Bledsoe (2002: 207).
5. Guyer (2004: 132–42). In these surveys, 'household' was defined in terms of co-residence and shared meals – 'eating from the same pot'. Recognizing the porosity of household boundaries, enumerators interviewed as many individual members of each household as they could, pooling the results to arrive at household figures.
6. The literature is too large to cite, but see, e.g., Comaroff and Roberts (1980), Berry (1993), Peters (1994), Guyer (ed.) (1995), B. Cooper (1997).
7. Awareness of the importance of disaggregating the household for purposes of policy design for use in African contexts owes much to the work of Guyer (1981), Guyer and Peters (1984), Moock (ed.) (1986), and others, in the 1980s.
8. World Bank statisticians acknowledged as much when they signed on to the Millenium Development Goals (World Bank, 2001).
9. In documenting the multidimensionality of global poverty, the World Bank counts assets, but does not discuss processes of acquiring them, or alterations in their value over time.
10. Neither the locations, nor the filmmakers' reasons for selecting them, are identified in the film – silences that appear to reflect and serve to reinforce common western misperceptions of Africa as one 'country' in which everyone is alike.
11. Studies of African household labour patterns show that girls often work longer hours than boys, on both domestic and directly productive tasks, especially in rural areas. See, e.g., Reynolds (1991); Bonilla-Chacin (2001).
12. For additional citations, see B. Cooper (1997: 86 n 31).
13. Much of this research was carried out by the Consultative Group for International Agricultural Research (CGIAR), a worldwide network of agricultural research institutes

established by the Ford and Rockefeller Foundations in the 1960s and 1970s. Scientists at CGIAR conducted research on plant breeding, insect and pest ecology, animal science, and other branches of agricultural and environmental science, and used their results to develop new technologies for raising agricultural productivity in low-income economies. Particular efforts were made to adapt new technologies to specific local agro-ecologies.

References

Amanor, K.S. (2001) *Land, Labour and the Family in Southern Ghana: a Critique of Land Policy Under Neo-liberalisation*. Uppsala: Nordiska Afrikainstitutet.

Ammassari, S. (2004) 'From Nation-building to Entrepreneurship: the Impact of Elite Return Migrants in Côte d'Ivoire and Ghana', *Population, Space and Place*, 10, 133–54.

Asad, T. (1973) *Anthropology and the Colonial Encounter*. Amherst, NY: Humanity Books.

Baim Lance, A. (2005) 'Who Cares? The Making of Citizens in South Africa'. Paper presented to the Institute for Global Studies Seminar, Johns Hopkins University.

Barnes, S. (1990) 'Women, Property and Power', in P. Sanday and R. Goodenough (eds) *New Directions in the Anthropology of Gender*. Philadelphia: University of Pennsylvania Press.

Beckett, W.H. (1944) *Akokoaso*. London: Percy, Lund Humphries.

Berry, S.S. (1985) *Fathers Work for Their Sons: Accumulation, Mobility and Class in an Extended Yoruba Community*. Berkeley: University of California Press.

Berry, S.S. (1993) *No Condition is Permanent: the Social Dynamics of Agrarian Change in Sub-Saharan Africa*. Madison: University of Wisconsin Press.

Berry, S.S. (2001) *Chiefs Know Their Boundaries: Essays on Property, Power and the Past in Asante, 1896–1996*. Portsmouth, NH: Heinemann.

Berry, S.S. (2004) 'Debating the land question in Africa', *Comparative Studies in Society and History*, 44(4), 638–68.

Bledsoe, C. (1990) "No Success Without Struggle": Social Mobility and Hardship for Foster Children in Sierra Leone, *Man*, 25(1) 70–88.

Bledsoe, C. (2002) *Contingent Lives: Fertility, Time and Aging in West Africa*. Cambridge: Harvard University Press.

Bonilla-Chacin, M.E. (2001) 'Family Structure and Time Allocation in a Development Context', Johns Hopkins PhD.

Bourdieu, P. (1985) 'The Forms of Capital', in J.G. Richardson (ed.), *Handbook of Theory and Research for the Sociology of Education*. New York: Greenwood Press.

Brokensha, D. (1966) Social Change at Larteh, Ghana. Oxford: Clarendon Press.

Brydon, L. (1987) 'Women in the Family: Cultural Change in Avatime, Ghana, 1900–80', *Development and Change*, 18, 253–89.

Brydon, L. and K. Legge (1996) *Adjusting Society: the World Bank, the IMF and Ghana*. London and New York: I.B. Tauris.

Carney, J. (1988) 'Struggles over Crop Rights and Labor Within Contract Farming Households in a Gambian Irrigated Rice Project', *Journal of Peasant Studies*, 15, 334–49.

Carney, J. and M. Watts (1990) 'Manufacturing Dissent', *Africa*, 60(2), 207–41.

Chen, S. and M. Ravallion (2004) *How Have the World's Poorest Fared Since the Early 1980s?*, World Bank Policy Research Working Paper 3341. Washington, DC: World Bank.

Clark, G. (1999) 'Negotiating Family Survival in Kumasi, Ghana', *Africa*, 69(1), 66–86.

Collinson, M. and A. Haugerud (1990) 'Plants, Genes and People: Improving the Relevance of Plant Breeding in Africa', *Experimental Agriculture*, 26, 341–62.

Comaroff, J. and S. Roberts (eds) (1980) *The Meaning of Marriage Payments*. New York: Academic Press.

Cooper, B. (1997) *Marriage in Maradi: Gender and Culture in a Hausa Society*. Portsmouth, NH: Heinemann.

Cooper, F. (1996) *Decolonization and African Society: the Labor Question in French and British Africa*. Cambridge: Cambridge University Press.

Cooper, F. and R. Packard (eds) (1997) *International Development and the Social Sciences: Essays on the History and Politics of Knowledge*. Berkeley: University of California Press.

Dasgupta, P. 'Economic Progress and the Idea of Social Capital', in P. Dasgupta and I. Serageldin (eds), *Social Capital: a Multifaceted Perspective*. Washington, DC: World Bank.

Deane, P. (1953) *Colonial Social Accounting*. Cambridge: Cambridge University Press.

Edelman, M. and A. Haugerud (eds) (2005) *The Anthropology of Development and Globalization: From Classical Political Economy to Contemporary Neoliberalism*. Malden, MA: Blackwell.

Edin, K. and M. Kefalas (2005) *Promises I Can Keep: Why Poor Women put Motherhood Before Marriage*. Berkeley: University of California Press.

Escobar, A. (1995) *Encountering Development: Making and Unmaking of the Third World*. Princeton: Princeton University Press.

Espeland, W. and M. Stevens (1998) 'Commensurability as Social Process', *Annual Review of Sociology*, 24, 313–34.

Fabian, J. (1983) *Time and the Other: How Anthropology Makes its Object*. New York: Columbia University Press.

Faubion, J. (1993) 'History in Anthropology', *Annual Review of Anthropology*, 22, 35–54.

Ferguson, James (1990) *The Anti-politics Machine: 'Development,' Depoliticisation and Bureaucratic Power in Lesotho*. Cambridge: Cambridge University Press.

Ferguson, James (1992) 'The Cultural Topography of Wealth: Commodity Paths and the Structure of Property in Rural Lesotho', *American Anthropologist*, 94, 55–73.

Foley, M. and B. Edwards (1999) 'Is it Time to Disinvest in Social Capital?', *Journal of Public Policy*, 19(2), 141–73.

Fortes, M. *et al.* (1948) 'The Ashanti Social Survey: a Preliminary Report', *Rhodes-Livingstone Journal Human Problems in British Central Africa*, 6, 1–36.

Fortes, M. *et al.* (1970) *Time and Social Structure and Other Essays*. London & New York: Athlone & Humanities Press.

Galletti, R. *et al.* (1956) *Nigerian Cocoa Farmers*. London: Oxford University Press.

Gledhill, J. ' "Disappearing the Poor?' a Critique of the New Wisdoms of Social Democracy in an Age of Globalization', *Urban Anthropology and Studies of Cultural Systems and World Economic Development*, 30(2–3), 123–56.

Goheen, M. (1996) *Men Own the Fields, Women Own the Crops: Gender and Power in the Cameroon Grassfield*. Madison: University of Wisconsin Press.

Guyer, J.I. (1981) 'Household and Community in African Studies', *African Studies Review*, 24 (2/3) 87–138.

Guyer, J.I. and P. Peters (eds) (1984) *Conceptualizing the Household: Issues of Theory, Method and Application* New York: Social Science Research Council.

Guyer, J.I. (ed.) (1995). *Money Matters: Instability, Values and Social Payments in the Modern History of West African Communities*. Portsmouth, NH: Heinemann.

Guyer, J.I. (2004) *Marginal Gains: Monetary Transactions in Atlantic Africa*. Chicago: University of Chicago Press.

Harper, R. (2005) 'The Social Organization of the IMF's Mission Work', in M. Edelman and A. Haugerud (eds), *The Anthropology of Globalization and Development* Oxford: Blackwell.

Haswell, M. (1963) *The Changing Pattern of Economic Activity in a Gambian Village*. London: Her Majesty's Stationery Office.

Haswell, M. (1975) *The Nature of Poverty: a Case History of the First Quarter Century after World War II*. London: Macmillan.

Haugerud, A. (1988) 'Food Surplus Production, Wealth and Farmers' Strategies in Kenya', in R. Cohen (ed.), *Satisfying Africa's Food Needs*. Boulder, CO: Lynne Rienner.

Hill, P. (1963) *Migrant Cocoa Farmers of Southern Ghana*. Cambridge: Cambridge University Press.

Hymes, D. (ed.) (1972) *Reinventing Anthropology*. New York: Pantheon.

Juul, K. and C. Lund (eds) (2002) *Negotiating Property in Africa*. Portsmouth, NH: Heinemann.

Lister, R. (2004) *Poverty.* Cambridge: Polity Press.

Lubeck, P. (1985) 'Islamic Protest Under Semi-industrial Capitalism: 'Yan Tatsine explained', *Africa*, 55(4), 369–90.

Manski, C. (2000) 'Economic Analysis of Social interactions', *Journal of Economic Perspectives*, 14(3), 115–36.

Maxwell, S. (1986) 'Farming Systems Research: Hitting a Moving Target', *World Development* 14(1), 66–77.

Maxwell, S. (2004) 'Heaven or Hubris: Reflections on the New "New Poverty Agenda" ', in R. Black and H. White (eds), *Targeting Development*. London and New York: Routledge.

Mitchell, T. (1991) 'America's Egypt: Discourse of the Development Industry', *Middle East Report*, March–April, 18–36.

Mitchell, T. (2002), *Rule of Experts: Egypt, Techno-politics, Modernity*. Berkeley: University of California Press.

Moock, J.L. (ed.), (1986) *Understanding Africa's Rural Households and Farming Systems*. Boulder, CO: Westview.

Moore, H. and M. Vaughan (1994) *Cutting Down Trees: Gender, Nutrition, and Agricultural Change in the Northern Province of Zambia, 1890–1990*. Portsmouth, NH: Heinemann.

Munn, N. (1992) 'The Cultural Anthropology of Time', *Annual Review of Anthropology*, 21, 93–123.

Odaga, A. (1995) *Girls and Schools in Sub-Saharan Africa: From Analysis to Action*. Washington DC: World Bank.

Okali, C. (1983) *Cocoa and Kinship in Ghana: the Matrilineal Akan*. London: Kegan Paul.

Osili, U.O. (2004) 'Migrants and Housing Investments: Theory and Evidence from Nigeria', *Economic Development and Cultural Change*, 52(4), 821–50.

Peel, J.D.Y. (1983) *Ijeshas and Nigerians: the Incorporation of a Yoruba Kingdom, 1890s–1970s*. Cambridge: Cambridge University Press.

Peters, P. (1994) *Dividing the Commons: Politics, Policy and Culture in Botswana*. Charlottesville: University of Virginia Press.

Peters, P. (2005) 'Rural Poverty in Malawi', unpublished paper.

Reynolds, P. (1991) *Dance Civet Cat: Child Labour in the Zambezi Valley*. London and Athens, OH: Zed Books and Ohio University Press.

Richards, A.I. (1939) *Land, Labour and Diet in Northern Rhodesia*. London: Oxford University Press.

Robertson, C. (1985) *Sharing the Same Bowl*. Madison: University of Wisconsin Press.

Robertson, S. and M. Camerini (1997) 'These Girls are Missing: the Gender Gap in Africa's Schools'. New York: Filmmakers Library.

Schroeder, R. (1999) *Shady Practices: Agroforestry and Gender Politics in Gambia*. Berkeley: University of California Press.

Shanin, T. (1972) *The Awkward Class: Political Sociology of Peasantry in a Developing Society: Russia 1910–1925*. Oxford: Clarendon.

Sharp, J. and A. Spiegel (1985) 'Vulnerability to Impoverishment in South African Rural Areas: the Erosion of Kinship and Neighborhood as Social Resources', *Africa*, 55, 133–51.

Stocking, G. (ed.) (1984) *Functionalism historicized: Essays on British Social Anthropology*. Madison: University of Wisconsin Press.

Uvin, P. (1998) *Aiding Violence: the Development Enterprise in Rwanda*. West Hartford, CT: Kumarian.

van der Geest, S. (1998) '*Ye bisa wo fie*: Growing Old and Building a House in the Akan Culture of Ghana', *Journal of Cross-Cultural Gerontology*, 13, 333–59.

Villalon, L. (1995) *Islamic Society and State Power in Senegal: Citizens and Disciples in Fatick*. Cambridge: Cambridge University Press.

Wade, R. (2004) 'Is Globalization Reducing Poverty and Inequality?', *World Development*, 32(4), 567–89.

World Bank (2001) *World Development Report 2000/01: Attacking Poverty*. Washington, D.C: Word Bank.

4
The Multidimensionality of Poverty: An Institutionalist Perspective

Alice Sindzingre

4.1 Introduction[1]

The multidimensionality of poverty is now a widely accepted concept, and as shown by Amartya Sen, dimensions of poverty include not only income-consumption poverty but also the deprivation of capabilities linked to health, education and participation in the activities of the society.[2]

This chapter argues that institutions and norms constitute pivotal causal elements in the levels, achievements, and stability of these dimensions and in the relationships between them. The impact of institutions on poverty has already been highlighted in the literature. Institutions, however, have not been analysed as determinants of the multidimensionality of poverty, with mental processes being themselves involved in the emergence and impact of institutions.

Institutions and norms are constitutive of these dimensions, and in two aspects. First, dimensions of poverty are dynamic phenomena, where each dimension may enter into a causal relationship with another one. Institutions and norms may determine the levels of several dimensions of poverty (income, health, education) and the relationships between them, with institutions constituting a 'hub' for these dimensions. The institutional environment 'filters' access to higher income, better health, the exercise of rights, and so on. Moreover, institutions are themselves multidimensional and composite phenomena; they include both 'forms' and 'contents', which multiplies the possible causalities involving institutions and the various dimensions of poverty. Causalities function both ways, from institutions to poverty and from poverty to institutions and this generates endogenous processes and poverty traps, or 'institutional poverty traps'.

Secondly, institutions and norms both determine and result from individual perceptions, mental models, expectations and behaviour regarding the desire, the capacity and the strategies for escaping poverty: individuals may, for example, pursue their own interest, enter into cooperative behaviour, or exclude themselves from society's activities because of the hopelessness created by norms of discrimination (Loury, 1999). Institutions and norms are cognitive mechanisms that generate in individuals' minds beliefs about states of the world, the beliefs of others and the behaviour that is appropriate to these states of the world.

Institutions and norms therefore contribute to the multidimensionality of poverty both directly (in shaping access to, for example, income opportunities or educational infrastructures) and via cognitive processes (which for a given individual shape perceptions of the various dimensions of poverty, as well as of the behaviour and types of social interactions that would improve the levels achieved in the various dimensions – for example, collective action, cooperation). Institutions and norms create feedback processes. These processes involve collective (shared) and normative mental representations that in turn stabilise institutions and norms and poverty equilibria that retroact on individual cognition. This may generate 'cognitive institutional traps'.

The chapter is thus divided as follows. Section 4.2 defines institutions and norms according to the new institutional economics perspective, as well as cognitive and evolutionary approaches: institutions are *per se* multidimensional and composite phenomena, which multiplies the causal paths involving institutions and the dimensions of poverty. Section 4.3 examines the *ex ante* indeterminacy of the effects of the dimensions of institutions on the dimensions of poverty – generating exclusion or cooperation. Section 4.4 presents the institutional causal mechanisms that underlie the multidimensionality of poverty, from institutions to poverty and from poverty to institutions. It highlights endogenous processes and 'cognitive institutional traps', through causal processes that go from mental representations to institutions, then to poverty, and finally back to norms and mental representations.

4.2   Institutions and norms as multidimensional phenomena

Perspectives from institutional economics: From institutions to economic outcomes

Defining institutions is a matter of intense debate, as institutions refer to different domains: market, non market, state, economic, social, and political, among others. Institutions are often equated with rules and norms, though these three concepts are distinct. Social norms are sometimes contrasted with official rules (for example, enforced by law).

Economics early on recognised institutions as key determinants of economic activity.[3] The definitions of institutions coined by Douglass North are now canonical. Institutions are 'the rules of the game in a society'; they are 'the humanly devised constraints that shape human interaction' (North, 1990: 3). Institutions consist of 'informal constraints (sanctions, taboos, customs, traditions, and codes of conduct) and formal rules (constitutions, laws, property rights)' (North, 1991: 97). For North (1989), norms are 'informal constraints on behaviour that are in part derivative of formal rules' (though the distinction between 'formal' and 'informal' does not correspond to empirical facts and cognitive mechanisms).[4] Institutions 'structure incentives in human exchange' (North, 1990: 3) and affect economic performance by their effects on the costs of exchange (transaction) and production (transformation), together with technology. The main function of institutions is to 'reduce uncertainty by establishing a stable (but not necessarily efficient) structure to human interaction' (North, 1990: 6).

In North's view, institutions allow one to understand the determinants of the divergence between societies. Determinants of economic growth emerge from the trade-offs between, on the one hand, low transaction costs in small-scale peasant societies but with limited division of labour and high production costs, and, on the other, economies of scale in market societies, which stem from specialization but generate high transaction costs and opportunities for free-riding.

The concept of institutions as an equilibrium outcome of a game has been explored by Aoki (2001), along with the issue of enforcement – that is, the endogenous generation of rules of the game and their self-enforcing character via the interactions between individuals. Institutions are interdependent: solutions and equilibria are multiple and institutional change is the selection of one equilibrium from many possible ones, which may be sub-optimal. The focus on enforcement leads to analysing the design of institutions that can implement given social goals in a manner that is compatible with the incentives of the players (Aoki, 2001: 6).

Understanding the modalities and conditions of rules enforcement is therefore crucial. Institutions and norms may be either self-enforcing or enforced by an external party given the environment, as shown by Greif in his studies of medieval Maghribi and Genoese traders and the contrast between 'collectivist' and 'individualist' institutions. The latter institutions provided examples of specific groups that developed markets through the creation of new economic institutions (business associations, 'coalitions', guilds). These institutions prevented opportunism via multilateral reputational devices (punishment of cheaters by other parties than the cheated) and credible commitments, coordination and enforcement mechanisms.[5]

Thanks to these mechanisms, impersonal exchanges are effective in the absence of legal systems guaranteed by a state (Greif, 1997). In combination with the external environment, these mechanisms generated norms and incentives for collective action and sanctions. These institutions have been crucial factors in economic growth.

Institutions may be distinguished according to several criteria. An important distinction separates institutions associated with transaction costs and exchange and addressing coordination failures from a second category of institutions that protect property rights.[6] Other types of rights may be considered, in particular political rights (democracy), given their importance in explaining the variations in income and human development levels in developing countries (Bardhan, 2005: chap. 1). The presence of transaction costs makes it so that different systems of property rights induce outcomes with variable degrees of efficiency. Private property rights create security, hence investment, therefore foster growth and are instruments for poverty reduction. The conceptual framework of property rights also explains the historical shift from rights over individuals (instituted, for example, by kinship systems, or slavery) to rights over goods.[7]

The emergence of cognitive theories of institutions

Explaining how and why individuals follow – or at least seem to follow – a rule is a complex problem that philosophers have long pondered.[8] Cognitive anthropology and philosophy view institutions as mental representations. They are not concrete

objects or actions, the latter being attributes of institutions. They are rules governing representations or meta-representations. When these representations include a
deontic content (at the pragmatic level, i.e., obligation, prohibition, permission
and so on), they are institutions that are internalized by a given group or society.
The mental representations that have the property to disseminate and replicate
the most widely, to be the most widely shared, are the representations and norms
which bring the largest cognitive gains for the least cost and effort: they are more
'relevant' (Sperber, 1985, 1990; Sperber and Wilson, 1986). Contexts are essential:
depending upon the situation, specific inferences are triggered; specific types of
information are more apt to be remembered, learned and disseminated. In a non-
cognitive perspective, Axelrod (1986) also argued that meta-norms are necessary
for norms to be stable: that is, norms that punish those who do not punish non-
compliance with a norm, though this view has been criticized by Elster (1989), as
norms change and violation may remain unpunished. Equally, for Searle (2005)
institutions are characterized by a collective acceptance and assignment of a status: institutions constitute behaviour and not only regulate it. These 'status functions' of institutions are constitutive of human societies, and the deontic dimension
of institutions stems from the power that they allow, as expressed by the terms of
rights, obligations, and permissions, which provide reasons ('incentives') for action
that are independent of individual preferences.

There remains an open debate regarding the mechanisms of transmission of
mental representations and rules. The analogy with natural selection is supported
by evolutionary approaches relying on the concepts of competition and selection.
It was popularized by Richard Dawkins (1976) with the concept of 'memes' – that
is, cultural units replicating by imitation from brains to brains. The controversy is
ongoing in regard to the characteristics of evolutionary processes (stability, spreading, adoption of mental models) and their causal role in behaviour, social interactions, and emergence of obligations. Mental representations and behaviour may
disseminate but not follow adaptive patterns of the type of natural selection. Contents
of representations change during transmission, with no guarantee that they are
identical in people's minds in the course of social interactions. Mechanisms of dis-
semination, transmission and stabilization of representations and norms seem to
be caused by various context-dependent and psychological domain-specific factors,
according to complex reasonings and inferences: for example the status of authority
(political, educational, kinship-related) of the individual that conveys the content of
norm, the credibility of the norm, the associated emotions, and so on.

Integrating cognitive approaches in the economic analyses of institutions

The central question of the new institutional economics is the relationship
between institutions and the level of development or poverty. It has progressively
integrated individual-centred and cognitive approaches, relying, for example, on
concepts such as preferences and beliefs. Institutions indeed are not observable:
what are observable are regularities of behaviour in individuals' interactions, who
are said to be a group when these individuals behave similarly. For Manski (2000),
for example, this similarity is explained by endogenous interactions (individual

behaviour varies with the behaviour of the group) or by contexts that are exogenous to individuals, or by correlated effects (individuals have similar characteristics, or they are obliged by the same institutions). Institutions are now analysed as the outcomes of repeated interactions, exchanges reinforcing shared beliefs, such as identity and trust.[9] Social norms and beliefs are now viewed as foundational in the action of exchange: they may limit rationality, or change preferences, or help to select and stabilise an equilibrium (Basu, 2000: chap. 4).

Similarly, North now conceives institutions as resulting from 'mental models', with mental processes, norms, behaviour and economic outcomes being endogenous to each other. For North, institutions are ultimately shaped by the 'subjective perceptions' of individuals to explain their environment, 'which in turn determine explicit choices of formal rules' and the evolution of norms (North 1997: 1). According to an evolutionary theory of learning, North now posits the existence of 'convergent mental models', shared beliefs and perceptions that derive from mental models, which evolve according to gradual or punctuated equilibria.[10] Social interaction implies and generates shared cognitive rules that provide a common framework for mutual understanding and interpreting perceptions and the environment.

Moreover, cognitive approaches have allowed for the understanding of the thresholds, the plurality of equilibria and traps that are generated by institutions. Small changes in perceptions may produce cascades of changes in behaviour and hence new equilibria. Threshold effects characterize collective behaviour according to the benefits or costs of imitating the others: similar preferences may generate positive and negative feedbacks and the related locking-in processes (Granovetter, 1978; Arthur, 1989). Collective action dynamics, and in particular the acceptance of a norm, depend on the distribution of individual thresholds of non-acceptance, which are determined by cost–benefits trade-offs and perceptions of the number of individuals who are above the thresholds or are expected to be in the future. In these models, perceptions that most individuals accept a norm create negative feedbacks and a stable equilibrium, even if an individual does not want to follow this norm because of the high costs of opposing a (perceived) majority. Above a certain critical threshold of non-acceptance, positive feedback may occur.

Institutions are increasingly defined as equilibria of shared beliefs. For Aoki (2001: 10), an institution is 'a self-sustaining system of shared beliefs about a salient way in which the game is repeatedly played'. Institutions are repeated games regulated by mechanisms of transmission of information.[11] Norms are self-enforcing patterns of behaviour, which solve coordination problems and constitute games equilibria (in various domains, property, statuses, contracts) (Young, 1998). Game theory helped to understand the well-known coordination problems of the 'tragedy of the commons', of how the lack of coordination among individuals pursuing their own ends impinges on the well-being of others and leads to a decreased well-being of all, for example the exhaustion of a common resource (for instance, via a classical prisoner's dilemma). Bowles (2004: 1) likewise defines institutions as the laws (central coercion), informal rules (social sanctions) or conventions (mutual expectations) that give a durable structure to social interactions among the members of a given group; they secure the conformity of behaviour and therefore may be represented as games or stable equilibria of underlying games, which explains institutional change.

The question of the origin and nature of institutions continues to be debated. In particular, Bowles has questioned the assumption of the contractual nature of social interactions that is assumed in neoclassical economics: many social interactions are obviously not contractual, especially in non-market contexts and in markets with incomplete contracts, which are governed by power and social norms. For behavioural economics, individuals pursue their objectives and with their behaviour being governed by cognitive routines (past experience). Individuals adapt to situations and to the behaviour of others and the perception of it. Individuals are heterogeneous and, as argued by Bowles (2004), their behaviour may be 'other-regarding' – that is, not governed by self-interest, improving the well-being of others at the expense of their own, and punishing those who violate ethical norms. This seems to be a universal trait of human societies, and it is expressed in developing countries by many traditional institutions.

The emerging fields of evolutionary economics and evolutionary psychology reinforced the analyses of institutions and norms as cognitive phenomena. The institutions and rules that regulate economic interactions result from historical processes and human intentions, but for evolutionary psychology,[12] the 'rules of the game' are also structured by cognitive specialised devices that are the outcomes of long-term adaptation to particular problems and domains (rather than of economic maximization). Sharing was a survival condition and hence an optimal rule for hunter-gatherers given the high uncertainty of their environment (Cosmides and Tooby, 1994).

Institutions as intrinsically multidimensional

New institutional economics sometimes confuses institutions and attributes of institutions; institutions are defined as property rights and incentives, while the latter are also particular attributes of institutions. Likewise, institutions and policies are often endogenous (Pritchett, 2005). In fact, institutions receive their mental content from their combination with the other existing institutions. Institutions are transformed by incentives that are provided by the existence of other institutions and markets, with markets obviously being institutions.

A more rigorous theoretical approach must therefore disaggregate institutions: institutions themselves are multidimensional. Because institutions are among the determinants of the various dimensions of poverty, institutions multiply the causal processes according to their own dimensions. Institutions are themselves composite and multilayered devices. They are characterized by their various forms (names, organizations) and contents (mental representations, functions) that actualize in their linkages with the forms and contents of other institutions.[13] Forms and contents of institutions are endogenous and shaped by other institutional forms and contents. Be they 'formal' or 'informal', all institutions exhibit forms and contents. Forms differ from contents: for example, the forms of a contract, an institutionalized exchange, a right, or a political institution such as democracy may differ from their effective contents – in other words, the mental representations that are associated with the actualizations of social norms in daily interactions.[14]

In this multidimensional view of institutions, forms and contents may evolve separately. The form of an institution that is 'filled' in the course of history with progressively changing contents may disappear finally. Individuals and groups may 'borrow' the form of an institution and not its content, which may remain filled by the 'traditional' contents. In developing countries for example, formal institutions may be 'filled' by the same representational contents that fill 'traditional' kinship rules.

This conception of multidimensionality of poverty, with the dimension of institutions being itself multidimensional, has important implications, as it reveals the limits of the measurement of institutions and econometric exercises that find a causality between 'institutions' and 'poverty'. Indeed, at the aggregate level, a large literature based on cross-country regressions highlights a variety of links between income growth and institutions. Econometric tools, however, have difficulty in analysing the links between variables with multiple and heterogeneous dimensions. The exact nature of the links and the direction of causalities are therefore often inconclusive.[15] The effects of institutions and norms on poverty depend on sets of mental representations and their relevance for individuals: the latter are composite phenomena, specific to individuals, and depend on contexts and types of interaction. These phenomena are difficult to predict *ex ante* and to measure.

4.3   Institutions and norms as generating both exclusion *and* cooperation

The *ex ante* indeterminacy of institutions and norms

The effects of institutional dimensions on the various dimensions of poverty – reducing or aggravating – are difficult to determine *ex ante* as they depend on contexts. As noted by Schlicht (2001) in regard to the concept of custom, institutions and norms cannot be said *ex ante* to be detrimental or optimal, to hinder or enable production and coordination. Many studies emphasize the fact that economic outcomes of institutions cannot be predicted with certainty. 'Institutions matter', but there is no certainty as to which specific institutions matter for growth. No particular institution seems necessary for growth. Transformation and adaptability appear to be more important ingredients for growth (Engerman and Sokoloff, 2003; Pritchett, 2002). For example, the same institutions that generate poverty may be exploited to escape poverty. Households may diversify their source of income in relying on the same traditional institutions – for instance, using demographic (large households) and migratory strategies, adapting tenure arrangements, choices of crops.[16]

Institutions and norms may be causes of exclusion, segmentation and poverty; but social norms and institutions also foster inclusion. They are inclusive-exclusionary devices that function in both subjective and objective terms. Social norms that define and regulate group memberships may limit social mobility, but help to increase income or welfare of group members. Inclusive or exclusionary outcomes of a given social institution are uneasy to determine *ex ante*, as they depend on individual or group characteristics. In particular, the social heterogeneity of the poor may prevent collective action and thus their demand for the provision of public goods.[17] Degrees of cooperation and collective behaviour may vary enormously depending on contextual conditions (economic, demographic, institutional, individual) that exhibit uncertain outcomes, such as the fact that rules are effectively shared or credible.

The institutions that regulate group memberships via various criteria, kin, ethnicity, occupation, or territory, are particularly pertinent in terms of the impact on poverty. They often exhibit significant enforcement capacity (compliance with the obligations and rights associated to these institutions even signals membership). In the 'weak states' of some developing countries, group membership is often more relevant that state allegiance. Poverty and exclusion – particularly in rural areas – may be determined by membership institutions, which may rely on individual characteristics (for example, physical), birth criteria, gender, age, and occupation, and create statuses, castes, and so on. Group membership may be a constraint on the access to resources even outside rural contexts, such as access to credit,[18] but group boundaries work as assets and devices facilitating trust, punishment of free riding, and access to capital.[19] Sharing and altruism, however, may stop at the borders of group memberships, lineages, and networks (the 'we'). Non-members are excluded from assistance and mutual insurance.[20]

This is where state institutions – and political institutions such as democracy – may be more welfare-enhancing than social institutions, in creating not group members but citizens, via norms of equality. Boundaries are extended beyond groups to that of the state boundaries and with altruistic norms extending beyond a limited number of individuals (for example, kin) to the ensemble of the citizenry. But state institutions also generate inequality among citizens, even in democracies if these institutions are mostly reduced to institutional forms. Political exclusion is indeed a major cause of poverty. For example, in Sub-Saharan Africa weak state institutions make it so that political regimes are associated with privileged access to resources and redistribution to specific groups that are close to rulers, together with the exclusion of regions or groups that are considered to be political threats.

Cooperation, reciprocity and altruism as evolutionary outcomes

Cooperative social norms and commitment to the goals of a group may be Pareto-optimal compared with non-cooperative games (Sugden, 2000; Harp, 2005). Evolution even seems to favour conventions that are egalitarian (Young, 1998). In repeated interactions, cooperation may arise as a rational outcome, as individuals may expect future benefits from their action. In their behaviour individuals take into account the fact that this generates a future reaction by others. If interactions are repeated and individuals value future payoffs more than current ones, this induces cooperative outcomes and the emergence of habits. Cooperative social norms may also be stable outcomes of the evolution of societies that face problems of management of commonly owned renewable resources: societies may select individuals who prefer collective activity, with cooperative norms therefore being internalized (Sethi and Somanathan, 1996).

Experimental economics approaches confirm that humans possess the desire to reciprocate, to avoid social disapproval and to be fair – fairness being defined as self-centred inequity aversion (Fehr and Fischbacher, 2004; Fehr and Falk, 2001). Evolutionary games show that individuals may be less motivated by self-interest than by other-regarding behaviour and altruism, which may result in altruistic norms, even if there are no repeated social interactions (Rabin, 1993). The various motives of individual behaviour (fairness, selfishness, cooperation, competition) interact with the economic environment according to the proportions of types of players, which give rise to different equilibria (Fehr and Schmidt, 1999).

Evolutionary psychology and games highlight the endogeneity of social preferences: because of evolution, social norms include the punishment of free-riders and exclusion as well as altruism. Reciprocity, in terms of responding to a hostile or prohibited action (punishment), may bring no benefit to the individual who achieve it but yield a benefit for the survival of its membership group. Reciprocal behaviour, however, differs from altruism. Altruism is defined as unconditional, and to this extent it differs from both cooperation (no expectation) and reciprocity (altruism is not a response). Altruism is an evolutionary outcome of interactions and competition between human groups, and Bowles makes a distinction between reciprocal altruism, kin altruism (with the expectation of a future reciprocal benefit), unconditional altruism and strong reciprocity (punishment of violators of norms even if there is no interest.[21])

Experimental economics show that reciprocity is more resilient when reciprocating another individual's behaviour that is itself perceived as negative rather than positive (Offerman, 2002). Reciprocity differs from the cooperation (or 'retaliation') found in repeated interactions: reciprocity is defined by responding to friendly behaviour in a more friendly way than predicted by the self-interest model ('positive reciprocity'), and responding to hostile behaviour in a more nasty way ('negative reciprocity'), even if reciprocity involves strangers, involves no reward, and is a costly one-shot game. The reciprocity model seems to predominate over the self-interest model. For experimental economics, this dominance of reciprocal behaviour entails cooperation and reinforces collective action and social norms. Specific characteristics of the institutional environment determine whether the self-interested or reciprocal behaviour will prevail (Fehr and Gächter, 2000).

Cooperation, however, may be a form of self-interest. Cooperation may be based on the social norm of conditional cooperation – that is, cooperation if the others cooperate. 'Other-regarding' behaviour, 'prosocial' behaviour, altruism or reciprocal behaviour may be the expressions of incentives as well as individual characteristics.[22] Indeed, the boundaries between categories of non self-interested behaviour are difficult to delineate: they are endogenous to group memberships and the associated social norms; they are both causes and effects of them. In traditional societies, for example, cooperative, reciprocal and altruistic behaviour may apply to individuals as they are related to a given individual – such as 'transitive' altruism with a friend's lineage members.

For evolutionary psychology, the detection and exclusion of cheaters show that some degree of ethics is ingrained in social relationships. As shown by Seabright

(2004), institutions built themselves on the evolution of psychology, which is inherited from hunter-gatherer societies that were based on rules such as division of labour and thus cooperation ('dealing with strangers'). Indeed, ethical norms appear to be a normative device that is a requisite for social exchanges in any society, even if norms are transgressed or limited to a very small number of members (for instance, the close kin).[23] The very fact of entering into an exchange with another individual supposes she is an addressee who is another individual. The 'cooperation principle', as coined by the philosopher H. Paul Grice, is a condition of social interaction and may be viewed as implying an ethical and other-regarding principle. Any act of conversational exchange implies some intention of relevance, and the assumption that the other recognises this intention (Grice, 1975; Sindzingre, 1987). Other-regarding reasoning may even be the general case: the 'team-directed' reasoning coined by Sugden (2000) explains problems such as the 'footballer's problem' better than individual-directed reasoning. Individual-directed reasoning may just be a case where the 'team' has only one member.

4.4 Institutional mechanisms underlying the multidimensionality of poverty: from institutions to poverty, from poverty to institutions

Multidimensionality is a dynamic phenomenon. Two types of feedbacks and causalities may be distinguished: from the dimensions of poverty to institutions and from institutions to poverty, which both operate at the macro and the micro levels.

From institutions to poverty

The line of causality from institutions to poverty is the object of many studies. In the first place, state institutions may be key determinants of poverty for individuals and groups. As coined by Harriss-White (2005) regarding groups of beggars in India, for certain groups the state may institutionalize situations of 'having nothing, being nothing and having no political rights'. State institutions guaranteeing the rule of law for the poor may exist, but their form may be filled by contents (such as traditional exclusionary norms) that diverge from their official purposes.[24] Their credibility for the poor may be weak. Similar state institutions may likewise have different impacts on poverty in different contexts if the similarity refers only to their forms: accountability *vis-à-vis* the poor and capacity of collective action of the poor in enforcing their rights may differ.[25]

Institutions regulating labour markets also have an impact on poverty. Among the various channels that link growth and poverty, the variation in the levels and sectors of employment is one of the most significant in terms of impact on poverty, and institutions influence the opportunities for participating in labour markets.

Rural institutions are likewise crucial in the causal relationship between institutions and poverty. Social norms, especially membership norms, may generate exclusion and poverty; in the context of social fragmentation, as often in Sub-Saharan Africa, the scope of exchanges and networks can be short and with little transitivity of trust and shared norms. In contrast, in East Asia large international trade networks have been associated with extensive trust and reputational mechanisms that have facilitated credit, capital mobility and investment (Malaizé and Sindzingre, 1998; Rauch, 2001). Similarly, differences in terms of growth of the agricultural sector in Sub-Saharan Africa and Asia have been explained by differences in population densities, through short-term economic effects and long-term effects on social norms. These differences have also been explained by patterns of access to land (more abundant land resources relative to population and labour force in Africa than in Asia) and land tenure (more communal and based on land use in Africa than in Asia). These norms were in turn less efficient in Africa for preventing the degradation of resources (Platteau and Hayami, 1998). The difference between 'poverty in men' (a low labour–land ratio) compared with 'poverty in resources' has long been a major analytical distinction characterising Sub-Saharan Africa (Iliffe, 1987). This 'poverty–geography–demography–institutions' nexus has explained the difficulties of state formation, the use of kin as risk mitigating, insurance and distributive devices, and norms favouring high fertility at the expense of children's quality in terms of health and education.

The shaping of poverty by social norms limits the room for state intervention. Social institutions change slowly and persist, even though they are inefficient or perpetuate income poverty for particular groups. Beliefs may be resilient: even in changing contexts, individuals may consider rural traditional institutions as more relevant than the state legal system, though the latter may provide opportunities for escaping poverty and be more equalizing than traditional norms. Rural poverty is indeed shaped by the coexistence of market and non-market institutions, which create externalities (for example, the possibility to participate or not in markets or in institutions that help escaping poverty). Rural poverty is also shaped by 'missing markets', which result not only from market conditions but also from institutional environments. This combination of institutions is dynamic, with incentives provided by markets combining with those provided by other institutions. In rural contexts, markets are also interlinked, which limits opportunities and is compounded by social norms: agricultural contracts may be locking-in devices if associated with social statuses, even if they are favourable in terms of income.

Institutional economics often equates institutions and property rights. This view, however, fails to fully explain the impact of institutions on poverty, especially for rural institutions in regions such as Sub-Saharan Africa. Rural institutions may be defined by many types of rights other than property rights, for example rights governing land and resource tenure rights, rights of access, and of temporary or permanent use.[26] In oral societies in particular, institutions are flexible and the result of negotiations. The establishment or titling of private property rights may trigger ownership and distributive conflicts,[27] while flexibility and negotiability of rights may mean inequality, exclusion and expropriation. Another limit of defining institutions via property rights is the latter's heterogeneity and the absence of linear relationships with growth. A further limitation is the linkages of property rights with other institutions in a given setting. The varieties of rights associated with a particular good by definition require other institutions to be recognised, i.e., other social contracts and legitimacy. It is also other institutions – political institutsions and power relationships – which make it so that a right can be claimed and exercised, or, on the contrary, denied.

Household institutions also typically generate poverty. In developing countries the model of the household tends to be collective rather than unitary. Types of productive activities, management of collective goods, intra-household resource allocation, use of profits, accounts, expenditure and consumption (for example, on food or education) are organized by social rules, which differentiate individuals according to age, gender, physical condition, social status, and so on. Poverty may be generated via the social norms that organize risk-sharing, mutual insurance, redistribution, transfers and loans.[28] These norms may be efficient devices of risk-pooling in the case of shocks affecting individuals or groups, but they also create unequal access to opportunities and resources.[29] They are also subject to problems of imperfect information and enforcement in case of opportunist behaviour. These norms smooth income shocks, but because the norms often rely on group membership they exclude from social protection non-members and individuals who are socially isolated for demographic or other reasons. Institutions thus may induce vulnerability, exposure to risks of income shocks and lack of access to consumption-smoothing mechanisms.[30]

Market institutions, however, may erode the equalizing and solidarity mechanisms of non-market norms, due to mobility, the increase in short-term transactions and the weakening of reputation effects and control of free-riding allowed by repeated interactions in small groups, particularly in Sub-Saharan Africa (Platteau, 2002; Arnott and Stiglitz, 1991).[31]

From poverty to institutions

At the aggregate level, lines of causality from poverty to institutions are generally inferred from cross-country growth regressions. The latter may show an impact of income levels on institutions (high income being associated with better institutions). A significant effect of income levels on institutions operates through the political economy channel: from aggregate poverty to specific types of political institutions – for example, democracy and participative institutions. For example, poverty, or low levels of literacy, could prevent the well-functioning of democratic institutions (as in Sub-Saharan Africa). Poverty could also favour the capture of institutions by patronage strategies.

At the micro level, poverty determines the access to institutions and, therefore, their nature and effectiveness: as argued by Zimmerman and Carter (2003), the rich have access to markets and institutions, especially financial institutions (credit), and may acquire portfolios with high returns. By contrast, the poor are limited to portfolios with lower risks and lower returns, and they are constrained to smooth their assets rather than their consumption.

In poor small-scale economies, poverty *per se* may perpetuate norms and institutions though they may be inefficient, such as rural traditional arrangements (risk-sharing, insurance) (Platteau, 1997, 2000a). There are thresholds of collective poverty under which redistributive social norms are inefficient (preventing savings and accumulation) or insufficient in case of covariate risks (natural disasters). The scope for customary exchanges may remain narrow and prevent the development of markets.[32] The capacity to enforce rules, punish and limit free-riding may be confined to members of networks.

Poverty *per se* may have a detrimental impact on collective action. As shown by Bowles (2006), the poor have difficulties in implementing large-scale coordinated collective action aimed at achieving more equal institutions, because they generally have less information than other members of the population. The poor are by definition more deprived in all assets than others. Moreover they do not form a homogenous group: there is no fixed set of necessary and sufficient criteria, nor affiliations to specific institutions which would constitute the poor as a 'natural' group.

Endogenous processes and poverty traps generated by institutions

Dimensions of poverty are endogenous to each other – income, health, employment, social relationships, status, and the norms that regulate them. Moreover, these endogenous processes reproduce themselves from one generation to the next (Dasgupta, 1997). Institutions create specific endogenous processes: they shape positive or negative feedbacks, poverty traps or virtuous paths out of poverty. For example, the cumulating of all dimensions in the same direction – low income, low education, institutional exclusion – builds poverty traps. Dimensions of poverty, however, do not necessarily evolve in the same direction, the status of women being an example, as in Sub-Saharan Africa – being sometimes wealthier because of their trading activities, but suffering lower rights in the household and social life.

Multidimensionality implies thresholds and nonlinearities between the different dimensions of poverty. Institutions contribute to this aspect of multidimensionality, because their own composite character generates threshold effects, depending on their effective content, their degree of internalization, and the presence of other institutions. Depending on contexts (on other political, economic, social institutions), the same institutional form can either aggravate or attenuate poverty. The presence of courts, for example, may help or lock-in the poor in their state of poverty, depending on whether formal legal institutions are linked to accountable or predatory regimes (Sindzingre, 2007).

Membership norms may be at the foundation of poverty traps,[33] and institutions may induce self-reinforcing dynamics that generate stable poverty traps: for example, predatory politics, corruption or social conflicts that stabilize expectations of future corruption and conflicts, all being both causes and effects of low income. In a relative poverty–social exclusion perspective *à la* Atkinson and Bourguignon (1999) (also focusing on the causal priority of dimensions), institutions may be pre-eminent when they are little affected by markets outcomes, such as social norms creating memberships by birth.

The concept of coordination failures causing multiple equilibria and poverty traps was analysed long ago,[34] as were concepts of cumulative causation and locking-in created by particular economic structures, or increasing returns and network externalities creating lock-in and path-dependence phenomena.[35] Multiple equilibria and paths may result from minor chance events. The concept of the poverty trap has been recently reactivated with the notion of 'institutional poverty traps', defined by Bowles as institutions 'that implement highly unequal divisions of the social product' and widespread poverty, and which persist over long periods of time despite their lack of efficiency *vis-à-vis* egalitarian institutions.[36] For Bowles, institutional poverty traps may be explained as outcomes of the uncoordinated actions of the members of a group, because they are self-enforcing and because the poor have difficulties in coordinating the modes of collective action that could transform an unequal set of institutions into a more equal one. Institutional poverty traps and coordination failures are also created by network effects, which in turn reinforces the resilience of social institutions within market economies (such as traditional kinship institutions), as shown by Hoff and Sen (2006).[37]

Political economy contributes to the formation of poverty traps. If there is a consensus that 'institutions matter', the ways they matter depend on both the political and the economic environment (Engerman and Sokoloff, 2003). Institutions may provide incentives for coordination, but institutions are obviously shaped by the power relationships and conflicts that generate them, maintain them and determine access to them. Power relationships set up the initial conditions of rights and the capacity to claim rights; they determine the distribution of rights and the economic outcome of this distribution. Institutions in unequal or polarized societies determine access to the satisfaction of basic needs as well as to social status. Political institutions are endogenous to existing balances of power, which makes it so that the implementation of 'rule of law' or democracy do not necessarily imply conditions that are favourable to the poor and more egalitarian. Political institutions may be entirely 'captured' by particular interest groups and elites, the rule of law and property rights being devised in order to maintain the status quo. Institutions create distributive conflicts and are simultaneously outcomes of them. In some Latin American countries, for example, the elites institutionalized laws and policies that gave them strong advantages; these institutions in turn contributed to the resilience of inequality (Engerman and Sokoloff, 2002).

'Cognitive institutional traps': from mental representations to norms, to poverty and back to norms and representations

The cognitive approach to institutions has enriched the analysis of the endogeneity between institutions and economic outcomes, in endogenizing beliefs, preferences, behaviour, economic and social interactions and the environment. Economic institutions such as markets influence the structure of social interactions, which in turn influence norms and preferences (Bowles, 1998). Social interactions may lead to feedbacks and increasing returns that generate multiple stable equilibria and lock-in effects, virtuous circles and poverty traps. Various events and shocks may generate 'equilibrium selection' and transitions – with some being dramatic (punctuated equilibria). Evolutionary dynamics make some equilibria more robust and others inaccessible. In an 'other-regarding' approach, institutions are resilient as long as individuals have an interest in their adherence, which is influenced by and endogenous to the fact that others do the same (Bowles, 2004).

It is argued here that the role of the institutions in the multidimensionality of poverty is a phenomenon that is stabilized by cognitive mechanisms. Institutions are cognitive phenomena that in turn generate institutions, which generate poverty in its different dimensions. Two types of causal processes may be distinguished, which are complementary.

In the first place, poverty is shaped by norms, because norms are psychological states, mental representations, and cognitive routines, which may make learning processes costly for individuals. This generates path-dependency and persistent differentiation in mental models and behavioural rules (Denzau and North, 1994), or 'cognitive traps'.[38] Because they are themselves composite phenomena, institutions multiply the causal paths. Beliefs and preferences shape norms, which in turn shape economic outcomes. Beyond subsistence, poverty is shaped by individual mental representations and norms, which impact on the other dimensions – for example, perceptions of having no right to claim rights, of being confined to a lower status, of having no prospects of social mobility, and the like. Prospects contribute greatly to differences in individuals assessments of their own poverty: if individuals perceive their society as enjoying high social mobility, the fact that they are poor does not imply for them that they will be poor in the future.[39] Individuals perceive their level of poverty depending on whether or not they believe in a 'just world' and that individual effort determines income, with these beliefs in turn influencing institutions (Benabou and Tirole, 2004a; Alesina and Angeletos, 2003).

The literature on subjective economic welfare confirms the dissonance between objective poverty and subjective perceptions of poverty. Even if there is a strong relationship between both indicators, it may be a non-linear one.[40] Poverty is also a psychological representation – the feeling that one is poor. The latter depends on income, health, education, and employment, but also on the resources of others (relative poverty), the perceptions of the other's perceptions, and on expectations as to future welfare, – that is, the perceptions of social mobility prospects offered by a society.

The multiple equilibria and endogenous effects that were highlighted at the aggregate levels of economic sectors likewise characterize social interactions between individuals. Multiple equilibria result from the beliefs that individuals have about what others will do within given membership groups. Incentives to behave similarly to others may lead to multiple equilibria and discontinuities ('phase transitions'; Brock and Durlauf, 2005). Group membership implies the attribution of characteristics to an individual by other members of a society (for example, prejudices) as well as their possible internalization by the recipient. Beliefs thus perpetuate poverty, as shown by Loury (2001) in the case of African-Americans: the social and normative construction of race induces an ingrained stigma and inhibiting effects on individuals. These beliefs appear difficult to revise. Cognitive mechanisms make it so that individuals tend to deny that these beliefs may be biased, as in the case of social discrimination.[41]

Poverty is maintained by mental representations that perpetuate poverty because these perpetuate powerlessness. The poor may not even consider institutions that could help them escape poverty. The poor lack incentives to claim their rights because of lack of bargaining power and asymmetries of information (Bowles, 2006). They lack incentives to participate in the market institutions and in the political institutions that could help them escape poverty, and they also lack the incentive to save, which, in turn, generates poverty traps and polarized societies (Mookherjee and Ray, 2000). These mechanisms work intergenerationally: the poor not only lack incentives to escape poverty but also transmit this lack of incentives to their children (their main assets), who will themselves lack the incentives, education or health that could incite them to participate in institutions or claim their rights. Trust is based on expectations that the others are worthy of trust or are altruistic: trust in institutions is a condition for the functioning of institutions, while in an endogenous way well-functioning institutions create trust in others and reinforce other-regarding behaviour.

Secondly, poverty is shaped by norms and institutions, as they shape mental representations and behaviour, in regard to individual status in particular, which builds cumulative causation and endogenous processes. For example, experiments in behavioural economics show that the institutional characteristics of markets (anonymity, competition) shape individuals' social preferences. Individuals are less social in anonymous environments, where the institution of the market appears to reduce the capacity to regard others; by contrast, the individuals are more social in environments of personal exchanges (Carpenter, 2005; Cardenas and Carpenter, 2005).

Institutions and norms generate mental processes and expectations that in turn maintain institutions. For instance, as shown by Hoff and Pandey (2004), in India low-caste individuals perform less well because they expect lower rewards; they think that they do not fully participate in certain institutions and that they will not have full access to the rights and rewards provided by these institutions. A particular institutional system of inequality here generates mental representations that sustain the institutions that support inequality. Poverty traps are created by institutions, which are in turn supported by expectations.

Poverty is also shaped by political institutions that generate specific mental representations. As Glaeser (2003) argues, political institutions provide incentives for true or false beliefs: false beliefs endure when they are costless, bringing large returns and when the incentives for true information are low. As is well known, political institutions, divisions and fragmentation may provide the incentives for psychological states and emotions such as hatred against particular groups (Glaeser, 2004).

4.5 Conclusion

This chapter has argued that institutions and norms are constitutive of the multidimensionality of poverty, according to a two-step causal process that is direct and involves cognitive phenomena. In the first place, institutions and norms determine access and achievements in various dimensions, in, for example, income, human development and social interactions.

Secondly, it has been shown that institutions as evolutionary cognitive phenomena play a key role in these causal processes. As psychological states, institutions and norms endogenously both determine and result from individual mental models, and are therefore also causes and effects of social interactions and types of behaviour regarding the capacity of escaping poverty – for instance, cooperation, altruism, self-interest. Institutions are themselves multidimensional, including forms and contents, which multiplies the causalities between dimensions of institutions and dimensions of poverty.

It has likewise been shown that because of these multiple cognitive causal chains, there is an *ex ante* indeterminacy of the effects of norms and institutions, which may be inclusive, cooperation enhancing and poverty reducing, or may be exclusionary. Causalities function both ways, from institutions to poverty and from poverty to institutions, which induce endogenous processes and may generate poverty traps, or 'institutional poverty traps'. Repeated social interactions may stabilize beliefs and norms, thus generating institutional poverty traps that are also 'cognitive institutional traps'.

Concepts from development economics, evolutionary institutionalism and psychology have been used in this analysis. The bridging of these disciplines is an increasingly promising field of research – in particular, regarding the concepts of norms and institutions. This cross-conceptualization should contribute to a better understanding of the multidimensionality of poverty.

Notes

1. A longer version of this chapter has been presented at the International Conference on 'The Many Dimensions of Poverty' organized by the International Poverty Centre, United Nations Development Programme (UNDP), Brasilia, 29–31 August 2005.
2. Among numerous studies, Sen (1987, 1993).
3. The 'old institutionalism' elaborated by Thorstein Veblen, among others.
4. Sindzingre (2006).
5. Among many studies, Greif (1989), Greif *et al.* (1994).
6. Property rights institutions have indeed been at the foundation of the neoinstitutionalist economic approach to institutions since Coase (1960).
7. Engerman (1973); on the case of Thailand, Feeny (1989).
8. For example, by Wittgenstein (1953), Quine (1960) or Kripke (1982).
9. Kranton (1996), Akerlof and Kranton (2000).
10. North (2005, 1996); Denzau and North (1994); Mantzavinos (2001, section 2).
11. Milgrom, North and Weingast (1990), or the many studies by Greif.
12. Rooted itself in evolutionary biology, as shown by Tooby and Cosmides (1992).
13. This is analysed in depth in Sindzingre (2005).
14. In a functionalist perspective (separating forms and functions), Rodrik (2003) explores the contrast between property rights in China and Russia.
15. On the lack of rigour in the use of institutional variables in econometric regressions, see Lindauer and Pritchett (2002), Sindzingre (2005).
16. See Hilhorst *et al.* (1999) on the example of Mali.
17. On caste and collective action in India, see Banerjee and Somanathan (2001).
18. Fafchamps (2000) on the case of supplier credit for manufacturers in Kenya and Zimbabwe.
19. On the concept of social exclusion, see Sindzingre (1999).
20. Goldstein *et al.* (2002) on the example of Southern Ghana.
21. Bowles (2004); on 'conditional cooperators' and 'altruistic punishers' as categories going beyond the debate on self-interest vs. altruism, Gintis *et al.* (2005).
22. Benabou and Tirole (2004b), Binmore (2006) for a critique of evolutionary explanations.
23. Norms of 'generalized morality', initial trust, may even be viewed as conditions for markets to properly function, Platteau (2000b).

24. On the impact of exclusionary norms on education and health in India, see Kozel (2003).
25. De Haan (2004) on the example of the state of Orissa.
26. For Sub-Saharan Africa, see Lambert and Sindzingre (1995), Lavigne-Delville *et al.* (2001), Chauveau (2000).
27. Berry (1993), Shipton and Goheen (1992), Platteau (1996).
28. Dercon (2004), Fafchamps and Lund (2003) on the example of the Philippines.
29. On the example of Côte d'Ivoire, Duflo and Udry (2003).
30. Such as lack of access to mutual insurance or formal financial institutions; on vulnerability or 'stochastic poverty', Morduch (1994).
31. In Sub-Saharan Africa colonization accentuated the erosion of intra-lineage and intra-household norms of cooperation (Leeson 2005).
32. Platteau (1994), Fafchamps (1992) on 'traditional' vs market societies.
33 They are reinforced by location effects (Durlauf 2002).
34. Rosenstein-Rodan (1943).
35. Arthur (1989); for a review, David (2001).
36. Bowles (2006, p. 2), Hoff (2000).
37. The concept of the poverty trap has been criticized as lacking empirical evidence when defined as zero growth; Easterly (2005), Kraay (2005), though they agree over the fact that institutions create poverty traps.
38. As coined by Egidi and Narduzzo (1997).
39. Alesina and La Ferrara (2001) on the case of the US; Alesina *et al.* (2001).
40. Ravallion and Lokshin (2002) on the discrepancies between objective income and self-rated welfare in Russia.
41. Because of 'cognitive inaccessibility': for a survey of neuroeconomics, Camerer *et al.* (2005).

References

Akerlof, Georges A. and Rachel E. Kranton (2000) 'Economics and Identity', *Quarterly Journal of Economics*, 115(3), 715–53.
Alesina, Alberto F. and George-Marios Angeletos (2003) *Fairness and Redistribution: US versus Europe*. Cambridge MA, MIT Department of Economics working paper 02–37.
Alesina, Alberto, Rafael Di Tella and Robert MacCulloch (2001) *Inequality and Happiness: Are Europeans and Americans Different?* Working Paper no. 8198. Cambridge, MA: NBER.
Alesina, Alberto and Eliana La Ferrara (2001) *Preferences for Redistribution in the Land of Opportunities*, Working Paper no. 8267. Cambridge, MASS: NBER.
Aoki, Masahiko (2001) *Toward a Comparative Institutional Analysis*. Cambridge, MA: MIT Press.
Arnott, Richard and Joseph E. Stiglitz (1991) 'Moral Hazard and Nonmarket Institutions: Dysfunctional Crowding Out or Peer Monitoring', *American Economic Review*, 81(1), 179–90.
Arthur, W. Brian (1989) 'Competing Technologies, Increasing Returns and Lock-In by Historical Events', *Economic Journal*, 99(394), 116–31.
Atkinson, Anthony and François Bourguignon (1999) *Poverty and Inclusion from a World Perspective*. Paris: World Bank, ABCDE Conference.
Axelrod, Robert (1986) 'An Evolutionary Approach to Norms', *American Political Science Review*, 80(4). 1095–111.
Banerjee, Abhijit and Rohini Somanathan (2001) *Caste, Community and Collective Action: the Political Economy of Public Good Provision in India*, mimeo. MIT, Department of Economics.
Bardhan, Pranab (2005) *Scarcity, Conflicts and Cooperation: Essays in the Political and Institutional Economics of Development*. Cambridge, MA: MIT Press.

Basu, Kaushik (2000) *Prelude to Political Economy: a Study of the Social and Political Foundations of Economics.* Oxford: Oxford University Press.

Benabou, Roland and Jean Tirole (2004a) *Belief in a Just World and Redistributive Politics*, mimeo. Princeton University, MIT and IDEI-Toulouse.

Benabou, Roland and Jean Tirole (2004b), *Incentives and Prosocial Behavior*, Discussion paper 4633. London: CEPR.

Berry, Sara (1993) *No Condition is Permanent: the Social Dynamics of Agrarian Change in Sub-Saharan Africa.* Madison: the University of Wisconsin Press.

Binmore, Ken (2006) 'Why Do People Cooperate?', *Politics, Philosophy and Economics*, 5(1), 81–96.

Bowles, Samuel (1998) 'Endogenous Preferences: the Cultural Consequences of Markets and other Economic Institutions', *Journal of Economic Literature*, 36(1), 75–111.

Bowles, Samuel (2004), *Microeconomics: Behaviour, Institutions and Evolution.* Princeton, NJ: Princeton University Press and Russell Sage Foundation.

Bowles, Samuel (2006) 'Institutional Poverty Trap', in Samuel Bowles, Steven N. Durlauf and Karla Hoff (eds), *Poverty Traps.* Princeton, NJ: Princeton University Press.

Brock, William A. and Steven N. Durlauf (2005) *Social Interactions and Macroeconomics*, mimeo. Madison, University of Wisconsin, Department of Economics working paper.

Camerer, Colin, George Loewenstein and Drazen Prelec (2005) 'Neuroeconomics: How Neuroscience Can Inform Economics', *Journal of Economic Literature*, 43(1), pp. 9–64.

Cardenas, Juan Camilo and Jeffrey P. Carpenter (2005) *Experiments and Economic Development: Lessons from Field Labs in the Developing World*, Middlebury, Middlebury College, Department of Economics Discussion Paper 05–05.

Carpenter, Jeffrey P. (2005) 'Endogenous Social Preferences', *Review of Radical Political Economics*, 37(1), 63–84.

Chauveau, Jean-Pierre (2000) *The Land Tenure Question in Côte d'Ivoire: A Lesson in History*, Drylands Programme Working Paper no. 95. London. IIED.

Coase, Ronald (1960) The Problem of Social Cost, *Journal of Law and Economics*, 3, 1–44.

Cosmides, Leda and John Tooby (1994) 'Better than Rational: Evolutionary Psychology and the Invisible Hand', *American Economic Review*, 84(2), 327–32.

Dasgupta, Partha (1997) 'Nutritional Status, the Capacity for Work, and Poverty Trap', *Journal of Econometrics*, 77, 5–37.

David, Paul A. (2001) 'Path Dependence, its Critics and the Quest for 'Historical Economics', in Pierre Garrouste and Stavros Ioannides (eds), *Evolution and Path Dependence in Economic Ideas.* Cheltenham: Edward Elgar.

Dawkins, Richard (1976) *The Selfish Gene.* Oxford: Oxford University Press.

De Haan, Arjan (2004) *Disparities within India's Poorest Regions: Why do the Same Institutions Work Differently in Different Places?*, mimeo, Washington DC, background paper for the World Development Report 2006.

Denzau, Arthur T. and Douglass C. North (1994) 'Shared Mental Models: Ideologies and Institutions', *Kyklos*, 47(1), 3–31.

Dercon, Stefan (2004) 'Income Risk, Coping Strategies and Safety Nets', in Stefan Dercon (ed.) *Insurance against Poverty.* Oxford: Oxford University Press.

Duflo, Esther and Chris Udry (2003) *Intrahousehold Resources Allocation in Côte d'Ivoire: Social Norms, Separate Accounts and Consumption Choices*, Washington D. C., BREAD working paper 016.

Durlauf, Steven N. (2002) *Groups, Social Influences and Inequality: a Memberships Theory Perspective on Poverty Traps*, mimeo, University of Wisconsin, Department of Economics.

Easterly, William (2005) *Reliving the 50s: the Big Push, Poverty Traps and Takeoffs in Economic Development*, mimeo, IFPRI/Cornell Conference on Threshold Effects and Non-Linearities in Growth and Development.

Egidi, Massimo and Alessandro Narduzzo (1997) 'The Emergence of Path-Dependent Behaviors in Cooperative Contexts', *International Journal of Industrial Organization*, 15(6), pp. 677–709.

Elster, Jon (1989) 'Social Norms and Economic Theory', *Journal of Economic Perspectives*, 3(4), 99–117.

Engerman, Stanley L. (1973) 'Some Considerations Relating to Property Rights in Man', *Journal of Economic History*, 33(1), 43–65.

Engerman, Stanley L. and Kenneth L. Sokoloff (2002) *Inequality Before and Under the Law: Paths of Long-Run Development in the Americas*. Oslo: Annual World Bank Conference on Development Economics.

Engerman, Stanley L. and Kenneth L. Sokoloff (2003) *Institutional and Non-Institutional Explanations of Economic Differences*, working paper 9989. Cambridge MA: NBER.

Fafchamps, Marcel (1992) 'Solidarity Networks in Preindustrial Societies: Rational Peasants with a Moral Economy', *Economic Development and Cultural Change*, 41(1), 147–74.

Fafchamps, Marcel (2000) 'Ethnicity and Credit in African Manufacturing', *Journal of Development Economics*, 61(1) 205–35.

Fafchamps, Marcel and Susan Lund (2003) 'Risk-Sharing Networks in Rural Philippines', *Journal of Development Economics*, 71(2), 261–87.

Feeny, David (1989) 'The Decline of Property Rights in Man in Thailand, 1800–1913', *Journal of Economic History*, 49(2), 285–96.

Fehr, Ernest and Armin Falk (2001) *Psychological Foundations of Incentives*, working paper 95. Zurich: University of Zurich, Institute for Empirical Research in Economics.

Fehr, Ernest and Urs Fischbascher (2004) 'Social Norms and Human Cooperation', *Trends in Cognitive Science*, 8(4), 185–90.

Fehr, Ernest and Simon Gächter (2000) 'Fairness and Retaliation: the Economics of Reciprocity', *Journal of Economic Perspectives*, 14(3) 159–81.

Fehr, Ernst and Klaus Schmidt (1999) 'A Theory of Fairness, Competition, and Cooperation', *Quarterly Journal of Economics*, 114, 817–68.

Gintis, Herbert, Samuel Bowles, Robert T. Boyd and Ernst Fehr (eds) (2005) *Moral Sentiments and Material Interests: the Foundations of Cooperation in Economic Life*. Cambridge, MA: MIT Press.

Glaeser, Edward (2003) *Psychology and the Market*, working paper 10203. Cambridge, MA: NBER.

Glaeser, Edward (2004) *The Political Economy of Hatred*, Discussion Paper 1970, third version. Cambridge MA, Harvard Institute of Economic Research.

Goldstein, Markus, Alain de Janvry and Elisabeth Sadoulet (2002) *Is a Friend in Need a Friend Indeed? Inclusion and Exclusion in Mutual Insurance Networks in Southern Ghana*, Discussion Paper 2002/25. Helsinki: WIDER.

Granovetter, Mark (1978) 'Threshold Models of Collective Behavior', *American Journal of Sociology*, 83(6) 1420–43.

Greif, Avner (1989), 'Reputation and Coalitions in Medieval Trade: Evidence on the Maghribi Traders', *Journal of Economic History*, 49(4), 857–82.

Greif, Avner (1997) *On the Social Foundations and Historical Development of Institutions that Facilitate Impersonal Exchange: From the Community Responsibility System to Individual Legal Responsibility in Pre-modern Europe*, Department of Economics working paper 97–016. Stanford: Stanford University.

Greif, Avner, Paul Milgrom and Barry Weingast (1994) 'Coordination, Commitment, and Enforcement: the Case of the Merchant Guild', *Journal of Political Economy*, 102(4), 745–76.

Grice, Herbert Paul (1975) 'Logic and Conversation', in Peter Cole and Jerry L. Morgan (eds), *Syntax and Semantics, vol. 3: Speech Acts*. New York: Academic Press.

Harp, Randall (2005) *Cooperation, Team Reasoning, and Rational Choice*, mimeo. Stanford University, Social Ethics and Normative Theory workshop.

Harriss-White, Barbara (2005) 'Destitution and the Poverty of Its Politics: With Special Reference to South Asia', *World Development*, 33(6) 881–91.

Hilhorst, Thea, Camilla Toulmin, Karen Brock and Ngolo Coulibaly (1999) *Sustainability amidst Diversity: Options for Rural Households in Mali*, London: International Institute for Environment and Development.

Hoff, Karla (2000) *Beyond Rosenstein-Rodan: the Modern Theory of Underdevelopment Traps*. Washington DC: the World Bank, Annual World Bank Development Economics Conference.

Hoff, Karla and Priyanka Pandey (2004) *Belief Systems and Durable Inequalities: an Experimental Investigation of Indian Caste,* policy research working paper 2875. Washington DC: the World Bank.

Hoff, Karla and Arijit Sen (2006) 'The Kin System as A Poverty Trap?', in Samuel Bowles, Steven N. Durlauf and Karla Hoff (eds), *Poverty Traps.* Princeton, NJ Princeton: University Press.

Iliffe, John (1987) *The African Poor: A History.* Cambridge: Cambridge University Press.

Kozel, Valerie (2003) *Local Power Relations and Poverty in India.* Washington DC: the World Bank, Poverty Day.

Kraay, Aart (2005) *Aid, Growth and Poverty,* mimeo, Maputo, IMF Seminar on Foreign Aid and Macroeconomic Management.

Kranton, Rachel E. (1996) 'Reciprocal Exchange: A Self-Sustaining System', *American Economic Review,* 86(4), 830–51.

Kripke, Saul (1982) *Wittgenstein on Rules and Private Language.* Cambridge, MA: Harvard University Press.

Lambert, Sylvie and Alice Sindzingre (1995) 'Droits de propriété et modes d'accès à la terre en Afrique: une revue critique', *Cahiers d'Economie et Sociologie Rurales,* 36, 95–128 (also *Land Reform,* (FAO), 1995, pp. 7–30).

Lavigne-Delville, Philippe, Camilla Toulmin, Jean-Philippe Colin and Jean-Pierre Chauveau (2001) *Securing Secondary Rights to Land in West Africa.* London: International Institute for Environment and Development.

Leeson, Peter T. (2005) 'Endogenizing Fractionalization', *Journal of Institutional Economics,* 1(1), 75–98.

Lindauer, David L. and Lant Pritchett (2002) 'What's the Big Idea? The Third Generation of Policies for Economic Growth', *Economia,* Fall, pp. 1–39.

Lokshin, Michael M. and Martin Ravallion (2002) *Rich and Powerful? Subjective Power and Welfare* policy research working paper 2854. Washington DC: World Bank.

Loury, Glenn C. (1999) *Social Exclusion and Ethnic Groups: the Challenge to Economics,* mimeo. Washington DC: the World Bank, Annual World Bank Conference on Development Economics.

Loury, Glenn C. (2001) *Racial Stigma: the Problem of Biased Social Cognition,* mimeo. Chicago: University of Illinois, Bertha Lebus Lecture.

Malaizé, Vincent and Alice Sindzingre (1998) 'Politique économique, secteur privé et réseau en Asie du Sud-Est et en Afrique de l'ouest', *Tiers-Monde,* 39(155), 647–73.

Manski, Charles F. (2000) 'Economic Analysis of Social Interactions', *Journal of Economic Perspectives,* 14(3), 115–36.

Mantzavinos, Chrysostomos (2001) *Individuals, Institutions and Markets.* Cambridge: Cambridge University Press.

Milgrom, Paul R., Douglass C. North and Barry R. Weingast (1990) 'The Role of Institutions in the Revival of Trade: the Law Merchant, Private Judges and the Champagne Fairs', *Economics and Politics,* 2(1), 1–23.

Mookherjee, Dilip and Debraj Ray (2000) *Contractual Structure and Wealth Accumulation,* mimeo, Boston University and New York University, McArthur Foundation Network on Inequality and Economic Performance.

Morduch, Jonathan (1994), 'Poverty and Vulnerability', *American Economic Review,* 84(2), 221–5.

North, Douglass C. (1989) 'Institutions and Economic Growth: An Historical Introduction', *World Development,* 17(9), 1319–32.

North, Douglass C. (1990) *Institutions, Institutional Change and Economic Performance.* New York: Cambridge University Press.

North, Douglass C. (1991) 'Institutions', *Journal of Economic Perspectives,* 5(1), 97–112.

North, Douglass C. (1996) *Economics and Cognitive Science,* mimeo. St Louis: Washington University.

North, Douglass (1997) *The Contribution of the New Institutional Economics to an Understanding of the Transition Problem.* Helsinki: WIDER Annual Lecture 1.

North, Douglass C. (2005) *Understanding the Process of Economic Change*. Princeton, NJ: Princeton University Press.

Offerman, Theo (2002) 'Hurting Hurts More than Helping Helps', *European Economic Review*, 46(8), 1423–37.

Platteau, Jean-Philippe (1994), 'Behind the Market Stage Where Real Societies Exist: Part1: The Role of Public and Private Order Institutions', *Journal of Development Studies*, 30(3) 533–77; 'Part 2: The Role of Moral Norms', 30(4), 753–817.

Platteau, Jean-Philippe (1996) 'The Evolutionary Theory of Land Rights as Applied to Sub-Saharan Africa: a Critical Assessment', *Development and Change*, 27(1), 29–85.

Platteau, Jean-Philippe (1997) 'Mutual Insurance as an Elusive Concept in Traditional Rural Communities', *Journal of Development Studies*, 33(6), 764–96.

Platteau, Jean-Philippe (2000a) *Community Imperfections*. Paris, the World Bank, Annual Bank Conference on Development Economics.

Platteau, Jean-Philippe (2000b) *Order, the Rule of Law and Moral Norms*. Bangkok: UNCTAD X, High-level Round Table on Trade and Development.

Platteau, Jean-Philippe (2002) *The Gradual Erosion of the Social Security Function of Customary Land Tenure Arrangements in Lineage-Based Societies*, discussion paper 2002/26. Helsinki: WIDER.

Platteau, Jean-Philippe and Yujiro Hayami (1998) 'Resources Endowments and Agricultural Development: Africa versus Asia', in Yujiro Hayami and Masahiko Aoki (eds), *The Institutional Foundations of East Asian Economic Development*. London: Macmillan in association with the International Economic Association.

Pritchett, Lant H. (2002) *A Conclusion to Cross-National Growth Research: A Foreword to 'The Countries Themselves'*, mimeo. Cambridge MA: Harvard University.

Pritchett, Lant H. (2005) *Reform is Like a Box of Chocolates: Understanding the Growth Disappointments and Surprises*, mimeo. Washington DC, the World Bank.

Quine, Willard Van Orman (1960) *Word and Object*. Cambridge, MA: MIT Press.

Rabin, Matthew (1993) 'Incorporating Fairness into Game Theory and Economics', *American Economic Review*, 83(5), 1281–302.

Rauch, James E. (2001) 'Business and Social Networks in International Trade', *Journal of Economic Literature*, 39(4), 1177–203.

Ravallion, Martin and Michael Lokshin (2002) 'Self-Rated Economic Welfare in Russia', *European Economic Review*, 46(8), 1453–73.

Rodrik, Dani (ed.) (2003), *In Search of Prosperity: Analytical Narratives on Economic Growth*. Princeton, NJ: Princeton University Press.

Rosenstein-Rodan, Paul N. (1943) 'Problems of Industrialization of Eastern and South-Eastern Europe', *Economic Journal*, 53, 210–11, June September, pp. 202–11.

Schlicht, Ekkehart (2001) *Custom*, discussion paper 2001–08. Munich: University of Munich, Department of Economics.

Seabright, Paul (2004) *The Company of Strangers: A Natural History of Economic Life*. Princeton, NJ: Princeton University Press.

Searle, John R. (2005) 'What is an Institution?', *Journal of Institutional Economics*, 1(1), 1–22.

Sen, Amartya (1987) 'The Standard of Living, Lecture I: Concepts and Critiques; Lecture II: Lives and Capabilities', in Geoffrey Hawthorn (ed)., *The Standard of Living*. Cambridge: Cambridge University Press.

Sen, Amartya (1993) 'Capability and Well-Being', in Martha C. Nussbaum and Amartya Sen (eds), *The Quality of Life*. Oxford: Clarendon Press.

Sethi, Rajiv and E. Somanathan (1996) 'The Evolution of Social Norms in Common Property Resource Use', *American Economic Review*, 86(4), 766–88.

Shipton, Parker and Mitzi Goheen (1992) 'Understanding African Landholding: Power, Land and Meaning', *Africa*, 62(3) 307–25.

Sindzingre, Alice (1987) 'Autres cultures, autres moeurs', *Autrement*, 93, 204–10.

Sindzingre, Alice (1999) 'Exclusion and Poverty in Developing Economies', in Gudrun Kochendörfer-Lucius and Boris Pleskovic (eds), *Inclusion, Justice and Poverty Reduction*.

Berlin: German Foundation for International Development/DSE, Villa Borsig Workshop Series, pp. 59–66.

Sindzingre, Alice (2005) *Institutions and Development: A Theoretical Contribution*, mimeo. The Hague: Institute of Social Studies (ISS), Economic Research Seminar.

Sindzingre, Alice (2006) 'The Relevance of the Concepts of Formality and Informality: A Theoretical Appraisal', in Basudeb Guha-Khasnobis, Ravi Kanbur and Elinor Ostrom (eds), *Linking the Formal and Informal Economy: Concepts and Policies*. Oxford: Oxford University Press and WIDER.

Sindzingre, Alice (2007) *Explaining Threshold Effects of Globalisation on Poverty: an Institutional Perspective*, Helsinki, UNU-WIDER Research Paper no. 2005/53 (in Machiko Nissanke and Erik Thorbecke eds., *The Impact of Globalization on the World's Poor: Transmission Mechanisms*. Basingstoke, Palgrave Macmillan, 2007).

Sperber, Dan (1985) 'Anthropology and Psychology: Towards an Epidemiology of Representations', *Man,* 20, 73–89.

Sperber, Dan (1990) 'The Epidemiology of Beliefs', in Colin Fraser and George Gaskell (eds), *The Social Psychological Study of Widespread Beliefs*. Oxford: Clarendon Press.

Sperber, Dan and Deirdre Wilson (1986) *Relevance: Communication and Cognition*. Cambridge, MA: Harvard University Press.

Sugden, Robert (2000) 'Team Preferences', *Economics and Philosophy*, 16(2) 175–204.

Tooby, John and Leda Cosmides (1992) 'The Psychological Foundations of Culture', in Jerome Barkow, Leda Cosmides and John Tooby (eds), *The Adapted Mind: Evolutionary Psychology and the Generation of Culture*. New York: Oxford University Press.

Wittgenstein, Ludwig (1953) *Philosophical Investigations*. New York: Macmillan.

Young, Henry Peyton (1998) 'Social Norms and Economic Welfare', *European Economic Review*, 42(3–5), 821–30.

Zimmerman, Frederick J. and Michael R. Carter (2003) 'Asset Smoothing, Consumption Smoothing and the Reproduction of Inequality under Risk and Subsistence Constraints', *Journal of Development Economics*, 71(2), 233–60.

5
The Subjective Dimension of Poverty: A Psychological Viewpoint

Joaquina Palomar Lever

Conceptualizing poverty is an extremely complex task, since, as is now widely acknowledged, it is a multidimensional phenomenon. When poverty is spoken of, reference is often made to the lack of or insufficiency of different attributes that are necessary for individuals to reach an acceptable standard of living. In 2001 the World Bank defined poverty along these lines, specifically as material deficiency, weak social relations, insecurity and precariousness, minimal self-confidence, and helplessness.

The first report by the technical committee for measuring poverty in Mexico – which emphasizes the limitations characterizing monetary measurements of poverty for representing non-monetary dimensions as components of well-being – states the following: 'multidimensional measurements would represent an ideal objective, particularly the *mixed* measurements that include both monetary and non-monetary indicators' (López-Calva and Rodríguez, 2005). Nevertheless, some questions still arise: What type of information is needed to be able to arrive at multidimensional measurements? What types of dimensions are relevant? And what kind of interaction takes place among the various dimensions? (Bourguignon and Chakravarty, 2003). The multidimensional conceptualization of poverty has important implications not only for the study and measurement of poverty, but also for the way in which social policy instruments are conceived of, and for the implementation of social policy (López-Calva and Rodríguez, 2004).

One aspect frequently ignored in studies of poverty and related social policies on poverty is its psychological dimension which, as I will attempt to demonstrate below, is a relevant factor for both explaining the phenomenon of poverty as well as the successful implementation of public polices aimed at reducing this phenomenon. The objective of this chapter is to offer an overall vision of what psychology and psychologists have contributed to the study of poverty. This contribution is focused primarily on five areas:

1. The study of how poverty is perceived, from different geographical locations and by different social actors (poor, not poor, men, women, liberals, conservatives, blacks, Latinos). This includes: (i) the perception of what it means to be poor; (ii) the perception of the causes of poverty; (iii) the relationship between beliefs

regarding the causes of poverty and how the possibilities for overcoming this condition are perceived; and (iv) how individuals classify themselves in terms of class (if they consider themselves to be poor or not poor) and the relationship between this identification and certain health variables as well as social mobility.

2. The psychological aspects of the culture of poverty. This encompasses the study of the impact of cultural aspects on the reproduction of extreme poverty or its eradication, through the socialization process of children, primarily in their homes, since this is the most important environment for the transmission of culture.

3. The study of the relationship between certain psychological variables and poverty (the degree to which poverty and economic hardship are associated with mental health) as well as of the effects that poverty may have on the process of socialization during childhood, youth and even adulthood.

4. The study of the relationship between certain psychological variables and the likelihood of experiencing upward social mobility.

5. The study of the relationship between the well-being of individuals living in poverty and their subjective perceptions.

5.1   The perception of poverty

(a) Psychological meaning

One of the modalities used in research on the perception of poverty is the study of *psychological meaning*. The notion of psychological meaning refers to the conceptual meaning or content that a given word or phrase has for a given person. According to Collins and Loftus (1975), the amount of information a person can generate with regard to any concept appears to be unlimited. Therefore, a concept can be represented as a node in a network and the properties of the concept can be represented as relational connections labelled with other concepts (nodes) in the network. Information stored in the semantic memory is located within a huge network, and each element is related to other elements through different connectors. Through the network, it is possible to discover the way in which a concept is represented in the memory and in this way, take note of its psychological meaning, the latter being the total network generated for a particular concept (Valdéz, 1994).

One of the ways of addressing *psychological meaning* is through the technique of semantic networks. This is a technique that emerged from the cognitivist theory in psychology, which attempts to explain the determinants of behaviour by using as a starting point the information that individuals have stored in the form of representations and symbols with a particular meaning. In order to achieve this objective, individuals are asked to define each *stimulus* word presented to them, with a minimum of five individual words, which may be names, pronouns, nouns, adjectives, verbs or adverbs, but without using prepositions, conjunctions or articles. After the words used to define the stimulus word have been written down, individuals are asked to place them into hierarchical order, based on the importance that each one has with respect to the stimulus word defined – in other words, in accordance with the degree to which they have the closest meaning to the stimulus word. Thus, individuals are asked to assign number one to the most important, number two to the next in importance and so on. What is obtained is a semantic network, understood as a set of concepts selected through processes of memory reconstruction, although this selection is not viewed as a simple association, since it is determined by the classes and properties of the elements of which it consists. The results can be analyzed qualitatively and quantitatively on the basis of an analysis of the semantic network, and will reflect the most important descriptors in terms of the frequency of appearance and the hierarchy assigned.

Thus in Mexico, Silva (2000) reports a study conducted with people living in poverty, and in which the subjects were offered 159 descriptors of 'poverty'. Those with the greatest semantic weight were: 'deficiency', 'scarcity', 'limitations', 'money', 'needs', 'sadness', 'malnutrition', 'dissatisfaction', and 'happiness'. According to the author of this study there appears to be two major dimensions in the perception of poverty, one tangible, observable and material-oriented, and the other, abstract. The first covers aspects such as 'money', 'house', 'clothes' and 'car' while the second refers to terms such as 'limitation', 'deficiency', 'shame' and 'sadness'.

In another study Palomar and Perez (2003) found in their study that a group of extremely poor subjects reported a greater number of descriptors in the category of 'personality characteristics', in comparison to a group of subjects who were not poor. These descriptors refer to aspects of the personality associated with poverty, as if possessing these characteristics makes individuals responsible for the situation in which they are living. There are other examples of studies that have used similar methodologies and have led to similar results.

(b) Perception of the causes of poverty

There are numerous studies on the perception of factors causing poverty is considerable. Feagin (1972, 1975) was the first to systematically study the multiple meanings of poverty for different social groups, developing a list of 11 types of beliefs regarding the causes of poverty, and grouping them into three categories: (1) individual or internal causes, which explain poverty in terms of the characteristics or lifestyles of poor people, such as a lack of skills, effort or savings; (2) social or external causes, which attribute poverty to unfavourable social and economic forces such as the inequitable distribution of wealth, exploitation of the poor, lack of education, low wages and absence of social opportunities; and (3) fatalism, including causes of poverty related to bad luck or a determination by inscrutable superior forces (God, fate).

The first type of belief is based on the perspective that poor people are responsible for their condition, while in the case of the two others, poor people are believed to suffer due to circumstances outside their control.

Studies conducted in other countries found factorial structures that are somehow different from this construct. Shek (2002), for example, stressed that beliefs regarding the causes of poverty referred to four factors: personal factors, lack of opportunities, exploitation and fate.

The results of research carried out in this field have made it possible to determine that, generally speaking, there is a tendency in developed countries to overestimate the power of individual factors as opposed to structural, situational or external factors, since it is believed that in a democratic society with equal opportunities for all, individuals are responsible for their own economic situation. In developing countries, by contrast, there is a greater tendency to attribute the causes of poverty to structural or fatalistic factors.

Beliefs regarding the causes of poverty have also been linked to certain variables, such as race, education, income, age, gender and social status. In terms of racial aspects, it has been observed that individuals tend to identify with the generalized experience of the group to which they belong, and to respond in accordance with this identification. Consequently, members of minorities tend to identify with the struggle and efforts of their reference group (Gurin, Millar and Gurin, 1980, cited in Hunt, 1996).

With respect to the education variable, it has been found that in social strata characterized by higher levels of education, there is a tendency to view poverty as a failure that should be attributed to individuals (Cryns, 1977, cited in An-Pyng Sun, 2001).

With respect to the socioeconomic level, it has been found that individuals who are in a favourable economic position tend to blame poor people for their situation, while they attribute their own favourable condition to their own merits. This is likely to be the result of a psychological need to distance themselves from poor people in order to enhance their own social identity and self-esteem. Poor people, for their part, tend to blame others – the *system*, government – for their own situation (Steele, 1994). As far as the gender is concerned, results have not been very consistent. It seems, however, that groups in less favourable economic conditions, including women and younger people, are more likely to attribute poverty to structural factors (Robinson and Bell, 1978).

(c) Perception of causes of poverty and perception of social mobility

There are many studies that link the type of beliefs held by individuals in relation to the causes of poverty with the way in which they perceive their own possibilities for overcoming this precarious condition. These studies generally show that individuals with a low socioeconomic level are more likely to have beliefs that connote victimization (for example, blaming society, God or the government) and that are associated with perceptions of a lack of control over their own lives, plus low self-esteem, low psychosocial adjustment, and a lack of optimism in regard to overcoming their poverty (Smith, 1985). Other studies found that individuals inclined to explain the causes of poverty in terms of the characteristics or lifestyles of poor people, tend more often to think that they have the means of overcoming poverty, in comparison to those adopting fatalistic or structural explanations. This is particularly true among young individuals with high levels of schooling (Palomar, 2005).

(d) Class identification and psychological health variables

Class identification is related to the way in which individuals locate their position within the social structure and to how they characterize their social preferences (the type of individuals with whom they enjoy socializing, the lifestyle they would like to have, and some other significant aspects of their lives). The way in which individuals define their background and identify with a social class has serious implications for their life opportunities, since this determines their behaviour in the face of economic deprivation (Marsh, 2003). Adler, Epel, Castellazzo and Ickovics (2000) thus found that physical and psychological health variables, such as certain styles for coping with stress, levels of stress, physical health and pessimism, are more related to the perceived than to the objective socioeconomic level.

5.2   Psychological aspects of the culture of poverty

The degree to which the cultural element is responsible for poverty has been a subject of discussion for a long time. Some theories attempt to explain poverty from a cultural perspective, defining culture as the factor that is ultimately responsible for this phenomenon. These theories have, however, been criticized for blaming poverty for its own misfortune.

Various authors, in Mexico as well as in other countries, analysed the most relevant aspects of popular culture and socialization in the culture of poverty, emphasizing the role played by family and social support networks in the survival of the poorest. In Mexico, literary figures such as Octavio Paz (1984), and psychoanalysts such as Santiago Ramírez (2002), focused on this issue, stressing also the role of history in popular idiosyncrasy.

In the Dominican Republic, Jorge Cela (1997) meticulously analysed some of the cultural and social characteristics of those living in extreme poverty in Santo Domingo, their sense of time, their lack of skills which prevents them from reaching their objectives, the intra-family violence in which they live (derived from authoritative use of power), their low self-esteem confronted through humour and aggressiveness and other aspects in their daily life which is marked by economic and emotional instability, a product of their experiences since very early ages.

> A characteristic feature of the culture of poverty is its institutional and emotional instability. Often families have been unstable. The number of cases in which couples have separated and found new partners is very high. Geographic mobility is very high. For many children, school is an unknown experience, or a very brief one. And for many, work does not represent an experience of institutional stability. Their reference to institutional stability is very weak, hence the lack of behavioral habits, such as perseverance, discipline, punctuality, coordination and planning. What is much stronger is the experience of insecurity. Emotional experience as a consequence is also marked by instability. Family instability, and the weak nature of other connections due to geographic, labour or school mobility, creates affectivity that is unanchored. (Cela, 1997, p. 68)

5.3   Poverty and psychological variables

Psychological research has also shown that economic deprivation in childhood – in addition to having adverse effects on the physical and mental development of individuals – increases risks of emotional and behaviour problems. Poverty places parents in a situation characterized by excessive daily demands, which can produce high levels of stress, depression and anxiety. This leads to less sensitivity on their part to the needs of their children, to the use of more severe discipline and to low levels of emotional support from their parents. All these elements increase the likelihood that their children will develop emotional problems (McLeod and Nonemaker, 2000).

Stress derived from economic hardship affects also marital relations, making it less likely that couples will express love, warmth, support and respect to each other. As a consequence couples are less able to solve their problems in common and this increases the level of hostility and stress between them. They then tend to less socialize with their children and often to show hostility toward their children's needs, leading to a deterioration in parent–child relationships (Ge, Conger Lorenz, Elder, Montague and Simons, 1992, cited in Ho, Lempers and Clark-Lempers, 1995).

The risk of an emotional disorder among children in poorer families is thus higher and they are in a situation of emotional and behavioural comorbidity that is three times higher than for other children (Costello, Farmer, Angold, Bums and Erkanli, 1997).

Poverty has been associated with numerous psychological variables such as depression, anxiety, self-esteem, strategies for coping with stress, achievement motivation, perception of social support, and locus of control, among others. I will present only a very general, compacted panorama of the research carried out in this regard.

In terms of the relationship between poverty and depression, a review of 47 studies addressing this issue in the literature reveals that in 28 of them statistically significant differences were not found between individuals with different socio-economic levels while they were found in 19 of them (Eaton, Muntaner, Bovasso and Smith, 2001). Most of the studies conducted currently on the relationship between socioeconomic status and depression are based on the stress paradigm, which relates this depression to a high degree of exposure to multiple stressors that foment this condition (Miech, Shanahan and Elder, 1999).

Three theoretical models have been developed in addressing the relationship between poverty and self-esteem. The first sustains that since socioeconomic level is an indicator of social status, a high socioeconomic level may promote high self-esteem, and a low socioeconomic level, low self-esteem (Rosenberg and Pearlin, 1978). The second affirms that individuals internalize the perceptions that others have of them so that if the socioeconomic level influences the way in which others treat us, this will be reflected in our self-esteem. The third model maintains that individuals have a broad repertoire of self-protecting strategies that serve as shields in relation to external feedback linked to socioeconomic level. Therefore, individuals from low social classes may blame external factors for their economic situation, and maintain their self-esteem by comparing themselves with others less fortunate (Twenge and Campbell, 2002). In any case, results on links between these two variables have been rather inconsistent (Rosenberg and Pearlin, 1978; Twenge and Campbell, 2002; Mullis, Mullis and Normandin, 1992, among others).

The relationship between poverty and strategies for coping with stress has been studied from various angles, and it has been found generally that poverty may promote ways of coping with stress that are passive (persons expect that circumstances on their own or other people will resolve their problems), emotional (persons focus on the emotions produced by a situation, more than on evaluating and confronting the situation in a rational manner), and evasive (persons avoid confronting the problem or situation that causes them stress, denying it or indefinitely postponing it) (Aldwin and Revenson, 1987).

In other research it has also been found that children who have grown up in an environment of extreme poverty have been subjected to high levels of stress so that when they become adults, they are not able to manage stress adequately. These adults are less likely to maintain a job, or to obtain the positions to which they aspire and this decreases the probability that they will experience upward social mobility (Corcoran, 1995).

Another variable that had an important role in the study of poverty from a psychological perspective is achievement motivation. This variable has been conceived of as a personality trait related to the search for independence and ongoing improvement in the activity in which one engages, as well as the desire of individuals to establish and meet personal goals. According to the main studies in this area, there exists a strong relationship between socioeconomic level and achievement motivation, since children who grow up in families with limited psychological resources assimilate feelings of fatalism, helplessness, dependence and inferiority – all of which are related to achievement motivation. Thus, individuals who have a strong achievement motivation have greater chances of escaping poverty (Cassidy, 2000; Cassidy and Lynn, 1991).

It is very important to continue research along these lines as it will improve our understanding of a phenomenon as complex as poverty. It is likely that social policies could be more effective, were these factors taken into account.

5.4   Social mobility and psychological variables

Social mobility can be defined as the transition or movement of an individual from one social position to another at a different level (Blejer, 1977), or the movement of persons within a social system that offers a certain degree of fluidity in the stratification of classes (Biswas and Pandey, 1996).

From a psychological perspective, the study of social mobility was centred on the impact that patterns of raising children, family structure and some psychological variables (such as values, attitudes and beliefs) have on social mobility (Aston and McLanahan, 1991; Biblarz and Raftery, 1993). According to this perspective, each social class instills in its members values that will encourage them to remain in that social class. On the contrary, individuals who are able to maintain a critical point of view with regard to the values of their reference group and adopt more independent behaviours and attitudes are more likely to move up and down from the social level in which they are (Balán, Blowing and Jelin, 1973).

The identification of the characteristics, attitudes and skills of the subjects who are socially mobile could thus lead to a greater effectiveness of public policies.

5.5   Poverty and subjective well-being

When we speak of poverty, we generally refer to a state of neediness, difficulty and a lack of what is indispensable for sustaining life, derived from individuals' economic situations. Nonetheless, poverty has characteristics that extend beyond an economic focus and have repercussions on individuals' levels of subjective well-being.

According to an economic approach to well-being one expects higher levels of income to be associated with higher levels of well-being through greater levels of material consumption. Existing studies in psychology have found, however, that such a positive relationship is weak so that a large percentage of human happiness remains unexplained. Other studies have indicated that psychological and personality variables have in fact an important impact on subjective well-being, since they explain a significant percentage of the variance in well-being and mitigate the impact of income. In other words, a high level of income does not necessarily promote a feeling of satisfaction or well-being, and a low level of income does not necessarily promote a feeling of dissatisfaction or a lack of well-being (López-Calva and Rodríguez, 2005). For example, a study conducted by Fuentes and Rojas (2001) found that income explained less than 5 per cent of the variance in subjective well-being and that the perception of satisfied material needs had a greater impact.

Of course, different perspectives have emerged to explain this type of result. What is relevant here, however, is the ability to pinpoint the factors and circumstances that determine the subjective well-being of individuals.

Research in psychology can thus contribute to the design of public policies that could promote the development of abilities and psychological and social resources among persons belonging to marginalized groups and, as a consequence, improve their living conditions.

These studies are important since they clearly establish that an increase in the well-being of individuals is not only a matter of satisfying basic needs by improving income or in-kind assistance (Weiss, Goebel, Page, Wilson and Warda, 1999; Petrosky and Birkimer, 1991; Elliot and Sheldon, 1997; Lenz and Demal, 2000; Palomar, Lanzagorta and Hernández, 2005).

Alleviating poverty is, however not sufficient because it is necessary to overcome the processes that generate poverty. It is therefore essential that government and other institutions do not neglect the study of the subjective factors that are related to poverty.

5.6   Conclusions

Poverty is a phenomenon that must be addressed from a multidisciplinary perspective, because of to its multidimensional nature. While the psychological dimension has often been ignored in these studies and in social policies, research in this field – although only in the early stages – points to its importance.

The results of psychological research have demonstrated that poverty is understood and explained in different ways, depending on the segment of the population and the geographic area from which the individual comes. Through this research it has been possible to discover that the majority of poor people in developing countries and, among them, the most disadvantaged groups (women and youth) attribute poverty to factors beyond their control and their lifestyles, and also that this type of belief is negatively associated with the likelihood of experiencing upward social mobility. It appears also that the well-being of a poor population is not mechanically associated with improved income.

It is therefore imperative to include psychosocial elements in designing public policies aiming at providing support to the most vulnerable groups in the population so that the target population fully understands the nature, orientation, functioning and scope of intervention programmes and shows assertive and proactive behaviour that will help to improve their situation.

Approaches of this type will encourage significant changes in the behaviour of participating social groups, guarantee a better allocation of the few available resources and prevent the implementation of paternalistic programmes and practices.

References

Adler, N.E., E.S. Epel, G. Castellazzo and J. Ickovics, (2000) 'Relationship of Subjective and Objective Status with Psychological and Physiological Functioning: Preliminary Data in Healthy White Women', *Health Psychology*, 19(6), 586–92.

Aldwin, C, and T. Revenson (1987) 'Does Coping Help? A Reexamination of the Relation Between Coping and Mental Health', *Journal of Personality and Social Psychology*, 53(2), 337–48.

An-Pyng Sun (2001) 'Perceptions Among Social Work and Non-social Work Students Concerning Causes of Poverty', *Journal of Social Work Education*, 37(1), 161–71.

Aston, N.M. and S.S. McLanahan (1991) 'Family Structure, Parental Practices and High School Completion', *American Sociological Review*, 56, 309–20.

Balán, J., H. Blowing and E. Jelin (1973) *Migración, Estructura Ocupacional y Movilidad Social (el caso Monterrey)*. Mexico: *Instituto de Investigaciones Sociales*, UNAM.

Biblarz, T.J. and A.F. Raftery (1993) 'The Effects of Family Disruption on Social Mobility', *American Sociological Review*, 58, 97–109.

Biswas, U.N. and J. Pandey (1996) 'Mobility and Perception of Socioeconomic Status among Tribal and Caste Group', *Journal of Cross-Cultural Psychology*, 27(2), 200–15.

Blejer, J. (1977) *Clase Social y Estratificación Social*. Mexico: Edicol.

Bourguignon, F. and S. Chakravarty (2003) 'The Measurement of Multidimensional Poverty', *Journal of Economic Inequality*, 1, 25–49.

Cassidy, T. (2000) 'Social Background, Achievement Motivation, Optimism and Health: a Longitudinal Study', *Counseling Psychology Quarterly*, 13(4), 399–413.

Cassidy, T. and R. Lynn (1991) 'Achievement Motivation, Educational Attainment, Cycles of Disadvantage and Social Competence: Some Longitudinal Data', *British Journal of Educational Psychology*, 61, 1–12.

Cela, J. (1997) *La Otra Cara de la Pobreza*. Dominican Republic: Centro de Estudios Padre Juan Montalvo, S.J.

Collins, A.M. and E.F. Loftus (1975) 'A Spreading Activation Model of Semantic Processing', *Psychological Review*, 82, 407–28.

Corcoran, M. (1995) 'Rags to Rags: Poverty and Mobility in the United States', *Annual Review of Sociology*, 21, 237–67.

Costello, F., E. Farmer, A. Angold, B. Burns and A. Erkanli (1997) 'Psychiatric disorders among American Indian and White Youth in Appalachia: The Great Smoky Mountains Study', *American Journal of Public Health*, 87, 827–32.

Cryns, A.G. (1997) 'Social Work Education and Student Ideology: A Multivariate Study of Professional Socialization', *Journal of Education for Social Work*, 13(1), 44–51.

Eaton, W.W., C. Muntaner, G. Bovasso and C. Smith (2001) 'Socioeconomic Status and Depressive Syndrome: the Role of Inter and Intra-generational Mobility, Government Assistance, and Work Environment', *Journal of Health and Social Behavior*, 42, 277–94.

Elliot, A.J. and K.M. Sheldon (1997) 'Avoidance Achievement Motivation: a Personal Goals Analysis', *Journal of Personality and Social Psychology*, 73(1), 171–85.

Feagin, J. (1972) 'Poverty: We Still Believe That God Helps Those Who Help Themselves', *Psychology Today*, 6, 101–29.

Feagin, J. (1975) *Subordinating Poor Persons: Welfare and American Beliefs*. Englewood Cliffs, NJ: Prentice-Hall.

Fuentes, N. and M. Rojas (2001) 'Economic Theory and Subjective Well-Being', *Social Indicators Research*, 53, 289–314.

Ge, X., R.D. Conger, F.O. Lorenz, G.H. Elder, R.B. Montague and R.L. Simons (1992) 'Linking Family Economic Hardship to Adolescent Distress' *Journal of Research on Adolescence*, 2, 351–78.

Gurin, P., A. Miller and G. Gurin (1980) 'Stratum Identification and Consciousness', *Social Psychology Quarterly*, 43, 30–47.

Ho, C.S., J.D. Lempers and D.S. Clark-Lempers (1995) 'Effects of Economic Hardship on Adolescence Self-esteem: a Family Mediation Model', *Adolescence*, 30, 117–32.

Hunt, M. (1996) 'The Individual, Society or Both? A Comparison of Black, Latino, and White Beliefs About the Causes of Poverty', *Social Forces*, 75, 293–322.

Lenz, G. and U. Demal (2000) 'Quality of Life in Depression and Anxiety Disorders: An Exploratory, Follow-up Study after Intensive Impatient Cognitive Behavior Therapy', *Psychopathology*, 33(6), 297–302.

López-Calva, L. and L. Rodríguez (2004) 'Cada quien habla de la feria...': Características Socioeconómicas de los Hogares y Percepciones sobre la Pobreza y la Política Social. Mexico City: *Secretaría de Desarrollo Social* (Sedesol), Series of research documents.

López-Calva, L. and L. Rodríguez (2005) 'Muchos rostros, un solo espejo: Restricciones para la medición multidimensional de la Pobreza en México'. Mexico City: *Secretaría de Desarrollo Social* (Sedesol), Series of research documents.

Marsh, R. (2003) 'How Important is Social Class Identification in Taiwan', *Sociological Quarterly*, 44(1), 37–59.

McLeod, J.D. and J.M. Nonemaker, (2000) 'Poverty and Child Emotional Behavioral Problems: Racial/ethnic differences in Processes and Effects', *Journal of Health and Social Behavior*, 41(2), 137–61.

Miech, R.A., M.J. Shanahan and G.H. Elder (1999) 'Socioeconomic Status and Depression in Life Course Perspective', Working Paper, No. 98-24. Madison, WI: Center for Demography and Ecology, Madison.

Mullis, A.K., R.L. Mullis and D. Normandin (1992) 'Cross-sectional and Longitudinal Comparisons of Adolescent Self-esteem', *Adolescence*, 27, 51–61.

Palomar, J. (2005) 'Percepción de las causas de la pobreza, factores psicológicos asociados y percepción de la movilidad social'. Mexico City: *Secretaría de Desarrollo Social* (Sedesol), Human development notebooks.

Palomar, J. and A. Pérez (2003) 'Un solo rostro y tres maneras de mirarlo: El significado de "Pobreza" según el nivel socioeconómico', *Revista Latinoamericana de Psicología*, 35(1), 27–39.

Palomar, J., N. Lanzagorta and J. Hernández (2005) 'Poverty, Psychological Resources and Subjective Well-being', *Social Indicators Research*, 73(3), 375–408.

Paz, O. (1984) El laberinto de la soledad. Mexico City: *Fondo de Cultura Económica*.

Petrosky, M.J. and J.C. Birkimer (1991) 'The Relationship Among Locus of Control, Coping Styles, and Psychological Symptom Reporting', *Journal of Clinical Psychology*, 47(3), 336–45.

Ramírez, S. (2002) *Infancia es Destino*. Mexico City: Siglo XXI.

Robinson, R. and W. Bell (1978) 'Equality, Success and Social Justice in England and the United States', *American Sociological Review*, 43, 125–43.

Rosenberg, M. and L.I. Pearlin (1978) 'Social Class and Self-esteem among Children and Adults', *American Journal of Sociology*, 84(1), 53–77.

Shek, D. (2002) 'Chinese Adolescents' Explanations of Poverty: the Perceived Causes of Poverty scale', *Adolescent*, 37(148), 789–803.

Silva, R. (2000) 'Dimensiones Psicosociales de la Pobreza, Percepción de una realidad recuperada'. Mexico City: *Universidad Nacional Autónoma de México, Escuela Nacional de Trabajo Social*.

Smith, K. (1985) 'I Made it Because of Me: Beliefs About the Causes of Wealth and Poverty', *Sociological Focus*, 5, 255–67.

Steele, S. (1994) 'On Being Black and Middle Class', in P. Kollack and V. O. Brian, J. (eds). The production of reality, Essays and readings in social psychology. Pine Forge Press, pp. 291–8.

Twenge, J.M. and W.K. Campbell, 2002 'Self-esteem and Socioeconomic Status: a Meta-analytic Review', *Personality and Social Psychology Review*, 24(4), 59–71.

Valdéz, J.L. (1994) 'El autoconcepto del mexicano. Estudios de validación. Doctoral dissertation', Mexico City: *Facultad de Psicología, Universidad Nacional Autónoma de México* (UNAM).

Weiss, S. J., P. Goebel, A. Page, P. Wilson and M. Warda (1999) 'The Impact of Cultural and Familial Context on Behavioral and Emotional Problems of Preschool Latino Children', *Child Psychiatry and Human Development*, 29(4), 287–301.

World Bank (2001) '*Voices of the Poor*. Washington, DC: World Bank.

Part II
On Poverty and Freedom

6
Choosing Dimensions: The Capability Approach and Multidimensional Poverty

Sabina Alkire[1]

There can be substantial debates on the particular functionings that should be included in the list of important achievements and the corresponding capabilities. This valuational issue is inescapable in an evaluative exercise of this kind, and one of the main merits of the approach is the need to address these judgmental questions in an explicit way, rather than hiding them in some implicit framework.[2]

6.1   Introduction

In the opening chapter of *Poverty and Inequality*, David Grusky and Ravi Kanbur observe that 'there is growing consensus among academic, policy makers, and even politicians' that attention to multidimensional poverty and inequality should not be treated as soft social issues that can be 'subordinated to more important and fundamental interests in maximizing total economic output'.[3] While the authors view this 'newfound concern with poverty and inequality' positively, they observe that it creates a set of conceptual questions that are really quite pressing. One such question is how to define the dimensions of concern. They argue that this question merits active attention because 'economists have not reached consensus on the dimensions that matter, nor even on how they might decide what matters'.[4]

The problem is not that poverty researchers refuse to select dimensions. On the contrary, in an increasing number of situations, researchers or practitioners do indeed choose dimensions. The problem is that they do not make explicit their reason for making a particular choice of dimensions. Without knowing the basis for their choice the reader is unable to probe the chosen dimensions and either trust them or question them. Was the choice one of convenience or are the researchers making a claim regarding people's values (and on what basis), or are they following a convention within the literature? As Robeyns suggests, a practice in which authors explicitly described *how and why they chose dimensions*, could itself be of tremendous value – even if it only consumed one short paragraph of a paper.[5] But what would such descriptions look like? And more importantly, what might be legitimate grounds for selecting dimensions?

The present chapter explores this conceptual issue, in the following terms: if poverty is conceived as capability deprivation, and if the task is to identify multidimensional poverty, what are the legitimate ways of defining dimensions? Put differently, by what methods should researchers decide 'what matters'. It may be worth emphasizing that the terms 'poor' and 'poverty' are used consistently across this chapter to mean capability deprivation, and never to mean only income poverty. After introducing the capability approach, the chapter situates the task of choosing dimensions of poverty within the wider task of multidimensional poverty measurement, and with respect to other kinds of poverty analyses that employ plural variables. It considers the debate regarding whether there should be one fixed 'list' of dimensions and argues in the negative. It then identifies five processes by which dimensions are *de facto* selected, and proposes when and how each could contribute to the task of selecting dimensions of multidimensional poverty. The five processes are: 1. Use existing data; 2. Make assumptions – perhaps based on a theory; 3. Draw on an existing list that was generated by consensus; 4. Use an ongoing deliberative participatory process; and 5. Propose dimensions based on empirical studies of people's values and/or behaviours. The chapter addresses the practical problem of selecting dimensions; the very real foundational considerations regarding whether to defend a consensus-based vs practical-reason-based vs theoretical approach, which are evidently important, are not treated here.[6]

6.2   Normative framework, technique, and method

In its essence, the capability approach is a normative framework for assessing alternative policies or states of affairs or options – whether in welfare economics, development, or poverty reduction. The capability approach proposes that social arrangements should be primarily evaluated according to the extent of freedom people have to promote or achieve plural functionings they value. It follows that the capability approach views poverty as a deprivation of these valuable freedoms and evaluates multidimensional poverty in the space of capabilities.[7]

As this chapter is set within a multidisciplinary book it is important to emphasize that as a conceptual framework the capability approach can engage with and draw upon a plethora of methodologies and analytical techniques. It does not *compete* with the techniques by which domains of interest may be identified, or kinds of data for multidimensional poverty comparisons. The capability approach can draw on quantitative, qualitative, participatory, and subjective data. It can examine income data – although income data alone is perhaps the crudest form of measurement.[8] Furthermore, the capability approach has been advanced by participatory methods; it has been represented by various indices and quantitative measures; it advocates empowerment, and draws attention to the critical role of social, political, legal and economic institutions in advancing capabilities over time. Within quantitative approaches, techniques that have been used to measure capabilities range from factor analysis and principal component analysis type tests, to fuzzy set theory, to multidimensional indices, to structural equation models, to dominance comparisons, to equivalent income measures and beyond.[9] The capability approach is a coherent framework that researchers can draw on in order to utilize diverse approaches to multidimensional poverty and well-being in a concerted and conceptually coherent fashion.

The capability approach can be – and, it is expected, will be – applied differently depending on the place and situation, the level of analysis, the information available, and the kind of decision involved. The methods will be plural. So if one expects the capability approach to generate one specific and universally relevant set of domains for all evaluative exercises, or to generate a specific and distinctive methodology by which to identify the domains of poverty any particular group values, one may be disappointed. This chapter will indeed discuss the processes by which to select the relevant domains for a particular evaluative exercise. But it will also argue that no single set of domains, or combining techniques, or levels of analysis will *always* be relevant and one of the important strengths of the capability approach is that researchers can employ many techniques, selecting those most relevant for each context. What the capability approach offers, fundamentally, is a framework with respect to which various research and policy questions about multidimensional poverty can be analysed, and the multiple deprivations which so many suffer can be reduced.

Turning now to the issue of selecting dimensions, the capability approach emphasizes the objective of *expanding* valuable freedoms and, conversely, of reducing capability poverty. One distinctive feature of the approach is the emphasis it places on identifying and prioritizing freedoms that people *value*. Thus when we turn to consider 'What are the methods by which domains can be identified and selected?', we can expect that a primary concern in the selection of domains are that they be things people value and have reason to value. A great deal of attention has been placed on which judgements are 'informed', on how to determine value, who determines value, and how to resolve conflicting value claims. For the purposes of this discussion, the salient point is that if the domains included in a comparison are intended to represent a community's well-being and to be used for policy purposes, then these domains should be able to be critically examined and challenged *by the people involved* on an ongoing basis, and amended if they fall short. As Sen clarifies, the process need not be one of formal democracy nor of deep deliberative participation, but some attention to people's present values seems essential.

> In the democratic context, values are given a foundation through their relation to informed judgements by the people involved... It is not so much a question of holding a referendum on the values to be used, but the need to make sure that the weights – or ranges of weights – used remain open to criticism and chastisement, and nevertheless enjoy reasonable public acceptance. Openness to critical scrutiny, combined with – explicit or tacit – public consent, is a central requirement of non-arbitrariness of valuation in a democratic society.[10]

The selection of dimensions of poverty represents only one quite narrow task in the application of the capability approach. The next two sections set the conceptual issue in its wider context both of potentially value-ridden measurement questions, and of alternative evaluative exercises.

6.3   Situating the question: multidimensional poverty measurement

Multidimensional poverty measures relate to the capability approach insofar as they provide information by virtue of which people's capability deprivations might be reduced more accurately. While this might seem quite a basic point, it is worth recalling, particularly if the conceptual tasks seem daunting. For what is needed in this context is not a quixotic search for the perfect measure, but rather domains and corresponding measures – and indeed other categories of information – that are *sufficient* to guide multidimensional poverty reduction efforts to critical objectives. Indeed, most or even all empirical outworkings of the capability approach have used drastic simplifications, and these can often be cheered and heralded as true advances, at the same time that their limitations may also be borne in mind. 'In all these exercises clarity of theory has to be combined with the practical need to make do with whatever information we can feasibly obtain for our actual empirical analyses. The Scylla of empirical overambitiousness threatens us as much as the Charybdis of misdirected theory'.[11]

Still, research underlying the empirical measurement of capability for welfare or poverty reduction exercises is strongly increasing. Figures 6.1 and 6.2 introduce the main areas of research and discussion on quantitative measures in the capability approach. As will be evident immediately, there are significant overlaps between capability-related measurement work and other approaches to multidimensional poverty.

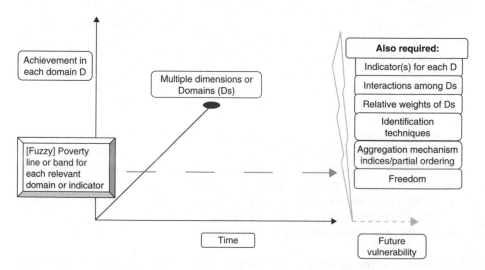

Figure 6.1   Multidimensional poverty for individual *i*: schematic overview

Figure 6.1 depicts multidimensional poverty in three-dimensional space. The vertical axis represents the achievement of individual i. The axis leading into the page, as it were, is segmented according to the 'dimensions' or domains of poverty. The dimensions or domains are discrete, hence this axis is not continuous (as Figure 6.2 clearly shows), but rather has one segment for each of the domains under consideration. For each domain there will be one or more indicators that proxy the capabilities (and these can be evaluated separately or aggregated). The horizontal axis represents time – and the dotted portion of the horizontal axis, after the vertical marker, represents the future. The 'future' section would be populated by estimations of vulnerability where vulnerability is understood to be the threat of future poverty.[12] The thick grey dotted line denotes an achievement level for a particular domain, beneath which a person or household is deemed to be poor (in the diagram this line is constant across time; the poverty line or band might also vary over time). Of course the poverty 'line' may be a fuzzy poverty band with the lower bound depicting the certainly poor and the upper bound, the certainly non-poor.[13]

Clearly, in order to populate the diagram, further specification is required. For example, one or more indicators must be selected for each domain (and indicator-specific poverty lines may then need to be set rather than domain-specific). A range of further issues require consideration in order to assess poverty across the multiple dimensions, such as:

- How to choose domains or dimensions (here I use these interchangeably).
- How to choose relevant indicators for the domains and related capabilities (these are usually output indicators).
- How to model the interaction among indicators and among dimensions and address endogeneity issues.
- How to set relative weights for each dimension (and for each indicator).
- How to identify who is 'multidimensionally' poor.
- How to aggregate across dimensions or, alternatively, to perform rankings and comparisons without prior aggregation.

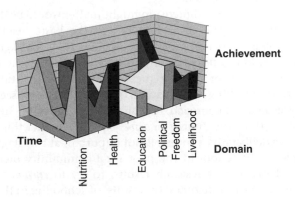

Figure 6.2   Example: achievement of individual i in five domains

- How to incorporate freedom and agency into multidimensional capability poverty measures.

This chapter will focus on only the first of these issues: how to choose focal domains or dimensions of poverty. But it is important to note that even if dimensions are chosen carefully, many other important questions remain that merit equally careful consideration. In some of these the capability approach might also be brought to bear.

6.4   Situating the question: instrument, result, and capability

On the face of it, there are distinct reasons that economists might consider certain dimensions to 'matter' and these vary a great deal depending upon the nature of the exercise. Consider three: instrumental importance for achieving *other* poverty reduction goals; anticipated outcomes of investments that are to be monitored; and direct poverty measures that represent a person's or a population's ill-being.

The first possible reason that a dimension might matter is that it has *instrumental* power. That is, the dimension is expected to contribute effectively to the reduction of one or more other dimensions of poverty and inequality. To take a slightly unlikely example, consider a poor rural community that believed that good cricket players became far more productive and socially adept members, both immediately and in the longer term, of the technological workforce which a great majority of the students attempted to join upon graduation. In this case, cricket skills might be included in a multidimensional measure of poverty. This would have nothing at all to do with the intrinsic value of cricket. Rather, information on cricket skills would be used in order to evaluate the local hypothesis on the empirical connection between cricket skills and subsequent poverty reduction. If cricket skills proved as instrumentally potent as was believed, a subsequent question might be how to foster it more widely. In a similar way, information on health and education might be collected, for example under an approach that viewed these 'dimensions' merely as instrumentally potent means to sustained economic growth and wished to probe more fully their instrumental features, but did not regard them to be of intrinsic value.

A very different reason that a dimension might matter would be if it represented an *intended outcome* of a project or activity – if the basic health clinics in a province were successful in terms of the outcomes they had agreed to create. Answering this question is important regardless of whether the intended outcomes were means or ends or simply represented what the institution was 'good at' (neonatal care, or installing lift irrigation, or introducing new seed varieties). In this monitoring/evaluation approach, the 'dimensions' are implicitly set *a priori* in the planning phase (how the dimensions are set, and whether this is based upon a more substantive deliberative process, is not important at this stage in our analysis). For example, if the school in the poor rural community mentioned above decided, on the basis of new research results, to try to *encourage* cricket skills among its pupils, then the 'outcomes' or 'results' of schooling in that community might include several dimensions such as exam results, athletic records, social activism, *and* the levels of cricket skills. Here the analysis might consider how effective the school had been in generating the intended results; it might also broaden the analysis to include certain unintended outcomes.

The above considerations are often vitally important strategic poverty-reducing interventions. It is with good reason that considerations of *instrumental effectiveness*, and the *intended outcomes* often guide the selection of dimensions. However, this chapter does not focus further on these exercises.

In other situations it is necessary to identify dimensions of poverty, of capability deprivation. Here the question is what dimensions *comprise* poverty itself? Does the inability to play cricket have this effect? While some schooling outcomes are solely useful in an instrumental sense, some outcomes directly contribute to people's well-being (as, perhaps, the ability to read whatever captures one's curiousity)? The remaining discussion focuses on this third question. The issue that emerges immediately is whether it is possible to have one list of dimensions of poverty to guide all multidimensional poverty research.

6.5   Should there be one list of capabilities or domains?

A single, 'one-size-fits-all', authoritative list of dimensions of poverty that could be shared internationally seems, on the face of it, quite an attractive proposition. It seems efficient, because researchers (whose expertise lies in other areas) would not have to pore over possible domains laboriously over and over again. It could inform the broad research agenda – such as the design of internationally comparable poverty related surveys, and so on. It may help to maintain a critical edge, as Martha Nussbaum (2000) argues in support of her list of Central Human Capabilities (see Table 6.5). Yet this chapter will argue against 'one' list despite its evident appeal (while arguing that one or more lists need to be developed precisely to guide internationally comparable survey work). As the issue of whether to have one authoritative list is the subject of a sharp and clear exchange between Martha Nussbaum (2003) and Amartya Sen (2004), we will briefly review the debate. Our focus at this point is on whether or not there should be one authoritative 'list' of core capabilities or domains of poverty. Whether this list should be the list Nussbaum proposes, or should comprise all human rights, or take a different form, is a separate question that only arises if we agree that there should be an authoritative list.

Nussbaum argues, as do others, that specification of one 'list' of domains or central capabilities is necessary to make sure that the content of the capability approach carries critical force. If the approach is too open-ended then there is a real, practical possibility that the wrong freedoms will be prioritized and expanded. She writes,

> [C]apabilities can help us to construct a normative conception of social justice, with critical potential for gender issues, only if we specify a definite set of capabilities as the most important ones to protect. Sen's 'perspective of freedom' is too vague. Some freedoms limit others; some freedoms are important, some trivial, some good, and some positively bad. Before the approach can offer a valuable normative gender perspective, we must make commitments about substance.[14]

Nussbaum repeatedly, and consistently, sets forth a set of central human capabilities that, she argues, should provide the basis of political guarantees (Table 6.6).

In response to all those who call for a more explicit set of capabilities, Sen writes, 'I have nothing against the listing of capabilities but must stand up against a grand mausoleum to one fixed and final list of capabilities'.[15]

Sen affirms that researchers need to select dimensions or capabilities (for the moment we can consider both terms because the structure of the problem is the same – although a dimension might encompass more than one capability). 'The problem is not with listing important capabilities, but with insisting on one predetermined canonical list of capabilities, chosen by theorists without any general social discussion or public reasoning'.[16]

A primary objection to having a fixed list or set of capabilities is that it sidelines ongoing public reasoning '[P]ure theory cannot "freeze" a list of capabilities for all societies for all time to come, irrespective of what the citizens come to understand and value. That would be not only a denial of the reach of democracy, but also a misunderstanding of what pure theory can do...'[17] And relatedly, 'To insist on a fixed forever list of capabilities would deny the possibility of progress in social understanding and also go against the productive role of public discussion, social agitation, and open debates'.[18]

An additional reason that a fixed list is inappropriate in practice is that the purposes (often called 'evaluative exercises') for which the lists will be used vary greatly in practice: 'What we focus on cannot be independent of what we are doing and why (e.g., whether we are evaluating poverty, specifying certain basic human rights, getting a rough and ready measure of human development, and so on)'.[19] In addition to the instrumental and evaluation analyses mentioned in the previous section, the appropriate elements (and the extensiveness of the list) will also depend in part on the social conditions as well as on the kind of public understanding of, and engagement with, the issues.

In the context of some types of social analysis – for example, in dealing with extreme poverty in developing economies, we may be able to concentrate, to a great extent on a relatively small number of centrally important functionings and the corresponding basic capabilities (for example, the freedom to be well nourished, well sheltered, and in good general health, the capability of escaping avoidable morbidity and premature mortality, the ability to move about freely, and so forth). In other contexts, the list may have to be longer and more diverse.[20]

In sum, Sen argues that key capabilities must be selected, but argues consistently against the specification of only one authoritative 'canonical' list of capabilities, that is expected to apply to all times and places.[21] The debate, which is here lightly sketched rather than analysed, might be caricaturized 'having a list' vs 'making lists for every occasion'. It might seem rather unfortunate, however, if we had to choose between these positions, to walk out one exit door or declare victory for one side or another. Sen's position leaves researchers without any systematic guidance as to *how* to choose capabilities or domains in different contexts. Not every evaluative exercise can be open to public discussion in the same way and it is not clear what criteria *besides* public scrutiny there might be. In addition, Sen's position would still seem very open to the charge that capabilities or dimensions could be specified – even with public discussion – in ways that are detrimental or even, as Frances Stewart has forcefully argued, fundamentally misguided.[22] Nussbaum's position seems, however, too limiting of public discussion and also, in practice, of limited relevance to many much narrower situations. Her list has generated criticism on grounds of its specificity, its prescriptivity, its unclear epistemological basis, and the fact that, being one author's list, it is not clear who decides – if it is to claim an overlapping consensus how is constructive disagreement with, or modification of, the list to proceed?[23] It may be that the debate has stopped prematurely, before a satisfactory alternative has been proposed.

6.6   How researchers select domains

By this time, it might seem that the problem of selecting dimensions is fiercely complex. However, in practical applications of the capability approach and related multidimensional approaches, it seems that the methods for identifying capabilities or dimensions of poverty are surprisingly straightforward. In particular, although as mentioned initially the discussion of the basis of choice is rarely explicit, it seems that most researchers draw implicitly on five selection methods, either alone or in combination. The five selection methods are:

Existing data or convention – to select dimensions (or capabilities) mostly because of convenience or a convention that is taken to be authoritative, or because these are the only data available that have the required characteristics.

Assumptions – to select dimensions based on implicit or explicit assumptions about what people do value or should value. These are commonly the informed guesses of the researcher; they may also draw on convention, social or psychological theory, philosophy, religion, and so on.

Public 'consensus' – to select dimensions that relate to a list that has achieved a degree of legitimacy due to public consensus. Examples of such lists at the international level are universal human rights, the MDGs, and the Sphere project; these will vary at the national and local levels.

Ongoing deliberative participatory processes – to select dimensions on the basis of ongoing purposive participatory exercises that periodically elicit the values and perspectives of stakeholders.

Empirical evidence regarding people's values – to select dimensions on the basis of empirical data on values, or data on consumer preferences and behaviours, or studies of which values are most conducive to mental health or social benefit.

What is very clear, immediately, is that these processes overlap and are often used in tandem. For example, rights-based approaches to development[24] might decide to make use of participatory processes to set specific priorities, and then choose indicators drawing on existing data. Psychological studies may make normative assumptions regarding human values then test these empirically. Nearly all exercises will need to consider data availability or data issues.

The following sections introduce each of the five methods briefly; Table 6.1 summarizes the analysis as to the strengths, weaknesses, and appropriate use of each of the five methods.

6.7 Existing data

One way to choose dimensions or capabilities is to draw on existing data or conventions, with or without explicit attention being given to the values that the choice of variables may or may not represent. Most or even all empirical outworkings of the capability approach eventually consider data issues, but for many, data form the *only* guiding criterion. The standard approach is to identify a problem and analytical framework, then to seek data which are both related to the problem and have the requisite characteristics to be useful in the analysis (for example, country coverage, number of data points, type of variables, etc). In many cases, only a few variables fit the criteria and researchers use these.

In some circumstances, selection according to existing data without any regard to a population's values is entirely appropriate. For example, after developing a proposed index of multidimensional poverty, Bourguignon and Chakravarty (2003) chose two dimensions from Brazilian data in order to test the index. 'Poverty includes two dimensions: income on the one hand, and educational attainment on the other'.[25] Their purpose in choosing the dimensions was to test the newly-defined index using relevant existing data in order to see whether it generated reasonable results, rather than to make any strong analyses of or prescriptions regarding poverty in Brazil. In this context (e.g. testing a technique), it was not necessary to consider the values issues. Existing data might be sufficient for a limited set of exercises – for example, descriptive historical research in which one observes the data a particular institution chose to collect.

However, we are focusing on the selection of dimensions of deprivation that people value, and in these kinds of exercises authors should combine consideration of data requirements with one or more of the other methods. The choice of dimensions for (and indicators for) the HDI was driven, in part, by the need to identify existing indicators of readily apparent importance for which cross-country comparable data were available for most countries and were relatively robust. However comparable data was not the *only* requirement (one could have compared, for example, wheat prices) – the data also had to relate to human development, and had to fit the political logic of the HDI, namely having a few readily comprehensible and arguably universally valued domains, and large country coverage. Fukuda-Parr also argued that the dimensions were chosen because they were arguably basic 'meaning their lack would foreclose many other capabilities'.[26] Those developing HDIs made quite transparent claims as to the data requirements and the logic behind these. They also made claims regarding the basic importance of each dimension: income, basic education and not dying

Table 6.1 Multidimensional poverty: domain, achievement and time

Method	Brief description	Weaknesses	When to use	Data
Existing data	Identify data that have the requisite technical features and that relate to the issue(s) of the study.	Does not raise values issues.	Only use in conjunction with another method, unless the exercise is a technical test and will not provide the basis for practical recommendations.	n/a
Normative assumptions	Make assumptions regarding what people should value based on researcher's views or drawing on social theory, religion, etc. It is deeply desirable that these assumptions should be communicated so that they become the subject of public scrutiny.	The assumptions may be inaccurate and even detrimental. May perpetuate inaccurate assumptions and inaccurate academic conventions. May be asserted ideologically rather than subjected to scrutiny and reasoned debate.	When the researcher has a clear view regarding the relevant dimensions (drawn from a theory or from their own informed experience), and is able to present them transparently such that public discussion that includes the poor could challenge or improve the view.	May be comparable across time and place; may also be modified or adjusted locally.
Public consensus	Use a set of dimensions that has generated some consensus and/or critical public discussion, as the basis for generating comparable data across time and space.	May mask conflict. May be inflexible. May not have involved poor people in the consensus.	When an instrument of consensus exists, preferably having been debated regularly, and when comparable data are required across a number of situations where the same instrument of consensus is held.	Comparable across time and place; may be modified or adjusted locally.

(Continued)

100

Table 6.1 (Continued)

Method	Brief description	Weaknesses	When to use	Data
Ongoing deliberative participation	Generate the set of dimensions directly through an ongoing, deliberative process in which participants articulate the dimensions of poverty that matter to them, and by sharing their reasons and improving their arguments, forge a set of dimensions that reflects their views.	May be hijacked by local elite If trust is low, 'values' discussions may be superficial and misleading. May be expensive and difficult to repeat. Unlikely to be feasible at a large scale. If dimensions change, data are not comparable across time.	When participation a) can be 'deep' and address value issues in a reflective manner where conflicting views are safely expressed; and b) can involve all relevant groups without being too distorted by power imbalances. It is difficult to use if there is a threat of violent conflict, or in the face of deep inequities between participants.	Unlikely to be comparable across place. May change over time.
Empirical evidence	Analyse data on people's values, beliefs, or behaviors to construct a set of dimensions that seems to represent their values.	Surveys may not include the relevant population. People cannot object if they disagree because they are treated as objects of study.	When data are available – whether on poor people's values (e.g. from past participatory poverty assessments) or other surveys – and when a third party view is necessary, for example because deep conflict precludes direct discussion.	Variable.

prematurely. These claims appealed to what they assumed to be a tacit public consensus. This transparent explanation enabled some people (those who could exercise certain democratic freedoms) to disagree with these claims or assumptions or propose improvements, or to state their support. The process of having communicated the reasoning publicly also meant that had no healthy criticism emerged (which in fact it did), the authors would have presumed tacit public consent.

In most situations, data considerations should not be the primary grounds on which to choose dimensions according to the capability approach (because splendid and robust data are not *necessarily* related to centrally valued capabilities). But eventually the feasibility of obtaining adequate data will influence the outworking of many different evaluative exercises.

6.8 Normative assumptions

In the case of the HDI, the authors assumed that people across cultures, regions, ages, genders, ethnicities, and even across individual sources of diversity, valued survival, income, and basic education. Furthermore, the authors made this assumption explicit. Making informed assumptions regarding the dimensions that matter to people is perhaps the most common method for selecting dimensions (although most researchers do not explicitly argue their case). In addition to drawing on the researchers' own informed views, normative assumptions might draw on social theory, on religious views, or on psychological views, or on conventions in the literature. For example, Ryan and Deci (2000) have suggested that people enjoy psychological well-being if they have a well-developed sense of *competence*, of *autonomy*, and of *relatedness*. In their theory these three features form the basic structure of well-being. Given this theory, Ryan and Deci might well choose dimensions that relate to their three features.[27] Maslow, as is well-known, provided a hierarchy of human needs that must be filled.[28] Similarly, many of the needs-based approaches to poverty reduction fall at least partly in this area, although they often mix this method with appeals to consensus and empirical evidence of the proposed needs (method five).

Nussbaum's list of Central Human Capabilities may be considered to fall at least partly in this category of normative assumptions. For although she argues that the list *could* be supported by overlapping consensus (and if it were then it would move into the next category), a public deliberative process has not yet engaged with this list to the same extent as it has engaged, for example, with human rights or the MDGs.

The strength of the normative or theoretical assumptions is deeply limited, from the perspective of the capability approach, *unless* the authors transparently communicate their assumptions in order to catalyse public discussion or scrutiny of these issues. If they do communicate these assumptions and encourage reflection, the list can become the subject of public debate – as occurred with the HDI. In the absence of the possibility of such public discussion, and especially if the dimensions are more than a very few or if the study addresses a local context, it can be difficult to know whether the normative or theoretical assumptions about which dimensions of poverty matter track the priorities of the poor.

6.9   Public consensus

Another approach is to use a set of dimensions that have been generated by some arguably legitimate consensus-building process at one point in time, and are relatively stable, thus not expected to be iterative or subject to ongoing participatory evaluation. There are many such lists in use – particularly within sectors or institutions. Some commonly known international and more 'holistic' lists at present in development activities are Human Rights, the Millennium Development Goals, and the Sphere project.

It would be inaccurate to claim that these lists represent an *actual* full consensus, for human rights and the MDGs in particular have been the subject of energetic criticism and ongoing debate – and the consensus explicitly involves heads of state rather than the general public. Yet in both cases a number of quite diverse groups have been able to support them, despite ongoing differences; furthermore the instruments themselves were shaped and changed in response to some criticisms. And their legitimacy in the public sphere stems at least in part from a wider claim to consensus.

Rights-based development – which has been advanced by the United Nations Development Program and national development agencies in, for example, the UK and Sweden – uses the framework of human rights and duties to guide development policy. Rights-based development draws attention not only to development outcomes, but also to development processes, insofar as it requires that no processes violate human rights. Framing development in rights terms can encourage individuals and communities to demand these rights and in some cases to engage formal legal instruments as well.

The Millennium Development Goals (MDG) are a set of eight goals, 18 targets and 49 indicators relating to poverty reduction, that have received widespread political support in different countries. Progress on the MDG indicators is being monitored annually by the international community, and in some cases is also monitored at the national level. Drawing on the information and the claim to consensus, the MDGs have influenced public priorities although their influence is highly variable across countries.

Another familiar resource in the humanitarian space is the Sphere project, which was set up in 1997 by NGOs, including the Red Cross and Red Crescent, to self-police their own activities. In emergency and disaster situations, Sphere provides guidance for those engaged in humanitarian assistance, particularly in situations in which the possibilities of beneficiary involvement are limited by time and situational factors. The Sphere *Handbook* emphasizes its basis in consensus: 'The Humanitarian Charter and Minimum Standards in Disaster Response are the product of the collective experience of many people and agencies'.[29] The project developed a set of universal minimum standards in core areas of humanitarian assistance, and a humanitarian charter and code of conduct. Thus unlike the MDGs, the Sphere approach includes processes as well as a 'list' of minimum standards. As the 2004 *Handbook* describes their approach, 'Sphere is three things: a handbook, a broad process of collaboration and an expression of commitment to quality and accountability'.[30] The consensus included the community delivering the support, not what Sen calls 'the people involved' as recipients.

One true advantage of such lists is their claim to legitimacy (although the question of who decide when there 'is' a consensus remains), and also authority because so much attention was given to their construction by persons with diverse experiences and priorities. In addition, because of their stability over time, they may provide incentives to develop a set of indicators or analyses that are comparable across communities and time and that can be periodically revised. Furthermore, their basis in a broad consensus gives rise to the anticipation that they will have some relevance to diverse contexts across time and space. This also means that they might be drawn on in emergencies as well as in national or international policy processes where time and circumstances prohibit more participatory processes. Furthermore, human rights and the MDGs are also the subject of vigorous criticism in the public space, and this criticism itself can be read by researchers and can inform their studies. Thus in some sense, researchers are able to take advantage of an ongoing public debate without having the cost of organizing participation itself. One disadvantage, of course, is that those who are most likely to engage in public debate may not be the poor population whose well-being is the concern of the study, and indeed their values may diverge significantly from the public consensus. This is important because capabilities are things people 'value and have reason to value' – and it is important to enquire whether or not the poor persons concerned value what others claim they do and agree they should. Furthermore the lists may be inflexible, and may not incorporate dissenting views.

It may be possible to combine a consensus-based set of dimensions or capabilities with some attention to processes of local specification and leadership, as the Sphere and some rights-based development approaches have done.

6.10   Ongoing deliberative participation

Another fundamental approach to the selection of dimensions is a process of ongoing deliberative participation. The processes of interest aim to draw out people's actual values and priorities using group discussions and participatory analyses – whether for the purposes of planning, assessment, policy, or interim monitoring and continuous improvement. They can be used at the local level – as in the example of the Pakistani NGO SUNGI's village development plans below – or at state or national levels, as in participatory poverty assessments or sector-specific participatory initiatives. The problems of combining conflicting views are amplified at the higher levels or scales.

Conceptually, participatory processes have a strong attraction because the value judgements are made and revised directly by the community concerned. Furthermore, the give and take of views and reasons may have constructive usefulness in improving the selected dimensions. In the case of vitally important functionings (or basic capabilities, or needs), an iterative participatory process can be used to

Box 6.1   Participatory Village Development Plans

SUNGI's social mobilization & development approach starts with the selection of an area/village for social organization under pre-determined criterion for all partner communities. These include (a) deprivation (b) remoteness of area (c) ecological degradation (d) willingness to be organized and work as partners with SUNGI and (e) ability of women to work in Women's Village Committees.

Once a village is selected the work of building a partnership with local community starts. The foundation block of this partnership consists of viable village committees at the grassroots levels. The formation of these village committees reflects unrelenting efforts of SUNGI field staff. The steps involved in creating a viable village committee include:

- Preparation of a village profile.
- Contacts with village activists.
- Group meetings with a cross-section of community members.
- Identification of primary groups.
- A joint village meeting to establish terms of partnership.
- Primary training in social organization.
- Group formation.
- Village development planning.

All these steps could take six to 12 months before a formal contract of partnership is finalized. The logic behind this partnership is to enhance the institutional capacity of communities to implement and manage their development programs through participatory approaches to serve as the primary advocates for institutional change...

[An] important feature of SUNGI's Social Mobilization approach is the facilitation of Village Development Planning process at the village level. In 1994, in an effort to develop a planning and analysis framework, which could reflect the development challenges of local communities accurately, SUNGI started using participatory analysis methods of Participatory Rural Appraisal (PRA) and Rapid Rural Appraisal (RRA). But the search for an alternative framework, which could serve as a bottom up planning tool continued until the concept of Village Development Plan was worked out. The process was initiated in 1997 [The process consists of a one- or two-day process in which the community considers the set of participatory analyses it has conducted over the past 6–12 months (with analyses by different groups – e.g. men and women – considered jointly). After reviewing the evidence, the groups select their priorities for a village development plan. If men and women meet separately then each group selects priorities independently and a compromise is negotiated if they differ]. So far SUNGI has completed 119 village development plan.[31]

identify the appropriate dimensions and, within the dimensions, the appropriate specific indicators or activities to pursue.[32] This process might include the following activities:

1. articulation of general dimensions or goals of special importance and social influenceability.[33]
2. identification of long-term valued goals and strategies for the community of interest (i.e. using participation).
3. establishment of vital priorities that seem feasible and instrumental to these goals in the short term for the community of interest.
4. implementation of a strategy such that negative freedoms are safeguarded and the goals and strategies can be influenced by public debate in an ongoing iterative manner.
5. mitigation of (especially vital) capability contraction that occurs either among the community of interest or among other groups, while meeting vital needs. This may require attention to externalities.[34]

Furthermore, in participatory processes it may be possible to deepen the level of deliberative discussion, and probe values issues more directly than in other methods. One approach to identifying relevant domains, that interfaces well with Sen's capability approach, involves a set of vague dimensions of human development. Earlier, drawing on the work of John Finnis (1980) I proposed the use of dimensions of human development to catalyze such discussions. While there need be no authoritative list of dimensions of value – nor a definitive number, or nomenclature, for the dimensions – nevertheless, some mental checklist of the categories of human purpose that many different cultures find to be central to well-being can be useful. Finnis proposes roughly seven dimensions, displayed in Box 6.2.

The use of this or other open-ended accounts of multidimensional poverty can deepen a deliberative process when it is important to have a relatively complete account of poverty and well-being. They may be of more general use also beyond the confines of poverty issues. Although some domains (such as friendship or

---

Box 6.2   Dimensions of Poverty or Human Flourishing

Life – survival, health, and reproduction.
Knowledge including understanding, education, and also aesthetic experience.
Meaningful Work and Play
Friendship and other valued kinds of human relationships
Self-Integration (inner peace)
Authentic **Self-Direction** (participation, self-determination, practical reason)
Transcendence 'peace with God, or the gods, or some nontheistic but more-than-human source of meaning and value'.

transcendence) are not usually considered relevant to poverty reduction and may not be amenable to measurement, in some cases it may be crucial to acknowledge these domains because *resistance* to poverty reduction initiatives may stem from perceptions of a trade-off between poverty reduction and such social or cultural values, or because a particular poverty reduction initiative does indeed lead to lower outcomes on some other dimensions.[35]

When it works well, ongoing deliberative participation seems to be the ideal process for selecting capabilities and dimensions. In practice, however, participatory processes may be subject to a number of distortions.[36] Power imbalances can derail the discussion so that the views of the elite dominate; in situations of low trust or conflict, it may not be possible to engage in a values discussion and many more obstacles arise. Thus it cannot be assumed that participatory processes always generate value judgements that establish and accurately reflect a group's values.[37] Furthermore, the problem of synthesizing conflicting views, which can be difficult enough at the local level, is compounded when participatory exercises held in a number of venues are combined or aggregated in some way to inform a regional or national set of priorities, so the exercises can be limited in scale. Finally, participatory processes, being dynamic, are likely to lead to different sets of dimensions at different times and for different groups, so if these form the basis for survey work the data generated will not be comparable across communities or across time, so when comparability is required a different process must also be included.

6.11   Empirical analyses

The final possibility is that the task of explicitly formulating and justifying a set of dimensions draws on expert analysis from various disciplines including quality of life literature, cross-cultural psychology, and other areas.

A number of psychologists articulate normative values that, they argue (usually but not always on the basis of empirical evidence) are required for healthy human flourishing. Surveys such as the *World Values Survey* has given rise to a significant empirical literature on cross-cultural values.[38] Furthermore, *Voices of the Poor* gathered and synthesized data regarding the views of poor people about issues related to poverty, well-being, and institutions.[39] There are also numerous surveys of consumer preferences and consumer behaviours. And a surging literature explores the causes and triggers of happiness, and while this data would have to be used quite carefully and in combination with other methods, it could be of interest.[40] The recent developments in, and insights and implications of, empirical and expert analyses of well-being and poverty, including those that draw upon survey data, may also inform the selection of capabilities, although the way that this data can complement or supplement the other approaches requires greater clarification.[41]

Empirical analyses have not often been used; however, the burgeoning studies of subjective well-being and its causes, as well as the increasing interchange between psychology and economics in behavioural economics, means that this interface may become increasingly active. The difficulty with empirical analyses based on a biological or psychological observation is that it sidelines practical reason and people's own aspirations, and studies them as objects. For this reason the empirical approach may be best used to inform participatory methods or participatory deliberations, but not as the sole basis for selecting dimensions. However, note that the *Voices of the Poor* study, in contrast, compiled poor people's considered reflections on their definitions of ill-being and well-being, and thus drew directly upon practical reason and aspirations.

6.12   Conclusion: explicit documentation of selection procedures

The preceding sections outlined the five methods that researchers use to select dimensions for multidimensional poverty analysis. It argued that considerations regarding data availability and adequacy permeate the study of multidimensional poverty, but are not sufficient to choose capabilities or domains of poverty. Empirical studies may introduce new information regarding interconnections between behaviours or situations and aspects of well-being, but alone these are insufficient to select dimensions; alternatively when they are used in combination with an approach that engages people's practical reason – such as participation or public debate – they may play a good role in informing the discussion and making it more balanced. Three additional methods were identified. The widely-used 'Assumptions' category draws on the researchers' opinions or on theoretical frameworks. Initially its relevance seems limited. However, if the researchers share their assumptions hence invite public dialogue and scrutiny of them, then the approach may be both efficient (being relatively quick) and constructive. In a similar way, while a prior consensus of a limited group of people is not necessarily authoritative for an existing group of persons in their own context, because instruments of consensus such as Human Rights and the MDGs are a magnet for public discussion, researchers may find it useful to draw on them (informed by the surrounding discussions). The fourth approach to identifying capabilities and domains of poverty, at least at a small scale, is deliberative participation. This approach appears to be very desirable, but only in those situations in which participation is not subject to distortions. Clearly in most cases researchers will use two or three methods in an iterative approach.

However the set of domains is generated – whether through participatory exercises, empirical study, or another manner (including data availability) – what is clear in every instance is that the domains should be, to some extent, open to public scrutiny and ongoing debate. To this end, Ingrid Robeyns has proposed that authors use four criteria for identifying the relevant domains and capabilities. These are:

1. *Explicit formulation*: The list [of domains and/or capabilities] should be made explicit, discussed and defended: why it is claimed to be something people value and have reason to value.

2. *Methodological justification*: The method that has generated the list should be clarified and defended (and open to critique or modification). For example, whether this domain was chosen on the basis of a participatory exercise, or through consultation of empirical studies of human values.
3. *Two-stage process: ideal-feasible*: If a set of domains aims at an empirical application or at implementable policy proposals, then the list should be drawn up in at least two stages. Each stage will generate a list at a different level, ranging from the level of ideal theory to more pragmatic lists. This means that only from the second stage onwards will constraints and limitations related to the measurement design and data collection, or to political or socioeconomic feasibility in the case of policy-oriented applications, be taken into account. Distinguishing between the ideal and the second-best level is important, because these second best constraints might change over time, for example as knowledge expands, empirical research methods become more refined, or the reality of political or economic feasibility changes.
4. *Exhaustion and non-reduction*: The capabilities on the [ideal] list should include all elements that are important: no dimensions that are relevant should be left out. For example, those capabilities related to the non-market economy should also be included in economic assessments.[42]

The advantage of such explicit documentation of selection procedures is that it enables technical artists of multidimensional poverty comparisons to articulate their methods, both for the purposes of instigating public discussion, and also in order to learn from and contribute to the academic discussion on this topic. As was mentioned at the opening of this chapter, such documentation is missing from the grand majority of papers on multidimensional poverty. Robeyns' third element – ideal vs feasible – opens space for researchers on multidimensional poverty to advocate plainly and consistently for 'more and better data' relating to valuable domains of poverty for which insufficient data exist.

This chapter has argued that we should not generate exactly one list of dimensions of poverty. For although it will be tremendously useful for some exercises (such as the ongoing improvement of international survey instruments) to generate such a list – and we should – that list will not be of use for local kitchen garden projects in Bolivia, or for health-related poverty assessments in Niger. But whereas researchers might feel quite daunted by the prospect of selecting domains transparently for their work, the options for selecting dimensions are really surprisingly few, and if the grounds of choice are clear, the project is really not that difficult. Grusky and Kanbur had observed that 'economists have not reached consensus on the dimensions that matter, nor even on how they might decide what matters'. While it may be highly unlikely that economists *will* reach consensus on these matters, this chapter has argued that it may be possible to identify a tittle more explicitly why they hold the views they do, and that this itself could be a step forward.

Table 6.2 Some domains of quality of life

Andrews & Withey 1976: concern clusters[1]	Allardt 1993: comparative Scandanavian welfare study[2]	Cummins 1996: domains of life satisfaction[3]	Anand & Sen 1994: basic features of well-being[4]	The Millennium Development Goals 2000[5]	Modules in World Bank Living Standards Measurement Survey (LSMS) questionnaires[6]
media societal standards weather government safety community house money job services recreation facilities traditions marriage children family relations treatment imagination acceptance self-adjustment virtues accomplishment friends religion health own education beneficence independence mobility beauty	*Having:* econ resources, housing, employment, working conditions, health, education *Loving:* attachments/ contacts with local community, family and kin, friends, associations, work-mates *Being* self-determination, political activities, leisure-time activities, meaningful work, opportunities to enjoy nature	Material well-being, Health, Productivity, Intimacy/friendship, Safety, Community, Emotional well-being	Longevity infant/child mortality preventable morbidity literacy nourishment personal liberty and freedom	(1) extreme hunger and poverty (2) universal primary education (3) gender equality and empower women (4) child mortality (5) maternal health (6) HIV/AIDS, malaria, and other diseases (7) environmental sustainability (8) global partnership for development	*Household:* Household Composition Food Expenditures Non-Food Expenditures Housing Durable Goods Non-farm self-employment Agro-pastoral activities Economic Activities Other income Savings and Credit Education Health Migration Fertility Anthropometrics *Community:* Demographics Economy and Infrastructure Education Health Agriculture

Notes:
1. Andrews and Withey 1976 pp. 38–39.
2. Allardt 1993 Categories used in a survey of 4,000 respondents from Scandanavia. See Article in Nussbaum and Sen 1993.
3. Cummins 1996: 303.
4. Anand and Sen 1994.
5. www.millenniumgoals.org.
6. http://www.worldbank.org/lsms/guide/lsmsbox1.html accessed 20 September 2006

Table 6.3 Participatory dimensions, human rights, and sphere project

Voices of the Poor Narayan et al. 2000[7]	*Chambers '95: dimensions of deprivation*[8]	*Max-Neef 1993: axiological categories*[9]	*Universal Declaration of Human Rights – index of articles*[10]	*Sphere project: minimum standards*[11]
Material well-being: having enough	Poverty	Subsistence	1–2 Human dignity, equality and non-discrimination	The sphere project has developed minimum standards around the following five areas:
Food	Social inferiority	Protection	3 Life, liberty and security	
Assets	Isolation	Affection	4 Slavery and slave trade	Water, sanitation & hygiene
Work	Physical weakness	Understanding	5 Torture and cruel/inhuman/degrading treatment or punishment	Food security
Bodily well-being: being and appearing well	Vulnerability	Participation		Nutrition
Health	Seasonality	Leisure	6–11 Legal rights	Food aid
Appearances	Powerlessness	Creation	12 Arbitrary interference	Shelter & settlement
Physical environment	Humiliation	Identity	13 Freedom of movement and residence	Non-food items (bedding, stoves)
Social well-being:		Freedom	14 Asylum	Health services
Being able to care for, bring up, marry and settle children			15 Nationality	
Self-respect and dignity			16 Marriage	
Peace, harmony, good relations in the family/community			17 Property	
Security:			18–19 Freedom of thought/conscience/religion/opinion/expression	
Civil peace			20 Peaceful assembly and association	
A physically safe and secure environment				
Personal physical security				
Lawfulness and access to justice				

Security in old age
Confidence in the Future
Psychological well-being:
Peace of mind
Happiness
Harmony (including a spiritual
life and religious observance)
Freedom of choice and action

21	Political rights
22	Social security and general recognition of socio-economic rights
23–24	Employment, trade union and rest
25	Adequate standard of living
26	Education
27	Cultural life
28	International order
29	Limitations (morality/public order/general welfare)

Notes:
7. Narayan 2000.
8. Chambers 1995.
9. Max-Neef 1989.
10. www.unhchr.ch/udhr accessed 20 Sept 2006.
11. www.sphereproject.org accessed 20 Sept 2006.

Table 6.4 Basic needs – practical applications

Braybrooke:[12]	Doyal & Gough 1992: intermediate needs[13]	Nielsen 1977 central elements' of human need[14]	Lane 1969 needs inform political behaviour[15]	Packard 1960 hidden needs towards which marketing theory is orientated[16]	Hamilton 2003: needs categories[17]
life-supporting relation to environment	Nutritional food/water	Love	cognitive needs – curiousity, learning, understanding	emotional security,	Vital needs
food & water	Protective housing	companionship	consistency needs – emotional, logical, veridical	self-esteem,	Adequate shelter
excretion	Work	security	social needs (affiliation, being linked)	ego gratification,	Sufficient clothing
exercise	Physical environment	protection	moral needs	recognition and status,	Required daily caloric intake
periodic rest, including sleep	Health care	a sense of community	esteem needs	creativity,	Periodic rest
whatever [else] is indispensible to preserving the body intact	Security in childhood	meaningful work	personality integration and identity needs	love,	Exercise
companionship	Significant primary relationships	adequate sustenance	agression expression needs	sense of belonging,	Social entertainment
education	Physical security	shelter	autonomy needs	a sense of power	Particular social needs
social acceptance and recognition	Economic security	sexual gratification	self-actualisation needs	a sense of immortality	Bald need-claims, i.e. the need for an efficient train service
sexual activity	Safe birth control/childbearing	amusement	need for instrumental guides to reality, object appraisal		Provision, i.e. the need for a television
freedom from harrassment	Basic education	rest			Consumption and production, i.e. the need for a car
recreation		recreation			Agency Needs
		recognition			Autonomy
		respect of person			Intersubjective recognition
					Active and creative expression

Notes:
12. Braybrooke 1987 p. 36.
13. Doyal and Gough 1991.
14. Nielsen 1977.
15. Lane 1969.
16. Packard 1960.
17. Hamilton 2003 pp. 23–4.

Table 6.5 Some philosophically defended dimensions of human value

Finnis:[18]	Griffin 1986 prudential values[19]	Galtung 1980 true worlds[20]	Davitt 1958: value areas[21]	Lasswell & Hoimberg 1969: human values[22]	Nussbaum 2000 central human capabilities[23]	Qizilbash 1996: prudential values for development[24]	Rawls' primary goods 1971[25]	Sen 1999 instrumental freedoms[26]
Life Survival Health Reproduction Knowledge Meaningful Work/opportunities, Livelihood Authentic Self-Direction/Agency Participation/Relationships Inner peace Harmony with a greater than human source of meaning and value *Environment & aesthetic*	Accomplishment components of human existence deciding for oneself/agency minimum material goods limbs & senses that work freedom from pain & anxiety liberty understanding enjoyment deep personal relations	input-output (nutrition, water, air) climate balance with nature (clothing, shelter) health community symbolic interaction and reflection (education)	Life and reproduction, Protection and security Title (property) sexual union decision-responsibility knowledge, art, communication, meaning	Skill Affection Respect Rectitude Power Enlightenment Wealth Well-being	Life Bodily health Bodily integrity Senses, thought imagination, Emotions Practical reason Affiliation Other species Play Control over one's environment	Health/nutrition/sanitation/rest/shelter/security Literacy/basic intellectual and physical capacities Self-respect and aspiration Positive freedom, autonomy or self-determination Negative freedom or liberty Enjoyment Understanding or knowledge Significant relations with others and some participation in social life Accomplishment (sort that gives life point/weight)	rights liberties opportunities income and wealth freedom of movement & choice of occupation social bases of self respect powers and prerogatives of offices and positions of responsibility	Political freedom, economic facilities, social opportunities transparency guarantees, protective security

Notes:
18. Finnis 1980.
19. Griffin 1986.
20. Galtung has listed different needs in different places. Galtung 1980.
21. Davitt 1968.
22. Lasswell and Holmberg 1969.
23. Nussbaum 2000.
24. Qizilbash 1996.
25. 'Things that every rational man is presumed to want' Rawls 1971 pp. 60–5, Rawls 1982 p. 162, Rawls 1988 pp. 256–7
26. Sen 1999 p. 10.

Table 6.6 Cross-cultural empirical studies of well-being and universal values

Rokeach-terminal values[27]	Schwartz 1994 universal human values[28]	Argyle 1991 causes of 'joy'[29]	Ryff dimensions of wellness[30]	Myers and diener: correlates of high subjective well-being[31]	Biswas-Diener and diener 12 life domains[32]
A comfortable life (a prosperous life)	Power	Social contacts with friends, or others in close relationship	Autonomy	1. Certain traits: self-esteem, personal control, optimism, extraversion	Morality
An exciting life (a stimulating, active life)	Achievement	Sexual activity	Environmental Mastery	2. Strong supportive relationships	Food
A sense of accomplishment (lasting contribution)	Hedonism	Success, achievement	Positive relations with others	3. Challenging work	Family
A world at peace (free of war and conflict)	Stimulation	Physical activity, exercise, sport	Purpose in live	4. Religious faith	Friendship
A world of beauty (beauty of nature and the arts)	Self-direction	Nature, reading, music	Personal growth		Material resources
Equality (brotherhood, = opportunity for all)	Universalism	Food and drink	Self-acceptance		Intelligence
Family security (taking care of loved ones)	Benevolence	Alcohol			Romantic relationship
Freedom (independence, free choice)	Tradition				Physical appearance
Happiness (contentedness)	Conformity				Self
Inner harmony (freedom from inner conflict)	Security				Income
Mature love (sexual and spiritual intimacy)					Housing
National security (protection from attack)					Social life
Pleasure (an enjoyable, leisurely life)					
Salvation (saved, eternal life)					
Self-respect (self-esteem)					
Social recognition (respect, admiration)					
True friendship (close companionship)					
Wisdom (a mature understanding of life)					

Notes:
27. Rokeach 1973.
28. Schwartz 1994.
29. Argyle 1991.
30. Ryff 1989 p. 1069–1081. Her work synthesizes ideas from Maslow, Jung, Rogers, Allport, Erikson, Buhler, Neurgartens and Jahoda. See Christopher 1999, who argues that it is culturally embedded.
31. Myers and Diener 1995 pp. 10–19.
32. Biswas-Diener and Diener 2001.

Notes

1. I am grateful for the comments of Cesar Calvo, Séverine Deneulin, Ian Gough, Javier Iguiñez, Nanak Kakwani, Mark McGillivray, Xavier Ramos, Ingrid Robeyns, Jacques Silber, Frances Stewart, and the participants of the Brasilia Conference in August 2005 on this paper or an earlier version of it, and to Afsan Bhadelia for research assistance; errors remain my own.
2. Sen (1999: 75).
3. Grusky, Kanbur and Sen (2006: 1) both quotes.
4. Ibid., p. 12.
5. Robeyns (2005).
6. Elsewhere I have proposed that Finnis' Aristotelian approach, which develops an objective account of human flourishing that is open to plural interpretations and is based on practical reasoning, be used to identify dimensions of human development in general, and that these be specified by deliberative participation that engages practical reasoning. Alkire (2002).
7. Additional principles or procedural considerations such as equity, efficiency, stability across time, sustainability, voice and participation, as well as additional information, for example pertaining to human rights and responsibility, might also be considered in an evaluation that fully reflects the capability approach as it has been developed within Sen's other writings on rationality and freedom. Robeyns (2000), Sen (2000: 477).
8. For example Reddy, Visaria and Asali (2006). See also section 7 of the Technical Annexe by Foster and Sen in Sen (1997).
9. See Alkire (2006), Kuklys (2005), Robeyns (2006).
10. Sen (1997: 206).
11. Sen (1985: 49).
12. Dercon (2005).
13. Chiappero-Martinetti (1994), Chiappero-Martinetti (1996), Chiappero-Martinetti (2000), Chiappero-Martinetti (2004).
14. Nussbaum (2003).
15. Sen (2004: 80).
16. Ibid., p. 77.
17. Ibid., p. 78.
18. Ibid., p. 80.
19. Ibid., p. 79.
20. Sen (1996: 57–8).
21. For a fuller account see Alkire (2002: Ch. 2 Section 1).
22. Stewart (2005). See also Robeyns (2005).
23. I have tried to elaborate these in Alkire (2002: Ch. 2).
24. The definition used by the Office of the High Commission for Human rights is: 'A rights-based approach to development is a conceptual framework for the process of human development that is normatively based on international human rights standards and operationally directed to promoting and protecting human rights'.
    'Essentially, a rights-based approach integrates the norms, standards and principles of the international human rights system into the plans, policies and processes of development'. http://193.194.138.190/development/approaches-04.html accessed 30 April 2006.
25. Bourguignon and Chakravarty (2003: 42).
26. (Fukuda-Parr, 2003 #390) at page 306
27. Chirkov, Ryan, Kim and Kaplan (2003), Ryan and Deci (2000), Ryan and Deci (2001).
28. Maslow (1943), Maslow (1948), Maslow (1959), Maslow (1963).
29. The Sphere Project (2004) p. 2.
30. Ibid., p. 5.
31. Adapted from http://www.sungi.org/ggovernance.asp accessed 10 May (2006). Bold mine.
32. This is argued in Alkire (2006) see also Alkire (2002) Ch. 5.

33. Sen (2004).
34. Alkire (2002), Alkire (2006).
35. Rao and Walton (2004).
36. Chambers (1997), Cooke and Kothari (2001), Deneulin (2006), Forester (1999).
37. The literature on participation, deliberation, and capability is large and growing. See Gutmann and Thompson (1996) and Fung and Olin Wright (2003) on deliberation and capability; Bohman (1996) on deliberation; Richardson (2006), Richardson (1994), Blackburn and Holland (1998), Chambers (1997), Cooke and Kothari (2001), Crocker (2006), Deneulin (2006), Forester (1999), Holland, Blackburn and Chambers (1998) and Richardson (1994) on democracy.
38. Biswas-Diener and Diener (2001), Inglehart (1997), Inglehart and Baker (2000), Kahneman, Diener and Schwarz (1999), Schwartz (1992).
39. Narayan-Parker (2000), Narayan (2000).
40. Alkire (2005), Alkire (2005), Argyle (1991), Clark (2005), Comim (2005), Diener (2000), Frey and Stutzer (2002), Layard (2005), McGillivray (2005), Ng (1997), Ng (2003), Oswald (1997), Ott (2005), Ryan and Deci (2001), Veenhoven (1993), Veenhoven and Data-book of (1994) *inter alia*.
41. Sen (1985: 48).
42. Robeyns (2003).

References

Alkire, S. (2002) *Valuing Freedoms: Sen's Capability Approach and Poverty Reduction*. New York, Oxford: Oxford University Press.

Alkire, S. (2005) 'Subjective Quantitative Studies of Human Agency', *Social Indicators Research*, 74(1).

Alkire, S. (2005) 'Why the Capability Approach?', *Journal of Human Development*, 6(1).

Alkire, S. (2006) 'Needs and Capabilities', in *The Philosophy of Need*, S. Reader. Cambridge: Cambridge University Press.

Allardt, E. (1993) 'Having, Loving, Being: An Alternative to the Swedish Model of Welfare Research', in M. C. Nussbaum and A. K. Sen Oxford, New York: Clarendon Press.

Anand, S. and A. K. Sen (1994) *Human Development Index: Methodology and Measurement*. New York: Human Development Report Office United Nations Development Programme.

Andrews, F. M. and S. B. Withey (1976) *Social Indicators of Well-Being Americans' Perceptions of Life Quality*. New York: Plenum Press.

Argyle, M. (1991) 'The Psychological Causes of Happiness', in *Subjective Well-Being: An Interdisciplinary Perspective*, F. Strack, M. Argyle and N. Schwarz. Oxford, New York: Pergamon Press.

Biswas-Diener, R. and E. Diener (2001) 'Making the Best of a Bad Situation: Satisfaction in the Slums of Calcutta', *Social Indicators Research*, 55(3).

Blackburn, J. and J. Holland (1998) *Who Changes? Institutionalizing Participation in Development*. London: Intermediate Technology.

Bohman, J. (1996) *Public Deliberation: Pluralism, Complexity, and Democracy*. Cambridge, MA: MIT Press.

Bourguignon, F. and S. R. Chakravarty (2003) 'The Measurement of Multidimensional Poverty', *Journal of Economic Inequality*, 1(1).

Braybrooke, D. (1987) *Meeting Needs*. Princeton, NJ: Princeton University Press.

Chambers, R. (1995) 'Poverty and Livelihoods: Whose Reality Counts?', *IDS Discussion Paper*, 347.

Chambers, R. (1997) *Whose Reality Counts?: Putting the First Last*. London: Intermediate Technology.

Chiappero-Martinetti, E. (1994) 'A New Approach to Evaluation of Well-Being and Poverty by Fuzzy Set Theory', *Giornale Degli Economisti e Annali di Economia*.

Chiappero-Martinetti, E. (1996) 'Standard of Living Evaluation Based on Sen's Approach: Some Methodological Questions', *Politeia*, 12(43/44).

Chiappero-Martinetti, E. (2000) 'A Multidimensional Assessment of Well-Being Based on Sen's Functioning Approach', *Rivista Internazionale di Scienze Sociali*, 108(2).

Chiappero-Martinetti, E. (2004) 'Complexity and Vagueness in the Capability Approach: Strengths or Weaknesses?'.

Chirkov, V., R. Ryan, Y. Kim and U. Kaplan (2003) 'Differentiating Autonomy from Individualism and Independence: A Self-Determination Theory Perspective on Internalization of Cultural Orientations and Well-Being', *Journal of Personality and Social Psychology*, 84(1).

Christopher, J. C. (1999) 'Situating Psychological Well-Being: Exploring the Cultural Roots of Its Theory and Research', *Journal of Counseling and Development*, 77(2).

Clark, D. A. (2005) 'Sen's Capability Approach and the Many Spaces of Human Well-Being', *Journal of Development Studies*, 41(8).

Comim, F. (2005) 'Capability and Happiness: Possible Synergies', *Review of Social Economy*, 63.

Cooke, B. and U. Kothari (2001) *Participation: The New Tyranny?* London, New York: Zed Books.

Crocker, D. (2006) 'Ethics of Global Development: Agency, Capability, and Deliberative Democracy – an Introduction', *Philosophy and Public Policy Quarterly*, 26(1/2).

Cummins, R. A. (1996) 'The Domains of Life Satisfaction: An Attempt to Order Chaos', *Social Indicators Research*, 38(3).

Davitt, T. E. (1968) *The Basic Values in Law: a Study of the Ethico-Legal Implications of Psychology and Anthropology*. Philadelphia: American Philosophical Society.

Deneulin, S. (2006) *The Capability Approach and the Praxis of Development*. Basingstoke: Palgrave MacMillan.

Dercon, S. (2005) 'Vulnerability: A Micro Perspective', in *ABCDE Europe Conference*, Amsterdam.

Diener, E. (2000) 'Subjective Well-Being – the Science of Happiness and a Proposal for a National Index', *American Psychologist*, 55(1).

Doyal, L. and I. Gough (1991) *A Theory of Human Need*. New York: Guilford Press.

Finnis, J. (1980) *Natural Law and Natural Rights*. Oxford, New York: Clarendon Press, Oxford University Press.

Forester, J. (1999) *The Deliberative Practitioner: Encouraging Participatory Planning Processes*. Cambridge, MA: MIT Press.

Frey, B. S. and A. Stutzer (2002) 'What Can Economists Learn from Happiness Research?', *Journal of Economic Literature*, 40(2).

Fromm, E. (1955) *The Sane Society*. New York: Rinehart.

Fung, A. and E. Olin Wright (2003) *Deepening Democracy: Institutional Innovations in Empowered Participatory Governance*. London: Verso Press.

Galtung, J. (1980) *The True Worlds: a Transnational Perspective*. New York: Free Press.

Griffin, J. (1986) *Well-Being: Its Meaning, Measurement, and Moral Importance*. Oxford Clarendon Press.

Grusky, D. B., S. M. R. Kanbur and A. K. Sen (eds) (2006) *Poverty and Inequality*. Stanford: Stanford University Press.

Gutmann, A. and D. Thompson (1996) *Democracy and Disagreement*. Cambridge: Belknap Press.

Hamilton, L. (2003) *The Political Philosophy of Needs*. West Nyack, NY: Cambridge University Press.

Holland, J., J. Blackburn and R. Chambers (1998) *Whose Voice?: Participatory Research and Policy Change*. London: Intermediate Technology.

Inglehart, R. (1997) *Modernization and Postmodernization: Cultural, Economic, and Political Change in 43 Societies*. Princeton, NJ: Princeton University Press.

Kahneman, D., E. Diener and N. Schwarz (1999) *Well-Being: The Foundations of Hedonic Psychology*. New York: Russell Sage Foundation.

Kuklys, W. (2005) *Amartya Sen's Capability Approach: Theoretical Insights and Empirical Applications.* Berlin: Springer.

Lane, R. E. (1969) *Political Thinking and Consciousness: the Private Life of the Political Mind* Chicago: Markham Pub. Co.

Lasswell, H. D. and A. R. Holmberg (1969) 'Toward a General Theory of Directed Value Accumulation and Institutional Development', in *Political and Administrative Development*, R. J. Braibanti. Durham, NC: Published for the Duke University Commonwealth-Studies Center by Duke University Press.

Layard, R. (2005) *Happiness: Lessons from a New Science.* London: Penguin.

Maslow, A. H. (1943) 'A Theory of Human Motivation', *Psychological Review*, 50.

Maslow, A. H. (1948) '"Higher" And "Lower" Needs', *Journal of Psychology*, 25.

Maslow, A. H. (1959) *New Knowledge in Human Values.* New York: Harper.

Maslow, A. H. (1963) 'Fusion of Facts and Values', *American Journal of Psychoanalysis*, 23(2).

Max-Neef, M. (1989) 'Human Scale Development: An Option for the Future', *Development Dialogue*.

McGillivray, M. (2005) 'Measuring Non-Economic Well-Being Achievement', *Review of Income and Wealth*, 51(2).

Murray, H. A. (1938) *Explorations in Personality; a Clinical and Experimental Study of Fifty Men of College Age.* New York, London etc.: Oxford University Press.

Myers, D. G. and E. Diener (1995) 'Who Is Happy?', *Psychological Science*, 6(1).

Narayan-Parker, D. (2000) *Can Anyone Hear Us? Voices of the Poor.* Washington, DC: World Bank.

Narayan, D. *et al.* (2000) *Crying out for Change: Voices of the Poor.* Washington, DC: World Bank Publications/Oxford University Press.

Ng, Y.-K. (1997) 'A Case for Happiness, Cardinalism, and Interpersonal Comparability', *Economic Journal*, 107(445).

Ng, Y.-K. (2003) 'From Preference to Happiness: Towards a More Complete Welfare Economics', *Social Choice and Welfare*, 20.

Nielsen, K. (1977) 'True Needs, Rationality and Emancipation', in *Human Needs and Politics*, R. Fitzgerald. Sydney: Pergamon Press.

Nussbaum, M. (2000) *Women and Human Development: The Capabilities Approach.* Cambridge: Cambridge University Press.

Nussbaum, M. (2003) 'Capabilities as Fundamental Entitlements: Sen and Social Justice', *Feminist Economics*, 9(2/3).

Nussbaum, M. C. and A. K. Sen (1993) *The Quality of Life.* Oxford: Clarendon Press.

Oswald, A. J. (1997) 'Happiness and Economic Performance'. *Oxford Labour Market Consequences of Technical and Structural Change Discussion Paper*, 107.

Ott, J. (2005) 'Level and Inequality of Happiness in Nations: Does Greater Happiness of a Greater Number Imply Greater Inequality in Happiness?', *Journal of Happiness Studies*.

Packard, V. O. (1960) *The Waste Makers.* New York: D. McKay Co.

Qizilbash, M. (1996) 'Ethical Development', *World Development*, 24(7).

Ramsay, M. (1992) *Human Needs and the Market.* Aldershot, Hants, England; Brookfield, Vt.: Avebury; Ashgate Pub. Co.

Rao, V. and M. Walton (2004) *Culture and Public Action.* Stanford: Stanford University Press, Stanford Social Sciences.

Rawls, J. (1971) *A Theory of Justice.* Cambridge, MA: Belknap Press of Harvard University Press.

Rawls, J. (1982) 'Social Unity and Primary Goods', in *Utilitarianism and Beyond*, A. K. Sen and B. A. O. Williams. Cambridge, New York: Cambridge University Press.

Rawls, J. (1988) 'The Priority of Right and Ideas of the Good', *Philosophy and Public Affairs*, 17(4).

Reddy, S., S. Visaria and M. Asali (2006) 'Inter-Country Comparisons of Poverty Based on a Capability Approach: An Empirical Exercise', *International Poverty Research Centre Working Paper Series*, 27.

Richardson, H. S. (1994) *Practical Reasoning About Final Ends*. Cambridge, New York: Cambridge University Press.

Richardson, H. S. (2006) *Democratic Autonomy: Public Reasoning About the Ends of Policy*. Oxford: Oxford University Press.

Robeyns, I. (2000) *An Unworkable Idea or a Promising Alternative? Sen's Capability Approach Re-Examined*. Leuren: University of Leuren.

Robeyns, I. (2003) 'Sen's Capability Approach and Gender Inequality: Selecting Relevant Capabilities', *Feminist Economics*, 9.

Robeyns, I. (2005) 'Selecting Capabilities for Quality of Life Measurement', *Social Indicators Research*, 74(1).

Robeyns, I. (2006) 'The Capability Approach in Practice', *Journal of Political Philosophy*, 17(3).

Rokeach, M. (1973) *The Nature of Human Values*. New York: Free Press.

Ryan, R. M. and E. L. Deci (2000) 'Self-Determination Theory and the Facilitation of Intrinsic Motivation, Social Development, and Well-Being', *American Psychologist*, 55(1).

Ryan, R. M. and E. L. Deci (2001) 'On Happiness and Human Potentials: A Review of Research on Hedonic and Eudaimonic Well-Being', *Annual Review of Psychology*, 52.

Ryff, C. D. (1989) 'Happiness Is Everything, or Is It? Explorations on the Meaning of Psychological Well-Being', *Journal of Personality and Social Psychology*, 57(6).

Schwartz, S. H. (1992) 'Universals in the Content and Structure of Values: Theoretical Advances and Empirical Tests in 20 Countries', *Advances in Experimental Social*, 25.

Schwartz, S. H. (1994) 'Are There Universal Aspects in the Structure and Contents of Human Values?', *Journal of Social Issues*, 50(4).

Sen, A. (1999) *Development as Freedom*. New York: Knopf.

Sen, A. K. (1985) *Commodities and Capabilities*. Amsterdam, New York: North-Holland; Elsevier Science Pub. Co, sole distributors for the USA and Canada.

Sen, A. K. (1996) 'On the Foundations of Welfare Economics: Utility, Capability and Practical Reason', in F. Farina, F. Hahn and S. Vannucci. Oxford: Clarendon Press.

Sen, A. K. (1997) *On Economic Inequality*. New York: Clarendon Oxford Press.

Sen, A. K. (2000) 'Consequential Evaluation and Practical Reason', *Journal of Philosophy*, 97(9).

Sen, A. K. (2004) 'Capabilities, Lists, and Public Reason: Continuing the Conversation', *Feminist Economics*, 10(3).

Sen, A. K. (2004) 'Elements of a Theory of Human Rights', *Philosophy and Public Affairs*, 234.

Stewart, F. (2005) 'Groups and Capabilities', *Journal of Human Development*, 6(2).

The Sphere Project (2004) *Sphere Handbook: Humanitarian Charter and Minimum Standards in Disaster Response*. Oxford: Oxfam Publishing.

Veenhoven, R. (1993) *Happiness in Nations: Subjective Appreciation of Life in 56 Nations, 1946–1992*. Rotterdam, Netherlands: Erasmus University of Rotterdam, Department of Social Sciences, RISBO, Center for Socio-Cultural Transformation.

Veenhoven, R. (1994) *Correlates of Happiness: 7838 Findings from 603 Studies in 69 Nations, 1991–1994*. Rotterdam, Netherlands: RISBO, Erasmus University Rotterdam.

Wilson, W. (1967) 'Correlates of Avowed Happiness', *Psychological Bulletin*, 67.

7
On the Concept and Measurement of Empowerment

Ruth Alsop

Empowering individuals and groups enhances their contribution to, and enables them to benefit from, poverty reduction. This chapter, which treats empowerment as 'enhancing an individual's or group's capacity to make purposive choice and transform that choice into desired outcomes', presents an analytic framework rooted in the concepts of asset-based agency and institution-based opportunity structure. After describing the framework and its component parts, the chapter references five country cases where the framework has been used to examine empowerment in a range of cultural and development settings.

7.1   Why is empowerment important?

Empowerment has both intrinsic and instrumental value. As Stern, Dethier and Rogers suggest, empowerment is both a goal and a driver of development.[1] Arguments for the intrinsic value of empowerment are found in the philosophical underpinnings of literature on democratization and decentralization,[2] non-monetary aspects of poverty reduction,[3] and human rights approaches to development.[4] Evidence suggests that empowerment also associates positively with achievements in other development outcomes, including growth and poverty alleviation.[5]

The conceptualization of empowerment as 'effective choice' complements utilitarian approaches to the measurement of poverty. Commonly, economic theory holds that economic actors make rational utility-maximizing decisions. Nuancing this approach, a power-based analysis holds that institutions are rarely neutral in their construction and impact, but tend to emerge to support the dominant ideology in any given context. These 'rules of the game' are devised by those with the greatest bargaining strength and often 'in the interests of private well-being rather than social well-being'.[6] In the absence of enforceable contracts and perfect information, power can be used by those with control over resources, information and decision-making power to compel people to do what they would not choose to do, sometimes through coercion or violence but often more subtly through the creation of consensus about, what to others outside of a particular context appear to be unfair, 'rules'.

The analytical framework introduced in this chapter provides both a theory of change to explain the instrumental value of empowerment and an operational tool with which to design and analyse empowering interventions. The framework goes beyond income-based and utilitarian approaches to poverty. Empowerment is based on tackling the differences in capabilities that deny actors the ability to make transforming choices.

7.2   Unpacking empowerment

Since Hobbes' discussion of the social contract and state–citizen relations, many other social and political scientists have explored power as a concept involving relations between individuals or groups.[7] If a person or group is empowered, they possess the capacity to make *effective* choices; that is, to translate their choices into desired actions and outcomes. As illustrated in Figure 7.1, this capacity is primarily influenced by two sets of interrelated factors: agency and opportunity structure.

Agency is defined as an actor's ability to make meaningful choices – that is, the actor is able to envisage and purposively choose options. Opportunity structure is defined as those institutional aspects of the context that determine their ability to transform agency into effective action. Working together, these factors give rise to different degrees of empowerment.

7.2.1   Agency

How can agency be captured or invested in? For the purposes of most analysis, a person's or group's agency can be largely predicted by their *asset endowment*. Assets are the resources that enable actors to be productive and to protect themselves from shocks. For the purposes of measurement (for monitoring or analysis) or consideration in operational work include psychological, informational, organizational, material, social, financial and human assets.

Some assets are easier to measure than others. For example, designing an intervention to enhance, or undertaking a survey to gather information on, human assets (such as skills or literacy) is less problematic than undertaking the same exercise for social assets (such as social capital) or – even more difficult – psychological assets (such as the capacity to envision).[8] Yet, all are critical in this treatment of empowerment which understands power to result from a combination of 'resources' and 'rules'.[9]

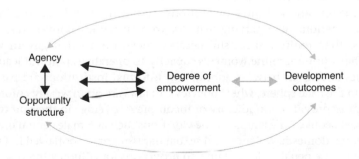

Figure 7.1   Correlates of empowerment

The complex interaction among assets also presents analytical challenges. The endowment of a single asset, such as ownership of land or capacity to aspire, can directly affect a person's or group's ability to make meaningful choices. However, command over one asset can also affect the endowment of another asset. For example, education (a human asset) often gives an actor greater access to information (itself an asset) and at times improves his/her capacity to envision alternative options (a psychological asset).[10] Similarly, for groups of people, collective savings (a financial asset) can give access to enhanced productive assets. In these cases, more than one asset contributes to the capacity to make meaningful choices. This has implications for data collection and analysis, as information is required on the range, quantity and value of asset endowments, and analysis can test for the effects of one asset on another as well as for their association with outcomes.

7.2.2　Opportunity structure

Utilitarian, preference-based approaches to analysis of choice assume that choice is a straightforward process. However, choice is often constrained by rules governing behaviour. These can be either formal or informal. Formal institutions touch the lives of most people – whether it is a country's legal framework, tax regulations or more local governance rules, such as what constitutes a quorum in a local committee or how pasture land is managed. Non-formalized social rules are also important and may be rooted in deeply entrenched cultural institutions. These are sometimes so habitual as to be 'naturalized'.[11] Women, for example, are often locked into a cultural framework which means they perceive their disempowerment to be right and proper. Those of us not living in Ethiopia, for instance, would find it hard to comprehend women's belief 'that a husband is justified in beating his wife for at least one of the following reasons', burning food (65 per cent of Ethiopian women agree), arguing with him (61 per cent), going out without telling him (56 per cent), or refusing sexual relations (51 per cent).[12] The effective use of assets is therefore often contingent upon the *formal and informal institutions* that shape an individual's and group's opportunity structure. These institutions include laws, regulatory frameworks and norms governing people's behaviour.

With both formal and informal institutions, it is not just the presence of rules which measurement efforts need to track; it is also the effectiveness and factors affecting the operation of these institutions. To illustrate, in India, the 1992 constitutional amendments reserving seats for women representatives was, in many places, less than entirely successful because social norms that govern women's public behaviour undermine women's capacity to operate as political leaders.[13]

Examples of tension between formal and informal institutions are particularly apparent in the legal sphere, where policies and laws are often weakly enforced, and in many cases provide contradictory or incomplete coverage in their protection of marginalized people. For example, while violations such as female genital mutilation, wife battering, domestic violence, and sexual harassment are outlawed in Ethiopia's Constitution, the penal code contains no provisions for adjudicating cases of such abuse, and existing laws are often applied by judges in a manner reflecting social norms rather than women's rights.[14] It is clear that the creation and presence of formal institutions does not always mean they operate effectively.

7.2.3   Interaction between structure and agency: degrees of empowerment

Empowerment requires addressing the differences in capabilities that deny actors the capacity to make transforming choices. This concept has similarities with Sen's notion of expanding human capabilities, or freedoms, by focusing on an individual's ability to 'enhance the substantive choices they have'.[15]

Prerequisite to empowerment is an opportunity structure that allows people to translate their asset base into effective agency – through raised consciousness and better information and also through more equitable rules and expanded entitlements. For example, an individual's human assets are improved through completion of secondary education, while at the same time new opportunities for citizen participation in budget allocations are opened up by the institutionalization of local-level budget planning processes. Using the new skills, confidence, and knowledge gained through formal education, and taking advantage of the opportunities opened up in the planning process, that individual is empowered to effectively participate in local-level decision making.

Measurement of or investments in assets and institutions provide *indirect* indicators of empowerment. *Direct* indicators of empowerment (effective choice) are extremely difficult to find in any national sample survey or poverty monitoring system. They are more common within project monitoring systems, but while attempts have been made to track empowerment outcomes, the indicators used are often rather limited. Prioritizing indicators used by these systems and embedding them within the discourse on power suggests that three direct measures are important for measuring or tracking empowerment. These are:

- whether an opportunity to make a choice exists (*existence of choice*).
- whether a person or group actually uses the opportunity to choose (*use of choice*).
- whether the choice results in desired outcomes (*achievement of choice*).

To illustrate, if a policy or project design team is trying to assess the degree of political empowerment among women, it would need to gather information on: (i) whether opportunities for political participation exist, such as whether elections are held; and, if so, (ii) whether women attempt to vote; and (iii) whether they actually vote. If the same team were using the information to design an intervention to politically empower women they would then need to ensure that the structures and processes of the intervention were such that these three ends were achieved, and monitored.

For several reasons – including the geographical, social, or economic positioning of a person or group – there may be no opportunity to make a desired choice. Take the case of a rural woman in the hills of Nepal who wants to send her daughter to primary school. If there is no actual school within walkable distance, she has no option. It may not matter that the formal opportunity structure – in this case a policy proclaiming education for all – exists, if the asset of a local school is not present, the opportunity for that woman to make a choice does not exist.

The use of choice involves measuring whether or not a person or group takes advantage of an opportunity to choose. To take the example above, if a school exists, does the Nepalese woman choose to send her daughter there? She may or she may not. If she does not, analysis of why would involve documenting the interplay between her assets and her opportunity structure. She may choose not to send her daughter to school because she cannot afford shoes to walk to school or to cover the bribe levied by the teacher – that is, her financial assets are insufficient. She may also not use the opportunity because her mother in law, with whom she lives, strongly feels that girls need no education and that the child is of more use herding the goats. Here there is interplay between informal institutions and economic assets. Or the fact that the woman does not send her daughter to school may simply be because her husband will beat her if she does – another informal rule coming into play. As these examples show, the framework of agency and opportunity structure helps in understanding why and what issues need addressing in operational work and what factors need tracking in monitoring systems. There is one further dimension of the capacity to use choice that needs to be considered. This is whether the use of choice is direct or indirect. The example of the Nepalese women was a direct use of choice. However, in many situations people may choose to indirectly use choice – for example, by accepting the legitimacy of an elected representative to engage on their behalf. This could occur in a local-level budgeting or planning exercise where the costs of direct use of choice are too high for individual citizens to bear.

The achievement of choice is a measure of how far a person or group is able to achieve their desired outcome. If the woman in Nepal has the option to send her daughter to school, and if she makes that choice, does her daughter actually attend school? Again, if she does not, the analytical framework suggests assessing whether there is something in the opportunity structure, such as that this is a low-caste girl and only Brahmins and Chettris (high-caste) children are allowed to attend the school and the girl was sent home on her first day. The lack of effectiveness of choice could also relate to the assets possessed by the girl or her family. She may not have the requisite skills to attend a class or she may not continue attending as the school may require a child to wear a uniform or shoes and the family cannot afford to buy them for her.

While these degrees of empowerment capture a person or a group's capacity to make effective choice, it is too simplistic to treat these three degrees of empowerment automatically as a continuum, with the final degree – the effective use of choice – considered as the most desirable degree of empowerment. The subject matter of choice has to be considered in relation to each degree. If, for example, in a well-functioning democracy an actor chooses not to go to a local council meeting because his/her/their elected representative is considered effective, this cannot be considered as a lesser degree of empowerment than if the person or group participated in the meeting. The person or group has chosen an indirect route of participation – one that many citizens in established democracies use. In this case, the operations of the formal institutions that influence an actor's choice to use an opportunity (the second degree of empowerment) are effective to the point that they result in indirect use of opportunity. Each degree, and the two key groups of factors associated with that degree, has therefore to be considered on their own merit.

7.2.4   Where empowerment takes place – domains and levels

The use of agency and opportunity structure to frame the analysis of empowerment is helpful, but prompts two further questions. First, does a person's or group's capacity to make effective choices vary according to *what* he/she/it is doing? Secondly, does empowerment vary according to the *level* at which a person or group is acting? The answer to both is yes. To illustrate, an Indian woman experiences a different form of empowerment when she is trying to exercise choice over domestic resources within the household from that which she experiences when in a bank trying to access a loan. Her experiences will also differ according to whether she is trying to operate in her village, at a market or office located at a distance from her village, or in a capital city.[16]

These added complexities in the measurement of empowerment are dealt with by conceptualizing three different *domains* and three different *levels* of actors' lives. This conceptualization is important to an analytical framework that seeks to span the multiple political, social, and economic conditions found in different countries. As the following discussion illustrates, this additional piece of the framework is viable in different contexts and, if required, can allow for cross-country comparisons of actual or changing relative degrees of empowerment for different people.

Domains

The three domains are:

>   *State*, in which a person or group is a civic actor;
>   *Market*, in which a person or group is an economic actor; and
>   *Society*, in which a person or group is a social actor.

These domains are further separated into eight sub-domains:

>   State is divided into the sub-domains of *justice, politics*, and *public services delivery;*
>   Market is divided into the sub-domains of *credit, labour*, and *private services;* and
>   Society is divided into the sub-domains of *family* and *community*.

In each of these sub-domains, the individual or collective actor experiences a certain degree of empowerment. This is likely to vary between people or groups and will vary according to whether an actor is in the position of a provider (supply side) or client (demand side). As Box 7.1 shows, this may vary between people or groups.

Box 7.1   Empowerment in Different Domains of Life

In the *state domain*, for example, citizens and their organizations may experience very different degrees of empowerment in terms of accessing justice, participating in politics, or accessing social services. In India, a well-educated, high-caste man with good social connections would experience a higher degree of empowerment in all state three sub-domains than his low-caste, illiterate counterpart.

In a perfect or 'complete' *market domain*, everyone plays by a set of equitable and transparent rules with highly efficient outcomes for the parties entering a transaction (Rajan, 2004). However, differences in control over resources and information, a lack of contract enforcement, or the ability to distort or control market prices through monopolistic practices, can result in highly inefficient and unequal outcomes. Hence a purchaser may enjoy a marketing monopoly or control price information, thus forcing producers to accept below-market prices.

In the *social domain*, social norms will combine with local implementation of formal institutions to affect the choices available to individuals and social groups. A son in an Indian household, for example, is likely to experience a higher degree of empowerment than a daughter, yet, in her community, a high-caste daughter would experience a higher degree of empowerment than the daughter of a low-caste family.

Source: Alsop, Bertelsen and Holland, 2006.

Levels

Within each domain and sub-domain, people operate and experience empowerment at different levels (administrative/political/geographical boundaries).

The *local level* comprises the immediate vicinity of a person's life. This is likely to be the level of an area contiguous with his (her) residence.

The *intermediary level* comprises a vicinity which is familiar but which is not encroached upon on an everyday basis. This is likely to be the area between the residential level and national level.

The *macro level* comprises a vicinity which is the furthest away from the individual. This is likely to be the national level.

For example, in Ethiopia, the macro level could correspond to the federal, the intermediary to the *woreda* and the micro to the *kebele*, or village. In India, the macro level might correspond to the state, the intermediary to the district and the local to the village.

7.2.5   The framework summarized

In summary, empowerment is experienced in different domains of a person's life (the state, the market, society) and at different levels (macro, intermediary and local). Each domain can be divided into sub-domains. At the intersection of domains and levels, people can experience different degrees of empowerment, addressing the issues of whether and to what extent a person or group is empowered. The degree of empowerment is contingent upon two clusters of interdependent factors – the agency and opportunity structure within which the actor operates. Thus, analysis of agency and opportunity structure helps explain why an actor is empowered to one degree or another. Table 7.1 summarizes the empowerment framework.

7.3   Using the framework for analysis and monitoring

The framework provides an analytical structure that can be used to: (1) focus empowerment practice by, for example, identifying determinants of empowerment that an intervention needs to focus upon, (2) structure efforts to monitor change and evaluate the impact of a specific project that has empowerment as one of its goals, (3) provide an analytic structure for in-depth research, (4) frame indicators for monitoring progress and changes in empowerment at a national level, and (5) frame indicators for tracking relative changes in empowerment among different countries.

Table 7.1   Summary of analytical framework

Domain		**Determinants and outcomes level**								
Sub-domain		*Macro*			*Intermediary*			*Local*		
		Agency (A)[1]	*Opportunity Structure (OS)*[2]	*Degree of Empowerment (DOE)*[3]	*A*	*OS*	*DOE*	*A*	*OS*	*DOE*
State	Justice Politics Public Service Delivery									
Market	Labour Goods Private Services									
Society	Intra Family Intra Community									

Notes:
1. Agency: measured through endowment of psychological, informational, organizational, material, financial, and human assets.
2. Opportunity Structure: measured through presence and operation of informal and formal rules.
3. Degree of Empowerment: measured through presence of choice, use of choice (direct or indirect), effectiveness of choice.

The objective and context of each intervention determines which aspects of the framework to use and how to collect and analyse data. The remainder of this chapter focuses on analysis and monitoring, using examples of five country cases where efforts were made to measure and analyze empowerment.[17]

7.3.1 The value added of an empowerment approach to poverty analysis

In the context of poverty analysis and monitoring, an empowerment perspective means that poverty is approached not only as a question of how much income a person generates or how much they consume or spend, but also as the absence of any opportunity to choose to act and move towards another standard of living or state of well-being. Treating poverty as a matter of deprivation in the exercise of choice assists on understanding of *why* some people are more likely than others to be impoverished. It moves analysis from the technical, involving the measurement of income, consumption or expenditure, to the relational, involving the measurement of the relative capability of people. This complements more conventional analyses of poverty based on income and consumption measures. It extends poverty analysis to an assessment of a person's relative capacity to achieve a desired outcome given their asset base and institutional environment.

7.3.2 Indicators and measurement[18]

Poverty reduction traditionally focuses on providing resources and services to address needs and increase material well-being. As suggested above, a focus on empowerment brings an additional emphasis on people's choices and opportunities and with it the need to analyse and track changes in these. Although empowerment is now seen as a legitimate developmental goal in its own right – and there is a growing body of anecdotal and case study evidence suggesting that empowerment also brings improved poverty reduction and other development outcomes – robust analysis of the association between (i) investments in empowerment and empowerment outcomes, and (ii) empowerment and development outcomes, is far from widespread.[19] This is not surprising given the challenges involved. Unlike more traditional measures of material poverty, an empowerment approach has to capture dynamic processes and relational changes that are less predictable, less tangible, more contextual and more difficult to quantify in data collection and analysis.[20] Furthermore, while poverty measurement is applied to individuals, or households as aggregate units, the process of empowerment can also require the collective expression of choice.[21]

Types of indicators and sources of data

This chapter distinguishes between *indirect* and *direct* measures of empowerment. Empowerment can be measured *indirectly* either by measuring asset endowments or by measuring opportunity structure. With respect to asset endowment, existing Living Standards Measurement Survey (LSMS) or Household Income and Consumption-type survey instruments generate plenty of data on asset ownership, including measures of human capital, social capital and access to productive assets. Table 7.2 provides examples of indicators of asset endowment.

Table 7.2   Indirect indicators of empowerment: asset endowment[22]

Asset endowment	Indicator (sex disaggregated)	Existing sources/instruments
Psychological assets	Capacity to envisage change	IQMSC (Integrated Questionnaire for the Measurement of Social Capital)
Informational assets	Frequency of radio listening	IQMSC
Organizational assets	Membership of organizations	IQMSC
Material assets	Land ownership	LSMS economic activities module
Financial assets	Household expenditure level	Household Budget Survey
Human assets	Literacy level	LSMS education module

Notes: IQMSC – Integrated Questionnaire for the Measurement of Social Capital; LSMS – Living Standards Measurement Survey.

With respect to opportunity structure, it is important to recognize in choosing indicators the gulf that often exists between the *presence* and *operation* of such institutions. In Ethiopia, for example, the opportunity structure for women's empowerment has been addressed through a government commitment to gender equality through the National Policy on Women (1993) and by the removal of discriminatory laws in the new Constitution (1995). Yet these institutions are poorly enforced, with no provision in the penal code for adjudicating them and a tendency amongst judges to pronounce in ways that do not take account of women's rights. International agencies such as Freedom House have identified indicators and developed indexes that track progress in the operation of institutions, particularly in the state domain. These and other national indicators can measure the operation of institutions to ensure and protect economic, political and social freedoms. Table 7.3 presents some examples of indicators for measuring the operation of empowering institutions.

In addition to recognizing the contributions of existing instruments, beginning with a review of existing data or potential future surveys reduces possibilities of duplication – where surveys are already undertaken in countries – and enhances opportunities to easily integrate parts of a 'base' empowerment modules into other national-level survey activities.

In terms of opportunity structure, the measurement of institutions is complicated by the gap between the presence of rules and the politicized, socially constructed reality of the enactment of those rules. The measurement of institutions therefore requires a mixed-methods approach that includes national-level tracking of legislation, regulations, and procedures and, ideally, local in-depth probing of the operation of informal institutions, or at least the specification of well-informed assumptions about the operation of informal institutions.

However, beyond aggregate measures of concepts such as rule of law, accountability and corruption, direct indicators empowerment are at an early stage of development,[23] although some themes, such as women's empowerment, have been subjected to more frequent attempts to measure change.[24] In general, however, data on degrees of empowerment are not currently available through any other survey instruments and therefore need to be collected as primary information.

Table 7.3   Indirect indicators of empowerment: opportunity structure

Domain	Indicator	Existing sources/ instruments
State (justice)	Index of civil liberties	Freedom House
State (political)	Index of political rights	Freedom House
State (public service delivery)	% budget allocation in line with PRSP (Poverty Reduction Strategy Paper)	PRSP policy matrix World Bank
	% population unable to access at least one basic service in the previous year due to (i) cost, (ii) physical distance, (iii) social distance	Country Policy and Institutional Assessment
Market (labour)	% employers complying with state regulations on core labor standards	N/A
Market (goods)	Distribution of productive asset ownership by income quintile	LSMS-type survey
Market (private services)	% women/ethnic/religious minorities accessing specified financial services in previous year	N/A
	No. of formal transparency and accountability mechanisms for financial service providers	N/A
Society (family)	No. of formal justice cases filed against violators of women's rights legislation (domestic abuse) per year	WB Country Policy and Institutional Assessment
Society (community)	Exclusion from community associational life based on social identity	N/A

Considerations of cost and time thus become important in survey design. Some recent innovative studies have combined short in-depth and interactive modules in large-scale surveys. Others have administered semi-structured interviews using participative techniques on a sub-sample of large scale household surveys. Both approaches are worthy of further use.

Diversity in measurement needs[25]

The application of the approach suggested in this chapter is not difficult, but does require context-specific application. The focus of any effort to measure and explain empowerment will determine which indicators are chosen and where they are clustered. For example, of the five cases refered to in this chapter, the Honduras case study examined whether the devolution of authority over schooling matters to community education councils led to the empowerment of parents in relation to school staff and to school staff in relation to the Ministry of Education. Indicators clustered in the service delivery and community sub-domain, at the local level. In Ethiopia, however, where the effects of a women's empowerment project provided the context for enquiry, indicators clustered at the local level in the sub-domains of household, community, legal services and goods.

Each of the five country case studies used the idea of 'power to' as their analytical reference point, as opposed to treating empowerment as a zero-sum game in which one person or group gains power at the expense of another person or group, that is has 'power over'. The country studies also recognized an iterative relationship

Table 7. 4 Case study analytic focus

Case country	Emphasis in analysis of empowerment	Level of measurement	Actors
Brazil	Changes in financial assets of municipalities (measure of agency) and formal institutions (measure of opportunity structure) for civil society participation and exercise of choice (measure of empowerment)	Groups at municipal (intermediary) level	General citizen organizations, elected representatives and government staff
Ethiopia	Association between legal, political and intra-household status of women, and range of assets	Individuals and groups at village (local) level	Women
Honduras	Citizens' participation in school management (degree of empowerment) associated with changes in assets (budgets, skills) and opportunity structures (formal decentralization of school management)	School management groups at village (local) level	General citizens, some focus on women, indigenous and poorest population
Indonesia	Change in capacity of the groups of villagers to manage conflict (degree of empowerment) – measure of the empowerment effect of new formal institutions on traditional informal institutions (opportunity structure)	Interest groups at village (local) level	General
Nepal	Empowerment impact of new formal rules (opportunity structure) imposed by an intervention on previously excluded (because of traditional social rules) people in terms of delivery of development benefits (development outcomes) and changes in effect of informal institutions	Caste and gender groups at village (local) level	Caste/ethnic groups, women

between individual or group agency and structure of opportunity, but differed in their analytical emphasis according to the project or initiative context (see Table 7.4). Those initiatives with delivery/accountability dimensions, particularly Brazil and Honduras, brought a stronger analytical focus to institutional change and transformed development outcomes through citizen participation. These projects were designed to emphasize the use of formal local institutions for empowerment and the creation of assets to support the operation of those institutions. The projects in Ethiopia and Nepal gave greater weight to agency-building through increasing investment in or access to a range of assets. The Indonesia case study prioritized the iteration of structure and agency by identifying 'deliberative spaces' created by a community-driven development project.

Because of the context-specific and relational nature of empowerment the depth of substantive coverage of data collection or analysis cannot be prescribed in the abstract. Neither can directions of causality be universally hypothesized. Specifying association and direction has to be at the discretion of those undertaking the measurement. This is deliberate. In developing this approach to measuring empowerment, fundamental elements of empowerment that could be measured and used within and across a range of countries and situations were identified. While the framework focuses on generic domains, levels, and degrees of empowerment, the indicators, variables, and their values are likely to be country- and context-specific.

In the five countries in which the framework was applied, each country team identified the domains and levels of analysis relevant to their interests, as well as the indicators to use for measurement and the values placed on variables. Some analysts may be uncomfortable with this flexibility, but mixed-methodology studies that include efforts to analyse prior information on the context are both a common feature of many research and monitoring efforts and have proved sufficient for analysts to hypothesize likely associations and causal relations for testing. The approach in this chapter provides users with an 'analytical lens' which sets out areas of enquiry and then allows adaptation to the specifics of a situation. In addition, in the common situation of scarcity of research or monitoring resources the framework assists in prioritization of focal areas.

7.3.3   Examples of application

The final part of this chapter outlines how each of the country studies approached the task of measuring and tracking empowerment, and provides examples of specific indicators used in each.

Measuring the collective empowerment effects of Participatory Budgeting in Brazil

The Brazil study measured empowerment within the state domain and, within that, the sub-domains of politics and service delivery. Also included were a small number of indicators in the social domain and, more specifically, the sub-domain of community. Since the locus of the analysis was municipal budgeting, analysis was concentrated at the intermediary level. Analysis of empowerment involved assessment of changes and the effects of changes in both the opportunity structure – as a result of the introduction of Participatory Budgeting (PB) institutions, and agency – by comparing the evolution of civil society organization's capacity for autonomous action in municipalities with and without PB.

The study addressed the effect of changes in opportunity structures by assessing trends in citizen engagement in municipal budgeting. Opportunity structure was measured on a continuum from clientelistic politics with no participation at one end and associational politics with binding forms of participation at the other. A municipality's position was determined through the analysis of four sets of indicators related to: (i) *the mode of engagement* – whether direct, delegated, mixed or none; (ii) *formalization of the process* – whether formal, informal or none, and the existence of rules and procedures governing the participatory inputs; (iii) *decision-making power* – whether they are of a consultative or binding nature or non-existent; (iv) *the scope of discussion*, capturing a range of governance functions the participatory processes had influenced – none, making general demands, budgets, policies or mixed.

Key variables to measure agency included: (i) civil society's access to information, which was seen as vital for active participation; and (ii) social and human capital factors within civil society. Changes in agency centred around two axes: (i) *mode of intermediation*, that is, the level of associationalism, the level of clientelism and the level of exclusion of civil society organizations; and (ii) *the degree of self-organization*, that is, the extent to which the organizations were dependent on other entities or individuals politically or economically or whether they were autonomous in terms of management as well as ideology.

Measuring women's empowerment in Ethiopia

The Ethiopia study gathered data on women's assets, their opportunity structure and degrees of empowerment in all three domains – the state, the market and society. Asset and degree of empowerment indicators mainly corresponded to the local and intermediary level. These included human, social, material and psychological assets. Opportunity structure indicators also encompassed the macro level and considered both the formal rules of the game, such as the existence of laws ensuring women's equal treatment within the justice and political systems, and the informal rules, such as those operating through the widespread traditional court system or influencing women's behaviour.

To illustrate, in the state domain/political sub-domain, the degree of empowerment indicators included the ratio of women to men represented in village and district councils as well as the question of how women were treated within the national judicial system and by traditional courts. Assets associated with an increase in women's representation and influence in district councils and their treatment in the judicial system included previous participation in associations (organizational assets) or numbers of people they could call on for help (social assets), as well as levels of education (human asset), self-confidence (psychological asset) and the extent of their awareness of their rights (informational asset). Opportunity structure indicators referenced formal rules of the game such as the existence of laws that ensured women equal treatment within the judicial system and granted them representation in community groups and councils. With regard to informal rules, indicators gauged the extent to which traditional gender norms operated, making women less likely to obtain justice than men, and/or less able to engage in political matters/public life.

In the market domain/labour sub-domain, one of the degrees of empowerment indicators was the extent to which women are able to choose their type of employment. Asset indicators captured women's education and income levels, their possession of job-specific skills, and the extent to which they had access to different sources of information. Opportunity structure indicators captured the extent to which cultural restrictions determined the nature of professions women were allowed to pursue, the amount of time women had to dedicate to household chores, and gendered rules governing access to productive assets and markets.

A project's monitoring system had established a series of empowerment indicators for the society domain/family sub-domain, such as the percentage of women who had decision-making power equal to that of their husbands over the number and spacing of children, the use of contraceptives, and conjugal relations. The interactive enquiry led the study team to hypothesize that the extent to which women had a say in these matters was associated with such assets as women's education, income, and self-confidence levels, their awareness of reproductive health issues, and their participation in women's groups. Analysis also tested for associations among opportunity structure indicators, such as customs that influence whether or not women were allowed to disagree with their husbands, and whether or not women were expected to play a subservient role regarding sexual conduct.

Measuring organizational and group empowerment in Honduras

This study addressed several aspects of empowerment resulting from educational decentralization. It assessed whether school councils were able to carry out devolved tasks and if different household and community members were able to participate meaningfully in school councils. The study focused its indicators on measuring empowerment within the state and societal domains. In the state domain, indicators focused on the sub-domain of service delivery. In the societal domain, indicators fell within the household and the community sub-domains.

Examples of assets associated positively with councils carrying out assigned functions included the amount of relevant information and training received by the councils. The opportunity structure for school council empowerment considered both formal rules, such as the regulations of the decentralization reform and the nature of the powers to be devolved to the school councils, and a range of informal rules that shaped the implementation of the reforms. The latter were found to mediate the ministry's provision of adequate information and training to communities as well as the regularity and timeliness of financial transfers that enabled councils to buy school supplies and pay teachers.

The degrees of a parent's empowerment indicators related to involvement in school council activities. Examples of assets included parents' prior engagement in or experience with other community organizations, as well their awareness of the right to participate in the council. The opportunity structure, in this case, referenced the formal or informal rules that determined whether certain groups could participate in public meetings and decision-making.

Measuring empowerment for conflict resolution in Indonesia

This study generated over 70 'conflict pathways' case studies. These sought to track and explain how social tensions and incidents of conflict played out with and without an external intervention (the Kekamatan Development Project). They looked at how different actors reacted to conflicts – either negotiating, failing to engage or engaging in a conflictual manner. Each case study included a summary of the case, its pre-history, evolution, attempts at resolution, impacts and aftermath. Case study sites were selected from project and non-project sites using propensity scoring.

The Indonesia analysis focused on the domains of state and society, concentrating on the intermediary and local levels. In the state domain it worked with (i) the legal sub-domain, looking at the ability of citizens to approach police and the ability of police and courts to apply the laws correctly and solve conflicts; and (ii) the political sub-domain, looking at the functioning and accountability of the local authorities and the citizen participation in the local decision-making processes. Within the societal domain, indicators centered on the community sub-domain, focusing on the associational and social interactions of people with different identities.

The study team used two key concepts – 'countervailing power' and 'routines' – to structure their analysis. People's 'countervailing power' was an indicator of agency. 'Routines' were understood to both reflect and construct the 'rules' that determined the outcomes of conflict. As such, in this case, routines were indicators of opportunity structure.

Measuring empowerment and social inclusion in Nepal

The Nepal country study covered the domains of the state and the society and concentrated on the intermediary and local levels. Data were collected on a wide range of assets hypothesized to have a relationship with empowerment outcomes. Assets included standard measures such as literacy and land ownership, as well as group membership, participation in training, and knowledge of rights. Indicators of opportunity structure focused on the rules (institutions) that governed social positioning, social interaction, physical mobility, violence, and economic security or vulnerability.

Degrees of empowerment indicators ranged from the ease with which people could approach legal services, to voting behaviour, to the degree of control over various aspects of domestic life that different household members enjoy. Indicators of intra-community engagement and the manner in which people behave or are able to behave in that setting were also gathered.

7.4 Summary

The approach suggested here for measuring empowerment is a simple one comprising three core concepts: agency; opportunity structure; and degree of empowerment. These are further refined into clusters of indicators. A broad range of assets are used as indicators of agency. Measurement of the presence and operation of formal and informal institutions provides indicators of opportunity structure. The existence of choice, the use of choice, and the effectiveness of choice are used as indicators of the degree of empowerment a person or group experiences. Three domains (state, market, and society) are divided into a number of sub-domains, or stages in or upon which actors live out their lives. These sub-domains are differentiated according to the level at which actors operate – the macro, intermediary, and local levels.

This framework can be used as the basis for in-depth research, for project- and national-level monitoring, and with certain caveats, for comparing the status of and changes in empowerment across countries. It can also be used to design interventions and policies intended to empower people or groups of people.[26] Empowerment is therefore firmly placed within the actionable remit of those involved in analysing and monitoring poverty policy and development interventions. An approach to operational and analytical work has been outlined, based on a review and translation of both historical and more recent discussions of the substance and nature of power. The resultant framework is one that can be used to measure empowerment and to provide a better understanding of the operational needs of implementing change to bring about empowerment. Diversity is crucial to a relational concept such as empowerment and the five country studies demonstrate that recognition of organizing principles does not mean uniformity of analysis when using such a framework.

Notes

1. Stern *et al.* (2005).
2. Dollar and Kraay (2002); Kaufmann *et al.* (2003); Moore and Putzel (1999).
3. Bourguignon *et al.* (2003); Sen (1999).
4. Alsop (2005); DFID (2000); Eyben (2003); Moser and Norton (2001).
5. Baiocchi *et al.* in Alsop, Bertelsen and Holland (2006); Lokshin and Ravallion (2005); Varshney (2005).
6. North (1990).
7. Key amongst these authors are Gramsci (in Hoare, 1978), Weber (1904), Lukes (1974), Parsons (1937), Giddens (1984) and Foucault (1980). In addition, this framework and its subsequent development owe much to the recent work of Bennett (2003); Bourdieu (1977); Clegg (1989); Kabeer (1999); Krishna (2003); Lukes (1974); Malhotra *et al.* (2002); Sen (1985, 1992); and Smulovitz, Walton, and Petesch (2003). Readers are referred in particular to the Bennett, Giddens, Lukes and Smulovitz publications for a discussion of the theoretical underpinnings of this framework.
8. Alkire (2005) surveys a series of subjective measures of agency; that is, measures that capture people's self-evaluation of whether or not they are free to act as agents. There is also a rich literature available on measuring social capital (**see** www.worldbank.org/socialcapital). Appadurai (2004) was the first to clearly articulate the idea of a 'capacity to aspire'.
9. Giddens (1984).
10. Research in India found that the addition of one more source of information to a person's repertoire increased participation in local level governance by more than five additional percentage points. Alsop *et al.* 2001.
11. Kabeer (1999); Bourdieu (1977).
12. Central Statistical Authority (2001).
13. However, without the force of the constitution, women would have experienced a much longer and harder fight to enter and operate effectively in the political arena.
14. World Bank (2004).
15. Sen (1997, 1999).
16. In this example, one Indian woman may well experience different degrees of empowerment from another. These differences can largely be explained by assets – such as education, information, and social capital – and opportunity structure – such as social norms of behaviour associated with caste and gender, or formal rules giving her access to loans, markets, or services.
17. The country case studies were undertaken as part of an initiative to understand and measure empowerment. Country studies were managed and written up by Lynn Bennett (Nepal), Arianna Legovini (Ethiopia), Mike Walton (Brazil), Mike Woolcock (Indonesia), and Emanuela di Gropello/Nina Heinsohn (Honduras). These task managers worked in

collaboration with the following international and local consultants: Kishor Gajural, Kim Armstrong and Sandra Houser (Nepal), the Ethiopian Economic Association (Ethiopia), Gianpaolo Baiocchi, Shubham Chaudhuri, Patrick Heller and the Centro de Assessoria e Estudios Urbanos (Brazil), Patrick Barron, Leni Dharmawan, Claire Smith, Rachael Diprose, Lutfi Ashari, Adam Satu, and Saifullah Barwani (Indonesia), and ESA Consultores (Honduras). For additional information please visit: www.worldbank.org/empowerment/.

18. Refer to Alsop, Bertelsen and Holland (2006) *Empowerment in Practice: From Analysis to Implementation*, Directions in Development series, (Washington DC: World Bank) for further discussion.
19. See Narayan (ed.) (2005), for a summary of multidisciplinary perspectives.
20. Graham and Pettinato (2005); Malhotra *et al.* (2002); Uphoff (2005).
21. Kabeer, op. cit.
22. Tables 7.2 and 7.3 were prepared by Jeremy Holland who also undertook the background research on the empowerment content of existing survey instruments.
23. Stern *et al.* (2005: 187).
24. Kabeer (1999).
25. This section is more fully described in Part II of Alsop, Berletsen and Holland (2006). The full range of indicators used in each country case study can also be found in that publication.
26. See Alsop *et al.* (2006) for a full description of the application of the framework to operations.

References

Alkire, S. (2005) 'Subjective Quantitative Studies of Human Agency', *Social Indicators Research*, 74(1), 217–68.

Alsop, R. (ed.) (2005) *Power, Rights and Poverty: Concepts and Connections*. Washington, DC: The World Bank.

Alsop, R., M. Bertelsen and J. Holland (2006) *Empowerment in Practice: From Analysis to Implementation*, Directions in Development series, World Bank Washington DC for further discussion.

Alsop, R. and N. Heinsohn (2005) 'Measuring Empowerment: Structuring Analysis and Framing Indicators', *Policy Research Working Paper*, No. 3510. Washington, D.C.: World Bank.

Alsop, R., A. Krishna and D. Sjoblom (2001) Inclusion and Local Elected Governments: The Panchayat Raj System in India, *Social Development Paper* No. 37. Washington DC: World Bank.

Alsop, R. and B. Kurey (2004) The Status of Empowerment in Ethiopia. Unpublished background paper for the Ethiopia Poverty Assessment.

Appadurai, A. (2004) 'The Capacity to Aspire: Culture and Terms of Recognition', in Rao V and M Walton (eds), *Culture and Public Action*. Stanford, CA: Stanford University Press.

Baiocchi, G., P. Heller, S. Chauduri and M. Silva (2005) 'Evaluating Empowerment: Participatory Budgeting in Brazilian Municipalities', Draft. World Bank, Brasilia.

Barron, P. and D. Madden (2003) 'Violent Conflict in "Non-Conflict" Regions: The Case of Lampung, Indonesia', *East Asia and Pacific Region, Working Paper*. Washington DC: World Bank.

Bennett, Lynn (2003) Empowerment and Social Inclusion: A Social Development Perspective on the Cultural and Institutional Foundations of Poverty Reduction. Washington DC: World Bank.

Bennett, Lynn and Kishor Gajurel (2004) Negotiating Social Change in Rural Nepal: Crosscutting Gender, Caste and Ethnic Dimensions of Empowerment and Social Inclusion. Draft. Washington, DC: World Bank.

Bennett, L. (2005) 'Nepal: Gender and Social Exclusion Assessment'. Draft. Kathmandu: World Bank.

Bourdieu, P. (1977) *Outline of a Theory of Practice*. Cambridge: Cambridge University Press.

Bourguignon, F., F. Ferreira and M. Menendez (2003) Inequality of Outcomes and Inequality of Opportunities in Brazil. Mimeo. Washington DC: World Bank.

Central Statistical Authority [Ethiopia] and ORC Macro (2001) *Ethiopia Demographic and Health Survey 2000*. Addis Ababa, Ethiopia and Calverton, MD: Central Statistical Authority and ORC Macro.

Clegg, I. (1989) *Frameworks of Power*. London: Sage Publications.

Dahl, R. (1961) *Who Governs? Democracy and Power in an American City*. Yale: Yale University Press.

DFID (2000) *Realising Human Rights for People*. Target Strategy Paper. London: Department for International Development.

Dollar, D. and A. Kraay (2000) 'Property Rights, Political Rights, and the Development of poor Countries in the Post-Colonial Period'. Draft. Washington, DC: World Bank. Development Economics Research Group.

Dollar, D. and A. Kraay (2002) 'Growth is Good for the Poor', *Journal of Economic Growth*, 7(3), 195–225.

Du Toit, A. (2003) 'Hunger in the Valley of Fruitfulness: Globalization, social exclusion and chronic poverty in Ceres, South Africa'. Paper presented at the conference on Staying Poor: Chronic Poverty and Development Policy, IDPM, University of Manchester, UK.

Evans, P. (2004) 'Development as Institutional Change: The Pitfalls of Monocropping and the Potentials of Deliberation', *Studies in Comparative International Development*, 38(4), 30–52.

Eyben, R. (2003) *The Rise of Rights: Rights Based Approaches to International Development*. IDS Policy Briefing Issue 17. Brighton: Institute of Development Studies.

Foucault, M. (1980) *Power and Knowledge: Selected Interviews and Other Writings 1972–77*. Ed. Colin Gordon. New York: Pantheon Books.

Fung, A. (2002) *Collaboration and Countervailing Power: Making Participatory Governance Work*. www.archonfung.net

Geertz, C. (1977) *The Interpretation of Culture*. New York: Perseus.

Gibson, C. and M. Woolcock (2005) 'Empowerment and Local Level Conflict Mediation in the Kecamatan Development Project in Indonesia: Concepts, Measures and Project Efficacy'. Draft Report. Washington DC: World Bank.

Giddens, A. (1984) *The Constitution of Society: Outline of the Theory of Structuration*. Polity Press, Cambridge, UK.

Gramsci, A. (1971) *Selections from Prison Notebooks*, London: Lawrence and Wishart.

Graham, C. and S. Pettinato (2005) Subjective Well-Being and Objective Measures: Insecurity and Inequality in Emerging Markets. In D. Narayan (ed.), 2005.

Grootaert, C. (2003) Assessing Empowerment in the ECA Region. World Bank ECA Region's study on the Non-Income Dimensions of Poverty. Paper presented at the World Bank Empowerment Workshop, 4–5 February, 2003. Accessed at http://www.worldbank.org/poverty/empowerment/events/feb03/papers.htm, 22 June 2003.

Gropello, E. di and N. Heinsohn (2004) 'School Based management in Central America: What are the Effects on Community Empowerment?' Draft Report. Washington DC: World Bank.

Hoare, Q. (ed.) (1978) *Antonio Gramsci: Selections from Political Writings (1921–1926)*. London: Lawrence and Wishart Ltd.

Kabeer, N. (1999) 'Resources, Agency, Achievements: Reflections on the Measurement of Women's Empowerment', *Development and Change* 30, 435–64.

Kaufman, D., A. Kraay and M. Mastruzzi (2004) 'Governance Matters III: Governance Indicators for 1996–2002', *World Bank Economic Review* 18(2), 253–87.

Kaufmann, D. (2000) 'Unbundling Governance and Corruption: Some New Empirical Findings and Collective Action Approaches' Paper presented at Anti-Corruption Summit. Washington, DC: World Bank Institute.

Krishna, A. (2003) 'Mapping Empowerment in a Comparative Perspective.' Consultant report for the Empowerment Team, Poverty Reduction Group, Poverty Reduction and Economic Management Network. Washington, DC: World Bank.

Legovini, A. (2005) 'Measuring Women's Empowerment in Ethiopia' Draft Report. Addis Ababa: World Bank.

Lokshin, M. and M. Ravallion (2003) 'Rich and Powerful? Subjective Power and Welfare in Russia', Development Research Group, World Bank. Paper presented at the World

Bank Empowerment Workshop, 4–5 February. http://www.worldbank.org/poverty/empowerment/events/feb03/papers.htm.

Lokshin, M. and M. Ravallion (2005) 'Self Rated Power and Welfare in Russia', in Narayan (ed.), *Measuring Empowerment: Cross Disciplinary Perspectives*. Washington, DC: World Bank, pp. 177–96.

Lukes, S. (1974) *Power: A Radical View*. London: Macmillan.

Malhotra, A., S. Schuler and C. Boender (2002) 'Measuring Women's Empowerment as Variable in International Development', paper commissioned by the Gender and Development Group of the World Bank, Washington DC, 28 June. Accessed at http://poverty.worldbank.org/library/view/13320/

Mansuri, G. and V. Rao (2004) 'Community-Based (and Driven) Development: A Critical Review', *World Bank Research Observer*, 19(1), 1–39.

Moore, M. and J. Putzel (1999) 'Thinking Strategically about Politics and Poverty'. *IDS Working Paper No 101*. Brighton: Institute of Development Studies.

Moser, C. and A. Norton (2001) *To Claim Our Rights: Livelihood Security, Human Rights and Sustainable Development*. London: Overseas Development Institute.

Narayan, D. (ed.) (2002) *Empowerment and Poverty Reduction: A Sourcebook*. Washington DC: World Bank.

Narayan, D. (ed.) (2005) *Measuring Empowerment: Cross Disciplinary Perspectives*. Washington, DC: World Bank.

North, D.C. (1990) *Institutions, Institutional Change and Economic Performance* Cambridge: Press Syndicate of the University of Cambridge.

Nussbaum, M. (2000) *Women and Human Development: The Capabilities Approach*. Cambridge: Cambridge University Press.

Parsons, T. (1937) *The Structure of Social Action*. New York: McGraw-Hill.

Parsons, T. (1963) 'On the Concept of Political Power', *Proceedings of the American Philosophical Society*, 107(3), 323–63.

Rajan, R. (2004) 'Assume Anarchy? Why an Orthodox Economic Model May Not be the Best Guide for Policy', *Finance and Development*, September, 56 7.

Rao, V. and M. Walton (2004) 'Culture and Public Action: Relationality, Equality of Agency, and Development'. in V. Rao and M. Walton, (eds), *Culture and Public Action*. Stanford: Stanford University Press.

Sen, A. (1985) *Commodities and Capabilities*. Amsterdam: Elsevier.

Sen, A. (1992) *Inequality Reexamined*. Cambridge, MA: Harvard University Press.

Sen, A. (1997) 'Editorial: Human Capital and Human Capability', *World Development*, 25(12), 1959–61.

Sen, A. (1999) *Development as Freedom*. New York: Anchor Books.

Smulovitz, C., M. Walton and P. Petesch (2003) Notes on Evaluating Empowerment. Draft, LAC, Washington, DC: World Bank.

Stern, N., J.-J. Dethier and H. Rogers (2005) *Growth and Empowerment: Making Development Happen*. Cambridge, MA: MIT Press.

Uphoff, N. (2005) Analytic Issues in Measuring Empowerment at the Community and Local Levels. In D. Narayan (ed.), 2005.

Varshney, A. (2002) *Ethnic Conflict and Civic Life: Hindus and Muslims in India*. New Haven: Yale University Press.

Varshney, A. (2005) Democracy and Poverty, in D. Narayan (ed.).

Weber, M. (1904) 'The Objectivity of the Sociological and the Social-Political Knowledge', in *Max Weber on the Methodology of the Social Sciences*, trans. and ed. E. A. Shils and H. A. Finch. Glencoe, IL: Free Press, 1949.

Weber, M. (1964) [1947] *The Theory of Social and Economic Organization*. Ed. Talcott Parsons, Free Press of Glencoe, New York.

World Bank (2004) 'The Poverty Reduction Strategy Initiative: An Independent Evaluation of the World Bank's Support Through 2003', Operations Evaluation Department. Washington DC: World Bank.

8
Participation, Pluralism and Perceptions of Poverty[1]

Robert Chambers

> The promise of both participatory research and the focus on well-being is that they will enable us to hear genuinely different voices, voices that speak from and about realities other than those configured by development discourse and institutions.
>
> (White and Pettit 2004: 95)

8.1   Introduction

Meanings of poverty and dimension

The words 'poverty' and 'dimension' are each used with many meanings. In this chapter, the meanings given to them are as follows:

Poverty includes bad conditions and/or experience of life. This means more than simply material poverty or lack. It is the meaning implied by the statement with which the World Development Report (WDR) 2000/01 *Attacking Poverty* opens 'Poverty is pronounced deprivation in wellbeing' (World Bank 2000: 15). 'Multidimensional poverty' is then the same as 'multidimensional deprivation'.[2] Well-being is the experience of good quality of life, and ill-being, its opposite, the experience of bad quality of life. This applies especially where material and other deprivations and disadvantages interact and reinforce each other (see Figures 8.1–8.4).

Dimension. In the literature, this is used in at least three senses.

First, the Research Group on Wellbeing in Developing Countries at the University of Bath (White and Pettit, 2006) describes three dimensions of well-being, and of its opposites, ill-being, poverty or deprivation. These are subjective, objective, and interactive or process. Subjective can be taken to mean what is experienced, objective to refer to conditions or causes outside a person, and interactive or process to encompass how subjective (internal and experiential) and objective (external) affect each other.

A second sense of dimension is that in the WDR 2000/2001 (see, for example, v, 1, 15 and *passim*) which 'sets out actions to create a world free of poverty in all its dimensions'. The multiple deprivations listed in the Report, besides low income or consumption, include lack of education, health, food and shelter, fear, powerlessness and voicelessness. And the WDR says that there is 'a powerful case for bringing vulnerability and its management to center stage' (ibid.: 32). The WDR implicitly separates some of the more experiential dimensions of poverty from their determinants (for example, ibid.: 34).

A third and broader usage includes the first two and extends dimension to include causes to a greater extent. Thus, for example, 'Corrupt and arbitrary governance constitutes a significant factor that defines and contributes to the various *other* dimensions of poverty' (Parasuraman *et al.*, 2003: 33, my emphasis). This was also the sense which evolved out of the Voices of the Poor process, in which participatory approaches and methods were used to enable poor people in close to 300 communities in 23 countries to express and analyze their realities (Narayan *et al.*, 2000). After stating that 'The dimensions of deprivation are multiple', ten 'Dimensions of Powerlessness and Illbeing' were elicited and described:

Capabilities:	lack of information, education, skills, confidence
Livelihoods and assets:	precarious, seasonal, inadequate
Places:	isolated, risky, unserviced, stigmatized
The body:	hungry, exhausted, sick, poor appearance
Gender relations:	troubled and unequal
Social relations:	discriminating and isolating
Security:	lack of protection and peace of mind
Behaviours:	disregard and abuse by the more powerful
Institutions:	disempowering and excluding
Organizations of the poor:	weak and disconnected

(Narayan *et al.*, 2000: 248–9 and Figure 2)

Many dimensions can thus be identified. As in other chapters in this book, they may be physical, material, economic, social, psychological, institutional, or legal, or related to capability, power or vulnerability. They may be experiential (or subjective) or external to a person (or objective). They may be related to interaction, process or cause. They may be combinations of any of these. To be open to the many realities and meanings of those who experience deprivations, there is little gain and perhaps some loss in any exclusive definition of dimension. I therefore allow the span of this chapter to cover these various and several senses, relying on other words and contexts to indicate particular meaning.

Orientations and reflexivity

We have travelled far in professional views of poverty. It is striking how the reductionist money-metric view of poverty has been, and to some extent remains, disproportionately dominant in much development discourse. For some economists and others it is a bedrock; for others, a default mode. Reviewing the important debates on poverty and the poverty line in India, Tony Beck observed (1994: 16) that 'the central preoccupation of the majority of authors on poverty has been the accuracy of the statistics and the statistical techniques used'. A tempting caricature of the concept of poverty implied by such debates could be of a top-down, centre-outwards, ivory tower, mathematical construct, overfed and driven by question-naires, statistics, computers, regressions, equations, graphs and tables. In this view, it could be seen as sustained by erudite, incestuous and self-reproducing systems of high-status organizations and departments, and by teaching, textbooks, inter-national conferences, prestigious journals and rigorous professional peer review. Economists, it might be suggested, construct their own reality of poverty based on reported income or consumption, provoking the verse:

> Economists have come to feel
> What can't be measured isn't real
> The truth is always an amount
> Count numbers, only numbers count

But those, like myself, who enjoy writing this sort of stuff about economists, also have to look closely at ourselves. We too find it useful and indeed necessary to refer to poverty lines; and their accuracy, what they represent, and the distribu-tions and trends they suggest, do matter. All of us development professionals have our biases and predispositions. Arguably, any writing on development should be preceded by a reflexive paragraph outlining those of which the author is aware. Let me list some of mine. As a lapsed biologist and historian, and now undisciplined social scientist, I take pleasure, and have sustained a livelihood, by looking for gaps between professions and aspects of realities that seem to have been over-looked or understudied. I recognise that I am liable to exaggerate the importance of such gaps, and am vulnerable to glee when I believe I have discovered a misper-ception of 'normal' professionalism and professionals. In my view, numbers and statistics are important, but often more flawed than their users recognize. I tend to privilege the knowledge, values and abilities of poor and excluded people over those of established groups, especially academics and powerful old men. I have been repeatedly astonished at the insights and capabilities that have been revealed by participatory behaviours, attitudes, approaches and methods. So about these of my predispositions and biases at least (and there are surely others) readers have now been alerted and warned.

8.2   Participation and poverty

In the past decade and a half we have come a long way in the invention, evolution and spread of participatory approaches and methods and their contributions to understanding poverty. A new pluralism of methodology and perception has opened up. A thousand flowers have bloomed. At the same time, many have turned into weeds, notably when disseminated by big bureaucracies. In parallel, however, there have been innumerable examples of good practice. Sourcebooks, guides and manuals of participatory practice have proliferated, and have then been increasingly superseded by eclectic creativity. Participatory methodologies capable of contributing to understanding poverty, and which have become best known and most widespread include: varied forms of participatory action research like cooperative inquiry (Reason and Bradbury, 2001); PRA (originally participatory rural appraisal, now often participatory reflection and action) and the more inclusive (Participatory Learning and Action) (Chambers, 1997); Popular Theatre (Mda, 1983; McCarthy with Galvao, 2004); Reflect (Education Action; Archer and Newman, 2003; Archer and Goreth, 2004); and many forms of Participatory Monitoring and Evaluation (PM and E) (McGillivray *et al.*, 1998; Estrella *et al.*, 2000 and Guijt, 2000). Well facilitated, these to varying degrees can enable and empower poor and marginalized people to conduct and learn from their own analyses, express their values and priorities, and provide insights into dimensions of poverty.

Five clusters of related innovation and insight stand out:

Participatory Poverty Assessments
Hidden and sensitive topics
Nets and webs of disadvantage and deprivation
Participatory numbers
Listening, learning and immersions

8.3 Participatory poverty assessments[3]

Participatory Poverty Assessments (PPAs) evolved in the early 1990s, notably in Ghana (1993–4), Zambia (1993–) and South Africa (1995–) and have since become widespread. By 2002 more than 60 countries had undertaken PPAs with assistance from the World Bank, with a similar number supported by other agencies (Robb 2002: 3). Increasingly, PPA-type studies have been carried out at subnational levels – for example, in Bolangir District in Orissa, India (PRAXIS 2001). Including all these, PPAs are now numbered in their hundreds.

A PPA was described in *The Rough Guide to PPAs* (Norton *et al.*, 2001: 6) as 'an instrument for including poor people's views in the analysis of poverty and the formulation of strategies to reduce it through public policy'. In many of these, focus groups have been combined with PRA methods of analysis. Groups have been facilitated to create and analyse their realities, often using visuals and tangibles for methods such as participatory mapping, preference ranking, matrix scoring, Venn diagramming, wealth or well-being ranking, and many others. They have covered many aspects of life and experience such as poor people's priorities, access and institutions, gender relations, causal linkages, seasonal variations, and trends and changes.

Repeatedly, PPAs have opened up aspects of poverty which had been relatively overlooked or given inadequate priority. Reviews of PPAs (Booth *et al.* 1998: 5–7) found that they highlighted:

- A sense of isolation, from services, markets, government institutions and information, with physical isolation a key factor
- The key importance of water supplies
- Security of life and livelihood as a primary concern
- Access to curative health as a consistently high priority

- Local visions of poverty relating to prevailing community norms
- Differential vulnerability according to inherent or socially constructed characteristics of individuals (gender, age, childlessness, health status, disability and individual pathologies such as drunkenness)
- Hunger and dietary inadequacy as a distinct dimension of deprivation
- The seasonality of access and vulnerability
- Intra-household poverty dynamics
- The decline of traditional, and insufficiency of, alternative safety nets
- Community-level poverty versus household or individual poverty

Caroline Robb concluded her review of PPAs (second edition, 2002: 104–5):

> The moral imperative for giving the poor a voice in the poverty debate is self-evident. The bonus is that engaging with the poor also leads to better technical diagnosis of problems and implementation of solutions. Through PPAs, the poor deepen our understanding of poverty and can influence policymaking. This new approach challenges traditional power relations ... when undertaken in an environment of increased trust, PPAs can present opportunities for a more open dialogue and greater understanding between the powerless and those in power.

The processes for Poverty Reduction Strategy Papers (PRSPs), which have superseded PPAs in prominence, have been criticized for inadequate consultation. Some, however, have drawn on PPAs, a clear example being Uganda where 'the PPA predated the PRSP concept, but was used extensively in revising the national strategy, which became the PRSP' (McGee *et al.*, 2002: 8). In Rwanda, a PPA process, *ubudehe*, has been developed and spread in which each commune conducts its own PPA leading to direct local learning and collective action. This process, with trained facilitators, has achieved extensive coverage (Joseph, 2005). Some PPAs have had a transformative learning impact through involving government and other staff in the fieldwork with poor communities and people. PPAs have indeed taken many forms and have many continuing potentials for informing pro-poor policy and practice.

8.4   Hidden and sensitive dimensions

Participatory methods, creatively evolved and carefully facilitated, have opened up aspects of life which have usually been thought too private, sensitive or dangerous to make public or to analyse. An early example (see also below) was wealth or well-being ranking, in which members of a community typically first draw a social map showing all households, then list these on cards, and then sort them into piles according to degrees of wealth or, more usually, some concept of well-being. Middle-class urban professionals often regard this as either impossible or unethical, supposing it will be demeaning and humiliating for those who are worse off. These fears have repeatedly proved unfounded. Three other areas are gender relations and sexual and reproductive well-being, violence, insecurity and social abuses, and defecation in the open.

The first example is the related areas of *gender relations, sexual behaviour* and *sexual and reproductive well-being*. Participatory approaches and methods have proved potent in bringing these into the open, and empowering women to take action. Gender relations, and how they have been changing, were a major theme in the Voices of the Poor study (Narayan *et al.*, 2000: chapter 6, 109–32). Much has been explored and documented as never before in *Realizing Rights: Transforming Approaches to Sexual and Reproductive Well-being* (Cornwall and Welbourn, 2002). The lives and realities of those who are marginalized, despised, excluded and ignored have been brought into the light. Sex workers, for example, come to life as people like other people, for whom respect, security and good relations matter as much as, as if not more than, they do for others. Participatory approaches to HIV/AIDS, especially through the group processes known as Stepping Stones (Welbourne 1995, 2002), have brought what was hidden or unspoken into the open, with frank talk about sex and death, concern for sensitive behaviour and relationships, acceptance of HIV-positive women and men, and counselling and care for the sick and dying. Participatory approaches and methods have also been developed for HIV/AIDS work with drug users (International HIV/AIDS Alliance 2003). Other areas are the sexual behaviours and preferences of adolescents[4] and of prepubescent children (unknown to their parents).

The second area is *violence, physical insecurity and social abuses*. Participatory studies of violence in Jamaica, Guatemala and Colombia have broken new ground, revealing wide differences between beliefs of policy makers about forms of violence and the realities experienced by ordinary people (Moser and McIlwaine, 2004). In Peru, participatory time lines, matrices and maps were used in Ayacucho as part of the Colectivo Yuyarisu ('We remember') process of the Truth Commission (Comision de la Verdad y Justicia): using these methods, over 100 groups recollected and reconstructed human rights violations which had taken place in the era of political violence 1980–94 (Francke, 2003, and *pers comm.*). In many contexts, domestic abuse and violence against women has been brought out into the open. An early example was an all-women's PRA activity in Tamil Nadu in 1990 (*pers comms.* Sheelu Francis and John Devavaram) in which women mapped households and marked with a yellow circle those where the husband was a drunkard. The Voices of the Poor study included perceived prevalence and trends of domestic violence against women. Another illustration is the Internal Learning System introduced into parts of India.[5] Women, both individually and in groups, keep visual diaries which they update every six months. In these they score from 1 to 5 for aspects of quality of life such as husbands drinking, domestic violence, Dalits having to drink out of separate glasses, Dalits being made to carry dead bodies or dead animals, and whether a girl can select her life partner (*pers comms.* Vimalanathan, S. Nagasundari and H. Noponen).

A third example is *open defecation*, widespread in South and Southeast Asia and a major source of sickness, mortality and ill-being for women who lack access to the privacy of a latrine. They are subject to gross gender discrimination, being compelled by custom, unlike men, to defecate unseen. Without latrines this means only before dawn or after nightfall. New participatory approaches are now enabling communities to confront and face the realities, often spurring them into action (Kar, 2003; Kar and Pasteur, 2005). A facilitator initiates the process. Community members are facilitated to make maps, usually on the ground, to show their communities and the areas where they defecate. They then walk and stand in those areas, face and smell the reality, draw flow diagrams to show pathways from faeces to food and mouths, calculate the cartloads of shit (the crude local word is used) produced and the amounts ingested, and are then encouraged to take action on their own. The communities in South Asia and Indonesia that have proudly declared themselves open defecation free now number thousands. The gains in well-being for women are suggested by an inscription on a wall in a totally sanitized village in Maharashtra: 'Daughters from our village are not married to villages where open defecation is practised'. In rural South Asia, where open defecation is widespread, the scale of potential gains in health, reduced mortality, and well-being for millions of women, children and men is so vast that it is difficult to grasp.

The importance of opening up these subjects can hardly be exaggerated. When they are not surfaced, analysed and confronted, much avoidable ill-being persists. Conversely, the potential for enhanced well-being from improving sexual and gender relations, from tackling and reducing or eliminating violence in its many forms, and from ending open defecation with gains in health and, in particular, for the well-being especially of women and children but also of men – each of these can only be described as phenomenal. Participatory approaches and methods, well facilitated, cannot solve these alone; but there is enough evidence now to realise that they can establish bridgeheads with the possibility of becoming transformative movements which spread on their own.

8.5   Nets and webs of disadvantage and deprivation

We now come to the issue of the multiplicity of dimensions of poverty. When dimension is used in the inclusive sense of this chapter, it includes many aspects of disadvantage. In the analysis of the Voices of the Poor study we faced difficult practical issues of how to analyse a large amount of data, most of it qualitative, but some also (see below, next section) amenable to aggregation and quantification.[6] We were continually impressed by how the dimensions of deprivation which emerged from the participatory data were interlinked, and we saw these links increasingly as a net or web in which poor people were trapped. Two diagrams were published (Figures 8.1 and 8.2).[7] And two others were not (Figures 8.3 and 8.4).

Figure 8.1, *Development as good change: From ill-being to well-being*, named five composite dimensions of ill-being and well-being, and their interlinkages. Development could be seen as shifting from illbeing to wellbeing with equity, with interventions to enhance wellbeing possible at any of the five points.

Figure 8.2, *Dimensions of powerlessness and ill-being*, expanded the circles to ten As the diagram indicates, each of these in turn can take various forms. They combine in powerlessness symbolized by the net.

By specifying these characteristics of disadvantage, Figure 8.2 again raises an agenda for intervention with any one of them, and questions of how they interlink

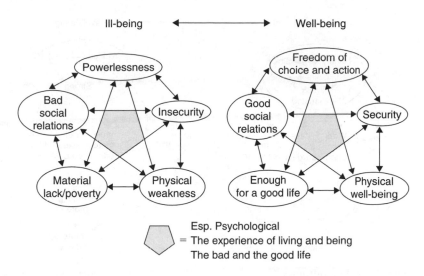

Figure 8.1 Development as good change: from ill-being to well-being

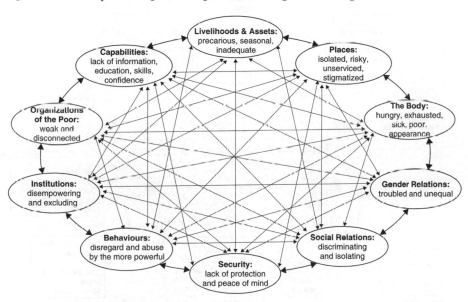

Figure 8.2 Dimensions of powerlessness and ill-being

and reinforce each other. In any story of the life of a poor person, linkages can be traced.

The versatility and power of these ways of presenting multiple dimensions and causal links can also be illustrated with two further diagrams.

Figure 8.3, also inspired by the Voices experience (and in part shown in Narayan *et al.* 2000: 97), shows two body syndromes. These express several ways in which a weak, hungry, exhausted body can be part of self-reinforcing syndrome, including

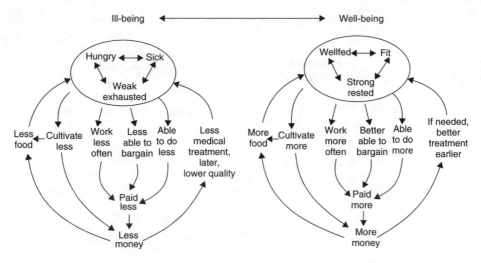

Figure 8.3   Body syndromes

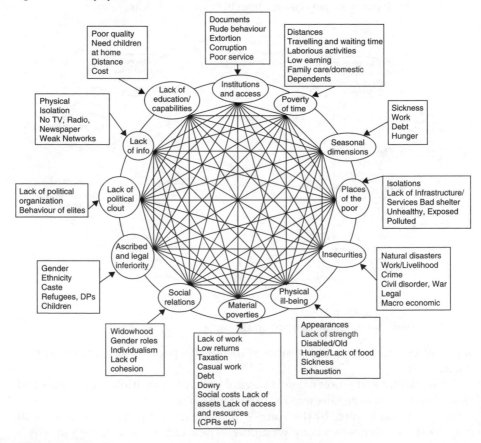

Figure 8.4   The web of poverty's disadvantages

reducing the power to bargain, and how less money can mean delayed and lower-quality medical treatment. These were both aspects of disadvantage which the Voices evidence presented.

Figure 8.4 goes further in complexity.

All 12 of these dimensions,

- material lack
- vulnerability and insecurities
- bad social relations
- physical weakness – the body, exhaustion
- location – places of the poor
- poverty of time
- seasonal dimensions
- capabilities
- ascribed and legal inferiority
- lack of information
- lack of access to services
- lack of political clout,

together with disregard and abuse by the more powerful, have been articulated and diagrammed by poor people, using variations and combinations of mapping, listing, Venn diagrams, pie diagrams, pile sorting, matrix scoring, pairwise ranking, time lines and seasonal diagrams, wealth and well-being ranking and sorting. The web has proved versatile, having been filled out for particular aspects: for sexuality by Susan Jolly[8] (2006) and for transgender and HIV/AIDS by Giuseppe Campuzano (2006).

These webs, especially the last, raise analytical and practical questions. We can ask which aspects and which linkages are found and function for any person, group or set of conditions. If we simplify by conflating or cutting out dimensions, do we risk failing to identify crucial disadvantages or connections? As the diagram indicates, each of the 12 can take a variety of forms. We can also ask whether Figures 8.2 and 8.4 overstress the negative, in ways in which Figures 8.1 and 8.3 do not because the latter indicate the potential for transitions (though, of course, these can go either way).

One question remains: whose analysis and categories are to be privileged? These are largely 'ours', those of professionals who are not ourselves poor, expressed in 'our' language. The words, concepts, categories and priorities of poor people, especially illustrated by the way they were elicited and expressed in the Voices of the Poor, were rich and varied, but with commonalities. There are trade-offs to be puzzled over: between 'their' realities and ours; between local participatory diversity and commensurability for aggregation; and between many categories representing poor people's realities and fewer categories more manageable for outsider professionals and for measurement.

8.6 Four neglected dimensions

Four dimensions have been relatively neglected in the professional literature.

Tropical seasonality

The interacting seasonal disadvantages include:[9]

- hard work in cultivation
- sickness (malaria, Dengue fever, diarrhoea, skin sores and diseases, snake bite, Guinea Worm Disease...)
- lack of food, especially in the hungry season
- poor quality and rapidly contaminated food
- physical weakness and exhaustion from combinations of the above
- shortage of money, loans in kind with high implicit interest rates
- isolation, with difficult or no access to markets and medical treatment
- late pregnancy and childbirth
- shelter and housing collapsing, leaking, flooded
- being wet and cold
- the high opportunity cost of not being able to work
- neglect and exposure of children

Season-proofed as they are against all of these, professionals living in urban centres lack a full appreciation of the multiple interactions of disadvantage for poor people living in rural areas during tropical rains, especially those areas which are 'remote'. During the rains, travel is often restricted to tarmac roads. Those off the tarmac and especially those 'cut off' during the rains, are not visited, met or heard.

Places of the poor

A whole chapter in Voices of the Poor (Narayan *et al.*, 2000: 71–88) came to be concerned with the places where poor people live and work. This was not foreseen in the planning of the study, but emerged as the findings were collected and sorted. The places where poor people live suffer combinations of isolation, lack of infrastructure, lack of services, crime, pollution, and vulnerability to disasters like drought, floods and landslips. Stigma of urban place can mean that place of residence must be concealed or dissembled when applying for a job. Inordinate amounts of time may be required for obtaining basics like water. The *Chronic Poverty Report 2004–05* devotes a whole chapter (CPRC 2005: 26–35) to 'Where do chronically poor people live?' and does a service by describing and analyzing spatial poverty traps, their ecological characteristics, poor infrastructure, weak institutions and political isolation. Place, whether rural or urban, as an interlocking dimension of deprivation is so obvious that it is strange that it has not received more prominence. It should be harder to overlook now that it has been named.[10]

Poverty of time and energy

Some of the poorest wish they had work. A very poor woman in a Bangladesh village said:

'These days I have no work,' she complains. 'If we had land, I would always be busy – husking rice, grinding lentils, cooking three times a day. You've seen how hard Jolil's wife works, haven't you? I have nothing to do, so I watch the children and worry. What kind of life is that?' (Hartmann and Boyce, 1983: 166–7)

There can be both poverty of too much time, and poverty of too little. The evidence from the Voices of the Poor study suggested that unwelcome surplus time was becoming more common for men with unemployment while poverty of both time and energy was becoming more common for women. This latter poverty of time and energy was recognized in the South African PPA (May with others, 1998: 108–9). It has become more acute for many women as they have become breadwinners in addition to their domestic and reproductive roles (Narayan *et al.*, 2000: 111–12). When asked what her dream was, a poor rural woman in Zambia said that it was to be able to go to town, spend time with her friends, and come back again.[11]

The body

The importance of the body, and of health and strength, to poor people shouts out from participatory study after study. The emergent categories from the Voices of the Poor study (Narayan *et al.*, 2000) led to a whole chapter entitled The Body. From their analysis of over 250 life-stories of poor people, Parasuraman and his co-authors derive a whole chapter of *Listening to People Living in Poverty* to 'The Labouring Body' (274–97). This, they point out, is often the only resource a person living in poverty is able to use.

The continuous exertion of their bodies in labour that is underpaid and undervalued leaves them exhausted. Their work is hazardous and, seasonal and leaves them vulnerable to outside harm. They are forced to use and sell their bodies as an instrument. They rarely have time to recuperate or rest, and are reduced to what their bodies can do. These processes inscribe on their bodies and leave them to diseases, degenerating illnesses and death (ibid.: 293).[12]

The central importance of the body to most poor people has been under-recognized in the literature. The slogan at the head of a poster of the trade union SEWA (the Self-Employed Women's Association) in India reads: OUR BODIES ARE OUR WEALTH. The body is more important to people living in poverty than it is to professionals. For many, it is their most important asset. But it is at the same time vulnerable, uninsured and indivisible. It has often been weakened by life experiences. It is exceptionally exposed and vulnerable – to hard and dangerous work and accidents, to violence, to sickness, to lack of nutrition, overwork and exhaustion. With an accident or illness it can flip suddenly from being main asset to liability, needing payment for treatment and having to be fed and cared for. It is a recurrent finding that many people fall into bad conditions of deep poverty because of what has happened to their bodies. Yet in general, the priority to poor people of quick, effective and affordable treatment has not been appreciated by professionals. In addition to human and ethical aspects, it may cost much less, and be more feasible, to provide good curative services so that poor people avoid becoming poorer than it is, once they are poorer, to enable them to claw their way back up again.

Negative synergies

These four neglected dimensions, like others, interact with negative synergies. A poor woman in the Gambia, referring to what could happen during the agricultural season of the rains, said: 'Sometimes we are overcome by weeds through sickness or accidents' (Haswell 1975). With seasonal vulnerability of the body, in places which are isolated or cut off, and with seasonal poverty of time and energy when time and energy have high opportunity costs, the disadvantages are compounded, but in ways which are not readily visible to professionals. The power and privileges of others make it worse. It is a cruel twist that poor people are kept waiting in clinics while better-dressed middle-class people see health staff straight away.[13] Counted as human well-being foregone by waiting, the time spent by the poor people can be worth so much more than that of those who are better off. But this is neither recognized nor acted on. Following any logic of optimizing wellbeing, it is the middle classes who should have to wait.

8.7 Participation and numbers

In recent years, increasing attention has been paid to combining qualitative and quantitative methods in research (see, for example, Booth *et al.*, 1998; Marsland *et al.*, 2000; Kanbur 2003). Complementarities have been recognized between the depth and detail contributed by qualitative research and the representativeness and statistical robustness contributed by quantitative research.[14] The benefits of such combinations are no longer seriously in dispute. They do, however, tend to overlook the power and potential of participatory approaches and methods, with two assumptions still quite common: first, that participatory approaches only generate

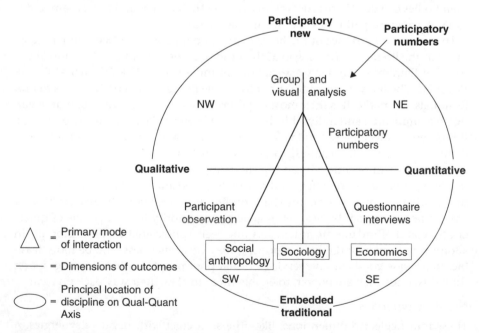

Figure 8.5   Dimensions of methodology and outcome

qualitative insights; and secondly, that quantitative data can only be produced by questionnaire surveys or scientific measurement.

To the contrary, many experiences have shown these assumptions to be false. Since the early 1990s, a quiet tide of innovation has developed a rich range of participatory ways by which local people can themselves produce numbers.[15] The methodological pioneers have rarely recognized the full significance of what they have been doing, written it up for publication, or made it easy for others to learn from them. They have worked in the NE quadrant of Figure 8.5.

The results have been as striking and exciting as they have been unrecognized in the professional mainstream. There are now many examples of numbers being generated by participatory processes and of statistical analysis of these.[16] The evidence to date indicates that participatory numbers tend to be much more accurate and often more useful than those from questionnaires. Some questionnaires will always be needed, and some, especially time series like the National Sample Survey in India, should surely continue. But for most investigations needing numbers questionnaires may now be best only a last resort.

Participatory analytical activities and applications can generate numbers through counting, measuring, estimating, valuing, ranking, and scoring. Making comparisons is often involved, giving numbers or scores to indicate relative values. Analytical activities are many, for example:

- Mapping
- Modelling
- Pile sorting
- Pie diagramming
- Card writing and sorting
- Matrix ranking and scoring
- Linkage diagramming
- Pocket voting
- Venn diagramming.

Applications of activities like these are numerous, including numerical comparisons of many sorts. Some of the more common derive from

- Resource mapping and modelling (including Participatory GIS) (*PLA* 2006)
- Social mapping
- Mobility mapping
- Household listing
- Well-being ranking
- Trend and change analysis
- Livelihood analysis
- Seasonal diagramming
- Causal linkage analysis
- The ten-seed technique (Jayakaran 2002, 2003)
- Aggregating from focus groups

Many illustrations are now accessible[17] in the literature. Much of it is grey, though some is beginning to be published in journals that are conventionally regarded as of higher status. On the statistical side, the Statistical Services Centre at Reading University[18] has been in the lead, especially with its remarkable pioneering work with partners in Malawi. To give a taste of some of the range, here are some examples of participatory numbers relating to poverty and to pro-poor programmes:

- *Mapping and counting in Nepal.* The earliest case of a large-scale survey with participatory visual analysis and no questionnaire may have been in 1992 with ActionAid's use of PRA-related methods, mainly mapping, classifying and counting, in over 130 villages in Nepal (ActionAid-Nepal 1992). This was a survey of utilization of services. It covered the whole population in the villages and generated 13 tables similar to those from a questionnaire. The population identified by the mapping summed to 35,414.

- *Pile sorting and coping strategies.* The NGO Save the Children (UK) study in 20 Districts in Malawi, Zambia, and Zimbabwe used pile sorting (subdividing piles of 60 stones or seeds) and other participatory methods for a retrospective study on how individual poor farmers coped with the 1992 drought (Eldridge 1995, 1998). The resulting tables were similar to those from a questionnaire survey.

- *The Bangladesh PPA.* In 1996 the UNDP PPA in Bangladesh convened focus groups of poor urban and rural women and men and facilitated their analysis of their priorities for 'doables', practical measures that would make a difference to their lives. These were aggregated by sex and location to produce cumulative prioritized problem indices which gave them comparative numerical values. These were presented in histograms. Among the findings were, for example, that the top priority for rural women was work, and for urban women water (UNDP 1996: 68).

- *The Participatory Poverty Index in China.* Ways are well known, if not always well practised, for enabling people living in poverty to reflect on and express their priorities. A major problem has been to combine this with comparisons of degrees or deprivation of different communities. Through participatory investigations and iterative pilot testing, a team in China identified eight common indicators as representing people's widespread priorities. Using these, a composite Participatory Poverty Index for each community was constructed from poor people's own allocation of personal priorities. This gave numerical expression to relative poverty between communities (Li *et al.*, 2002; Li and Remenyi and others, 2004; Remenyi in draft).[19] This was, however, lost when the method was taken rapidly to a vast scale (*pers comm.* Joe Remenyi 2005).

- *Violence in Jamaica, Guatemala and Colombia.* Focus groups facilitated to undertake participatory studies of urban violence in Jamaica, Guatemala and Colombia identified different types of violence, their seriousness, and the importance, positive or negative, of different related institutions. Their findings were aggregated, including those from Venn diagramming (Moser and Holland, 1997; Moser and McIlwaine, 2000, 2001 and 2004). In the Guatemala study this led to a table derived from 176 focus group listings which showed the frequency of mention of 22 different strategies for coping with violence (Moser and McIlwaine, 2001: 140). Contrary to common professional belief, violence categorized as economic was found to be much more widespread than that which was political.

- *Voices of the Poor.* Aggregation from focus groups was also undertaken in the Voices of the Poor study (Narayan *et al.* 2000) in 23 countries. This involved the views of many hundreds[20] of discussion groups in close to 300 communities on, for example, directions of change in violence against women (ibid.: 124–31) and characteristics of institutions (ibid.: 184 and 199–202). The results of these were presented in pie charts and tables.
- *The Malawi starter pack study.* A participatory study was undertaken in Malawi of the 'starter pack' (of seeds, fertilizer, etc.) programme and of small farmers' ideas of sustainability (Cromwell *et al.* 2001). In each of 30 villages, analysis by three focus groups, each bringing together a different category of farmer, included pairwise ranking of the relative importance of 15 indicators of sustainability. The results were combined in a table of mean values across villages by region.
- *The Malawi census.* When a major debate with pro-poor policy implications arose in Malawi about the size of the rural population as enumerated in the national census, participatory mapping and household listing were undertaken in a carefully selected sample of 54 villages and combined with household visits. Extrapolation indicated a population of 11.5 million compared with the census figure of 8.5 million (Barahona and Levy 2003). The Government census office was not willing to discuss the discrepancy. In their paper, Barahona and Levy elaborate the statistical principles relevant for rigour in such studies.
- *The Malawi Targeted Inputs Programme (TIP) study.* An ingenious and sensitive sequence of participatory methods, using community mapping with cards, was devised, tested and applied in Malawi to identify what proportions of those who were food secure, food insecure, and extremely food insecure had received inputs from the TIP programme. The programme was intended for the poor. All of the extremely food insecure should have received the inputs, and none of the food secure. The study found that 21 per cent of recipients were food secure, 38.5 per cent food insecure, and 40 per cent extremely food insecure, the corresponding figures for non-recipients being 33, 40 and 27 per cent respectively (Levy 2003).
- *Wealth/well-being ranking.*[21] In wealth, or more usually well-being ranking, household lists are usually derived from participatory social maps, and written on cards which are then sorted into piles, often by several groups which then meet to triangulate and explain the criteria implicit in their allocations. In recent years this has been rapidly adopted as a part of insightful poverty-related research. For the May 2004 Toronto Conference *Q-Squared in Practice: a Conference on Experiences Combining Qualitative and Quantitative*

Methods in Poverty Appraisal, 14 papers were selected from over 60 proposed. In the research reported in these 14, 10 had used PRA-type visuals or tangibles, and no less than 8 had used wealth/well-being ranking. One of the papers (Hargreaves *et al.*, 2004a) described a breakthrough in South Africa with a household wealth index that made comparisons of poverty possible between people in different communities.[22]

Despite experiences like these, major research organizations like the Independent Evaluation Group of the World Bank are still stuck with old ways of finding out, most notably large-scale long questionnaires. Given what we now know, this is inefficient and increasingly unprofessional.

A feature of most of these methods and applications has been the time taken to experiment, test and modify them in the field with people in communities, with eclectic borrowing, adaptation and improvisation of methods and sequences in order to assure rigour and a good fit. With the Malawi starter pack study, this was a team activity for an intensive three weeks (*pers comm.* Fiona Chambers). In the case of the China PPI it was longer, with iterations. These methods were thus tailor-made and tested for fit. They were not taken off the shelf. Together they give some indication of potential, showing that there can be many alternatives to questionnaires that can lead to better insights and more accurate numbers.[23] The scope for invention appears unlimited.

Three words of caution are in order. First, the ethical issues of participatory research (as of other research) deserve careful and sensitive attention. Secondly, the training, behaviour and attitudes of facilitators are critical for good results. This was stressed, in particular, in the South African wealth/well-being ranking where training and mentoring of facilitators was intensive and sustained (*pers comm.* Anton Simanowitz). Thirdly, given the evidence it is difficult to imagine that approaches like these will not be much more widely adopted, indeed that they are a wave of the future; but experience with other participatory approaches and methods suggests that progress will be slow and accompanied by bad practice. Professional conservatism in bureaucracies, the reproduction of normal professionalism by universities and training institutions, so often the last to learn and change, and inappropriate behaviour and attitudes, can be expected to remain major obstacles.

8.8   Listening, learning and immersions

In learning about poverty in a participatory mode, the behaviours and attitudes of the contextually powerful – the would-be learners, whether senior staff, middle management, field facilitators or researchers – have proved more important than the methods used. They include "don'ts" such as don't lecture, don't criticize, don't be important, don't dominate, dont's rush... and do's such as do be sensitive, respect, sit down, listen, learn, facilitate, take time, be nice to people...

Three streams of activity have contributed much here.

The first is listening and learning. An outstanding example is Harsh Mander's (2001) book *Unheard Voices: Stories of Forgotten Lives*. These are accounts of the lives and struggles of people in India 'who in many ways, have been pushed to the extreme edges of society... street children, sex workers, women, dalit and tribal survivors of atrocities, riot victims, especially women, homeless and destitute people, scavengers of night soil, and those living with leprosy and HIV' (ibid.: ix), and people displaced by big development projects, survivors of famines, and human-made and natural disasters. Some are excruciating to read, and tell of realities and resilience which are beyond normal middle-class imaginations. Another is *Listening to People Living in Poverty* (Parasuraman *et al.*, 2003) based on in-depth reading of over 250 life stories of poor people in Vietnam, Pakistan, Nepal, India and Bangladesh. It presents 29 of these, and then derives basic concepts and a framework from them 'in an open-ended structure that is continuously evolving.' (ibid.: xiv). This, as might be expected, stresses multidimensionality, (for example 'depletion of bodily resources': ibid.: 202), and power relations between poor people and institutions. Institutions are differentiated into discriminatory, contractual and affirmative, and interactions into constructive, nurturing, redistributive, prof-itable, maintenance, damaging, punitive, depriving and destructive (ibid.: 206–14).

The second is what are known as immersions or reality checks (Eyben, 2004; Irvine *et al.*, 2004; IDS Participation Group, 2005).[24] These are direct experiences by development professionals who spend a time, usually a few days and nights, living in poor communities with poor people. Pioneered in an organized form as the Exposure and Dialogue Programme by Karl Osner and others in Germany, practices have been spreading and emerging spontaneously in different forms. Senior managers in the World Bank have had their own programme. Perhaps the best known and most influential immersion or reality check was that of Ravi Kanbur, when he was directing the World Development Report 2000/01 in which part of his account was published (World Bank, 2000: 2). The trade union SEWA in India has internalized immersions as part of the induction for new staff, who now spend time living and working with their members. Some staff in the INGO ActionAid International practise immersions for their own learning: in the Western Region of Kenya, all 35 staff members have undertaken and experienced these reality checks twice a year, resulting in 'a huge change in the way we think, the way we work' (*pers.comm.* Ashish Shah August 2005).

To my knowledge, the third has not been repeated, but just might be a wave of the future. It is another form of immersion that had remarkable results. In 2002 SDC (the Swiss agency for Development and Cooperation) organized a four-week participatory and qualitative study of 26 poor households, with careful and sensi-tive training and facilitation. SDC staff spent entire days, from waking to sleeping, and without taking notes – to avoid distraction and so that their hands could be free – living and working with the families. There were striking insights such as how much more important shelter and the quality of housing were to poor people than had been supposed (Jupp 2003, 2004). For the researchers, the experience proved personally and professionally transformative. They reflected, for example, 'We had no idea what poverty was really like until we were involved in this study' and 'I thought I knew about village life as my roots are in the village and I still visit family in my village from time to time. But I know nothing about what it is like to be poor and how hidden this kind of poverty can be' (Jupp 2004: 4 and *pers comm.*). As Dee Jupp, the trainer and facilitator, observed, despite the risks, the outcomes of the exercise were extraordinary.

8.9   Participation, creativity and pluralism: a pro-poor paradigm?

One difficulty in writing this chapter has been a sense of an explosion of poverty-related participatory activities in recent years. Perhaps we development professionals, especially negative academics, have been so aware of bad practice in the name of participation that we have overlooked the trend of improving and at times brilliant innovative practice.[25] It is scattered, and often unconnected, and quite often short-lived. Much of it is by NGO staff and dispersed and isolated in small organizations and countries of the South. Much of it turns standard labelling and branding, central ownership and control, and the ego associated with these, on their heads.[26] There is a telling example in the history of Reflect. In its early days, after piloting, Reflect had a Mother Manual. But this was quickly abandoned. The idea of a centralized, standardized, detailed correct way of doing things was a paradigmatic misfit. It is the principles, not the details of practice, or even the label, that matter. Reflect in Nepal now has 16 different local names, each taking its own form with local ownership and fit (*pers comm.* Bimal Phnuyal). Similar isolated creativity and diversity are found with the work of consultants who innovate in a participatory mode. Unfortunately, the one-off nature of most consultancy means that they lack time, sponsorship or even inclination to reflect on, record, share or spread what they have evolved; and those who commissioned their work rarely provide for such activities. Instead they tick the box of satisfactory completion, and move on to other things. Much promising participatory innovation is, thus, isolated or still-born.

Using the word paradigm to mean concepts, ideas, perceptions, values, methods, behaviours and relationships which are mutually supporting and reinforcing, we can identify here an emergent paradigm of participation and pluralism, and, with it, of perceptions of poverty. Participation goes with changing power relations and behaviours, and sharing; pluralism goes with openness, mutual learning, eclectic improvisation and creativity; and a plurality of perceptions of poverty are those both of professionals and of people living in poverty. In this paradigm, it is the experience, conditions and realities of poor people, and their analysis and expression of these, that come first. For this to happen well, professional *un*learning has its part to play. As with PPAs, with sensitive and hidden topics, with nets or webs of disadvantage, with participatory numbers, and with listening, learning and immersions, the primary role of professionals is to convene, facilitate, learn and then later communicate. This is not to undervalue trained professional competences. It is not to substitute one fundamentalism for another. It is, rather, to correct an imbalance. It is to start in another place, upending the normal, and empowering those who lack power through enabling them to conduct their own analysis and supporting them. It is then that the diversity of deprivations becomes more evident, and the many forms that multidimensional poverty can take. It is then, too, that we may conclude that there is no one final best set of concepts, ideas, perceptions, methods or behaviours, but only continuous mixing, adoption, adaptation, improving, improvising and creativity, energized by commitment and informed by search, practice, doubt, and reflection. Participation and poverty both take many forms. And the potentials for combining them to enhance the well-being of those who suffer multiple deprivations have scarcely begun to be tapped. Poverty may never be made history. But we can ask whether a precondition for its sharp reduction is that powerful professionals become more participatory and get closer to and learn more from those who live their lives in poverty; and then act on what they experience, learn and feel.

Notes

1. For comments on an earlier version of this paper I am grateful to participants in the Conference on The Many Dimensions of Poverty at the International Poverty Centre, Brasilia, in August 2005. I thank Francisco Filho and Dee Donlan for support and assistance with the diagrams and editing.
2. I recognize that many usages are possible. In another context I used deprivation to encompass more than poverty. Poverty was 'a condition of lack of physical necessities, assets and income. It includes, but is more than, income-poverty. Poverty can be distinguished from other dimensions of deprivation'. Deprivation was 'lacking what is needed for well-being. Deprivation has dimensions which are physical, social, economic, political and psychological/spiritual. It includes forms of disadvantage such as social inferiority, physical weakness, isolation, poverty, vulnerability, powerlessness and humiliation. (Chambers 1997: xiv, xv).
3. For PPAs see Holland with Blackburn (1998) for accounts and analysis of Ghana, Zambia, South Africa and Mozambique; and Norton *et al.* (2001) and Robb (2002) for authoritative reviews.
4. For example, a group of seven schoolgirls in M'tendere Compound, Lusaka, matrix scored a typology of sex partners and preferences, with 16 categories of male partners scored against 5 criteria (Shah 1999: 52).
5. For the Internal Learning System see chapters by Nagasundari, Narendranath and Noponen in Brock, K. and Pettit, J. (eds) forthcoming *Springs of Participation*.
6. For a self-critical review of the process see Chambers (2002).
7. For a more extended analysis of the origins and process of developing these diagrams, see Chambers (2002: 147–8).
8. The web of disadvantages has been expanded and filled out from the same categories for sexuality by Susan Jolly (s.jolly@ids.ac.uk), and for transgender and for HIV/AIDS by Giuseppe Campuzano.
9. For more on the multiple adverse interactions of tropical seasonality for poor people see Robert Chambers, Richard Longhurst and Arnold Pacey (eds) (1981). *Seasonal Dimensions to Rural Poverty*, Frances Pinter, London (out of print). For an update in 1993, see Chapter 4 in my book *Challenging the Professions*, Intermediate Technology Publications, which also has a short bibliography. This remains a lamentably neglected subject despite its profound policy implications for pro-poor policy and practice.
10. This is not to suggest at all that this is a new insight. For the UK, for example, see Friedrich Engels, *The Conditions of the Working Class in England* (1845) and Charles Dickens, *Hard Times* (1854). The question is whether the multiple interactions of disadvantage which have spatial dimensions have been adequately appreciated by professionals.

11. The source is a video of a PRA training in Zambia in 1993, entitled *The PRA Report*, made by World Vision, Australia.
12. The authors refer at the end of this paragraph to Scarry (1985), but these conclusions also flow from their own analysis.
13. This was a repeated complaint in focus groups in the *Voices of the Poor* study (Narayan *et al.*, 2000: chapter 5).
14. For an attempt to summarize the benefits of quantification see Chambers (2003a).
15. For an early comparison with questionnaire approaches see Mukherjee (1995).
16. For an overview and sources in mid-2003, see Robert Chambers 'Participation and Numbers', *PLA Notes* 47, August 2003: 6–12, itself a revision and update of Chambers 2003a 'The Best of Both Worlds' in Kanbur (ed) *Q-Squared*, 2003: 35–45. See also Mayoux and Chambers (2005). These articles present more evidence and reference more sources than this current chapter which, however, includes some new material.
17. A rich source is the journal *PLA Notes* now *Participatory Learning and Action*. Other sources include the websites of the Statistical Services Centre at Reading University www.reading.ac.uk/ssc (accessed 19 October 2006) and of the Participation Group at the University of Sussex www.ids.ac.uk/ids/particip (accessed 19 October 2006) See also Mukherjee (2001).
18. Work of the Statistical Services Centre at Reading University can be found at www.reading.ac.uk/ssc.
19. The method is described in the sources. It would take too much space to describe it here.
20. A precise figure cannot be given for two reasons: the total number of discussion groups was not recorded for every country, though it was probably over 1,500 (Narayan *et al.*, 2000: 298–305); and not all discussion groups produced relevant comparable data suitable for analysis.
21. For an early treatment of wealth/well-being ranking see *RRA Notes, 15 Special Issue on Applications of Wealth Ranking*, (IIED, London, 1992).
22. See also Hargreaves *et al.* (2004b). The Hargreaves *et al.* sources also refer to Simanowitz and Nkuna (1998, 2000).
23. My assertion of accuracy would need a further paper. I would be delighted to discuss this with anyone who is interested. Earlier evidence was in my book *Whose Reality Counts?* (1997), chapters 6 and 7.
24. For an outline of the history of immersions, see Eyben (2004). Immersions have been promoted and provided by the Association for the Promotion of North–South Dialogue (www.exposure-nsd.de/engl.html). In 2006 ActionAid International (contact Sonya. ruparel@actionaid.org) trained facilitators and planned to provide immersion opportunities in initially nine countries.
25. For example, the book edited by Cooke and Kothari, *Participation: the New Tyranny?* (2001), focused on bad practices and drew attention away from evolving good practice and potentials, now, however, more recognized is its successor Hickey and Mohan (eds), *Participation: from Tyranny to Transformation?* (2004).
26. For an insightful reflection on ego and branding in the case of Reflect, see Archer (forthcoming).

References

Action Aid-Nepal (1992) Participatory Rural Appraisal Utilisation Survey Report Part 1. (Rural Development Area Sindhupalchowk, Monitoring and Evaluation Unit, ActionAid-Nepal, PO Box 3192, Kathmandu.
Archer, D. (forthcoming 2007) 'Seeds of Success are Seeds for Potential Failure: Learning from the Evolution of Reflect,' in Brock and Pettit (eds), *Springs of Participation*. Rugby: ITDG Publishing.

Archer, D. and K. Newman (compilers) (2006) *Communication and Power: Reflect Practical Resource Materials*. London N19 5PG: ActionAid, 2003 www.reflect-action.org. accessed 17 August 2006.

Archer, D. and N.M. Goreth (2004) 'Participation, Literacy and Empowerment: the Continuing Evolution of Reflect,' *Participatory Learning and Action*, 50, 35–44.

Barahona, C. and S. Levy (2003) *How to Generate Statistics and Influence Policy Using Participatory Methods in Research: Reflections from Malawi 1999–2002*, Working Paper 212. Brighton: IDS.

Beck, T. (1994) *The Experience of Poverty: Fighting for Respect and Resources in Village India*. London: Intermediate Technology Publications.

Booth, D., J. Holland, J. Hentschel, P. Lanjouw and A. Herbert (1998) *Participation and Combined Methods in African Poverty Assessment: Renewing the Agenda*. Report commissioned by DFID for the Working Group on Social Policy, Special Program of Assistance for Africa.

Brock, K. and R. McGee (eds) (2002) *Knowing Poverty: Critical Reflections on Participatory Research and Policy*. London and Sterling, VA: Earthscan.

Brock, K. and J. Pettit, (eds) (2007) *Springs of Participation*. Rugby, UK: Practical Action Publishing (formerly ITDG Publishing).

Campuzano, G. (forthcoming 2007) *Struggles for Transgender Rights in Peru*. (IDS Working Paper.

Chambers, R. (1997) *Whose Reality Counts? Putting the First Last*. Rugby, UK: ITDG Publications.

Chambers, R. (2002) 'Power, Knowledge and Policy Influence: Reflections on an Experience,' in Brock and McGee (eds), *Knowing Poverty*. London: Earthscan, pp. 135–65.

Chambers, R. (2003a) 'Qualitative Approaches: Self-criticism and What Can be Gained From Quantitative Approaches,' in Kanbur (ed.). Toronto: *Q-Squared*, pp. 22–7.

Chambers, R. (2003b) 'The Best of Both Worlds', in Kanbur (ed.). Toronto: *Q-Squared*, pp. 35–45.

Chambers, R. (2005) *Ideas for Development*. London and Sterling VA: Earthscan.

Cooke, B. and U. Kothari (eds) (2001) *Participation: the New Tyranny?* London, New York: Zed Books.

Cornwall, A. and A. Welbourn, (eds) (2002) *Realizing Rights: Transforming Approaches to Sexual and Reproductive Well-being*. London: Zed Books.

CPRC (2005) 'The Chronic Poverty Report 2004–05'. Chronic Poverty Research Centre, Institute for Development Policy and Management, University of Manchester, Manchester UK.

Cromwell, E., P. Kambewa R. Mwanza and R. Chirwa with KWERA Development Centre (2001) *Impact Assessment Using Participatory Approaches: 'Starter Pack' and Sustainable Agriculture in Malawi*. Network Paper No. 112, Agricultural Research and Extension Network, Overseas Development Institute, London.

Dickens, C. (1854) *Hard Times* (1854, reprinted 2004, New York, Bantam Classics and many others).

Education Action (2006) 1994–2006 continuing twice a year in four languages (ActionAid, London, www.reflect-action.org, accessed 17 August 2006).

Eldridge, C. (1995) 'Methodological Notes, Instructions to Facilitators, Household Responses to Drought Study in Malawi, Zambia, and Zimbabwe'. UK: Save the Children.

Eldridge, C. (1998) 'Summary of the Main Findings of a PRA Study on the 1992 Drought in Zimbabwe' (2001) UK: Save the Children.

Eldridge, C. (2001) *Investigating Change and Relationships in the Livelihoods of the Poor Using an Adaptation of Proportional Piling*. UK: Save the Children.

Engels, F. (1845) *The Conditions of the Working Class in England*. 1845, reprinted 1987, London: Penguin, and many others.

Estrella, M. with J. Blauert, D. Campilan, J. Gaventa, J. Gonsalves, I. Guijt, D. Johnson and R. Ricafort (eds) (2000) *Learning from Change: Issues and Experiences in Participatory Monitoring and Evaluation*. London: Intermediate Technology Publications.

Eyben, R. (2004) *Immersions for Policy and Personal Change*. IDS Policy Briefing Issue 22, IDS Sussex, UK, July.

Francke, M. (2003) 'Including the Poor Excluded People of Ayacucho in the Construction of the Truth: Reflections on Methods and Processes for the Realisation of Rights'. (Unpublished paper available from mfrancke@pucp.edu.pe.)

Guijt, I. (2000) 'Methodological Issues in Participatory Monitoring and Evaluation,' in Estrella with others (eds), *Learning from Change*, pp. 201–16.

Hargreaves, J.R, L. Morison, J.S.S. Gear, D.H Porter, M.B, Makhubele, J.C Kim, J. Buzsa, C. Watts, and P.M. Pronyk (2004a) 'Hearing the Voices of the Poor: Assigning Poverty Lines on the Basis of Local Perceptions of Poverty: a Quantitative Analysis of Qualitative Data from Participatory Wealth Ranking in Rural South Africa'. Paper presented to Q-Squared in Practice: a conference on experiences combining qualitative and quantitative methods in poverty appraisal, Toronto, 15–16 May.

Hargreaves, J.R, L. Morison, J.S.S. Gear, D.H. Porter, M.B. Makhubele, J.C. Kim, J. Buzsa, C. Watts and P.M. Pronyk (2004b) 'The Assessment of Household Wealth in Health Studies in Developing Countries; a Comparison of Participatory Wealth Ranking and Survey Techniques from South Africa' typescript (correspondence to James Hargreaves, Clinical Research Unit, London School of Hygiene and Tropical medicine, Keppel St, London WC1E 7HT email jimharg@soft.co.za).

Hartmann, B. and J. Boyce (1983) *A Quiet Violence: View from a Bangladesh Village*. London: Zed Press.

Haswell, M. (1975) *The Nature of Poverty: a Case History of the First Quarter-century after World War II*. London and Basingstoke: Macmillan.

Hickey, S. and G. Mohan, (eds) (2004) *Participation: From Tyranny to Transformation?* London and New York: Zed Books.

Holland, J. with J. Blackburn (eds) (1998) *Whose Voice? Participatory Research and Policy change*. London: IT Publications.

IDS Participation Group (2005) 'Immersions and Reality Checks', source materials (available from Jane Stevens, Participation Group, Institute of Development Studies, Sussex BN1 9RE, UK j.stevens@ids.ac.uk.

International HIV/AIDS Alliance (2003) *Developing HIV/AIDS Work with Drug Users: a Guide to Participatory Assessment and Response*. Brighton: International HIV/AIDS Alliance.

Irvine, R., R. Chambers and R. Eyben (2004) Learning from Poor People's Experience: Immersions, Lessons for Change in Policy and Organisations No. 13. Brighton: IDS.

Jayakaran, R. (2002) *The Ten Seed Technique*, World Vision, China. (ravi_jayakaran@wvi.org).

Jayakaran, R. (2003) Participatory Poverty Alleviation and Development, a comprehensive manual for development professionals', World Vision, China. (ravi_jayakaran@wvi.org).

Jolly, S. (2006) 'Sexuality and Development', *IDS Policy Briefing* Issue 29, April 2006, http://www.ids.ac.uk/ids/bookshop/briefs/PB29.pdf (accessed 17 August 2006).

Joseph, S. (2005) *Rwanda Ubudehe: Local Collective Action*, updated June 2005, Kigali, Rwanda.

Jupp, D. (2003) *Views of the Poor: the Perspective of Rural and Urban poor in Tanzania as Recounted Through Their Stories and Pictures*, Swiss Agency for Development and Cooperation, Berne, May.

Jupp, D. (2004)'Views of the Poor: Some Thoughts on How to Involve Your Own Staff to Conduct Quick, Low Cost but Insightful Research into Poor People's Perspectives' (available on request from djupp@btinternet.com.

Kanbur, R. (2000) 'Basrabai's story', in *Attacking Poverty*. Washington DC: World Bank; Oxford: Oxford University Press.

Kanbur, R. (ed.) (2003) *Q-Squared: Qualitative and Quantitative Methods of Poverty Appraisal*. Permanent Black, D-28 Oxford Apartments, 11, I.P. Extension, Delhi 110092.

Kar, K. (2003) *Subsidy or Self-respect? Participatory Total Community Sanitation in Bangladesh*, Working Paper 184. Brighton: IDS.

Kar, K. and K. Pasteur (2005) *Subsidy or Self-Respect? Community Led Total Sanitation. An Update on Recent Developments*, Working Paper 257. Brighton: Institute of Development Studies.

Levy, S. (2003) Are we Targeting the Poor? Lessons from Malawi', *PLA Notes* 47, 19–24.

Li, X. *et al.* (2002) *Preparing a Methodology for Development Planning in Poverty Alleviation under the New Poverty Strategy of PRC*, ADB/TA3610-PRC. Manila: Asian Development Bank.

Li, X., J. Remenyi, Sibin W. LiZhou, Z. Chuntai, and L. Yonggong (2004) 'Who's Poverty? Making Poverty Mapping and Monitoring Participatory', typescript. College of Humanities and Development, China Agricultural University.

MacGillivray, A., C. Weston and C. Unsworth (1998) *Communities Count! a Step by Step Guide to Community Sustainability Indicators*. London: New Economics Foundation.

Mander, H. (2001) *Unheard Voices: Stories of forgotten Lives*. New Delhi, London, New York, Victoria, Toronto, Auckland: Penguin Books.

Marsland, N., I.M. Wilson, S. Abeyasekera and U.K. Kleih (2000) *A Methodological Framework for Combining Quantitative and Qualitative Survey Methods: Statistical Guide*. Statistical Services Centre, University of Reading, Reading UK www.reading.ac.uk/ssc.

May, J. with H. Attwood, P. Ewang, F. Lund, A. Norton and W. Wentzal (1998) *Experience and Perceptions of Poverty in South Africa*. Final Report of the South African PPA. Durban: Praxis Publishing.

Mayoux, L. and R. Chambers (2005) 'Reversing the Paradigm: Quantification, Participatory Methods and Pro-poor Impact Assessment', *Journal of International Development*, 17, 271–98.

McCarthy, J. with K. Galvao (2004) *Enacting Participatory Development: Theatre-based Techniques*. London and Sterling, VA: Earthscan.

McGee, R. with J. Levene and A. Hughes (2002) *Assessing Participation in Poverty Reduction Strategy Papers: a Desk-based Synthesis of Experience in Sub-Saharan Africa* IDS Research Report 52. Brighton: IDS.

Mda, Z. (1983) *When People Play People: Development Communication Through Theatre*. London: Zed Books.

Moser, C. and J. Holland, (1997) *Urban Poverty and Violence in Jamaica*, World Bank Latin American and Caribbean Studies Viewpoints. Washington DC: World Bank.

Moser, C. and C. McIlwaine (2000) *Urban Poor Perceptions of Violence and Exclusion in Colombia*, Latin American and Caribbean Region, Environmentally and Socially Sustainable Development Sector Management Unit. Washington DC: World Bank.

Moser, C. and C. McIlwaine (2001) *Violence in a Post-Conflict World: Urban Poor Perceptions from Guatemala*, Latin America and Caribbean Region, Environmentally and Socially Sustainable Development Sector Management Unit. Washington, DC: World Bank.

Moser, C. and C. McIlwaine, (2004) *Encounters with Violence in Latin America: Urban Poor Perceptions from Colombia and Guatemala*. New York and London: Routledge.

Mukherjee, N. (1995) *Participatory Rural Appraisal and Questionnaire Survey: Comparative Field Experience and Methodological Innovations*. Concept Publishing Company, A/15-16, Commercial Block, Mohan Garden, New Delhi 110059.

Mukherjee, N. (2001) *Participatory Learning and Action – with 100 field methods* Concept Publishing Company, A/15-16, Commercial Block, Mohan Garden New Delhi 110059.

Narayan, D., R. Chambers, M.K. Shah and P. Petesch (2000) *Voices of the Poor: Crying Out for Change*. Oxford: Oxford University Press for the World Bank.

Norton, A. with B. Bird, K. Brock, M. Kakande, and C. Turk (2001) *A Rough Guide to PPAs: Participatory Poverty Assessment – an Introduction to Theory and Practice*. London: Overseas Development Institute.

Parasuraman, S., K.R. Gomathy, and B. Fernandez B. (2006) *Listening to People Living in Poverty*. Books for Change, 139 Richmond Road, Bangalore 560 025 www.booksforchange.net (2003) accessed 19 October.

PLA Notes (2006) (formerly *RRA Notes*, and now *Participatory Learning and Action*), triannual, (International Institute for Environment and Development, 3 Endsleigh Street, London WC1H ODD. Email sustag@iied.org Website www.iied.org) Accessed 18 Aug 2006.

PLA Mapping for Change: Practice, Technologies and Communication (Participatory Learning and Action 54, April 2006).

PRA Report Video (Video by World Vision, Australia, of a PRA Training in Zambia 1993).

PRAXIS (2001) *The Politics of Poverty: a Tale of the Living Dead in Bolangir*. Bangalore: Books for Change.

Reason, P. and H. Bradbury (eds) (2001) *Handbook of Action Research: Participative Inquiry and Practice*. London, Thousand Oaks, New Delhi: Sage Publications.

Remenyi, J. (forthcoming) 'Poverty Analysis, Poverty Mapping and Participation in China' in K. Brock and J. Pettit, (eds), *Springs of Participation*. Rugby, UK: ITDG Publishing.

Robb, C. (2002) *Can the Poor Influence Policy? Participatory Poverty Assessments in the Developing World*. Washington DC: The World Bank and International Monetary Fund.

RRA Notes 15 (1992) *Special Issue on Applications of Wealth Ranking*. London: International Institute for Environment and Development.

Scarry, E. (1985) *The Body in Pain: the Making and Unmaking of the World*. New York: Oxford University Press (cited in Parasuraman *et al.*).

Sen, A. (1999) *Development as Freedom*. Oxford: Oxford University Press.

Shah, M.K. (1999) 'A Step-by step Guide to Popular PLA Tools and Techniques', Chapter 2 in Shah *et al.* (eds), *Embracing Participation in Development*.

Shah, M., S. Kaul, D. Kambou and B. Monahan (eds) (1999) *Embracing Participation in Development: Worldwide Experience from CARE's Reproductive Health Programs*. USA: CARE, 151 Ellis Street, Atlanta, Georgia 30303.

Simanowitz, A. and B. Nkuna (1998) *Participatory Wealth Ranking Operational Manual*. Small Enterprise Foundation, Tzaneen, South Africa (contact a.simanowitz@ids.ac.uk).

Simanowitz, A., B. Nkuna and S. Kasim (1996) Overcoming the Obstacles to Identifying the Poorest Families, unpublished Report (contact a.simanowitz@ids.ac.uk).

UNDP, Bangladesh (1996) *UNDP's 1996 Report on Human Development in Bangladesh, Volume 3 Poor people's perspectives*. Dhaka: UNDP.

Walker, S. and Matin, I. (2006) 'Changes in the Lives of the Ultra Poor: an exploratory Study', *Development in Practice* 16(4), 80–4.

Welbourn, A. (1995) *Stepping Stones: a training Package on Gender, HIV, Communication and Relationship Skills*. Manual and video, Strategies for Hope. London: ActionAid.

Welbourn, A. (2002) 'Gender, Sex and HIV: How to Address Issues That No One Wants to Hear About', in Cornwall and Welbourn (eds), *Realizing Rights*. New York: Zed Books, pp. 99–112.

White, S. and Pettit, J. (2004) 'Participatory Methods and the Measurement of Well-being', *Participatory Learning and Action 50*, 88–96.

White, S. and Pettit, J. (2006) 'Participatory Approaches and the Measurement of Human Well-being', in Mark McGillivray (ed.) *Human Well-Being: Concept and Measurement*. London: Palgrave Macmillan.

World Bank (2000) *Attacking Poverty: World Development Report 2000/01*. New York: Oxford University Press for the World Bank.

9

A Human Rights-Based Approach to Poverty: The South African Experience

Linda Jansen van Rensburg

> Poverty is a human rights violation, and freedom from poverty is an integral and inalienable human right.
>
> United Nations Development Programme, January 1998

9.1   Introduction: a human rights-based approach to poverty

There exist numerous definitions of poverty. Traditionally, poverty has been associated with a lack of resources.[1] The more recent concept of social exclusion[2] is now no longer seen as an alternative to the poverty concept, but as a more comprehensive concept, which concerns much more than money. In fact, poverty (referring to a lack of disposable income) can be seen as part of the multidimensional and dynamic concept of social exclusion (referring to multifaceted failure). Social exclusion, therefore, has to be understood with reference to the failure of any one or more of the following: (i) the democratic and legal system (civic integration); (ii) the labour market (economic integration); (iii) the welfare state system (social integration); and (iv) the family and community system (interpersonal integration).[3]

Conversely, social participation, being the positive counterpart of social exclusion, is to be determined with reference to all four systems.[4] Or, as an ILO/UNDP study remarks, the notion of social exclusion links together both social rights and material deprivation. It encompasses not only the lack of access to goods and services, which underlie poverty and basic needs satisfaction, but also exclusion from security, justice, representation and citizenship.[5] It concerns inequality in many dimensions – economic, social, political, and cultural.[6]

UNICEF[7] describes poverty as follows:

> *Poverty is a denial of human rights*[8] *and human dignity*. It means not having a good primary school or health centre to go to and not having access to safe drinking water or adequate sanitation. It means insecurity, powerlessness, exposure to violence and discrimination and exclusion from the mainstream of society. It also means not having a voice to influence decision-making, living at the margin of society and being stigmatized. *Obviously, poverty reduction involves more than crossing an income threshold.*[9]

A broad definition of poverty as 'the lack of basic capabilities to live in dignity'[10] seems to be the most appropriate for purposes of this chapter.

The above description of poverty and social exclusion clearly recognizes that poverty constitutes a denial of human rights and human dignity.[11] A human rights-based approach provides legal protection for basic human dignity.[12] Human dignity is, for example, considered to be one of the core constitutional values in the Constitution of the Republic of South Africa 1996.[13] The universal aim and basis for the existence of rights pertaining to poverty is to protect a person's right to human dignity.[14] Accordingly, in South Africa, human dignity, as a fundamental constitutional value[15] as well as a fundamental right[16] contained in the Bill of Rights, plays a very important role with regard to fundamental rights of the poor and the equal treatment of those who are historically deprived.[17]

UNICEF[18] describes a human rights-based approach as follows:

> A human rights-based approach means that the situation of poor people is viewed not only in terms of welfare outcomes but also in terms of *the obligation to prevent and respond to human rights violations*. For example, any action that excludes a specific group of children from school or discriminates against girls constitutes such a violation. The human rights approach aims to empower families and communities to secure assistance and advocates a fair and just distribution of income and assets.[19]

In other words, a human rights-based approach implies protection by law of fundamental freedoms and entitlements needed for a decent standard of living.[20] This implies that a number of rights may be infringed at a given moment when the situation of poor people is viewed.[21] For example, denying squatters access to housing rights also implies that there is an infringement on their rights to health, human dignity, water, food, freedom from discrimination and, depending on the circumstances, social assistance. This is a typical situation where poor people are socially excluded, marginalized and placed in a vulnerable position and therefore seek social protection from the state.

I thus propose that when the fundamental rights relating to poverty are infringed, such a person needs social protection. The type of social protection will differ depending on the type of right that has been infringed upon. For example, when a person's right to social assistance is denied, such a person is entitled to some kind of social grant. Social protection is usually connected to social security, but has a much wider meaning. The primary objective of social security – and especially social assistance – is to combat poverty. The definition that is going to be suggested will cover a much broader terrain of poverty issues and may in fact be seen as a method to address poverty. It must be kept in mind that the package that will be suggested will be entitlements and not welfare measures since we are working from a human rights-based approach.

9.2   The case of South Africa

South Africa is an upper-middle-income country, but despite this relative wealth, the experience of most South African households is that of outright poverty or of continuing vulnerability to being poor.[22] The main reason for this is the fact that Apartheid has left South Africa with an exceptionally divided society, with extensive social and economic inequality.[23] A consequence of this social and economic inequality is that the distribution of income and wealth in South Africa is among the most unequal in the world, and many households still have unsatisfactory access to education, health care, energy and clean water, as well as to wealth-generating assets and opportunities.[24]

To address the problems of poverty, a human rights-based approach may be used. I have chosen South Africa to serve as an example of how such an approach may be applied for the following reasons.

First, as indicated above, many South African households face outright poverty and the distribution of income and wealth in South Africa is among the most unequal in the world.[25]

Secondly, South Africa lacks a comprehensive social protection system aimed at combating poverty. Permanent social assistance grants in South Africa are highly categorized. It only covers children from infancy to 14 years (Child Support Grant), children in foster care (Foster Child Grant), people with disabilities (Disability Grant), children with disabilities (Care Dependency Grant) and the elderly (Old Age Grant). In addition to the Old Age and Disability Grant, one can apply for a Grant-in-Aid. This entire grant system is subject to a strict means test under the new Social Assistance Act 13 of 2004.[26] There are no social assistance grants available for people without disabilities from the age of 14 to 60/65, depending on whether you are a women or a man. This implies that a large section of the population is still excluded from the social security (or protection) programme which serves as the main safety net in South Africa, if one is not contributing to the Unemployment Fund or the Compensation for Occupational Sickness and Diseases Fund (Social Insurance) or to any private scheme.

Thirdly, South Africa has a unique Constitution that contains a number of 'fundamental rights for the poor'.[27] These rights are justiciable and have been positively enforced by the highest court on constitutional matters in South Africa, namely the Constitutional Court.[28]

I will now discuss the fundamental rights of the poor as contained in the South African Constitution. Then I will examine the way the South African Constitutional Court is prepared to enforce the rights of the poor by way of a rights-based approach. The aim is to establish to what extent the courts may enforce the fundamental rights of the poor when a government fails to realize programmes and policies (international or national) aimed at alleviating poverty in a particular country. Weaknesses and strengths will be deducted from the South African experience in order to make recommendations on how the rights-based approach may be used in other foreign and (possibly) international jurisdictions.

A committee appointed by the cabinet recently developed a definition for social protection that is adapted to the unique circumstances of South Africa. The report by the Committee of Inquiry into a Comprehensive System of Social Security for South Africa[29] suggested that the current categorized social security system must be phased out. The Committee indicated that the current social security system in South Africa is unequal, exclusionary and inequitable and will not stand the test of reasonableness as defined in the *Grootboom* case.[30] The Committee further stressed the importance of compliance of the social security system with international standards.[31] The Committee suggested a comprehensive social protection (CSP) package in the place of the current categorized social security system.

> Comprehensive social protection is broader than the traditional concept of social security, and incorporates development strategies and programmes[32] designed to ensure, collectively, at least a minimum acceptable living standard for all citizens. It embraces the traditional measures of social insurance, social assistance and social services, but goes beyond that to focus on causality through an integrated policy approach including many of the developmental initiatives undertaken by the state.[33]

The committee further developed 'minimum' requirements for the comprehensive social protection package (CSP). It remarks that CSP will work through a variety of mechanisms, embracing a package of social protection interventions and measures. In identifying the practical aspects of such an approach, and taking into account necessary adaptations for South Africa, the Committee has arrived at the following measures: (i) measures to address 'income poverty' (provision of minimum income); (ii) measures to address 'capability poverty' (provision of certain basic services); (iii) measures to address 'asset poverty' (income-generating assets) and (iv) measures to address 'special needs' (for example, disability or child support).

In the CSP package, the first three are core elements of the CSP basic platform that should be available to all South Africans and certain categories of noncitizens. In general, so the Committee opines, these components need to be established as a universal-as-possible package of income transfers, services and access provided in a non-work-related manner and whose availability is not primarily dependent on the ability to pay.[34] A minimum level or measure of provision should be made available to everyone. The key components of this relate to the (eventual) introduction of a Basic Income Grant, the immediate extension of the Child Support Grant to gradually cover children under the age of 18, and maintaining the state Old Age Grant. The scrapping of the means test across the board is also recommended.

Other elements of the package include, amongst others, free health care (the Committee advocates the eventual introduction of a National Health Insurance system), free primary and secondary education, free water and sanitation, free electricity, access to affordable and adequate housing, access to jobs and skills training, and a reformed disability grant, foster care grant and child dependence grant.[35]

It is clear that the social protection package suggested by the Committee entails not only a human rights-based approach to development but also a rights-based approach to respect and uphold the human dignity of the poor by providing him or her with their basic needs.

9.3   Fundamental rights of the poor in the South African Constitution

> Civil and political rights cannot prevail if socioeconomic rights are ignored, and stability of political democracy depends on the extent of balance between the two groups of rights.[36]

Along with the birth of the final Constitution and the Bill of Rights came the existence of 'fundamental rights for the poor'. These are rights placing an obligation on the state to act positively in favour of everyone – especially the poor, marginalized and vulnerable. Socioeconomic rights, and specifically those rights pertaining to the alleviation of poverty, are contained in different sections of the Bill of Rights. Section 27(1)(c) states that 'everyone has the right to have access to social security, including, if they are unable to support themselves and their dependants, appropriate social assistance'. Section 27(1)(c) makes direct reference to the concept of social protection, as a measure to combat poverty. As already indicated social protection is a measure that combats social exclusion, poverty, marginalisation and vulnerability.

Other provisions in the Bill of Rights make indirect reference to the concept of social protection as a measure to combat poverty. Section 26 grants everyone the right to have access to adequate housing while section 27(1)(a) provides for the right to access to health care services, including reproductive health care; and section 27(1)(b) provides for the right to access to sufficient food and water.

Textually linked[37] to sections 26(1) and 27(1) respectively are sections 26(2) and 27(2) which internally limit the obligation of the state to only take reasonable legislative and other measures, within its available resources, to achieve the progressive realization of [this] right'.[38] Section 29 further provides that everyone has the right (i) to a basic education, including adult basic education; and (ii) to further education, which the state must take reasonable measures to make progressively available and accessible.

Section 28 specifically addresses the socioeconomic rights of children. Section 28(1)(c) grants every child the right to basic nutrition, shelter, basic health care services and social services. It does, however, not contain a similar qualification as contained in section 26(2) and 27(2) concerning 'reasonable measures' and 'progressive realization'.

9.4   South African jurisprudence

This section explains the importance of the human rights-based approach followed by the South African Constitutional Court in the protection of the rights of the poor. Traditionally, it has been argued that the Courts cannot enforce socioeconomic rights because it is expected that the Courts will not interfere in government policy. An example of this is where the Court orders an organ of state to act positively. It is therefore, highly commendable that the South African Constitutional Court on several occasions acknowledged these positive obligations of the state.

9.4.1 Government of the Republic of South Africa and others v Grootboom and others

9.4.1.1 Facts of the case

The *Grootboom* case raised the state's obligations under section 26 of the Constitution, which gives everyone the right to access to adequate housing, and section 28(1)(c), which affords children the right to shelter. The respondent in this case, Mrs Grootboom, was one of a group of 510 children and 390 adults living in appalling circumstances in Wallacedene informal settlement. They illegally occupied nearby land earmarked for low-cost housing, but were forcibly evicted; their shacks were bulldozed and burnt and their possessions destroyed in the process. The land they had occupied in Wallacedene had been taken over by others and in desperation they settled on the sports field and in an adjacent community hall.

9.4.1.2 Considering international law

9.4.1.2.1 Similarity between Sections 26(2) and 27(2) of the South African Constitution and Article 2(1) of the International Covenant on Economic Social and Cultural Rights (CESCR).
Section 26(2) states that the state must take reasonable legislative and other measures, within its available resources, to achieve the progressive realization of each of these rights. Almost the same formulation and phrasing are found in article 2(1) of the ICESCR. The observations and comments of the supervisory committee of the ICESCR (namely the Committee on Economic, Social and Cultural Rights) may serve as a valuable source for interpreting the South African provisions.

9.4.1.2.2 International similarities and deviation.
Sections 26(2) and 27(2) of the South African Constitution state that the state must realize the rights 'within its available resources', as opposed to the language of the Covenant which states 'to the maximum of its available resources'.

The United Nation Committee on Economic Social and Cultural Rights (UNCSECR) is of the opinion that if the state is a developing country or is experiencing some economic difficulties, it must at least realize minimum core obligations. The UNCESCR makes the following statement with regard to minimum core obligations.

> The Committee is of the view that a minimum core obligation to ensure the satisfaction of, at the very least, minimum essential levels of each of the rights is incumbent upon every State Party.[39]

The UNCESCR further states that:

> If the Covenant were to be read in such a way as to not establish such a minimum core obligation, it would largely be deprived of its *raison d'être*.[40]

> The failure by the state to provide for the basic subsistence needs of the population and in effect the fundamental rights of the poor may be considered as a *prima facie* violation of the Covenant.[41]

The South African Constitutional Court noted that the General Comment of the UNCESCR does not specify precisely the meaning of 'minimum core'.[42] The Court further stressed that the minimum core obligation is determined generally by having regard to the needs of the most vulnerable group that is entitled to the protection of the right in question. It is in this context that the concept of minimum core obligations must be understood in international law.

The Court argued that it is not possible to determine the minimum threshold for South African purposes due to the fact that, unlike the UNCESCR, the Court does not have comparable information.[43] The Court mentioned that the UNCESCR developed the concept of 'minimum core' over the course of many years of examining reports submitted by individual states.[44] The Court therefore concluded that the real question in terms of the South African Constitution is whether the measures taken by the state to realize social rights are reasonable.[45] For these reasons the Court deviated from the recognized international principle of minimum core obligation.

9.4.1.2.3   Reasonableness and fundamental values.

The Court then went further and interpreted the relevant limitation by considering reasonableness. First of all, the Court stated that the court will not enquire whether other more desirable or favourable measures could have been adopted, or whether public money could have been better spent.[46] The Court stressed further that the policies and programmes must be reasonable both in their conception and their implementation.[47] The Court stated further that.

> Reasonableness must also be understood in the context of the Bill of Rights as a whole. A society must seek to ensure that the basic necessities of life are provided to all if it is to be a society based on human dignity, freedom and equality. To be reasonable, measures cannot leave out of account the degree and extent of the denial of the right they endeavour to realize. Those whose needs are the most urgent and whose ability to enjoy all rights therefore is most in peril, must not be ignored by the measures aimed at achieving realization of the right. It may not be sufficient to meet the test of reasonableness to show that the measures are capable of achieving a statistical advance in the realization of the right. Furthermore, the Constitution requires that everyone must be treated with care and concern. If the measures, though statistically successful, fail to respond to the needs of those most desperate, they may not pass the test.[48]

9.4.1.2.4   Progressive realization.

The UNCESCR summarizes the position of the 'progressive realization' of socioeconomic rights as follows:

> On the other hand, the phrase must be read in the light of the overall objective, indeed the *raison d'être*, of the Covenant which is to establish clear obligations for State parties in respect of the full realization of the rights in question. It thus imposes an obligation to move as expeditiously and effectively as possible towards the goal.[49]

The UNCESCR further mentions that:

> ...any deliberately retrogressive measures would require the most careful consideration and would need to be fully justified by reference to the totality of the rights provided for in the Covenant and in the context of the full use of the maximum of available resources.[50]

It then states that the ultimate objective of the Covenant is the 'full realization'[51] of the rights. The fact that the 'full realization' is subject to the condition of progressiveness is merely a recognition of the fact that the full realization of all socioeconomic rights will generally not be able to be achieved in a short period of time.

In the *Grootboom* case, the court drew on the UNCESCR's interpretation of the phrase 'progressive realization'. The court stated that 'progressive realization' contemplates that rights cannot be realized immediately, but that the goal of the Constitution is for the basic needs of all in our society to be met effectively; the requirement of progressive realization means that the state must take steps to achieve this goal.

9.4.1.3   *Priority to the most vulnerable*

As already indicated, the Court remarked that a society must seek to ensure that the basic necessities of life are provided to all if it is to be a society based on human dignity, freedom and equality. In this case the Court revealed a hesitant, context-sensitive approach by taking the position of the weakest members of society into account when deciding whether policies of the government are reasonable.[52] This confirms that socioeconomic transformation cannot always occur overnight and that in some cases formal equality and identical treatment must be postponed in order to avoid unnecessary harm to the weakest and poorest members of society.

It is clear that the Court makes use of the constitutional values in the Constitution to give content to socioeconomic rights.[53] When investigating an infringement of a specific socioeconomic right, such investigation must take place in conjunction with all other socioeconomic rights in the Bill of Rights. The Court emphasizes that socioeconomic rights must not be seen in isolation from one another. They must thus be read within the Constitution as a whole.[54]

The conclusion can be made that the state cannot realize all the rights of the poor immediately, and that the Courts must keep this in mind, and that the material needs of those persons who are the most vulnerable ought to enjoy priority.[55] It is a difficult task to determine the infringement of a particular socioeconomic right and each specific situation of alleged infringement must be evaluated on a case-by-case basis.[56] It is clear from the *Grootboom* case that the Courts will more readily interfere, where it appears that the state has not realized the basic needs of a vulnerable group.

9.4.1.4   *Decision of the Court*

The Court made a declaratory order requiring the state to fulfill its obligations in terms of section 26. Section 26(2) of the Constitution requires the state to devise and implement within its available resources a comprehensive and coordinated programme progressively to realize the right of access to adequate housing. This includes the obligation to devise, fund, implement and supervise measures to provide relief to those in desperate need.[57]

9.4.2   Minister of Health and others v Treatment Action Campaign and others 2002 (10) BCLR 1033 (CC)

9.4.2.1   Facts of the case

This case deals with the provision of anti-retroviral drugs to pregnant mothers that would not otherwise have the means to afford them. The case was based on section 27(1)(a) of the Bill of Rights, which determines that everyone has the right to access to health care, including reproductive health care. Section 27(1)(a), like most other socioeconomic rights in the Bill of Rights, is limited by the following provision contained in section 27(2), namely that the state must take reasonable legislative and other measures, within its available resources, to progressively realize these rights.

Only three remarks on this case will be made. First, the way the court interpreted section 27; secondly, the approach of the court towards the consideration of international law; and thirdly, the boundaries of judicial activism in this particular judgement.

9.4.2.2   Interpretation of section 27

In line with the *Grootboom* decision, the Court denies the existence of the international law principle of 'minimum core entitlement' or basic minimum realization of every socioeconomic right. The Court interprets this as part of the question as to whether the state had a reasonable programme to realize socioeconomic rights.[58] The Court indicates that the court is

> ...not institutionally equipped to make the wide-ranging factual and political enquiries necessary for determining what the minimum-core standards called for by the first and second *amici*[59]

The Court recognizes its inability to consider social and economic factors and further notes that a court is not in the position to make orders that can have social and economic consequences for the community.[60]

The Court's contention that it is impossible to give everyone access even to a 'core' service has immediate merit. At least the court in this specific case indicated that government programmes must at least satisfy the basic needs of the most vulnerable. Unfortunately, courts as adjudicating forums can only enforce those rights that are alleged by a specific party in a specific case. This has the implication that other members of the community, whose basic need of access to socioeconomic rights are infringed but who do not have the resources to approach the courts, cannot be satisfied.

It must, however, be stressed that it is the minimum core approach that provides economic and social rights with a determinacy and certainty.[61] It is suggested that nothing prevents the Court from giving instructions to executive and legislative authorities[62] to start with programmes and to identify the 'minimum core obligation' of each right. This, however, again requires a specific party in a specific case alleging infringement of a socioeconomic right.

9.4.2.3   Boundaries of judicial activism

One positive step by the Court is the way in which the court views the doctrine of the separation of powers. The Court acknowledges that

> ...there are no bright lines that separate the roles of the legislature, the executive and the courts from one another, there are certain matters that are pre-eminently within the domain of one or other of the arms of government and not the others.

The Court further acknowledges that the different spheres of government must respect each other's different functions, but recognizes that the Court may make orders to impact on policy.[63] The Court[64] elaborates further that if state policy is inconsistent with the Constitution, the Court has to examine this to comply with its Constitutional duties. If the executive act is inconsistent with the Constitution, it can be considered as an intrusion mandated by the Constitution itself.

9.4.2.4   Decision by the Court

The Court made a declaratory order requiring government to devise and implement within its available resources a comprehensive and co-ordinated programme to realize progressively the rights of pregnant women and their newborn children to have access to health services to combat mother-to-child transmission of HIV. The programme must include reasonable measures for counselling and testing pregnant women for HIV, counselling HIV-positive pregnant women on the options open to them to reduce the risk of mother-to-child transmission of HIV, and making appropriate treatment available to them for such purposes.[65]

9.4.3   Khosa and Others v Minister of Social Development and Others; Mahlaule and Another v Minister of Social Development and Others 2004 (6) BCLR 569 (CC)

9.4.3.1   Facts of the case

In a most recent case, *Khosa and Others v Minister of Social Development and Others; Mahlaule and Another v Minister of Social Development and Others*[66] the Court addressed the constitutionality of some of the provisions in the Social Assistance Act 59 of 1992[67] and the requirements to qualify for some of the grants in the grant administration process in South Africa.

The applicants in both cases are permanent residents. The applicant in the *Khosa* case challenged section 3(c) of the Social Assistance Act 59 of 1992 because it only reserves grants for the elderly for South African citizens and thereby excludes permanent residents. In the *Mahluale* case section 4(b)(ii) and 4(B)(ii) of the Social Assistance Act 59 of 1992 was challenged because it only reserves child support grants and care-dependency grants for South African citizens again, excluding permanent residents. The applicants in both matters would qualify for social assistance, except for the fact that they did not meet the citizenship requirement.[68] Because the two matters are related and involve similar considerations and arguments of law, they had been heard together both in the High Court and the Constitutional Court.[69] The Constitutional Court found these provisions to be unconstitutional emphasizing the fact that permanent residents are a vulnerable group and they need special constitutional protection.

Only three remarks on this case will be made. First, reference will be made to the intersecting rights (so-called special approach) the Court refers to in its interpretation of the rights of a particular poor and socially excluded group. Secondly, reference will be made to the objects and aims of social assistance. Thirdly, reference will be made to the way in which the Court examines the social expenditure budget along with the drastic remedy the Court gives with relation to the argument of judicial activism.

9.4.3.2   Intersecting rights

The Court referred to the foundational values in the Constitution – namely human dignity, equality and freedom.[70] It recognized that all rights are interdependent, mutually related and equally important and emphasized that this specific case concerned intersecting rights which reinforce one another at the point of intersection.[71] The implication of this remark in this particular case is the fact that a number of rights are alleged to be infringed and this requires that the Court adopts a special approach. The Court[72] comments that:

> when the rights to life, dignity and equality are implicated in cases dealing with socioeconomic rights, they have to be taken into account along with the availability of human and financial resources in determining whether the state has complied with the constitutional standard of reasonableness. This is, however, not a closed list and all relevant factors have to be taken into account in this exercise. What is relevant may vary from case to case depending on the particular facts and circumstances. What makes this case different from other cases that have previously been considered by this Court is that, *in addition to the rights to life and dignity, the social-security scheme put in place by the state to meet its obligations under section 27 of the Constitution raises the question of the prohibition of unfair discrimination.*[73]

The Court remarked that where the state argues that they cannot afford to pay benefits to everyone entitled under section 27(1)(c) the criteria for excluding a specific group, for example permanent residents, must be consistent with the Bill of Rights as a whole.[74] As indicated, the state chose to differentiate between citizens and non-citizens in their Social Assistance legislation. The Court[75] remarked that this differentiation must be constitutionally valid and cannot be arbitrary, irrational or manifest a naked preference.

There must be a rational connection between differentiating law and the legitimate government purpose it is designed to achieve. A differentiating law or action which does not meet these standards will be in violation of section 9(1) and section 27(2) of the Constitution.

It is clear from the Court's approach that when it comes to the infringement of the rights of the poor it is possible that civil and political rights such as human dignity and equality can also be infringed, along with the typical rights of the poor or so-called socioeconomic rights.

9.4.3.3   The objects and aims of social assistance

The Court further referred to the testimony of the Director-General of the Department of Social Development that described the object of social assistance legislation as (i) a strategy to combat poverty, (ii) to realize the objectives of the Constitution and the Reconstruction and Development Plan and (iii) to comply with South Africa's international obligations.[76]

The Court further remarked that the aim of social security – and especially social assistance – is to ensure that society values human beings by providing them with their basic needs.[77] This statement is of particular relevance for the human rights-based approach and the protection such an approach must provide in order to protect the human dignity of the poor.[78] The Court states explicitly that the effect of excluding permanent residents from the social assistance system is that it limits their rights and fundamentally affects their dignity and equality.[79] As proposed, a social protection system is one way to respect and protect and realize the rights of the poor.

9.4.3.4   Judicial activism

Regarding the argument about the availability of resources,[80] the respondents argued that the inclusion of permanent residents in the Social Grant System would impose an unsustainably high financial burden on the state.[81] The respondents indicated a progressive trend in government expenditure on social security spending.[82] In the absence of providing clear evidence of the additional cost in providing social grants to permanent residents, the respondents made some assumptions on the groups and numbers of eligible permanent residents, and came to the conclusion that this inclusion would cost the state an additional R243 million – R672 million per annum.

The Court, taking the above numbers into account, decided that the cost of including permanent residents in the system would be only a small portion of the cost compared with the total budget spent on social grants.[83] In this case the Court considered evidence on the budget and decided, as the judicial branch of government, whether the financial burden on the executive branch of government is acceptable or not. This may be seen as an infringement of the separation of powers argument. It is my submission that the Court did not directly calculate the budget or interfere with the budget. They only examined the evidence before them and did what was expected of them, namely giving social protection to the poor by providing an appropriate remedy. The Court clearly described the human rights-based approach they used when they[84] came to the following conclusion.

There can be no doubt that the applicants are part of a *vulnerable group* in society and, in the circumstances of the present case, are worthy of constitutional protection.

We are dealing here with *intentional, statutorily sanctioned unequal treatment of part of the South African community*. This has a strong *stigmatizing* effect. Because both permanent residents and citizens *contribute to the welfare system* through the payment of taxes, the lack of congruence between benefits and burdens created by a law that denies benefits to permanent residents almost inevitably creates the impression that permanent residents are in some way *inferior* to citizens and less worthy of social assistance.[85]

Referring to the impact of the exclusion, the Court also stressed the burden that permanent residents without social assistance benefits place on other members of the community, such as their families and friends, and how this affects their dignity.[86] This exclusion is unfair, because permanent residents are outcast to the margins of society and are deprived of those rights that may be essential for them to enjoy their other constitutional rights.[87] The Court further ruled that this unfairness would not be justified under the general limitation clause[88] of the Constitution.[89]

9.4.3.5 Decision of the Court

The Court decided that the most appropriate order to make was the 'reading-in' of the words 'permanent resident' in the challenged legislation. This again may be seen as a drastic remedy and an interference with the other branches of government by the Constitutional Court. In this case the remedy was chosen because of the urgency of the matter.[90]

9.5 Conclusion

Poverty is more than a lack of income. It can better be described as social exclusion from the democratic and legal system, the labour market, the welfare state system and the family and community system. With relation to rights, poverty may be seen as a denial of human rights and human dignity. Human dignity and equality as fundamental values and rights in the South African Constitution, are infringed if they are denied to the poor because of their economic status.

From a rights perspective, poverty is about a denial of human rights. A human rights-based approach implies protection by law of fundamental freedoms and entitlements needed for a decent standard of living. It is further important to keep in mind that a number of rights may be infringed at a given moment when the situation of poor people is viewed. This may include civil and political rights such as human dignity and equality on the one hand, and socioeconomic rights such as the rights to social security, health, food and water on the other.

Where there is poverty or social exclusion, a human rights-based approach demands action to rectify the situation. If possible, and financially viable, the poor may approach the Court for help, as happened in the cases of *Grootboom, TAC* and *Khosa*. The fact that this is possible in South Africa, because we have justiciable socioeconomic rights, is a strength of the system. However, approaching the courts is not only an expensive exercise but also one that only remedies, in most cases, the situation of those people who brought the action before the court. This may be seen as a weakness of the current system of enforcement.

A better solution may be to provide social protection, where the fundamental rights relating to poverty are infringed. The type of social protection will differ depending on the type of right that has been infringed upon. Social protection is a measure that combats social exclusion, poverty, marginalization and vulnerability. A committee appointed by the cabinet recently developed a definition of social protection adapted to the unique South African circumstances. This definition lies out the perfect tools to protect the poor. It includes measures to address 'income poverty', measures to address 'capability poverty', measures to address 'asset poverty' and measures to address 'special needs'.

Unfortunately, this approach was not included in the new Social Assistance Act 13 of 2004. The new Act was only aimed at the consolidation of legal requirements and provisions for social assistance in the Republic, and to create uniform norms and standards, which can apply countrywide. It has been indicated that no new policy shifts will be made in the new Social Assistance Act and that the act is tabled to remove the assignment to the provinces as indicated in the Memorandum.[91] One may only ask why they did appoint a committee to examine a comprehensive social protection system. Lack of political commitment and will to help the plight of the poor may be seen as a further weakness in the human rights-based approach where a proper remedy may only be obtained by approaching the courts and trying to enforce the rights of the poor. A further disadvantage, as already mentioned, is that remedies are given in isolation and are only applicable to a specific case.

In the *Khosa* case the Court referred to the foundational values in the Constitution, namely human dignity, equality and freedom. As in the *Grootboom* and *TAC* cases it recognized that all rights are interdependent, mutually related and equally important and emphasized that the *Khosa* case concerned intersecting rights which reinforce one another at the point of intersection. The Court remarked that what makes this case different from other cases that have previously been considered by this Court is that, in addition to the rights to life and dignity, the social security scheme put in place by the state to meet its obligations under section 27 of the Constitution, raises the question of the prohibition of unfair discrimination. It is clear from the Court's approach that when it comes to the infringement of the rights of the poor it is possible that civil and political rights such as human dignity and equality can also be infringed along with the typical rights of the poor or so-called socioeconomic rights.

To conclude, the Constitution in South Africa set the way for the development and usage of a human rights-based approach. According to UNICEF,[92] all countries, even those at low levels of income, can achieve the realization of at least the rights of the most vulnerable. Universal access to basic social services and the pursuit of socioeconomic rights do not have to wait until rapid economic growth is achieved.

Notes

1. United Nations Children's Fund, 2000, p. 5.
2. This concept apparently has its origin in the European Union context, dating back to the second half of the 1980s: Berghman, 1997, 3–22. The most significant innovation in the recent poverty literature in the developed world is the emergence of the concept of 'Social Exclusion'. Noble, Ratcliffe and Wright, 2004, p. 11.

3. Olivier and Jansen van Rensburg, 2006, p. 109. See Noble, Ratcliffe and Wright, 2004, p. 7, Adato, Carter and May, 5.
4. Berghman, 1997, 6 refers to the comment by certain European researchers that 'one's sense of belonging in society depends on all four systems'. Compare Commins, 1993, p. 4, which continues as follows: 'Civic integration means being an equal citizen in a democratic system. Economic integration means having a job, having a valued economic function, being able to pay your way. Social integration means being able to avail oneself of the social services provided by the state. Interpersonal integration means having family and friends, neighbours and social networks to provide care and companionship and moral support when these are needed. All four systems are therefore, important... In a way the four systems are complementary: when one or two are weak the others need to be strong. And the worst off are those for whom all systems have failed...'. For a similar appreciation of the distinction between the (narrower) income-related poverty concept and the (wider) multi-dimensional social exclusion concept, see Rodgers, 1994, pp. 2–3, 8.
5. Rodgers, 1994, p. 8.
6. As discussed in Olivier and Jansen van Rensburg, 2006, p. 110.
7. United Nations Children's Fund, 2000, p. 45. See United Nations Development Programme, 1998, as referred by De Gaay Fortman, 2001.
8. For exactly the similar definition see Committee on Economic, Social and Cultural Rights, 2001, paras 1–2 and Piron, 2003, p. 19.
9. Own emphasis.
10. Piron, 2003, p. 19.
11. United Nations Children's Fund, 2000, p. 19. De Gaay Fortman, 2001, see Committee on Economic, Social and Cultural Rights, 2001, paras 1–2 and Piron, 2003, 19.
12. De Gaay Fortman, 2001.
13. (Hereafter the Constitution.) Section 1 of the Constitution states that the Republic of South Africa is one sovereign democratic state founded on the values of human dignity, the achievement of equality and advancement of human rights and freedoms, non-racialism and non-sexism. Section 7(1) further states that the Bill of Rights is the cornerstone of democracy in South Africa. It enshrines the rights of all people in our country and affirms the democratic values of human dignity, equality and freedom.
14. *Government of the Republic of South Africa and Others* v *Grootboom and Others* 2000 11 BCLR 1169 (CC) para. 23 (hereafter *Grootboom*). See Piron, 2003, p. 19.
15. Sections 1 and 7(1) of the Constitution.
16. Section 10 of the Constitution reads as follows: 'Everyone has inherent dignity and the right to have their dignity respected and protected'.
17. The South African courts have consistently stated that there is close correlation between the right to equality and the protection of a person's dignity: *Hoffmann* v *SA Airways* 2000 21 *ILJ* 2357 (CC); *Walters* v *Transitional Local Council of Port Elizabeth & Another* 2001 BCLR 98 (LC).
18. United Nations Children's Fund, 2000, pp. 3–4.
19. Own emphasis.
20. De Gaay Fortman, 2001.
21. See discussion of *Khosa and Others* v *Minister of Social Development and Others; Mahlaule and Another* v *Minister of Social Development and Others* 2004 (6) BCLR 569 (CC) below and the reference to intersecting rights.
22. Adato, Carter and May, 2004, 1–4.
23. Noble, Ratcliffe and Wright, 2004, p. 13.
24. Olivier and Jansen van Rensburg, 2006, p. 105. See Noble, Ratcliffe and Wright, 2004, p. 4.
25. Adato, Carter and May, 2004, 1–4.
26. The Act recently replaces the previous Social Assistance Act 59 of 1992. Commencement date of Act excluding Chapter 4: 1 April 2006. R 15/GG 28652/31-03-2006. The two Acts are very much the same when it comes to their categorical nature towards social grants.
27. Also known as socioeconomic rights, red rights or second-generation rights.
28. See heading 9.3 below.

29. Committee of Inquiry Into a Comprehensive System of Social Security for South Africa, 2002, p. 61.
30. South African Human Rights Commission, 2002/2003, 5–7. See below for discussion on *Grootboom* case. In the *Grootboom* judgement the Court held that socioeconomic policies and programmes must be reasonable both in their given priority and their needs must be addressed effectively.
31. South African Human Rights Commission, 2002/2003, 5–7.
32. This suggests a rights-based approach to development. See Malone and Belshaw, 2003, 76–89 and Piron, 2003, pp. 1–28. Due to the restricted length of this chapter and the complexity of the rights-based approach to development as a separate topic, this topic will only be referred to.
33. Own emphasis.
34. Committee of Inquiry Into a Comprehensive System of Social Security for South Africa, 2002, pp. 41–2. See also Olivier and Jansen van Rensburg, 2002.
35. Committee of Inquiry Into a Comprehensive System of Social Security for South Africa, 2002, pp. 42–3. See also Olivier and Jansen van Rensburg, 2002.
36. Arat, 1991, p. 4. See Arambulo, 1999, p. 107. In the Proclamation of Teheran adopted on 13 May 1968 during the International Congress on Human Rights paragraph 13 the above has been affirmed: 'Since human rights and fundamental freedoms are indivisible, the full realization of civil and political rights without the enjoyment of economic, social and cultural rights is impossible. The achievement of lasting progress in the implementation of human rights is dependent upon sound and effective national and international policies of economic and social development'.
37. As discussed in *Minister of Health and Others* v *Treatment Action Campaign and Others* 2002 (10) BCLR 1033 (CC) para. 30. (Hereafter *TAC*.)
38. Almost the same formulation and phrasing are found in article 2(1) of the International Covenant of Economic Social and Cultural Rights (ICESCR), 1966.
39. Committee on Economic, Social And Cultural Rights, 1990, para. 10.
40. Ibid.
41. Ibid.
42. *Grootboom*, para. 30.
43. Ibid., para. 32.
44. Ibid., para. 32.
45. Ibid., para. 33.
46. Ibid., para. 41.
47. Ibid., para. 43.
48. Ibid., para. 44.
49. Committee on Economic, Social And Cultural Rights, 1990, para. 9.
50. Ibid.
51. Sections 26(2) and 27(2) of the South African Constitution reads that the state must 'achieve the progressive realization of each of these rights' and not the full realization of these rights.
52. Van der Walt, 2001, 11.
53. So-called dignitarian approach.
54. *Grootboom*, para. 44.
55. Ibid., para. 43.
56. Ibid., para. 20.
57. Ibid., para. 96.
58. *TAC*, para. 34.
59. An *amicus* joins proceedings of the court, as its name suggests, as a friend of the court. An *amicus curiae* assists the court by furnishing information or argument regarding questions of law or fact.
60. *TAC*, para. 39.

61. Van Bueren, 1999, 57. See further Brand and Russell, 2002, pp. 1–21.
62. An example thereof is the baseline approach recommended by the Committee of Inquiry Into a Comprehensive System of Social Security for South Africa, 2002.
63. *TAC*, para. 98.
64. Ibid., para. 99.
65. Ibid., para. 135.
66. Hereafter *Khosa*.
67. As amended in some instances by the Welfare Laws Amendment Act 106 of 1997.
68. *Khosa*, para. 3.
69. For purposes of this discussion these cases will be referred to as one case, as only one judgement was made.
70. *Khosa*, para. 40.
71. Ibid. Referring to the judgement in *Grootboom*.
72. *Khosa*, para. 44.
73. Own emphasis.
74. *Khosa*, para. 45.
75. Ibid., para. 53.
76. Ibid., para. 51.
77. Ibid., para. 52.
78. United Nations Children's Fund, 2000, p. 19, De Gaay Fortman, 2001.
79. *Khosa*, para. 84.
80. Ibid., para. 19.
81. Ibid., para. 60.
82. For example, in the last three years, the spending on social grants (including administrative cost) increased from R16.1 billion to R26.2 billion and a further increase to R44.6 billion is estimated in the following three years. The respondents further estimated that there are about 260,000 permanent residents residing in the country. The respondents failed to furnish the court with statistical evidence on the number of permanent residents that might be eligible for social grants if the citizenship requirement is removed. *Khosa*, paras 60–1.
83. *Khosa*, para. 62.
84. Ibid., para. 74.
85. Own emphasis.
86. *Khosa*, paras 76, 80 and 81.
87. Ibid., para. 77.
88. Section 36.
89. *Khosa*, paras 80, 83 and 84.
90. Ibid., paras 92 and 95.
91. Memorandum on the objects of the Social Assistance Bill B 57A-2003. As amended by the Portfolio Committee on Social Development (National Assembly). (As introduced in the National Assembly as a section 76 Bill; explanatory summary of Bill published in *Government Gazette* 25340 of 8/08/2003).
92. United Nations Children's Fund, 2000, p. 46.

References

Adato, M. M. Carter and J. May (2004) 'Sense in Sociability? Social Exclusion and Persistent Poverty in South Africa' *Basis Brief CRSP*, no. 25 1–4 available on the internet http://www.basis.wisc.edu/live/basbrief25.pdf.
Arambulo, K. (1999) *Strengthening the Supervision on the International Covenant on Economic, Social and Cultural Rights: Theoretical and Procedural Aspects.* Antwerp: Intersentia.

Arat, Z.F. (1991) *Democracy and Human Rights in Developing Countries*. London: Lynne Reinner Publishers.

Berghman, J. (1997) 'The Resurgence of Poverty and the Struggle against Exclusion: a New Challenge for Social Security?', *International Social Security Review*, 50, 3–22.

Brand, D. and S. Russell (2002) *Exploring the Core Content of Socio-economic Rights: South African and International Perspectives*. Menlo Park: Protea.

Commins, P. (1993) *Combating Exclusion in Ireland 1990–1994: A Midway Report*. Brussels: European Commission.

Committee of Inquiry Into a Comprehensive System of Social Security for South Africa (2002) *Transforming the Present – Protecting the Future Consolidated Report*. Pretoria: Government Press.

Committee on Economic, Social and Cultural Rights (2001) *Poverty and the International Covenant on Economic, Social and Cultural Rights*, E/C.12/2001/10 (Other Treaty-Related Document) (10 May). Available on the internet http://www.unhchr.ch/tbs/doc.nsf/(Symbol)/E.C.12.2001.10.En?Opendocument.

Committee on Economic, Social And Cultural Rights (1990) *The Nature of States Parties Obligations No. 3*, E/1991/23 (14 December). Available on the internet http://www.unhchr.ch/tbs/doc.nsf/(symbol)/CESCR+General+comment+3.En?OpenDocument.

De Gaay Fortman, B. (2001) *Pro Poor Growth, the State and the (Non)-Implementation of the Rights of the Poor* (Unpublished Paper) Lecture for the Ministry of Foreign Affairs and the RAWOO, The Hague, Foreign Ministry, 26 April.

Government of the Republic of South Africa and Others v *Grootboom and Others* 2000 (11) BCLR 1169 (CC).

Hoffmann v *SA Airways* 2000 21 *ILJ* 2357 (CC).

International Covenant of Economic Social and Cultural Rights G.A. Res. 2200A (XXI), U.N. GAOR Supp. (No. 16) at 49, U.N. Doc. A/6316 (1966) U.N.T.S. entered into force 3 January 1976.

Khosa and Others v *Minister of Social Development and Others*; *Mahlaule and Another* v *Minister of Social Development and Others* 2004 (6) BCLR 569 (CC).

Malone, M. and D. Belshaw (2003) 'The Human Rights-Based Approach to Development: overview, context and critical issues', *Transformation*, 20(2), 76–89.

Noble, M., A. Ratcliffe and G. Wright (2004) *Conceptualizing, Defining and Measuring Poverty in South Africa – an Argument for a Consensual Approach*. Oxford: CASASP.

Olivier, M.P. and L. Jansen van Rensburg (2002) 'Addressing the Alleviation of Poverty Through Social Welfare Measures'. Unpublished paper presented at a joint session between CROP and the International Sociological Association (ISA) Research Committee on Sociology of Poverty, Social Welfare and Social Policy at the XVth World Congress of Sociology, entitled *Issues in Pro-poor Policy in Non-OECD Countries*, Brisbane, Australia, 7–13 July.

Olivier, M.P. and L. Jansen van Rensburg (2006) 'South African Poverty Law: The Role and Influence of International Human Rights Instruments', in L. Williams (ed.), *International Poverty Law: An Emerging Discourse*. London: Zed Books.

Piron, L.H. (2003) *Learning from the UK Department of International Development's Rights-Based Approach to Development Assistance*. Bonn: German Development Institute.

Rodgers, G. (1994) *Overcoming Social Exclusion*. A contribution to the World Summit for Social Development. Switzerland: International Institute for Labour Studies, ILO.

South African Human Rights Commission (2002/03) '5th Economic and Social Rights Report – The right to Social Security'. Available from the Internet http://www.sahrc.org.za/esr_report_2002_2003.htm.

Minister of Health and Others v *Treatment Action Campaign and Others* 2002 (10) BCLR 1033 (CC).

United Nations Development Programme (1998) *Integrating Human Rights with Sustainable Development*. New York: UNDP.

United Nations Children's Fund (2000) *Poverty Reduction Begins with Children*. New York: UNICEF.

Van Bueren, G. (1999) 'Alleviating Poverty Through the Constitutional Court', *South African Journal of Human Rights*, 15, 52–74.

Van der Walt, A.J. (2001) 'Tentative Urgency: sensitivity for the paradoxes of stability and change in social transformation decisions of the Constitutional Court', *South African Public Law*, 16(1), 1–27.

Walters v *Transitional Local Council of Port Elizabeth & Another* 2001 BCLR 98 (LC).

Part III
Extending the Concept of Multidimensional Poverty

10
Identifying and Measuring Chronic Poverty: Beyond Monetary Measures?

David Hulme and Andy McKay

10.1   Introduction

Despite the renewed commitment over the past 15 years to the reduction of poverty as the core objective of international development discourses and policies, progress to this end remains disappointing. (UNDP, 2003; UN Statistics Division, 2004). This inadequate progress raises important questions about the policies and strategies adopted to achieve poverty reduction, as well as about key international issues, including aid, debt, trade and conflict reduction. It also raises important questions about our very conception and understanding of poverty. While perspectives on poverty have evolved significantly over this period, with widespread acceptance of the multidimensional nature of poverty, and of the importance of considering the depth and severity of poverty, there has been slower progress in recognising and responding to the persistence of much poverty over time (Clark and Hulme, 2005); in other words, the phenomenon of *chronic poverty*. For many people poverty is not a transitory experience or a seasonal problem: it is a situation from which escape is very difficult, most emphatically illustrated by deprivation which is transmitted from one generation to the next. At present, chronic poverty is still not seen as a distinct and important policy focus. This is a significant area of neglect both because a substantial proportion of poverty is likely to be chronic (CPRC, 2004), and because it is likely to call for distinct or additional policy responses that can tackle deep structural obstacles.

Existing work on chronic poverty and poverty dynamics in general have so far been conceptualized in narrow terms, focusing on income or consumption poverty measured using household panel survey data. This has created important limitations in our understanding. Further, much of the focus has been on the identification of chronic poverty and finding correlates, without developing an understanding of the underlying processes by which some people are trapped in persistent poverty while others escape. A broader multidimensional – and multidisciplinary – perspective needs to be brought to the understanding of chronic poverty.

This chapter argues that analysis and policy debate around chronic poverty need to be based on a broader understanding of the concept. The argument is set out as follows. The next section discusses current approaches to the analysis of chronic poverty and poverty dynamics, leading into a discussion about the limitations of monetary measures. The following two sections discuss two alternative approaches, one based on assets, and the other on concepts of needs or human development. This leads into a discussion of progress to date in terms of implementing some of these approaches at the micro level. The final section synthesizes interim conclusions.

10.2   Analysing chronic poverty

Historically, the idea that some people are trapped in poverty while others have spells in poverty was a central element of analysis. For example, officials and social commentators in eighteenth-century France distinguished between the *pauvre* and the *indigent*. The former experienced seasonal poverty when crops failed or demand for casual agricultural labour was low. The latter were permanently poor because of ill health (physical and mental), accident, age, alcoholism or other forms of 'vice'. The central aim of policy was to support the *pauvre* in ways that would stop them from becoming *indigent*.

The work of the Chronic Poverty Research Centre (CPRC 2004; Hulme and Shepherd 2003) identifies four main ways in which people may experience chronic poverty.

- Those who experience poverty for a long time. Hulme and Shepherd (2003) suggest five years, but this has been challenged.
- Those who experience poverty throughout their entire lives (lifecourse poverty)
- The transfer of poverty from parents to children (intergenerational poverty)
- Those who experience a premature death that was easily preventable.

In this chapter, chronic poverty refers to these four experiences, and/or mixes of these experiences.

In contemporary times this durational aspect of poverty has been relatively neglected. Conceptual development, and more particularly measurement, has focused on severity/depth and multidimensionality.[1] In economics serious work on duration only began to emerge in the late 1980s (Bane and Ellwood, 1986; Gaiha, 1988, 1989). An implicit assumption of much research was that the persistence of poverty at the individual and household level was highly correlated with the severity of poverty. During the early 1990s such work began to proliferate based on available panel data sets, and in 2000 the first collection of papers on this topic was published (Baulch and Hoddinnott, 2000).

There are three important points to note about the contemporary empirical literature on chronic poverty (see Clark and Hulme, 2005 for a fuller discussion). First, it is dominated by economists and econometricians using panel datasets to distinguish chronic poverty from transient or transitory poverty and to identify variables that correlate with mobility, or lack of mobility.[2] Secondly, virtually all of the empirical work conducted by economists and econometricians uses income or consumption measures of poverty as its main variable.[3] Of the 28 panel datasets that cover developing countries and for which information is available, 26 assess poverty or standard of living in terms of income or consumption measures and 23 use these measures exclusively (Lawson, McKay and Moore, 2005). Thirdly, these variables were almost entirely quantitative and findings were, at best, only partially contextualized.[4] Examples of the use of combined quantitative and qualitative work in relation to poverty dynamics have only very recently begun to emerge (Adato *et al.*, 2004; Howe and McKay, 2007; Kabeer, 2005; Lawson, McKay and Okidi, 2006).

There are a number of reasons why the study of chronic poverty in developing countries has followed this path. Here we can only briefly identify some of them. Most obvious is that the approaches and methods used to analyse chronic and transient poverty in OECD countries, and especially the USA, have been transferred to the panel datasets that emerged belatedly in developing countries. In effect, '[t]he technically sophisticated econometric analysis that forms the basis of the poverty research industry today...' in the USA (O'Connor, 2001: 3) colonized work on poorer countries. Secondly, much contemporary empirical economics places a strong focus on quantitative analysis, and adopts a perspective of methodological individualism,[5] rather than work on collectivities such as classes or social groups. In Europe, where the other social sciences are rarely positivist and quantitative, this meant that chronic poverty analysis was seen as the domain of economists and not as a topic for cross-disciplinary efforts. Thirdly, there remained ambivalence within sociology, anthropology, political science and geography (SAPG) about the concept of poverty. Research more often focused on inequality because of doubts about the idea of an objective poverty line and a belief that it is unequal social and political relations that underpin deprivation and social problems[6] (see Green and Hulme, 2005, for a more detailed discussion). Even when exemplary studies were produced – such as Iliffe's (1987) *The African Poor: A History* which contrasted structural and conjunctural poverty – this did not lead to further conceptual development or a set of comparative empirical studies. Other social scientists lauded this work but did not systematically extend it.

This situation left a void in policy-oriented poverty analysis that was increasingly filled in the 1990s by Participatory Poverty Assessments (PPAs) and participatory methods as exemplified in *Voices of the Poor* (Narayan *et al.*, 2000). Krishna (2006) has developed the 'Stages of Progress' approach that uses participatory, group-based methods and recall to track the changes in well-being and poverty in rural areas over 25-year periods. These approaches need to be carefully distinguished from the concepts and methods used by SAPG researchers. Indeed, they are criticized by some SAPG researchers (Mosse, 1994; Cooke and Kothari, 2001) for generating elite-biased and inaccurate accounts of 'who' is poor and 'why' people are poor.

In summary, the prevailing approach in relation to chronic poverty remains dominated by monetary indicators derived from household panel datasets. We now consider some of the limitations of this approach in more detail, before considering the scope to develop a broader approach in the rest of this paper.

10.3 The limitations of monetary measures: conceptual and empirical

A major reason why income- or consumption-based measures of well-being are insufficient for considering well-being or poverty (in static or dynamic terms) is that these indicators relate to the means to achieve ultimate ends rather than the ends in themselves. Such ultimate ends can be conceptualized in terms of Sen's capabilities framework (Sen, 1985), later extended to distinguish instrumental and intrinsic freedoms (Sen, 1999). The capabilities framework moves beyond a focus on consumption commodities to emphasize the characteristics of these commodities and the functionings that these commodities – along with other factors such as the environment – enable individuals to achieve. Examples of key functionings may include the ability to avoid preventable premature mortality or an ability to live with dignity in the community.

The key issue is that individuals differ in their ability to convert commodities and their associated characteristics into the achievement of functionings for a variety of personal, social and environmental factors. This has particular significance for people who are chronically poor because they are more likely to have personal characteristics (such as physical disability), social characteristics (for example, tribal status) or live in environments (such as remote, rural areas) that mean that their ability to convert commodities into functionings is lower than that found in the wider population. Human functioning also depends on the public provision of key services, the value of which is typically not included (and is, in any case, conceptually and practically difficult to value) in monetary measures of well-being. Solely emphasizing the income or commodities that an individual can command is insufficiently focussed on the ultimate ends of well-being. While in practice micro data suggest that income and the achievement of most ultimate ends tend to be positively correlated with each other across individuals or households, such correlations are often modest (Appleton and Song, 1999). Thus, for a given income level there can be a wide variation in non-monetary welfare outcomes. In addition, an increasing amount of literature finds only a weak correlation between income and measures of happiness in comparisons across and within countries (Stutzer, 2003; Frey and Stutzer, 2001), although it has also been argued by some capability theorists that there is an equally weak association between happiness and well-being.

Another important and widely stressed issue in relation to income or consumption measures is that these will almost invariably (for practical reasons) be measured at the household level and so not capture intra-household variations, which may be substantial (Haddad and Kanbur, 1990). In looking at welfare issues the appropriate focus is clearly at the individual level, but it is very difficult to measure individual income or consumption due to factors such as shared income and purchases, or joint consumption, within the household. This also invites an alternative approach, as those experiencing chronic poverty (and/or have the lowest prospects of social mobility) are commonly discriminated against within the household. This includes young females (and especially informal 'maids'), widows and people with learning disabilities.

Aside from these conceptual issues, income or consumption measures of well-being typically show large fluctuations over time, and this is often especially significant for the poorest. Indeed, these fluctuations, and the vulnerability they imply, are a key aspect of ill-being. Many non-monetary indicators, such as adult literacy or nutritional status, are much less subject to fluctuations. Thus monetary indicators (even consumption, which is generally preferred over income) more than almost any others fail to provide an adequate measure of long term well-being status when measured at just one point in time, based on a one-off survey or even on repeated cross-sections. This is likely to be particularly the case for the poorest for whom consumption smoothing is most difficult. For this reason panel data offers the promise of looking at longer term dynamics when using income or consumption measures. Thus, in Uganda there was a large reduction in consumption poverty over the 1990s from 55.7 per cent in 1992 to 35.2 per cent in 1999; but these figures fail to capture the substantial mobility over this period revealed by panel data where significant numbers of households fell into income poverty while at the same time many others escaped (Lawson, McKay and Okidi, 2006: 1231).

There are also a number of practical issues involved with the use of longitudinal income or consumption data to look at poverty dynamics. One is that the number of waves in panel data is typically small – frequently just two or three periods with significant time gaps in between. A second issue is the extent of attrition which typically affects panel datasets, with households dropping out (e.g. due to mobility, or refusal to be re-interviewed), a phenomenon which is likely to show systematic patterns (Alderman *et al.*, 2000; Falaris, 2003). Related to this, inevitable changes over time in household composition mean that it is not always easy to identify panel households unambiguously, an issue which is especially important for the potentially more interesting panel data sets covering longer periods of time.

Another important limitation is the extent of measurement error typically associated with measuring income or consumption. These are complex variables to measure given the variety of different types of consumption or sources of income; there will inevitably be significant recall error; and measurement methods to increase accuracy (such as using short recall methods) also introduce increased volatility into the data (Scott, 1992). These issues are less serious when looking at averages (that is, patterns of poverty) across groups of households, but can also be substantial at the individual household level – the level at which poverty dynamics must be considered. It follows that household-level income or consumption data in panel surveys display greater volatility over time than is really the case, due to the impact of measurement error. This will mean that mobility will be exaggerated and chronic poverty is likely to be underestimated. While some studies have attempted to correct for measurement error (Dercon and Krishnan, 2000), such corrections are inevitably imperfect because of the lack of information to form a firm judgement about the extent of measurement error. For some non-monetary dimensions of poverty (which may themselves correspond more closely to ultimate welfare outcomes) the measurement difficulties may be less severe, though the difficulties in estimating indicators such as illiteracy or stunting should not be underestimated.

In addition, as already noted, the ways in which panel data have been used in analysis have generally been limited to the measurement of chronic and transitory poverty and the identification of correlates of poverty transitions or non-transitions (being trapped in poverty). Typically, the range of correlates considered has been quite limited, reflecting the range of information typically collected by surveys. The correlates identified are generally plausible (McKay and Lawson, 2003), but only provide partial insights about causes. In general, what is required is to develop an understanding of the processes underlying poverty transitions (or traps) and household surveys used in isolation are generally not well adapted to provide such insights. This is partly a limitation of a purely quantitative analysis, and this has been recognised in the recent development of combined qualitative and quantitative approaches.[7] For the most part, however, these still remain strongly focused on money-metric poverty.

There is scope to analyse dynamics of important non-income indicators using panel datasets – for example, whether children are enrolled at school, or anthropometric indicators. While anthropometric data in particular could offer a major opportunity, in practice this is often not possible in practice because of the common habit of only collecting data over a very limited age range, typically pre-school children. This in part reflects concerns about the extent to which anthropometric indicators can be standardized for older children, an issue on which there is disagreement among researchers.

It is also important to raise questions about alternatives to panel data. On a very practical level, in the large majority of low-income countries panel data are unavailable – but the issue of chronic poverty is clearly still important. The question of alternatives is also important because of the significant cost and also the difficulty of collecting panel data (for example, tracking and matching individuals and households (Wilson and Huttly, 2003)). In the absence of panel data, are there other adequate ways of analysing chronic poverty? One potential opportunity could be offered by pseudo-panel methods (Bourguignon *et al.*, 2004, looking at vulnerability), but such methods typically require very large sample sizes, much bigger than those in the majority of multipurpose household surveys currently available.[8]

There are many points that might be drawn from the above discussion. From the perspective of this chapter, the main one is that to date the creation of knowledge about chronic poverty remains highly dependent on the work of economists examining income or consumption dynamics. That said, it is important to recognise that the distinction between chronic and transitory poverty is much more relevant for income or consumption poverty compared to other dimensions. Social scientists from other disciplines have generally engaged much less with the concept of chronic poverty. This is much more the case for chronic poverty than it is for poverty in general terms.

This leads to two arguments that inform the rest of this chapter. The first is that the conceptualization and operationalization of chronic poverty, currently shaped largely by economists, needs to be as rigorous as it can be – otherwise, the overall understanding of poverty dynamics may be distorted or inadequate. The second is the need to look for ways in which chronic poverty is not analysed through an excessively narrow lens. Table 10.1 illustrates the ways in which different requirements for human flourishing, derived from a review of six human development listings, relate to chronic poverty. Can concepts from other disciplines be incorporated into chronic poverty analysis by economists, and/or can cross-disciplinary or combined quantitative and qualitative approaches be developed? We consider now a range of potential alternative approaches.

Table 10.1 Requirements for human flourishing and their relation to chronic poverty*

Requirement	Relationship to Chronic Poverty
Bodily well-being	• Preventable and premature death deprives a person of all capabilities and functionings for the 'lost' years. • Chronic ill-health and terminal illness, especially of the main 'breadwinner' of a household, are closely associated with chronic poverty. • Poor people frequently cite ill-health as a cause and consequence of chronic poverty. • Disability correlates with chronic poverty.
Material well-being	• Income/consumption poverty is the most commonly used indicator of chronic poverty. Asset measurements have been increasingly proposed recently.
Mental development (and mental health)	• Low levels of human capital (education, knowledge, skills) are commonly reported as a factor trapping people in poverty. • Mental health problems are significantly associated with homelessness and extreme poverty in OECD countries. Little is known about mental health in developing countries, but there are reports that mental health problems are common for the homeless and destitute.
Work	• Chronic poverty is closely associated with low-paid, irregular and insecure work. • Work-related ill-health (injuries, lung disease) are causes of chronic poverty.
Security	• Regions and countries experiencing violent conflict typically have high levels of chronic poverty. • Physical insecurity raises the probability of chronic poverty. • Lack of access to basic social security encourages risk averse behaviours that lower productivity – these can become poverty traps.
Social relations	• Low levels of social capital/social networks are seen as an asset condition predisposing households to chronic poverty. • Social relations, in terms of social exclusion and adverse incorporation, are viewed by many SAPG researchers as the fundamental cause of chronic poverty.
Spiritual well-being	• Rarely explored in the literature on chronic poverty. • Anecdotally, chronically poor people explain their circumstances through reference to the spiritual e.g. 'will of God', witchcraft, 'evil eye'.
Empowerment and political freedom	• Disempowerment and lack of rights/abuse of rights are often argued to be key causes of chronic poverty.
Respect for other species	• In some cases environmental degradation is identified as a factor contributing to chronic poverty. This is not usually framed as [lack of] respect for other species.

Note: * The framework is taken from Ranis, Stewart and Samman (2005: 4) based on a review of 'six lists' of needs/human development which have differing philosophical approaches and justifications.

10.4   What are the alternatives? Part 1: an asset-based approach

Many of the limitations of monetary measures are quite widely accepted in the literature, but a key difficulty has often been the identification of alternative approaches which retain a strong focus on chronic poverty or poverty dynamics. One important potential alternative approach is to focus on asset ownership, given that assets capture longer-term dynamics much better than a measure of income at one or two points in time. For this reason having longitudinal data may be less crucial. In addition, assets can in principle be considered in a range of different dimensions, including social capital.

An asset-based approach: static and dynamic thresholds

The assets that a household possesses, or to which it has access, can be related to household income in that the latter may be conceptualised as returns to these assets. In this view a household's income reflects the assets it commands and the returns it is able to earn on these assets, which in turn depend on many factors. Assets are also likely to be important to households in their own right, besides their role in generating income; as well as representing wealth and status, having a sufficient level of assets also offers security, such that households can insure themselves against shocks, and gain easier access to credit. Ownership of key assets may be a good indicator of well-being in its own right (although any evidence for this has typically been judged in relation to income or consumption indicators). Compared to income or consumption, assets are likely to be much less subject to fluctuations in the short to medium term. Important issues to consider, however, are which assets should be included in any asset-based measure of well-being and biases due to the under-reporting of assets.

One important example of placing assets in a central role in the analysis of persistent poverty is the work of Michael Carter and associates (Carter and Barrett, 2006; Carter and May, 2001). This moves beyond a distinction between chronic and transitory (income) poverty, to introduce asset poverty and distinguish between structural and stochastic poverty. Consider a transitorily poor household that is poor in the first period but above the poverty line in the second period. This may reflect structural change, because, for example, the household has been able to accumulate assets over this period. Alternatively, it may reflect stochastic factors: the fact that the household was poor (non-poor) in the first (second) period may have been simply a reflection of bad (good) luck in that specific period. This distinction can be made by considering the assets owned by the household and asking (based on a relationship between income and assets) whether *on average* that level of assets is sufficient to place a household above the poverty line. Thus, it is possible to identify an asset poverty line corresponding to a given income poverty line based on an average relationship between income and assets. In this way it is possible to distinguish among the income poor (non-poor) between those for whom this situation appears to be temporary because they have (do not have) a sufficiently high level of assets, and those for whom this seems to be permanent. This enables a more sophisticated understanding of the poor/non-poor distinction, contingent on the relationship between income and assets.

Building on ideas of poverty traps and multiple livelihood strategies, Carter and Barrett (2006) extend this concept to identify a dynamic asset threshold, taking account of households' ability to save or have access to credit. In their model (with two livelihood strategies), the dynamic asset threshold is the level above which households will save and accumulate assets (keeping them above the poverty line), and below which they will reduce their asset holdings and find themselves in a situation of poverty over the longer term. Of course, the challenge here is to estimate this dynamic asset poverty threshold. As part of this a key issue to consider is which assets should be considered and how diverse categories of assets can be aggregated. There are various solutions to this latter question; for instance, Sahn and Stifel (2000) have used factor analysis to construct a one-dimensional household asset index, though this technique does not take account of the relative importance of different assets in generating income.

This focus on assets adds considerably to the distinction between chronic and transitory poverty based on income data alone, but income still plays a central role in this approach; both static and dynamic asset thresholds are still defined in relation to income poverty lines. It has also focused to date on a relatively narrow range of productive assets, and it provides little discussion of the factors affecting the returns to these assets. There are also important questions about the reliability with which the relationship between assets can be established. Is there scope to consider assets in their own right as indicators of chronic poverty status?

Assets in a livelihoods framework

The livelihoods approach (Carney, 1998; DFID, 1999–2001; Scoones, 1998; Ellis 2000) is widely used in poverty analysis. In its orthodox form it recognises five 'capitals' that capture the assets households utilize to generate consumption and accumulate (or liquidate) for future use: natural capital, physical capital, human capital, social capital and financial capital. Hulme *et al.* (2001) adapt this by dividing social capital into sociocultural and sociopolitical assets and by proposing other potential categories (security and psychological); see also Moore (2001).

Potentially, this framework could be utilized to estimate the total asset set that a household controls. A hypothetical example of this is developed by Johnson, Hulme and Ruthven (2005). However, operationally the livelihoods framework falls back on less comprehensive devices to assess the level of poverty or wealth of households. Ellis (2000) points to the conventional economic devices of income and consumption and makes a strong case for consumption measures to be preferred. The example he provides in his book, however, recommends the use of participatory wealth rankings to assess who is poor, and these fall back on a small number of natural and physical assets (presumably because these are the easiest to identify and measure in practice): ownership of land, cattle, housing quality and a number of context specific key physical assets (ibid; 206–7).[9] Varying mixes of these natural and physical assets are used to 'designate' whether a household is presently 'low income', 'middle income' or 'high income'. Low-income households are assumed to be poor. The logic behind this is not presented, but it would appear to be that low levels of these key assets reveal directly that the household has low levels of natural and physical capital and indirectly that there are also low levels of financial, human and social capital. In effect, the last three capitals are assumed to closely correlate with the levels of the key assets.

While the livelihood framework appears to have the potential to allow a comprehensive assessment of assets, in practice this seems either difficult to utilize (because of the problems in measuring or placing values on financial, human and social capital) or unnecessary (as the assets that can be easily measured serve as surrogate measures for the others).[10] The latter, however, remains an empirical issue to be demonstrated.

10.5 What are the alternatives? Needs and human development approaches

Asset-based approaches to identifying and measuring poverty and deprivation have also been heavily criticized, for instance, because of the limited range of assets, because of difficulties of measurement, and because they are insufficiently linked to ultimate ends. An early alternative to this was the basic needs approach originally developed by the ILO in the 1970s (with a focus on goods and services), and revamped in the early 1980s by Paul Streeten *et al.* (1981), and Frances Stewart (1985) and associates (with a focus on outcomes) (see Stewart, 2006). This was in recognition of the fact that economic growth was frequently not associated with improvements in key education and health outcomes. However, basic needs approaches have also been criticized for seeing poverty reduction as essentially about access to goods and services, as well as for their universalist nature. While this criticism is appropriate of the early version developed by the ILO in the 1970s, it is less applicable to more recent variants of the needs approach (see Alkire, 2002a; Clark, 2006; Stewart, 2006).

Later work by Doyal and Gough (1991) sets out a much more comprehensive needs-based perspective. As with the basic needs approach, they argue strongly for the importance of recognising fully universal needs and they reject arguments based on cultural relativism that purport to challenge this. Doyal and Gough identify health and autonomy as the two key basic needs that, '[all] *humans must satisfy in order to avoid the serious harm of fundamentally impaired participation in their form of life...*' (Gough, 2004) Individual autonomy of agency depends on three key variables (Gough, 2004)

(a) Cognitive and emotional capacity
(b) The level of cultural understanding an individual has about himself (herself), and
(c) Critical autonomy: 'the capacity to compare cultural rules, to reflect upon the rules of one's own culture, to work with others to change them and, *in extremis*, to move to another culture' (Doyal and Gough, 1991, p. 187).

These basic needs are universal, but the means of satisfying them (the basic needs *satisfiers*) can be culturally specific. However, Doyal and Gough seek to identify universal satisfier characteristics – characteristics of goods, services, activities or relationships which enhance physical health or autonomy in all cultural contexts, by identifying a set of 11 intermediate needs (Table 10.2). This list, they argue, is drawn up based on codified and experiential knowledge. How these intermediate needs are satisfied, however, still depends on the social context.

In practice, there remains a major challenge in how to identify indicators for these basic and intermediate needs. Another major criticism which has been levelled at this approach it is paternalistic as it does not permit people to define their own needs.

Another approach has been developed by a prominent group of philosophers and social scientists, such as Amartya Sen (1984, 1985, 1999), Mahbub ul Haq (1995) and Martha Nussbaum (1988, 1995, 2000), which can be loosely grouped under the heading of human development.[11] Many lists of the dimensions of human development have been published. Alkire (2002a: 39) identifies 139 of these,[12] Saith (2001) reviews six and Clark (2002, ch.3) provides an overview of over 15 lists. Here, in order to illustrate the space that human development covers, we reproduce Nussbaum's list (Table 10.3). Her list is not definitive and can, according to the author, be revised. This list overlaps with Doyal and Gough's basic and intermediate needs but there are also significant differences (Gough, 2004, sets out a comparison between these two approaches).

Table 10.2 Doyal and Gough's 11 intermediate needs

Nutritional food and clean water
Protective housing
A non-hazardous work environment
A non-hazardous physical environment
Safe birth control and child-bearing
Appropriate health care
A secure childhood
Significant primary relationships
Physical security
Economic security
Appropriate education

Source: Gough (2004).

Table 10.3 Nussbaum's central human capabilities

Life
Bodily health
Bodily integrity
Senses, thought, imagination
Emotions
Practical reason
Affiliation
Other species
Play
Control over one's environment

Source: Nussbaum (2000: 72–5).

While there are many differences, and sometimes disagreements, between these approaches a number of common features (many of which they share with the Needs approaches discussed above) can be observed.

(i)   Their focus is on the achievement of ultimate ends, often envisioned as 'human development' or 'well-being', rather than on the means to achieve ends.

(ii) They are much more multi-dimensional than asset-based approaches, usually recognising at least six dimensions of human development and in some cases more than a dozen (and often dimensions are divided into several distinct sub-dimensions and multiple indicators may be used to assess these).

(iii) They temper the materialism of flow and asset-based approaches through a focus on non-material aspects of human development such as affection, friendship, autonomy and security (the last, however, is sometimes defined, at least in part, in material terms).

(iv) To varying degrees,[13] they allow for participatory processes in the identification and specification of the dimensions of poverty so that different cultures, or the preferences of poor people, influence the lists that are produced.

(v)   Concepts and methods from moral philosophy and ethics are used extensively and economics often plays only a secondary role.

While such 'lists' make great efforts to present a conceptually coherent account of human well-being and/or the 'good life', they all aspire to making some practical contribution to identifying, measuring and understanding poverty and low levels of well-being, so that more effective action can be undertaken. But in terms of the identification, measurement and analysis of chronic poverty, it can be argued that none of them have made a significant impact. They have pointed out the limitations of commodity-based approaches, but have not managed to generate a widely used operational alternative for empirical studies on poverty or specifically in relation to chronic poverty. There have been many attempts to make the capability approach operational, but there are very few attempts to introduce dynamic analyses into the capabilities approach (though see Clark and Hulme, 2005).

Why have they failed to make more headway? According to Alkire (2002b: 193), there are three main reasons why a synthesis has not emerged from this work: they are biased to western sources; the mechanisms for 'empirical testing' and/or 'participatory processes' are unclear; and the items on the lists 'vary slightly'. One can also add that the intellectual leader of this field, Amartya Sen, refuses to provide a list while his esteemed peer, Martha Nussbaum, has provided a list and is accused of 'overspecifying' the concept.

Philosophically, there may be strong grounds for resisting a synthesis that inevitably compromises the internal logic of each individual approach to some degree. Practically, however, there are dire consequences: the analysis of chronic poverty and poverty dynamics remains dominated by monetary approaches or by researchers who simply 'do what everyone else is doing'. As Qizilbash (2002b) points out, most of the human development literature has 'shared values' and confronts 'common foes', but it has focused excessively on examining differences within its constituent parts.

While Sen's capabilities framework has much to recommend it, there are at least three significant problems. First, the focus on a very broad range of capabilities may be appropriate when thinking of well-being and flourishing, but in poverty studies it may be better to focus on a smaller sub-set of 'basic capabilities' (Stewart quoted in Alkire, 2002b: 184). Secondly, while there are strong grounds for arguing for pluralist and/or participatory strategies to identify capabilities (Alkire, 2002a,b; Clark, 2002, etc.), this makes empirical work time consuming and expensive and may make cross-community, cross-national and longitudinal analysis difficult or even infeasible. Thirdly, there are questions about whether commodities and capabilities are mutually separable (Clark, 2002: ch. 2; 2005), leading to questions about whether commodities need to be a component of a capability approach (as for the HDI).

But the opportunity to operationalize human capabilities approaches remains open. Here we illustrate possible ways of applying these theories for empirical work. The challenge now is to move beyond using capabilities frameworks to criticize income/consumption and asset measures, and to generate alternatives that can challenge or displace these.

10.6 The scope to implement non-money-metric alternatives

As discussed above, a number of attempts have been made to implement asset-based approaches to poverty (and chronic poverty) measurement. However, these have typically been based on a relatively narrow range of assets (typically physical and natural, and sometimes human capital) as in the construction of asset indices or the implementation of livelihoods frameworks; and/or have been strongly linked to income poverty in any case (as in the work of Carter and Barrett). These approaches are typically limited to forms of assets that are in some sense measurable, and asset indices have frequently been criticised because of the relatively arbitrary – and non-context-specific – weightings that they employ. An analogous criticism of course applies to the Human Development Index.

Here we consider three alternative approaches that have been implemented.

Klasen's deprivation measure

Stephan Klasen has pointed to the shortcomings of money-metric measures of poverty and deprivation and experimented with a 'deprivation index [that] examines capability outcomes directly' (Klasen, 1997; 2000: 57). Here our focus is on the deprivation measure itself and not on empirical comparisons of the deprivation and expenditure poverty measures. Klasen refers extensively to Sen's work as the conceptual inspiration for his measure, which assesses deprivation in terms of 14 'components' of well-being (Table 10.4). This is not an attempt 'to propose the definitive measure of well-being, but simply to contribute to a debate about possible ways to capture well-being more directly than relying on expenditures...' (ibid.: 43). Households are scored in each component based on responses to questions in the 1993 Southern Africa Labour and Development Research Unit (SALDRU) survey in South Africa (PSLSD, 1994).

This measure has clear advantages over the monetary measure for assessing chronic poverty as: (i) it focuses on capabilities rather than means; (ii) it bypasses many of the problems associated with aggregation and equivalence scales; and (iii) it is less sensitive to measurement error.

However, it is not unproblematic. In particular, it can be challenged in terms of its choice of components, its scoring system and the weighting of components in the index, as Klasen (ibid.: 36) recognises (though he argues some of these things are likely to be uncontroversial). Clark and Qizilbash (2005) point out that Klasen does not clearly explain the choice of components. Essentially, they appear to be selected pragmatically from all of the possible SALDRU[14] indicators that relate to capabilities. Arguably, only 11 of the components selected can be directly related to capabilities. Two are commodities – income and wealth – and one – perceived well-being – is a measure of utility. So, conceptually, the measure could be challenged for mixing indicators of capabilities with commodities and utility. However, Klasen also constructs a 'core deprivation index' of seven components, concentrating on 'the most basic human capabilities' (see Table 10.4). This simpler measure has the conceptual advantage of not including commodities or perceived well-being as components. Practically, it has the advantage of requiring less data. It also has the advantage of using variables which are easier to measure. Empirically, it produces results that are very similar to the fuller index.

The second major criticism is of the scoring system used for each indicator. While Klasen argues that 'in most cases... the scoring system is quite intuitive and

Table 10.4   Components of a composite measure of deprivation (Klasen)

Component	Description of indicator used
Education[#]	Average years of schooling of all adult (16+) household members
*Income	Expenditure quintiles (as used throughout paper)
*Wealth	Number of household durables (list includes vehicles, phone, radio, TV, geyser, stoves, kettle, bicycles)
*Housing [#]	Housing characteristics
*Water[#]	Type of water access
Sanitation	Type of sanitation facilities
Energy	Main source of energy for cooking
*Employment[#]	Share of adult members of households employed
Transport	Type of transport used to get to work
Financial Services	Ratio of monthly debt service to total debt stock*
*Nutrition[#]	Share of children situated in household*
*Health Care[#]	Use of health facilities during last illness*
Safety[#]	Perception of safety inside (i) and outside (o) of house, compared to 5 years ago
Perceived Well-being	Level of satisfaction of household

Notes: * Households with missing values in these indicators were assigned a value based on their race, location (rural/urban/metro), and expenditure quintile.
[#] These seven components are used for the 'core deprivation index'.
Source: Klasen (2000, p. 40).

unlikely to stir much debate' (ibid.: 39), Clark and Qizilbash (2005) do query the arbitrariness of this and there are quite obvious challenges that might be made. For example, why should a non-poor individual who has a luxury flat close to his work and the privilege of walking to work each morning (despite owning two cars) be scored as deprived in terms of transport/mobility? Similarly, why should a domestic servant living in almost slave-like conditions be assessed as least deprived in terms of housing when she sleeps on the kitchen floor in her employer's house? In addition, the way in which these scores operate means that the measure is of relative and not absolute deprivation.

Thirdly, there is the inevitable questioning of the weighting of components in the index. Giving all components the same weight implies a complex set of value judgements. For example, can nutrition (child stunting that may reduce an individual's capabilities over her lifecourse) be weighted the same as transport/mobility (where a low score may be a temporary inconvenience)? There is another issue that Klasen does not mention: that this approach is paternalistic, in that it does not allow respondents to say what well-being, or more accurately lack of well-being, means for them.

Finally, and of central importance from the point of view of this chapter, Klasen's approach was not intended to be focused specifically on chronic poverty. Not all of the 14 indicators clearly correspond to chronic poverty rather than poverty as a whole; a more limited set of indices would be appropriate in measuring chronic poverty.

Despite these problems Klasen's index, or something similar to it, would represent a potentially important alternative to the income/consumption/expenditure approaches that have dominated chronic poverty analysis in South Africa and elsewhere. They may focus on relative deprivation – but in countries with large numbers of poor people such as South Africa, those who are relatively deprived in terms of capabilities are likely to be in absolute poverty.

Clark and Qizilbash's core poverty

Over recent years Mozaffar Qizilbash (2000, 2002a, 2003, 2005) has been exploring approaches that deal explicitly with the vagueness of what poverty is, and of how boundaries distinguishing the poor from the non-poor might be specified. These ideas have been empirically operationalized with David Clark in an approach that is strongly linked to capabilities – and to Sen's work in particular (Clark and Qizilbash, 2002, 2005). Their approach seeks to deal with the 'horizontal vagueness' of the dimensions of poverty and the 'vertical vagueness' of the minimal critical levels (for given dimensions) at or below which someone must fall to be classed as poor (Qizilbash, 2003: 50).

Following Fine's 'supervaluationalist' approach (Qizilbash, 2003), they develop a method that can identify admissible specifications for poverty. A statement about poverty is 'super true' only if it is true in all admissible ways of making it more precise. They refer to someone who is poor in this sense as 'core poor', meaning that they are unambiguously poor. To be core poor, a person must be poor in any single core dimension of poverty (i.e. one that is part of all admissible specifications for poverty) and must fall at or below the lowest critical level in that dimension. Other people who are ambiguously poor in a core dimension (i.e. poor in terms of at least one but not all admissible specifications of the corresponding poverty threshold), are classified as 'vulnerable'. In this usage, '...vulnerability relates to the possibility of being classified as poor, rather than any risk of becoming poor' (Qizilbash, 2003: 52). It is important to note that this approach does not aggregate scores in different dimensions. If a person is below the critical minimum level in a core dimension s/he is unambiguously poor regardless of their scores in all other dimensions.

Clark and Qizilbash (2002, 2005) have applied this approach by asking a randomly selected sample of 'ordinary people' from disadvantaged regions in South Africa about 'which needs and capabilities... are basic, and where they draw the line between the poor and non-poor' (ibid.: 9). The focus is on 'the essentials of life' rather than broader living conditions. Their interviewers administered a questionnaire that '...asked people about the level of achievement required to 'get by' as opposed to that to 'live well'' (ibid. 10). Interviewees were asked open ended questions about what they regarded as essential to 'get by' in their context and later were asked about a set of pre-defined human needs or capabilities.

A method was required to identify which of the dimensions specified by interviewees were 'core', and what counted as critical minimal levels. A natural criterion for a dimension to class as core poverty would be 100 per cent endorsement by all 941 respondents; however, no dimension received such a complete endorsement and 'it is sensible to allow for some margin of error in the interviewing process and to allow for at least a tiny proportion of answers which can be excluded' (ibid.: 13). Consequently, Clark and Qizilbash select a 'relaxed 95 per cent rule' i.e. any dimension of the essentials of life that is endorsed by 95 per cent of respondents (ibid.: 15). Correspondingly, a relaxed 5 per cent rule (requiring endorsement by at least 4.5 per cent of respondents) is used to identify the critical minimum level below which a person is classified as unambiguously poor in a particular dimension (ibid.: 18).[15]

This exercise suggests a large number of admissible dimensions of poverty (Table 10.5), of which the top 12 are core dimensions (i.e. 95 per cent of people identified these dimensions in their responses to open-ended questions). In the later parts of their paper the data from the nationally representative 1993 PSLSD survey of South Africa are analysed in terms of these core dimensions and minimum critical levels. Interestingly, all seven components of Klasen's (2000: 43) 'core deprivation index [of] the most basic capabilities' are included in this list of 12 'core dimensions'.

What would such an approach mean for the identification, measurement and analysis of chronic poverty? Potentially, it offers a number of advantages. The method means that the selection of the capabilities/components/dimensions that are sufficient to 'get by' (avoid poverty), can be held to be legitimate not because of 'intuition' (Klasen) or authorative judgement (Barrientos, see below), but because impoverished communities have specified them. The argument for the setting of the minimum level has a similar legitimacy. In addition, the procedure used can avoid challenges of paternalism as the people who experience poverty, or live alongside those who do, are selecting the measures and criteria that are to be used.

Table 10.5 Ordinal ranking of the top 30 essentials of life in three impoverished communities in South Africa (Clark and Qizilbash)

1 Housing/Shelter	16 Land and Livestock
2 Food	16 Own business/Enterprise
3 Water	16 Religion
4 Work/Jobs	19 Furniture
5 Money/Income	20 Happiness and Peace of Mind
6 Clothes	21 Community Development
7 Education/Schools	22 Love
8 Health/Health Care	23 Freedom/Independence
9 Electricity/Energy	24 Better Life
10 Safety and Security	24 Oxygen
11 Transport/Car	24 Respect
12 Family and Friends	27 Blankets
13 Sanitation	27 Heat/Temperature
14 Infrastructure	29 Sexuality
15 Leisure/Leisure Facilities	29 Sunlight

Source: Clark and Qizilbash (2005: 32).

A final advantage of this approach is that it does not require the construction of an index or the computation of adult equivalence. Challenges about the scoring and weighting of components do not arise.

Inevitably, there are potential disadvantages with this approach. The first, and perhaps most obvious, relates to the justification of the 95 per cent and 5 per cent rules – why not 99 per cent or 90 per cent... why not 1 per cent or 10 per cent? Clark and Qizilbash argue, however, that their rule is robust. The setting of these rules can be argued to be arbitrary – the method deals with vagueness by making a vague assumption. In fairness to Clark and Qizilbash, the selection of these cut-off points is discussed in detail, but still these end up as judgements rather than unambiguous criteria.

A second challenge relates to the issue of not aggregating data. According to this approach, it would be possible for someone who is just above the lowest admissible threshold in all dimensions to be classed as vulnerable (that is, not unambiguously poor) despite their relatively desperate circumstances. Someone else who is well above all of the highest admissable critical minimum levels in all dimensions except work/jobs (because they lost their job yesterday/recently) would be classed as core poor. Can this be justified?

A third problem is that this approach might be difficult or impossible for comparative work. As it is likely that people in different countries, or even in different parts of a country, would come up with different sets of dimensions and different minimum levels for unambiguous poverty, could these measures ever be used for cross-country comparisons? It is also not likely to be applicable in longitudinal studies – the key approach for analysing poverty dynamics. If the full method is applied each time a panel dataset is to be analysed, should the analyst apply the criteria (dimensions and levels) from the original survey or should a new exercise be conducted? If one opts for the former, one is imposing an old value set on the people interviewed, and not permitting them to revise their values over time. If one opts for the latter, then the criteria are likely to change, making it difficult to track the dynamics of poverty? This issue would need clarification.

Finally, there is the issue of the additional costs that this approach would impose on poverty analysis. At the very least, it would require an additional survey to be undertaken in each country (or region of a country) to derive the dimensions and levels that 'ordinary people' feel are important. This is not a vast amount, but it is likely to mean additional costs of $100,000 to $200,000 in most countries. It might, of course, be included in standard existing household surveys, but does represent a significant change in methodology.

Clark and Hulme (2005) have conceptually outlined a means by which Clark and Qizilbash's core poverty framework might be integrated with chronic poverty. However, this has already been challenged by Qizilbash (2005: note 9) and their approach has not been empirically tested as yet. Clark and Hulme (2005) have begun to explore ways of integrating the core poverty framework with the chronic poverty approach (see also Qizilbash, 2005 for some early reactions). Most of the work that has taken place is conceptual and typically involves introducing an additional layer of vagueness (vagueness about the duration of poverty) and a new sub-set of analytical categories, which are essentially hybrids of those used in the core poverty and chronic poverty frameworks (see Clark and Hulme, 2005: table 2). To qualify as *chronically core* poor in the extended framework, a person must fall at or below the lowest admissible poverty threshold in any core dimension for *all* admissible time periods (Clark and Hulme, 2005: 27; Qizilbash, 2005: 19). Much work remains to be done in terms of refining this framework and making these ideas operational.

Barrientos's measure of multidimensional deprivation

The third example considered here is Barrientos's (2003) construction of a multidimensional measure of deprivation to assess the impacts of non-contributory pensions on older people in Brazil and South Africa. His focus is 'on developing basic tools of multidimensional analysis of well being, and demonstrating that these can be effective in the evaluation of public policy'. He makes it clear that he has concerns about the inadequacies of standard monetary measures of poverty, and that Sen, along with Doyal and Gough and Nussbaum, have provided theoretical guidance in this exercise. His approach is explicitly less ambitious than Clark and Qizilbash's as he has a policy evaluation goal and strives for simplicity.

The indicators (Table 10.6) he selects (and he does call these indicators rather than specifying components or dimensions and then choosing indicators) fix 'on a range of achieved functionings rather than on capabilities, as the latter involves greatly more demanding information on opportunity and choice' (ibid.: 7). Deprivation is envisaged as failure in terms of certain basic functionings and these are chosen pragmatically in the light of data availability.

How the minimum levels that identify deprivation are selected is not clearly explained. These seem to have been set by personal judgements after consultations with other evaluators and older people in Brazil and South Africa. Each

Table 10.6 Well-being indicators (Barrientos)

Label	Description	Values	Deprivation
Health	Self-reported health status	1 very poor 2 poor 3 average 4 good 5 very good	1
Life satisfaction	Self-reported assessment 'Taking everything into account, how satisfied is this household with the way it lives these days?'	1 very dissatisfied 2 dissatisfied 3 neither satisfied not dissatisfied 4 satisfied 5 very satisfied	1, 2
Safety	Change in perception of safety from two years before	1 worse 2 same 3 better	1
Social participation	Number of social organisations the respondent belongs to	0–8 (Brazil) and 0–10 (South Africa). Brazil: senior centre, church group, community organisation, sports club, school organisation, political party, trade union. South Africa as Brazil plus: women's club, stokvel, burial society.	0
Political participation	Number of citizen actions	0–4 (participation in community meeting, or general meeting, complaints to authorities, work for political candidate)	0
Financial control	Responses to the question: 'How much of own money are you able to keep for yourself?'	1 none 2 very little 3 some 4 a reasonable amount 5 all	1
Debt service	Monthly debt repayments as proportion of total debt	1 if $x = >0.5$; 2 if $0.5 > x > = 0.2$; 3 if $0.2 > x > = 0.1$; 4 if $0.1 > x = >0.01$; 5 if $x < 0.01$	1, 2
Durables	Number of durables in household	0–11 (phone, stove electric or gas, stove paraffin or wood, electricity, tv, radio or stereo, fridge or freezer, sewing machine, car, bicycle, motorcycle)	1–5

(Continued)

Table 10.6   (Continued)

Label	Description	Values	Deprivation
Water	Main source of drinking water	1 other (river, dam, rainwater) 2 borehole 3 public tap/water carrier 4 piped water on site, neighbour 5 piped water in dwelling	1
Expenditure	Quintiles of equivalised per capita household expenditure	1–5	1, 2

Source: Barrientos (2003).

indicator is scored on a scale, ranging from 1 to 3 or from 0 to 11, and a different cut-off point is specified for each (see Table 10.6).

Aggregation at the individual level is computed by simple addition/counting, so that each person has a deprivation score out of 10. A score of zero indicates that a person is experiencing no deprivations, while a score of 10 indicates that someone is experiencing deprivation in all of the assessed dimensions. Barrientos is fully aware of the implications of equally weighting all dimensions in this way – 'aggregating the different indicators into a single measure of deprivation involves strong ethical implications, and it is important to bring these out... this amounts to assuming perfect substitution across deprivations' (ibid.: 9).

Barrientos sums up his approach as follows: 'The strategy adopted here – involving the counting approach, binary indicators of deprivation, and the assumptions regarding the weights attached to different deprivations, and their relationship – delivers the simplest approach to multidimensional evaluation' (ibid.: 10). Indeed, it has great simplicity, is readily understood by policy makers and a lay public, and produces persuasive findings about the contribution that non-contributory pensions can make to the well-being of older people.

As with all of these examples of operationalization of a human development approach to poverty assessment, it is open to many challenges. The first relates to the choice of indicators. His pragmatic approach has clear policy implications, but there are significant conceptual concerns about the method. While the indicators clearly derive from the literature on well-being there is no explicit theoretical rationale for their selection. The measures involve functionings (for example, health, social participation, political participation), capabilities (financial control, level of debt servicing), commodities (expenditure quintile and durables) and utility (self-reported satisfaction with life). This is more complex than the 'basic functionings' discussed in the methodology would suggest. Can all of these different things be put together? There are also omissions of key dimensions of deprivation that appear on many analysts 'lists'. For example, the analysis of both Klasen and Clark and Qizilbash (see above) include education, housing, employment and nutrition in their basic dimensions. Why are these excluded from Barrientos's list? In the cases of education and employment, it may be that for public policy purposes for older people it is 'too late' for intervention, or at least perceived as such. If that is the case it would be good to know it. However, for nutrition and housing it is much more difficult to explain why these are not included in the indicators.

The second criticism is the issue of thresholds. There is no clear explanation of how these have been selected. While their levels may seem reasonable they are not unproblematic. For example, a score of zero for political participation could mean an individual has full capability in this space but has exercised his (her) agency by deciding not to function in the political sphere. So, a zero functioning reflects a 100 per cent capability. Similarly, why 5 or less durables should be a threshold, rather than 4 or 6, needs some explanation.

Then there is the issue of aggregation. While his method is elegantly simple it faces standard challenges. For example, can the deprivation of poor health be equated to the lack of one or two durables? The former may be a catastrophic capability failure occasioned by weaknesses in public policy. The latter may reflect the capability of someone to function in a way that is environmentally friendly and leaves their life uncluttered.

Finally, there is the criticism of paternalism. By selecting the dimensions and indicators and choosing threshold levels has Barrientos deprived older people in Brazil and South Africa of their right to say what deprivation means for them?

As with the other examples, there is a long list of theoretical and methodological criticisms, but these need to be offset by considering the purpose of the exercise. It provides substantial evidence that non-contributory pensions can improve the well-being of older people, rather than just their income or expenditure, and reduces the measurement errors that a purely monetary assessment would have introduced to the evaluation. It is highly imperfect, but still may be better than the alternative – a unidimensional approach.

10.7   Conclusions: the current situation and possible future options

As our exploration has shown, monetary measures for assessing chronic poverty, and especially flow measures, are inadequate in both conceptual and practical terms. Their apparent precision masks the evidence that, at best, they are rough and partial surrogates; indeed, they may be quite imprecise as a result of measurement problems. Because of this they are likely to give an incomplete and possibly incorrect understanding of the poverty dynamics of households and populations. The reason for the focus on monetary measures in poverty dynamics work is understandable, because of all poverty indicators these may be the ones that have greatest difficulty in identifying longer-term living standards from a single observation.

Without doubt there are major challenges in developing measures of specifically chronic poverty that move beyond the monetary dimension, and none of the approaches considered here are yet completely convincing. Clearly, assets based approaches (section 10.4) offer new insights into the nature of poverty traps and there is much room for further elaboration.

The needs and human development approaches discussed in sections 10.5 and 10.6 provide detailed insights into the dimensions that might be included in a measure and of the operation of aggregation and dominance rules. Is there any way that these varying attempts to operationalize human development approaches might be brought together to agree to a single, common, practical measure that can be used over time and across countries? There are two potential alternatives here. Ruhi Saith (2001) argues that common ground can be identified. In the six human development lists she reviews, health, nutrition and education emerge as commonly agreed capabilities (see also Clark, 2002: ch. 3). An individual or household-level common capabilities index (CCI) might be constructed using a health indicator (for example, the quality of access to basic health services, last period of illness or a subjective assessment of health status), a nutrition indicator (such as BMI or degree of stunting and/or wasting) and an education indicator (years of schooling).

The second approach might be to construct a household-level human development index (HHDI) based on the dimensions used in UNDP's national-level HDI. This would have a similar degree of legitimacy and criticism as the HDI. While there would be plausible arguments pointing out the imperfect nature of the HHDI, it is hard to see what arguments could be made to demonstrate that the HHDI is inferior to per capita household income or consumption as a measure of human development. An HHDI would comprise a life expectancy indicator (for example, district/sub-district life expectancy adjusted for occupation of head of household),[16] an education/literacy indicator (for example, the percentage of literate adults and the average years of schooling per adult) and an income/consumption indicator (income or consumption per adult equivalent).

In both cases, however, significant difficulties arise, especially in relation to current and likely future data availability. In the former case there are issues about which indicators should be chosen, and which thresholds. It is difficult to derive satisfactory comparative measures of some dimensions within and across countries, including quality of access to health care services and (more problematically) subjective health care status. Stunting and wasting are typically only measured for young (often pre-school) children, who obviously will not be present in many households. In the latter case enrolment cannot be used in an indicator defined across all households because many households will not have school-aged children, and estimating variations in life expectancy across households is particularly problematic. In both cases also there is a need for aggregation to the household level, losing variations between individual household members.

This then raises the issue of why a single multidimensional measure of poverty is required. At national level the HDI has been convenient in providing a unique ranking of countries, but performance across different dimensions varies – and the specific dimension is often of greater relevance for policy purposes. A similar point arises at the household level: education indicators are the ones of greatest relevance for education sector policy. In other words, there is a strong argument for *not* aggregating different dimensions into a single indicator, but, rather, to consider different dimensions separately. In any case any proposed single indicator of multidimensional chronic poverty will inevitably omit some dimensions.

Whatever progress is made with assets-based or human development frameworks two foundational difficulties remain: one is conceptual and ideological and the other is ethical.

(i) How to capture social relations and power within an analytical framework; and,
(ii) 'who' has the moral right to specify what poverty is.

With regard to the first, the main device that is currently used is to view social relations as social capital, based on Coleman's (1990) conceptualization rather than that of Bourdieu (1986), and to measure social capital in terms of a household's social network. An oft-cited example is Narayan and Pritchett (1997) who measured social capital in Tanzania in terms of households' involvement with local and community organizations. This has the great advantage of being operationally feasible and also providing a measure that can be incorporated into assets and/or livelihoods frameworks. Unfortunately, this ignores the fact that social relations are about much more than 'civic engagement' and that social relations are of many different qualities (weak or strong, cooperative or exploitive, mutual or asymmetric, universal or particularistic). In Harriss's (2001: 113) words this 'obscure[s] class politics and power... [and provides] a way of talking about 'changing social relations' – but without seriously questioning existing power relations and property rights'. It also ignores the 'dark side' (ibid.: 115) of social capital – mafias, gangs and cartels which are actively anti-social. It depoliticizes development so that policy options are presented as technical decisions rather than political choices. To get around these criticisms this version of social capital has been deepened to recognise bonding capital (ties that give communities a sense of identity and common purposes), bridging capital (ties that transcend various social divides) and, linking capital (that connects the poor and marginalized to the more powerful), but these still do not respond to many of the key concerns raised above. However, recent innovative work by Kabeer (2005) suggests that it is possible to undertake quantitative work that examines the assets of households and, alongside it, use qualitative data collection and analysis methods to explore social relations and power, but without seeking to measure social capital or relations.

The second foundational problem concerns the question of 'who' should determine what poverty is and how it might be assessed. While much of this chapter has looked at the feasibility of reconciling different conceptual approaches and/or different lists of needs, capabilities or functionings (theorist versus theorist) there is the question of whether the abstract ideas of elites should override the experiences and understandings of those living in poverty (theorists versus poor people). Letting a theorist, or an amalgam of theorists, determine what poverty is can be seen as paternalistic and even disempowering. Qizilbash and Clark (see section 10.6) provide a mechanism for permitting poor communities to set the parameters for poverty assessment. They point out that most of the parameters set by poor South Africans are not dissimilar to the human development lists produced by theorists. However, as mentioned earlier, this approach might not allow for comparisons over space and over time as it has a non-universalist view of poverty.

Acknowledgments

Our special thanks to David Clark for advice on the design and content of this chapter. We also received excellent research assistance from David Clark and Karen Moore and David Hulme's contribution was supported by the Economic and Social Research Council's (ESRC) Global Poverty Research Group (Universities of Manchester and Oxford).

Notes

1. This paragraph and the next draw heavily on Clark and Hulme (2005).
2. The Chronic Poverty Research Centre (CPRC) has explicitly set out to be multidisciplinary but a high proportion of its publications remain based on quantitative analyses of panel data (see www.chronicpoverty.org and Hulme and Shepherd 2003).
3. For a rare exception see Baulch and Masset (2003).
4. As Hulme and Toye (2006) point out 'the benefits of [disciplinary] specialization brought with them various costs, most particularly an erosion of the overall coherence of the concept of poverty'.
5. Even when the unit of analysis is the household this is commonly treated as behaving like *homo economicus*.
6. A fine example is sociologist/social historian Charles Tilly's (1998) *Durable Inequality*. Much of the content of this volume could be viewed as exploring the persistence of poverty in the USA. However, the term poverty is not even listed in the index. Tilly's insistence that analysis must focus on social relations and social categories means that methodological individualism, and phenomenalogical individualism, are seen as ineffective tools at best.
7. But do note that du Toit (2005) argues that most attempts at combination simply 'add on' a little qualitative analysis. They do not seriously attempt to relate quantitative work to critical social theory.
8. Gibson (2001) claimed to develop a method for distinguishing transitory and chronic poverty without a panel, but in fact his approach is about more accurate measurement of poverty and not about poverty dynamics.
9. Note, however, that in practice getting reliable responses on land and livestock ownership is often difficult due to the sensitivity of these issue, and because these assets are less easily observed than, say, housing quality.
10. The LADDER project (2001–2003), directed by Frank Ellis, elaborated on his earlier work. However, its focus was on key natural assets (LADDER Research Team, 2001) and data collection on social capital was limited or absent.
11. See also the volumes edited by Hawthorn (1987), Nussbaum and Sen (1993), Nussbaum and Glover (1995), and Fukuda-Parr and Kumar (2003). The human development approach incorporates the basic needs approach to development as well as the capability approach, the emerging literature on development ethics and the UNDP's highly influential *Human Development Reports*. The Human Development and Capability Association's web site can be accessed at http://www.hd-ca.org.
12. However, only 15 are listed in a journal article published in the same year (Alkire, 2002b).
13. To what degree is a heated debate? For example, Nussbaum (2000, 2003) claims to allow for additions and modifications to her list that permit agency and different cultures to shape the content of what constitutes well-being. However, many would say this is mere lip-service.
14. See PSLSD (1994).
15. Technically, a person is classified as definitely poor if she or he falls below the lowest critical minimum to get an endorsement of at least 4.5 per cent. This is because Clark and Qizilbash's questionnaire asked people what they thought was necessary to 'get by'.

16. The computation of a household life expectancy indicator is probably the greatest challenge to an HHDI and merits a paper in its own right.

References

Adato, M., M. Carter and J. May (2004) 'Sense in Sociability? Social exclusion and persistent poverty in South Africa'. Available at: http://www.sarpn.org.za/documents/d0001127/index.php

Alkire, S. (2002a) *Valuing Freedoms: Sen's Capability Approach and Poverty Reduction*. Oxford: Oxford University Press.

Alkire, S. (2002b) 'Dimensions of Human Development' *World Development*, 30(2), pp. 18–205.

Alderman, H., Behrman, J., Kohler, Maluccio J, and Cotts Watkins, S., (2000) 'Attrition in Longitudinal Household Survey Data: Some Tests for Three Developing-Country Samples', *Policy Research Working Paper 2447*. Washington, DC: World Bank.

Appleton, S. and L. Song (1999) 'Income and Human Development at the Household Level', Background paper for the World Development Report 2000/2001.

Bane, M. and D. Ellwood (1986) 'Slipping into and out of Poverty: The Dynamics of Spells', *Journal of Human Resources*, 21(1), 1–23.

Barrientos, A. (2003) 'Non-Contributory Pensions and Well-being among Older People: Evidence on Multidimensional Deprivation from Brazil and South Africa', *Development Economics and Public Policy Working Paper 1*, Institute for Development Policy and Management, University of Manchester, UK. Available at http://www.sed.manchester.ac.uk/idpm/publications/wp/depp/depp_wp01.pdf.

Baulch, B. and J. Hoddinott (2000) (eds), *Economic Mobility and Poverty Dynamics in Developing Countries*. London: Frank Cass.

Baulch, B. and E. Masset (2003) 'Do Monetary and Non-Monetary Indicators Tell the Same Story about Chronic Poverty? A Study of Vietnam in the 1990s', *World Development*, 31(3), 441–53.

Bourdieu, P. (1986) 'The Forms of Capital', in J. Richardson (ed.), *Handbook of Theory and Research for the Sociology of Education*. New York: Greenwood, pp. 241–58.

Bourguignon, F., Goh, C., and Kim, D. (2004) 'Estimating Individual Vulnerability to Poverty with Pseudo-Panel Data', *Policy Research Working Paper 3375*, Washington, DC: World Bank.

Carney, D. (ed.) (1998) *Sustainable Rural Livelihoods: What Contribution Can We Make?* London: Department for International Development (DFID).

Carter, M and C. Barrett (2006), 'The Economics of Poverty Traps and Persistent Poverty: an Asset-based Approach', *Journal of Development Studies*, 42(2), 178–99.

Carter, M. and J. May (2001), 'One Kind of Freedom: Poverty Dynamics in Post-Apartheid South Africa,' *World Development*, 29(12), 1987–2006.

Clark, D.A. (2002) *Visions of Development: A Study of Human Values*. Cheltenham: Edward Elgar.

Clark, D.A. (2005) 'Sen's Capability Approach and the Many Spaces of Human Well-Being', *Journal of Development Studies*, 41(8), 1339–68.

Clark, D.A. (2006) 'Capability Approach,' in D. A. Clark (ed.), *The Elgar Companion to Development Studies*. Cheltenham: Edward Elgar, pp. 32–45.

Clark, D.A. and D. Hulme (2005) 'Towards A Integrated Framework for Understanding the Breadth, Depth and Duration of Poverty', *GPRG Working Paper 20*, Universities of Manchester and Oxford, UK. Available online at http://www.gprg.org/pubs/workingpapers/pdfs/gprg-wps-020.pdf.

Clark, D.A. and M. Qizilbash (2002) 'Core Poverty and Extreme Vulnerability in South Africa', *Discussion Paper No. 2002-3*, School of Economics, University of East Anglia, UK. Revised version: http://www.geocities.com/poverty_in_southafrica.

Clark, D.A. and M. Qizilbash (2005) 'Core Poverty, Basic Capabilities and Vagueness: An Application to the South African Context', *GPRG Working Paper 26*, Universities of Manchester and Oxford, UK. Available online at http://www.gprg.org/pubs/workingpapers/pdfs/gprg-wps-026.pdf.

Coleman, J. (1990) *Foundations of Social Theory*. Cambridge, MA: Harvard University Press.

Cooke, W. and U. Kothari (2001) *Participation: The New Tyranny?* London: Zed Books.

CPRC (2004) *The Chronic Poverty Report 2004/05*, Chronic Poverty Research Centre (CPRC), University of Manchester, UK. http://www.chronicpoverty.org.

Dercon, S. and P. Krishnan (2000) 'Vulnerability, Seasonality and Poverty in Ethiopia', *Journal of Development Studies*, 36(6), 82–100.

DFID (1999–2001), *Sustainable Livelihoods Guidance Sheets*. London: DFID. Available at http://www.livelihoods.org/info/info_guidancesheets.html.

Doyal, L. and I. Gough (1991). *A Theory of Human Need*. London: Macmillan.

du Toit, A. (2005) 'Poverty Measurement Blues: Some Reflections on the Space for Understanding "chronic" and "Structural" Poverty in South Africa', *Chronic Poverty Research Centre Working Paper* 55, University of Manchester, UK. Available at http://www.chronicpoverty.org/resources/working_papers.html.

Ellis, F. (2000) *Rural Livelihoods and Diversity in Developing Countries*. Oxford: Oxford University Press.

Falaris, E. (2003) 'The Effect of Survey Attrition in Longitudinal Surveys: Evidence from Peru, Côte d'Ivoire and Vietnam', *Journal of Development Economics*, 70(1), 133–57.

Frey, B.S. and A. Stutzer (2001) *Happiness and Economics: How the Economy and Institutions Affect Human Well-Being*. Princeton, NJ: Princeton University Press.

Fukuda-Parr, S. and A. K. S. Kumar (eds) (2003) *Readings in Human Development*, New York: Oxford University Press.

Gaiha, R. (1988) 'Income Mobility in Rural India', *Economic Development and Cultural Change*, 36(2), 279–302.

Gaiha, R. (1989) 'Are the Chronically Poor also the Poorest in Rural India?', *Development and Change*, 20(2), 295–322.

Gibson, J. (2001) 'Measuring Chronic Poverty Without a Panel', *Journal of Development Economics*, 65, 243–66.

Gough, I. (2004) 'Lists and Thresholds: Comparing Our Theory of Human Need with Nussbaum's Capabilities Approach', *WeD Working Paper No. 1*, University of Bath.

Green, M. and D. Hulme (2005) 'From Correlates and Characteristics to Causes: Thinking About Poverty from a Chronic Poverty Perspective', *World Development*, 33(6), 867–79.

Haddad, L. and R. Kanbur (1990) 'How Serious is the Neglect of Intra-Household Inequality?', *Economic Journal*, 100(402), 866–81.

Harriss, J. (2001) *Depoliticising Development: The World Bank and Social Capital*. London: Anthem Press.

Hawthorn, G. (ed.) (1987) *The Standard of Living*. Cambridge: Cambridge University Press.

Haq, Mahbub ul (1995) *Reflections on Human Development*, Oxford: Oxford University Press.

Howe, G. and A. McKay (2007) 'Combining Quantitative and Qualitative methods in Assessing Chronic Poverty: The Case of Rwanda', *World Development*, 35(2), 197–211.

Hulme, D., K. Moore and A. Shepherd (2001), 'Chronic Poverty: Meanings and Analytic Frameworks', *Chronic Poverty Research Centre Working Paper* 2, University of Manchester, UK. Available at http://www.chronicpoverty.org/resources/working_papers.html.

Hulme, D. and Shepherd, A. (2003) 'Conceptualizing chronic poverty', *World Development*, 31(3), 403–24.

Hulme, D. and Toye, J. (2006) 'The Case for Cross-disciplinary Social Science Research on Poverty, Inequality and Well-being', *Journal of Development Studies*, 42(7), 1085–107.

Iliffe, J. (1987) *The African Poor: A History*. Cambridge: Cambridge University Press.

Johnson, S., D. Hulme and O. Ruthven (2005) 'Finance and Poor People's Livelihoods', in C. J. Green, C. Kirkpatrick and V. Murinde (eds), *Finance and Development: Surveys of Theory, Evidence and Policy*. Cheltenham: Edward Elgar.

Kabeer, N. (2005) 'Snakes, Ladders and Traps: Changing Lives and Livelihoods in Rural Bangladesh (1994–2001)', *Chronic Poverty Research Centre Working Paper 50*, University of Manchester, UK. Available online at http://www.chronicpoverty.org/pdfs/50%20Kabeer.pdf.

Klasen, S. (1997) 'Poverty, Inequality and Deprivation in South Africa: an Analysis of the 1993 SALDRU Survey', *Social Indicator Research*, 41, 51–94.

Klasen, S. (2000) 'Measuring Poverty and Deprivation in South Africa,' *Review of Income and Wealth*, 46, 33–58.

Krishna, A. (2006) 'Pathways Out of and Into poverty in 36 Villages of Andhra Pradesh, India', *World Development*, 34(2), 271–88.

LADDER Research Team (2001) 'Methods Manual for Fieldwork', *LADDER Working Paper 2*, School of Development Studies, University of East Anglia.

Lawson, D., A. McKay and K. Moore (2005) 'Panel datasets in developing and transitional countries (version 1 – 07, 2003)', Chronic Poverty Research Centre, University of Manchester, UK. Available at http://www.chronicpoverty.org/pdfs/PanelDatasetsVersion1-July%202003.pdf.

Lawson, D., A. McKay and J. Okidi (2006) 'Poverty Persistence and Transitions in Uganda: A Combined Qualitative and Quantitative Analysis', *Journal of Development Studies*, 42(7), 1225–51.

McKay, A. and D. Lawson (2003) 'Assessing the Extent and Nature of Chronic Poverty in Low Income Countries: Issues and Evidence', *World Development*, 31(3), 425–39.

Moore, K (2001) 'Frameworks for Understanding the Intergenerational Transmission of Poverty and Well-being in Developing Countries', *Chronic Poverty Research Centre Working Paper 8*, University of Manchester, UK. Available online at http://www.chronicpoverty.org/resources/working_papers.html.

Mosse, D. (1994) 'Authority, Gender and Knowledge: Theoretical Reflections on the Practice of Participatory Rural Appraisal', *Development and Change*, 25(3), 497–525.

Narayan, D. and L. Pritchett (1997) 'Cents and Sociability: Household Income and Social Capital in Rural Tanzania', *Policy Research Working Paper 1796*. Washington, DC: World Bank, Social Development Department and Development Research Group.

Narayan, D., R. Chambers, M. Kaul Shah, and P. Petesch (2000) *Voices of the Poor: Crying Out for Change*. New York: Oxford University Press for the World Bank.

Nussbaum, M.C. (1988) 'Nature, function and capability: Aristotle on political distribution', *Oxford Studies in Ancient Philosophy*, Suppl. Vol., pp. 145–84.

Nussbaum, M.C. (1995) 'Human Capabilities, Female Human Beings', in Martha C. Nussbaum and Jonathan Glover (eds), *Women, Culture and Development*. Oxford: Clarendon Press, pp. 61–104.

Nussbaum, M.C. (2000) *Women and Human Development: the Capabilities Approach*. Cambridge: Cambridge University Press.

Nussbaum, M.C. (2003) 'Capabilities as Fundamental Entitlement: Sen and Social Justice', *Feminist Economics*, 9(2–3), 33–59.

Nussbaum, M.C. and J. Glover (eds) (1995) *Women, Culture and Development*. Oxford: Clarendon Press.

Nussbaum, M.C. and Sen, A.K. (eds) (1993) *The Quality of Life*. Oxford: Clarendon Press.

O'Connor, A. (2001). *Poverty Knowledge: Social Science, Social Policy and the Poor in Twentieth Century US History*. Princeton: Princeton University Press.

PSLSD (1994) *South Africans Rich and Poor: Baseline Household Statistics*. Cape Town: Southern Africa Labour and Development Research Unit, University of Cape Town.

Qizilbash, M. (2000) 'Vagueness and the Measurement of Poverty', *Discussion Paper No. 200003*, School of Economic and Social Studies, University of East Anglia.

Qizilbash, M. (2002a) 'A Note on the Measurement of Poverty and Vulnerability in the South African Context', *Journal of International Development*, 14, 757–72.

Qizilbash, M. (2002b) 'Development, Common Foes and Shared Values', *Review of Political Economy*, 14(4), 463–80.

Qizilbash, M. (2003) 'Vague Language and Precise Measurement: the Case of Poverty', *Journal of Economic Methodology*, 10(1), 41–58.

Qizilbash, M. (2005) 'Philosophical Accounts of Vagueness, Fuzzy Poverty Measures and Multidimensionality', *Discussion Paper No.2005-1*, School of Economics, University of East Anglia, Norwich.

Ranis, G., F. Stewart and E. Samman (2005) 'Human Development: Beyond the HDI', *Economic Growth Centre Discussion Paper* 916, Yale University. Available at http://www.econ.yale.edu/~egcenter/EGCdp4.htm (Later published in the *Journal of Human Development*, 7(3), 2006, 323–51).

Sahn, D.E. and D.C. Stifel (2000) 'Poverty Comparisons Over Time and Across Countries in Africa', *World Development*, 28 (12), 2123–55.

Saith, R. (2001) 'Capabilities: the Concept and its Operationalisation', *QEH Working Paper Series 66*, Queen Elizabeth House, University of Oxford.

Scoones, I. (1998) 'Sustainable Rural Livelihoods: A Framework for Analysis', *IDS Working Paper* 72. Brighton: Institute for Development Studies.

Scott, C. (1992) 'Estimation of Annual Expenditure from One Month Cross Sectional Data in a Household Survey', *Inter-Stat*, 8, 57–65.

Sen, A.K. (1984) *Resources, Values and Development*. Oxford: Basil Blackwell.

Sen, A.K. (1985) *Commodities and Capabilities*. Oxford: Elsevier Science Publishers.

Sen, A.K. (1999) *Development As Freedom*. Oxford: Oxford University Press.

Streeten, P., Shahid J. Burki, Mahbub ul Haq, Norman Hicks, and Frances Stewart (1981) *First Things First: Meeting Basic Human Needs in Developing Countries*. New York: Oxford University Press.

Stewart, F. (1985). *Planning to Meet Basic Needs*. London: Macmillan.

Stewart, F. (2006) 'Basic Needs Approach', in D. A. Clark (ed.), *The Elgar Companion to Development Studies*. Cheltenham: Edward Elgar, pp. 14–18.

Stutzer, A. (2004) 'The Role of Income Aspirations in Individual Happiness', *Journal of Economic Behavior and Organization*, 54(1), 89–109.

Tilly, C. (1998) *Durable Inequality*. Berkeley: University of California Press.

UN Statistics Division (2004) Progress towards the Millennium Development Goals, 1990–2004, Available at: http://millenniumindicators.un.org.

UNDP (2003) *Human Development Report 2003*. Oxford: Oxford University Press.

Wilson, I., and S. R. A. Huttly (2003) *Young Lives: A Case Study of Sample Design for Longitudinal Research*. London: Save the Children UK.

11
Risk and Vulnerability to Poverty

Cesar Calvo and Stefan Dercon

About a quarter of the rural population survive by exchanging labour at market wages and commanding food with what they earn. For them a variation of the exchange relationships can spell ruin. There is, in fact, some evidence that in recent years in Bangladesh the wage system itself has moved more towards money wages, away from payments in kind – chiefly food. More modern, perhaps; more vulnerable, certainly.

Sen (1981: 150)

11.1   Introduction

Human deprivation is not confined to consumption shortfalls. Recent literature is crafting both analytical and empirical frameworks that will reshape our understanding of poverty as a multidimensional condition. Low consumption, below some minimal standard, is but one of the faces of poverty, and indeed the predicaments of the poor may be often due to some other forms of deprivation, such as disease, illiteracy, malnutrition, and also a sense of insecurity and defencelessness as they endeavour to survive in an environment characterized by uncertainty about the future. In this chapter we focus on this last component, and claim that such lack of 'peace of mind' is a relevant form of deprivation, as argued for instance by Chambers (1989) and Narayan, Patel *et al.* (2000).

Indeed, in recent decades, poverty measures have been provided with welfare-economic foundations both in the unidimensional space, as in Sen (1976) and Atkinson (1987), and later in the multidimensional case, as in Atkinson and Bourguignon (1982), and Bourguignon and Chakravarty (2003). Consequently, poverty measures consistent with social welfare functions have found their way into applied research, using state-of-art methods and data analysis – Foster, Greer and Thorbecke (1984) and Ravallion (1994) are well-known examples, to take two among various others. However, the entire analysis so far tends to take place in a world of certainty: poverty measures are defined after all uncertainty surrounding the individual welfare indicator has been resolved. In this chapter, we take a step backwards, and address issues arising at a stage when uncertainty has not been lifted yet. For simplicity, we focus on one well-being dimension, and let uncertainty regarding its final outcomes act as the second dimension where a dent on well-being may result.

In many instances, full certainty is a suitable assumption. For example, when assessing the impact of a new transfer scheme after it has been introduced, data on its actual impact and the resulting poverty outcomes are obviously relevant. However, when deciding to commit resources to competing schemes *ex-ante*, evaluating which one will be more effective to reduce poverty will have to pay attention to as many potential outcomes as possible states of the world. Uncertainty cannot be ignored.

Furthermore, uncertainty also matters in the following sense, which is crucial in our analysis. The possibility of serious hardship must contain information relevant for assessing low well-being. For example, consider two families, both with the same expected consumption, above some accepted norm, but one with a positive probability of hardship, and the other one facing no uncertainty. Neither is expected to be poor, and *ex-post* we may observe them to exhibit identical consumption levels, but surely the possibility of downside risk for the former has some bearing on the *ex-ante* analysis of welfare.

It is surprising that the calculus of risk has not systematically entered normative economic analysis of poverty until fairly recently. Even Sen's (1981) seminal contribution on famines is, in its welfare analysis, concerned with the *ex-post* consequences of the crisis in terms of poverty and destitution. Policy analysis is done with the benefit of hindsight, even though the sequence of events unfolding during the Bangladesh famine in 1974 and the realized outcomes were just one set among a number of possible scenarios *ex-ante*.

In this chapter, we consider the *ex-ante* consequences of the possibility of *future* hardship. In particular, we focus on the concept and measurement of *vulnerability*, which we view as the magnitude of the *threat of poverty*, measured *ex-ante*, before the veil of uncertainty has been lifted.

Many authors have made use of the term 'vulnerability', with increased frequency since it was brought to the spotlight by the 2000/1 World Development Report, where 'vulnerability measures the resilience against a shock – the likelihood that a shock will result in a decline in well-being' (World Bank, 2001: 139). This definition, however, did not remain uncontested for too long, since various other views have been proposed. Nonetheless, the resulting variety does not obscure a common thread, which can probably be reduced to some sense of insecurity, of potential harm people must feel wary of – *something bad* can happen and 'spell ruin'.

For instance, vulnerability is sometimes equated to low expected welfare, whereby the concept is conveniently ensured to be sensitive to risk exposure. However, we argue in this chapter that vulnerability is not a mere tantamount for the welfare loss due to general risk. The concept necessitates some explicit reference to 'danger' or 'downside risk'. Even in common parlance, someone is vulnerable if she is capable of being hurt or wounded. The etymological root '*vulnerare*' is Latin for the verb 'to wound'. The term clearly relates to *dangers*, or *threats*, as opposed to uncertainties in general.

For instance, in the example from Sen quoted above, we could say that, before the floods in Bangladesh in 1974, the future of wage-earners was overall more promising and less uncertain than that of subsistence farmers – yet their exposure to severe destitution in case of floods and rising food prices was greater, and they were more vulnerable than the farmers.

There is a broader sense of the term 'vulnerability' as 'defencelessness', referring to a general frailty or chronic helplessness of people. While our measure of vulnerability will include those who are bound to be poor in all states of the world, our focus in this chapter is largely on exploring the implication of considering different possible states of the world, which both may or may not drive people into poverty.

In short, this chapter aims to contribute to the ongoing debate by proposing vulnerability measures which we will claim to be faithful to this fundamental sense of *vulnerability as exposure to 'threats', to 'downside risks'*. We will derive these measures from a set of axioms, including, crucially, what we will call the 'focus axiom'. This axiom will allow us to separate out threats from overall expectations, or in other words, downside risks from general uncertainty. Going back to Sen's quotation, even if Bangladeshi wage-earners expect a 'better future' than subsistence farmers, we will allow them to be more vulnerable than the latter.

We discuss the small, largely empirical, but closely related literature that has introduced other concepts of vulnerability. Among the most important examples are Bourguignon *et al.* (2004), Christiaensen and Subbarao (2004), Chaudhuri *et al.* (2002), Kamanou and Morduch (2005). Ligon and Schechter (2003) provide a conceptually careful attempt to bring poverty considerations into an expected utility framework for a well-defined concept of vulnerability. The analysis in this chapter is fundamentally different by its normative welfare-economic focus, providing axiomatic foundations to measurement issues. It is non-welfarist in spirit, not relying on the utility framework. Furthermore, we place the notion of 'downside risk' at the core of our analysis.

The chapter draws heavily on the results in Calvo and Dercon (2006). Proofs and more detailed mathematical formulations can be found there, as we focus here on the main intuitions and arguments emerging in the vulnerability debate.

The structure of the chapter is as follows. Section 11.2 will discuss further our view of vulnerability. Section 11.3 continues this clarification, as we expand on the meaning and implications of an axiom which lies at the heart of our analysis and which we call a 'focus' axiom. Sections 11.4 and 11.5 then turn to propose and discuss measures of individual and aggregate vulnerability, respectively. Section 11.6 concludes.

11.2 The concept of vulnerability

To describe life in an environment tainted by uncertainty, we imagine a world where future outcomes differ across possible states of the world. Let m states exist and each i-state be characterized by an outcome level y_i and a probability p_i. Vectors **y** and **p** summarize this world, together with the poverty line z.[1]

It may be easiest to think of the relevant outcomes as consumption levels, but we shall avoid such language as an effort to stress that our measure is suitable to other well-being dimensions (say, health or leisure). In any case, we do impose that no exchange in outcomes will take place across states. This does not necessarily mean that neither formal nor informal insurance mechanisms are allowed to exist. It suffices to imagine that all desired and feasible exchanges have already been made. In other words, outcome smoothing across states has been taken as far as it was possible and convenient (say, for instance, with the maximization of expected utility as driving criterion).

We view vulnerability as *the magnitude of the threat of future poverty*. To be more explicit, we can use our notation to relate this 'magnitude of the threat' both (i) to the likelihood of future states where poverty obtains (that is, to the set of p_i for all *i* where $y_i < z$), and (ii) to the severity of poverty in those cases, as given by some suitable comparison of y_i with z. Individuals dread the possibility of future poverty episodes, and they are said to be vulnerable to the extent that poverty cannot be ruled out as a possible scenario. By the same token, their vulnerability is greater when there is a worse danger to fear, when poverty threatens to be more severe.

Note that vulnerability is in this sense an *ex-ante* statement about *future* poverty, before the veil is lifted and the uncertainty is replaced by the knowledge of the actual facts. Indeed, authors were prompted to resort to the term 'vulnerability' by the sense that the predicament of the poor is not only about insufficient command on resources, but also about insecurity and risks. The usual poverty concepts and measures do not capture the burden placed by this insecurity on the shoulders of the poor, as they typically focus on observed states of deprivation, making statements about singular or multiple dimensions of well-being. They invoke an *ex-post* concept of poverty, devoid of the *ex-ante* uncertainty which compounds the distress of the poor. In a sense, the notion of vulnerability was meant to amend this omission.

To put it differently, we may say that we refer here to 'vulnerability to future poverty' – for instance, we understand expressions such as 'vulnerability to an epidemic' as a shortcut to 'vulnerability to poverty due to an epidemic'. Of course, this highlights that some particular concept of poverty is required. In this chapter, we simply follow the mainstream. By imposing a constant z, we see poverty as the failure to reach some absolute standard of living (as measured by overall consumption, or nutritional levels, or any other dimension of human well-being). Outcomes below this poverty line are socially unacceptable.

More formally, let vulnerability be measured by

$$V^* = V(z, \mathbf{p}, \mathbf{y}).$$

This definition will hold until section 11.5, when we deal with aggregate vulnerability. To begin with, we intend to assess only how vulnerable each individual or household is, and not the extent of vulnerability among a group of them. We can thus rank families according to their vulnerability levels, or describe the evolution of household vulnerability over time – but vulnerability comparisons across regions or countries remain unexplored until section 11.5.

11.3   The focus axiom

We take the following condition as our starting point. As long as outcomes are above the poverty line, our vulnerability measure will ignore changes in those outcomes.

This requirement is based on our view of vulnerability as a burden caused by the threat of future *poverty*, which it is crucial to keep conceptually separate from the gain deriving from simultaneous (*ex-ante*) possibilities of being well off. The individual may compare both this threat and this gain and conclude that either outweighs the other, possibly using maximum expected utility as her ultimate target – but still, they remain distinct. Again, good overall expectations are not the same as, nor do they ensure, low vulnerability.

For instance, imagine that a farmer faces two scenarios: rain (no poverty) or drought (poverty). Does she become less vulnerable if the harvest in the rainy scenario improves? Our answer is 'no'. *Poverty is as bad a threat as before!* It is as likely as before, and it is potentially as severe as before. Likewise, take again the example of subsistence farmers and wage-earners in Bangladesh: the fact that the latter would have probably thrived and outperformed the former in almost every other state of the world apart from the floods does not make them less vulnerable.

A further example can be found in Sen, whose discussion of the famine in Sahel includes the following point:

> Compared with the farmer or the pastoralist who lives on what he grows and is thus vulnerable only to variations of his own output (arising from climatic considerations or other influences), the grower of cash crops, or the pastoralist heavily dependent on selling animal products, is vulnerable both to output fluctuations and to shifts in marketability of commodities and in exchange rates. ... *while commercialization may have opened up new economic opportunities, it has also tended to increase the vulnerability of the Sahel population.*
>
> (Sen, 1981: 126; added emphasis)

This condition may be formalized as follows. V^* satisfies the FOCUS AXIOM if

$$V(z,\mathbf{p},\mathbf{y}) = V(z,\mathbf{p},\tilde{\mathbf{y}}), \text{ where } \tilde{y}_i = \text{Min}[z,y_i].$$

The uncensored vector $\mathbf{y}$ will not add any relevant contribution to the information already contained in $\tilde{\mathbf{y}}$, where outcomes are censored at z. Greater or lower outcomes in 'non-poor states' of the world do not make individuals more or less vulnerable to poverty.

Ignoring the focus axiom would lead to some odd conclusions. For instance, even if severe destitution is one possible scenario, a household could still be found not to be vulnerable, provided other scenarios are promising enough to compensate for the risk of starvation.

To clarify this further, take the following two examples. Firstly, let us imagine that each week the poor buy a state lottery ticket – they spend a very small sum of money, but 'you never know', and there is a 0.001 per cent chance of winning the top prize of $10,000. With no focus axiom, the following 'policy' measure would make these households less vulnerable: increase the top prize to $10 million!

For a second example, assume rain and drought are the only two states of the world possible, and the poverty line is estimated to be 100. With no focus axiom, imagine John (with outcomes (80,50), under rain and drought respectively) is found to be more vulnerable than his neighbour Peter (with outcomes (120,30)).

Imagine now that the poverty line had been overestimated (say because the researcher wrongly thought that John and Peter had special needs). If the real poverty line is 70 and vulnerability is recalculated, should we still expect John to turn out to be more vulnerable than Peter? We find, however, no strong intuition to *a priori* discard a ranking reshuffle, and it is the focus axiom that ensures that such a reshuffle is possible. In fact, when the true poverty line is used, John's future has some scope for hope – should the weather be benevolent and the rain plentiful, he would escape poverty, along with Peter. Nevertheless, if the line is overestimated, John is doomed to destitution, even in the best scenario, whereas Peter's hopes remain upbeat. If we take the poverty line seriously, then this should have relevant consequences in our assessment of vulnerability. With no focus axiom, such consequences would be overlooked, and the reason lies in the peripheral role of the poverty line. In our view of vulnerability, this line is placed at the core of the analysis, by virtue of the focus axiom.

11.4   A family of measures of individual vulnerability

Let us propose the following family of measures of individual vulnerability:

$$V_{(\alpha)} \equiv 1 - E[x^{\alpha}], \text{ with } 0 < \alpha < 1 \tag{11.1}$$

where we define $x_i \equiv (\tilde{y}_i / z)$ as the rate of coverage of basic needs, which implies $0 \leq x_i \leq 1$. In this section, we discuss a number of convenient features of this measure.

We should note that this is reminiscent of the measure of *individual* poverty implicit in Chakravarty (1983), where *aggregate* (*ex-post*) poverty in a group of n individuals is determined by

$$P_{(\alpha)} = \frac{1}{n} \sum_{j=1}^{n} \left(1 - x_j^{\alpha} \right), \text{ with } 0 < \alpha < 1.$$

Vulnerability measures proposed elsewhere also resemble some poverty measure. In fact, vulnerability is often seen as nothing else than 'expected poverty', so that *any* tractable poverty measure is taken as the starting point in the task of measuring vulnerability – for instance, as in Christiaensen and Subbarao (2004), Suryahadi and Sumarto (2003), Kamanou and Morduch (2005), and Chaudhuri *et al.* (2002). Our proposal here is thus not far removed from the existing literature, except we do reject most poverty measures as suitable building blocks. In this section, we argue that only the Chakravarty index, along with a few other functions of x_j (which to our knowledge have not been advanced as poverty measures), can provide a safe foundation to the measurement of vulnerability.

To understand why, consider the behaviour of (11.1) in the face of an increase in risk, as defined by a probability transfer 'from the middle to the tails', in keeping with one of the Rothschild-Stiglitz senses of risk. If we define the expected censored outcome as $\hat{y} \equiv E[\tilde{y}]$, then it will be useful to think of the imaginary case where $\hat{y}$

occurs with certainty or, to put it differently, where the probabilistic weight falls entirely on $\hat{y}$. As compared with this full-certainty case, the actual array of possible outcomes **y** seems to spread the weight away from the expected outcome, towards the tails. Given $0 < \alpha < 1$, this increase in risk (probability transfer from the middle to the tails) always results in a rise in our vulnerability measure $V_{(\alpha)}$, since

$$V(z,\mathbf{p},(\hat{y},\hat{y},\dots,\hat{y})) - V(z,\mathbf{p},\mathbf{y}) = -\left(\sum_{i=1}^{m} p_i \tilde{y}_i\right)^{\alpha} + \sum_{i=1}^{m} p_i \tilde{y}_i^{\alpha} < 0$$

where we make use of the focus axiom (and let $\tilde{y}_i$ replace y_i), as well as of the concavity of function $f(u) = u^{\alpha}$, for $0 < \alpha < 1$. This also shows that as α approaches 1, concavity turns weaker and $V(z,\mathbf{p}, (\hat{y},\hat{y}, \dots, \hat{y})) - V(z,\mathbf{p},\mathbf{y})$ approaches 0, such that risk makes little difference.

Our proposed measure thus imposes that vulnerability should be lower if the expected censored outcome $\hat{y}$ were attained with certainty – that is to say, if with no need to increase outcome expectations, uncertainty were removed by making the final outcome independent of the state of the world realization. Put it differently, the existence of risk leads to greater vulnerability. Needless to say, this links up with our first intuition about vulnerability, as a concept aiming to capture the burden of insecurity, the fact that hardship is also related to fear for the future, to threats. The cash-crop farmer in Sahel must be more vulnerable to poverty if output prices are more variable (say due to more limited connections to the market), even with no change in their expected value.

More generally, we may define a RISK SENSITIVITY axiom, requiring V^* to satisfy

$$V(z,\mathbf{p},\mathbf{y}) > V(z,\mathbf{p}, (\hat{y},\hat{y}, \dots, \hat{y})),$$

for every $(z,\mathbf{p},\mathbf{y})$. Alternatively, one may formulate this axiom in terms of a certainty-equivalent y^c, as follows:

$$y^c < \hat{y}, \text{ where } V(z,\mathbf{p},\mathbf{y}) = V(z,\mathbf{p},(y^c,y^c,\dots,y^c)).$$

This second formulation stresses that some form of 'efficiency loss' occurs, due to the uneven distribution of outcomes across states of the world. Intuitively, imagine it were possible to remove all uncertainty (so that $\hat{y}$ becomes the risk-free outcome level) – the individual could then give up $\hat{y}-y^c$ outcome units and remain as vulnerable as at the outset. In other words, the existence of uncertainty means that outcomes will to some extent fail to translate into low vulnerability. In this sense, an efficiency loss exists.

Measures building on other poverty indices can also exhibit this risk sensitivity. For instance, the single-parameter FGT-family can be consistent with this axiom, if their determining parameter is conveniently chosen. Thus, in the case of a vulnerability measure

$$V_{(b)} \equiv E[(1 - x)^b],$$

risk sensitivity would hold only if $b > 1$.[2] As Ligon and Schechter (2003) were first to point out, it is, however, common to find empirical pieces where this condition is not met. In particular, both the probability of being poor ($b = 0$) and the expected poverty gap ($b = 1$) fail to react to changes in the degree of risk exposure.

In some sense, the well-known drawbacks of $b = 0$ and $b = 1$ with regards to poverty measurement carry over to the sphere of vulnerability. For instance, just as the poverty gap is insensitive to the distribution of outcomes among the poor, $b = 1$ implies that the vulnerability measure will pay no attention to the probability distribution of outcomes below the poverty line. In other words, it assumes risk-neutrality. As for $b = 0$, it can be shown readily that it assimilates (11.1) only if outcomes are for some unlikely reason bound to be zero in every state of the world where the individual is poor.[3]

Nonetheless, even under $b > 1$, an FGT-based vulnerability measure exhibits some undesirable features in its treatment of risk. As Ligon and Schechter also pointed out, this case entails that better outcomes will exacerbate the extent to which the individual dreads an increase in risk exposure. Much empirical evidence to the contrary exists (for instance, Binswanger 1981), and it is usually seen as a safe assumption to impose that risk aversion decreases in wealth.

To ensure that risk sensitivity does not follow odd patterns, we may prefer to formulate an explicit axiom fully specifying its behaviour and ruling out undesirable properties. For instance, under CONSTANT RELATIVE RISK SENSITIVITY, V^* should be such that for every $(z, \mathbf{y}, \mathbf{p})$,

$$y^c(z, \mathbf{p}, \mathbf{y}) = \frac{y^c(z, \mathbf{p}, \kappa \mathbf{y})}{\kappa}, \text{ where } \kappa > 0.$$

A *proportional* increase by κ in the outcomes of all possible states of the world leads to a similar *proportional* increase in the certainty-equivalent outcome y^c. While RISK SENSITIVITY ensures $y^c / \hat{y} < 1$, we now further impose that this ratio must remain constant if all state-specific outcomes increase proportionally – in other words, the 'efficiency loss' due to uncertainty is determined as a constant proportion of expected outcome.

Our measure in (11.1) abides with this condition. Of course, risk sensitivity could be assumed to behave otherwise, probably on the grounds of empirical investigations into perceptions of risk and attitudes towards it. To take a simple example, one may propose that the *absolute* increase in the certainty-equivalent outcome equates the *absolute* increase in state-specific outcomes, so that the 'efficiency loss' is a constant value $y^c - \hat{y}$. In this case, vulnerability would be measured by

$$V_{(\beta)} = E\left[\frac{e^{\beta(1-x)} - 1}{e^{\beta} - 1}\right], \text{ where } \beta > 0.$$

We had mentioned earlier that a vulnerability measure is linked to some particular index of poverty, at least in the 'expected-poverty' vein of vulnerability measures.

Taking $V_{(\beta)}$ as an example, we see that the corresponding poverty index $\sum_{j=1}^{n}(e^{\beta(1-x_j)}-1/e^{\beta}-1)$ is by no means one of the usual choices in the literature. Hence, its suitability for vulnerability analysis would pass unnoticed if no specific attention were paid to the risk-related properties of the resulting vulnerability measure. Likewise, the FGT family may be (and has been) wrongly taken as suitable if these properties were overlooked.

To fully characterize the measure in (11.1), Calvo and Dercon (2006) develop a set of axioms including SYMMETRY OVER STATES, PROBABILITY-DEPENDENT EFFECT OF OUTCOMES, PROBABILITY TRANSFERS, SCALE INVARIANCE and NORMALIZATION.[4] Details on the definitions of these conditions, and on how these conditions combine and yield (11.1) can be found in that reference. If anything, we will only point out here that by virtue of the PROBABILITY-DEPENDENT EFFECT OF OUTCOMES axiom, we discard any form of 'subjective' cross-effects between any two states of the world. For instance, as we assess the impact of a low outcome in state *i*, it will not be allowed to argue 'there could be some relief in considering that one could have done much better had the odds been more fortunate' – outcomes and probabilities of states other than *i* will be irrelevant in this assessment. To a large extent, our focus on 'objective' (as opposed to 'subjective') valuations of outcome shortfalls is akin to the 'absolute' (as opposed to 'relative' or 'positional') nature of most poverty measures, where poverty of individual *j* is independent of the outcomes of her peers.

To close this section, we will make some observations about the relation between our measure (11.1) and those proposed elsewhere, outside the expected-poverty approach. First, consider studies where vulnerability is equated to 'low expected utility', as in Cunningham and Maloney (2000), Ligon and Schechter (2003), and Elbers and Gunning (2003). The focus axiom turns out to be the crucial difference between the two views.[5] For instance, while Ligon and Schechter do specify their notion of 'low' by defining some minimum socially acceptable level of *expected utility*, we go further and let the threshold act *before* state-specific outcomes merge into $E[x^{\alpha}]$. Thus, they do allow fortunate states to compensate for episodes of misfortune, whereas our concept of vulnerability remains always distinct from the possibility of being well off. We presented the arguments underpinning our choice in section 11.3.

Secondly, our approach differs from the one in which vulnerability is opposed to poverty, used, for instance, in Suryahadi and Sumarto (2003). For studies in this second vein, a vulnerable individual is *not* currently poor, but not sufficiently above the poverty line to feel safe and discard the risk of poverty – it is not unconceivable that a shock in the future might be negative and large enough to push her below the poverty line. In our case, an individual can be both very poor *and* very vulnerable, if both the present and the future are grim. Furthermore, individuals who are certain to be poor in the future are highly vulnerable – for them, since vulnerability is about threats, certainty of being poor is but a dominant, irresistible threat. The concept is not restricted to those whom the winds might blow into poverty or out from it.

Lastly, in some other studies, vulnerability is understood as inability to isolate well-being from income shocks, for example as in Amin, Rai and Topa (2003). For instance, in a regression of consumption on income and other variables, the income coefficient would be construed as a measure of consumption-vulnerability. In such view, outcome changes are all that matters. Outcome levels are irrelevant, as well as the concept of a critical outcome level (as the poverty line). Likewise, probabilities of shocks occurring play no role – these measures focus on the reaction to the shock, given the shock occurs. Clearly enough, this approach to vulnerability is so far removed from our framework, that in fact comparisons are hardly possible.

11.5   A family of measures of aggregate vulnerability

The related literature offers fewer alternative views when addressing aggregate vulnerability. A society is typically thought to be more (or less) vulnerable if its individual members are more (or less) vulnerable, so that simple averages of individual vulnerability indices are enough to measure aggregate vulnerability. This is in fact the case for the vast majority of vulnerability studies where some aggregation has been rehearsed.

To imagine a general case where a suitable measure of aggregate vulnerability AV^* depends on a whole matrix $\mathbf{Y}$ (whose columns $\mathbf{y}_j$ contain the set of state-specific outcomes for each individual j), we may write

$$AV^* = AV(z,\mathbf{p},\mathbf{Y}).$$

Thus, a simple average-based approach would impose the following specification on function AV:

$$AV(z,\mathbf{p},\mathbf{Y}) = \frac{1}{n}\sum\nolimits_{j=1}^{n}\varphi\left(V_j^*\right)$$

where $V_j^* = V(z,\mathbf{p},\mathbf{y}_j)$ may (or may not) be defined as in (11.1). Function φ is $\varphi(u) = u$ in the case of simple averages, but can take more sophisticated forms if necessary. For instance, $\varphi(u) = 1/\rho\, u^\rho$ would allow some concern for inequality in the distribution of vulnerability – however, we know of no study exploiting this possibility.

While averages dominate the scene, exceptions exist. The most important departures from the mainstream are provided by Ravallion (1988) and Kamanou and Morduch (2005), whose analyses are theoretical and empirical, respectively. In both cases, aggregate vulnerability is seen as expected aggregate poverty.[6] Interestingly, also in both cases, this results in an approach where aggregation *across states of the world* is preceded by aggregation *across individuals*. In other words, much unlike the case of simple averages, aggregate vulnerability does not build on individual vulnerability measures, but on a set of aggregate poverty indices, one for each possible state of the world.

While averaging individual vulnerability indices may be useful in many cases, here we prefer to explore a different path. Our stance is similar to that of Ravallion, and Kamanou and Morduch, except that we do not pay much attention to state-specific aggregate poverty indices – again, we would find that existing poverty measures are mis-starters if the consequences of risk exposure are intended to receive sensible treatment. We do however continue to place aggregation across individuals first, as we propose the following measure:

$$V_{(\gamma)} = E\left[\left(\prod_{j=1}^{n} x_j\right)^{\frac{\gamma}{n}}\right] - 1, \text{ with } \gamma < 0 \qquad (11.2)$$

Again, Calvo and Dercon (2006) provide a full discussion of the properties of this index, and also of the axiomatic structure underlying our proposal. Since the set of axioms exhibits greater complexity in this case, as compared with the individual space, we prefer not to present these desiderata, not even briefly. We make an exception with the axiom on CORRELATION SENSITIVITY, which in our view lies at the core of the difference between individual and aggregate measures.[7] Here, we draw on the multivariate risk literature, especially on Richard (1975) and Epstein and Tanny (1980).

Take the following example, where $n = 3$, $k = 3$, $z = 10$, and $\mathbf{p} = (1/3,1/3,1/3)$, so that all states of the world are equally likely. Two different sets of outcomes $\mathbf{Y}$ and $\mathbf{Y'}$ determine two alternative scenarios:

$$\mathbf{Y} = \begin{bmatrix} 15 & 7 & 18 \\ 25 & 12 & 8 \\ 5 & 20 & 14 \end{bmatrix} \begin{pmatrix} \text{drought} \\ \text{normal} \\ \text{floods} \end{pmatrix}, \quad \text{and} \quad \mathbf{Y'} = \begin{bmatrix} 5 & 7 & 8 \\ 15 & 12 & 14 \\ 25 & 20 & 18 \end{bmatrix} \begin{pmatrix} \text{drought} \\ \text{normal} \\ \text{floods} \end{pmatrix}$$

For instance, $\mathbf{Y}$ implies that only the third state (floods) is a poverty threat for the first individual ($y_{31} < z$). For illustrative purposes, imagine she lives by the river and would lose everything if its banks overflowed. The second individual is a farmer, highly dependent on generous rainfall ($y_{12} < z$). The third individual is a speculative food trader, whose business profits from others' distress ($y_{23} < z$).

Evidently, $\mathbf{Y'}$ calls for a different story – we would probably need to say that all individuals are farmers, differing only in the particular crop they grow. However, the switch from $\mathbf{Y}$ to $\mathbf{Y'}$ *does not make any individual more nor less vulnerable*. As each state is equally likely, states can 'swap' individual outcomes with no bearing on individual vulnerability, at least if a definition as in (11.1) is in place.

Thus, $V_1^*(\mathbf{Y}) = V_1^*(\mathbf{Y'})$, $V_2^*(\mathbf{Y}) = V_2^*(\mathbf{Y'})$, and $V_3^*(\mathbf{Y}) = V_3^*(\mathbf{Y'})$. Under an average-based approach, we are compelled to conclude $AV^*(\mathbf{Y}) = AV^*(\mathbf{Y'})$ – nevertheless, there is a sense in which *society as a whole could be said to be more vulnerable under* $\mathbf{Y'}$. Even though individuals might be indifferent, the threat of poverty at the aggregate level can be argued to be milder under $\mathbf{Y}$ than under $\mathbf{Y'}$. In this second scenario, society must contemplate *the possibility of widespread poverty* if it is hit by a drought, while no such concern arises under $\mathbf{Y}$.

In some way, one could argue that the fear of widespread destitution is never absent from the study of poverty and development. For instance, it clearly underlies the vast literature 'concerned with famines and other transient "crises", which may or may not include open starvation, but do involve a sudden eruption of *severe deprivation for a considerable section of the population* (for example, in the recent East and Southeast Asian economic crises)' (Sen, 1999: 160. The italics are ours).

Take the viewpoint of the policy maker. While a few groups of the population could suffer poverty with no major political consequences, the prospect of widespread destitution is menacing. Except perhaps for dictatorial governments with no need to respond to public needs, the expectation of good 'overall' economic performance is not enough – policy makers cannot fail to pay attention to some particularly distressing states of the world.

Sen illustrates the point with a reference to 'the massive Chinese famines of 1958–1961'. Even before the recent economic reforms, China had been much more successful than India in economic development in many significant respects. (...) Nevertheless, there was a major failure in China in its inability to prevent famines. The Chinese famines of 1958–61 killed, it is now estimated, close to thirty million people – ten times more than even the gigantic 1943 famine in British India' (p. 181). So to speak, a democratic government in China would have feared the prospect of a famine and put into practice effective preventive measures.

In practice, this concern for the threat of widespread poverty brings to a forefront role the *correlation of individual outcomes over the set of all possible states of the world*. Under Y', all individuals face greatest hardship in the case of a drought. As they are all farmers, they are all particularly sensitive to water dearth. From the point of view of society, one could say that there is very little diversification – individual outcomes are highly correlated across society, and this is precisely the source of social concern.

Using the terminology of the multidimensional poverty literature, individuals may be seen as 'substitutes' in the assessment of aggregate vulnerability – in a state of the world where some individuals are poor, society would avoid distress only if some other individuals do escape poverty. If such 'compensation' (substitution) does not occur, then widespread poverty exists and society must dread this state of the world.

As discussed in Bourguignon and Chakravarty (2003), this substitutability-based view imposes a positive cross-derivative on the individual index of multidimensional poverty (here, on the state-specific index of aggregate poverty). In the case of (11.2), this can be readily verified, since for any state i, and any pair of individuals g and h,

$$\frac{\partial^2 AV_{(\gamma)}}{\partial x_{ig} \partial x_{ih}} = p_i \frac{\gamma^2}{n^2} \frac{\left(\prod_{j=1}^{p} x_{ij}\right)^{\frac{\gamma}{n}}}{x_{ig} x_{ih}} > 0$$

11.6   Concluding remarks

Standard poverty analysis makes statements about deprivation after the veil of uncertainty has been lifted. This implies that there is no meaningful role for risk as part of an assessment of low states of well-being; the only role is instrumental. In this chapter, we introduced a concept of vulnerability, as a threat of poverty. This allows us to explore a dimension of well-being deprivation which has been largely ignored in the literature – namely, the stress deriving from the mere possibility of future hardship in any other particular dimension, such as consumption or health.

In recent years, a number of empirical papers have been produced using some concept of vulnerability not dissimilar to our own. However, our contribution in this chapter remains original, since we are very careful to ensure that risk is given a consistent and acceptable treatment in our proposed measures of both individual and aggregate vulnerability.

Further research along this path may reveal important insights in a setting where in each state of the world, individual well-being is allowed to depend on more than one dimension. In this chapter, we have only considered one relevant outcome y_{ij}, for individual j in state i. For instance, if a second relevant dimension (say health, if y was defined as consumption) exists, then vulnerability would refer to the threat of multidimensional poverty, and we should expect its assessment to be sensitive to how both dimensions correlate over the set of possible states of the world, for each individual. The relevance of these outcome correlations would come in addition to the well-known role of outcome correlations over the set of individuals. We think this can prove a fruitful avenue for further work.

Notes

1. Domains are $\mathbf{y} \in \{(y_1, y_2, \dots y_m) | y_i \in [0, \infty]\}$ and

$$\mathbf{p} \in \left\{ (p_1, p_2, \dots, p_m) | p_i \in [0,1] \wedge \sum_{i=1}^{m} p_i = 1 \right\}.$$

2. $b < 0$ would also ensure risk sensitivity, but it must be discarded, since vulnerability cannot be allowed to increase in outcomes.
3. To prove it, simply say $x_i = 0$ if $i \le n^* \le n$ and $x_i = 1$ if $i > n^*$. $V^* = \sum_{i \le n} p_i$ will follow immediately.
4. Due to SYMMETRY, the measure is not sensitive to permutations of the states of the world, so that all states receive the same treatment. As far as vulnerability is concerned, the only relevant difference between two states of the world s and t is the difference in their outcomes (y_s, y_t) and probabilities (p_s, p_t). All other features are uninteresting, and states of the world can swap 'labels' with no information loss. By imposing PROBABILITY-DEPENDENT EFFECT OF OUTCOMES, the effect of a change in y_s is ensured to depend *only* on p_s and y_s, that is to say, neither outcomes nor probabilities in states of the world other than s matter. The PROBABILITY TRANSFERS axiom requires that, if y_s is less than or at most equal to y_t, then vulnerability cannot increase as a result of a probability transfer from state s to state t. For instance, the Sahelian farmer will become more vulnerable if a drought becomes more likely, at the expense of the rainy scenario. Finally, SCALE INVARIANCE conveniently allows our measure not to depend on the unit of measure of outcomes, and NORMALIZATION imposes 0 and 1 as lower and upper boundaries, for the sake of a direct interpretation of the measure.
5. Measures based on expected utility also typically fail to satisfy SCALE INVARIANCE unless a logarithmic form is imposed on utility, and in this case it comes at the cost of discarding states where outcomes fall to zero.
6. More precisely, Ravallion does not resort to the term vulnerability, perhaps because it had not been coined yet. The spirit of his analysis is otherwise similar to that of more recent studies where vulnerability is addressed explicitly.

7. We may also point out that NORMALIZATION applies only partially, so that the measure is only bounded from below, at zero.

References

Amin, S., A. Rai and G. Topa (2003) 'Does Microcredit Reach the Poor and Vulnerable? Evidence from Northern Bangladesh', *Journal of Development Economics*, 70, 59–82.

Atkinson, A. (1987) 'On the Measurement of Poverty', *Econometrica*, 55, 749–64.

Atkinson, A. and F. Bourguignon (1982) 'The Comparison of Multi-dimensioned Distributions of Economic Status', *Review of Economic Studies*, 49, 183–201.

Binswanger, H. P. (1981) 'Attitudes Toward Risk: Theoretical Implications of an Experiment in Rural India', *Economic Journal*, 91, 867–90.

Bourguignon, F. and S. Chakravarty (2003) 'The Measurement of Multidimensional Poverty', *Journal of Economic Inequality*, 1, 25–49.

Bourguignon, F., C. Goh and D. Kim (2004) *Estimating Individual Vulnerability Using Pseudo-Panel Data*, World Bank Policy Research Working Paper 3375. Washington DC: World Bank.

Calvo, C. and S. Dercon (2006) *Vulnerability to Poverty*. Mimeo.

Chambers, R. (1989) 'Editorial Introduction: Vulnerability, Coping and Policy', *IDS Bulletin*, 20, 1–7.

Chakravarty, S. (1983) 'A New Index of Poverty', *Mathematical Social Sciences*, 6, 307–13.

Chaudhuri, S., J. Jalan and A. Suryahadi (2002) *Assessing Household Vulnerability to Poverty from Cross-sectional Data: A Methodology and Estimates from Indonesia*, Columbia University Discussion Paper 0102–52.

Christiaensen, L. and K. Subbarao (2004) *Toward an Understanding of Household Vulnerability in Rural Kenya*, World Bank Policy Research Working Paper 3326. Washington DC: World Bank.

Cunningham, W. and W. Maloney (2000) *Measuring Vulnerability: Who Suffered in the 1995 Mexican Crisis?*, IBRD mimeo.

Elbers, C. and J. Gunning (2003) 'Growth and Risk: Methodology and Micro-evidence', Tinbergen Institute Discussion Papers 03-068/2.

Epstein, L. and S. Tanny (1980) 'Increasing Generalized Correlation: A Definition and Some Economic Consequences', *Canadian Journal of Economics*, 13, 16–34.

Foster, J., J. Greer, and E. Thornbecke (1984) 'A Class of Decomposable Poverty Measures', *Econometrica*, 52, 761–6.

Kamanou, G. and J. Morduch (2005) *Measuring Vulnerability to Poverty, in S. Dercon* (ed.), *Insurance Against Poverty*. Oxford: Oxford University Press.

Ligon, E. and L. Schechter (2003) 'Measuring Vulnerability', *The Economic Journal*, 113, C95–C102.

Narayan, D., R. Patel *et al.*, (2000) *Can Anyone Hear Us?* New York: Oxford University Press.

Ravallion, M. (1988) 'Expected Poverty under Risk-Induced Welfare Variability', *The Economic Journal*, 98, 1171–82.

Ravallion, M. (1994) *Poverty Comparisons: Fundamentals of Pure and Applied Economics Volume LVI*. Chur: Harwood Academic Publishers.

Richard, S. (1975) Multivariate Risk Aversion, Utility Independence and Separable Utility Functions', *Management Science*, 22, 12–21.

Sen, A. (1976) 'Poverty: An Ordinal Approach to Measurement', *Econometrica*, 44, 219–31.

Sen, A. (1981) *Poverty and Famines: An Essay on Entitlement and Deprivation*. Oxford: Oxford University Press.

Sen, A. (1999) *Development as Freedom*. Oxford: Oxford University Press.

Suryahadi, A. and S. Sumarto (2003) 'Poverty and Vulnerability in Indonesia Before and After the Economic Crisis', *Asian Economic Journal*, 17, 45–64.

World Bank (2001) *World Development Report 2000/2001: Attacking Poverty*. New York: Oxford University Press.

Part IV
Critical Policy Issues

12
On the Political Economy of Poverty Alleviation[1]

Marcelo Côrtes Nerì[2] and Marcelo Casal de Xerez[3]

12.1 Introduction

The management of social policy has become more complex and challenging than ever. The decentralization of public actions allied to the growing involvement of NGOs and private firms creates a widespread diversity of simultaneous actions. On the other hand, the internationalization process of economies, concomitant with contagious macroeconomic instabilities, broadens the scope of opportunities for the realization of transfers of resources and social technology between countries.

The question of interest is: how should we increase the returns obtained by society from this myriad of actions? It is up to the diverse levels of public activity (multi-lateral entities, several levels of the state, and civil society) to act simultaneously towards common goals. These involve the coordination of diffused efforts through the settlement of targets and the design of mechanisms providing the incentives to achieve them.

The Millennium declaration, recently promulgated, proposes not only social indicators, but also values and deadlines to be pursued at the global level. Our proposal is that specific administrative entities – in particular, those at the sub-national level – announce a commitment to the global targets as they have been specified. In practice, this implies that states and municipalities, aside from nations, attempt to convince their respective population to reach the proposed targets. An example: state A, or district B, would adhere to the target of reducing by one half the proportion of its population with income per capita below US$1.00 daily at PPP by the year 2015. The recent international experience with inflationary targets enlightens the strength of tangible objectives.

Now why should we only adhere to the Millennium goals and not to others? (a) The proposed indicators have already been formulated and monitored, thereby benefiting from inherent credibility. (b) The uniformity of the goals may contribute to the convergence of social efforts at the global scale by guaranteeing a positive externality. (c) The fact that the deadline for the global goals outlasts the mandate of a single government inhibits discontinuity of actions between political mandates; in other words, external goals tend to establish temporal consistency in decisions. (d) The perceived exogeneity of the goals across locations also provides a neutral

231

ground for agreements across different government levels, allowing a better integration of social efforts. The goals ideally belong to society and its citizens, who can be perceived as being independent from the idiosyncrasies of specific governments. In other words, it provides regional consistency to policies.

Of course, after the many detailed discussions on multidimensional indicators developed throughout the book one may want to use a broader social indicator than that used by the Millennium Development Goals (MDGs). However, the main argument approached here is the advantage of sharing common worldwide goals. One may assume in this chapter that we have at hand the ideal social indicator (the Holy Grail).

Aside from the coordination and mobilization characteristics of the social targets, the conditioning of the financial elements on the observed social outcome – whether at the individual or at the governmental level – is an interesting illustration of how to deal with the principal–agent issue. The same idea that led to rewarding poor families only if their children attend school (which is at the core of the *Bolsa Família* in Brazil or *Oportunidades* in Mexico among other conditional cash transfers programs) can be applied to the annual reallocation of the social budget at various administrative levels. The process of rewarding, with additional resources, those units progressing swiftly, may be applied towards the lower levels of government: from the federal to the state realm, from the state to their respective municipalities and from the latter to their respective administrative regions. The Demographic Census provides a vast array of social information that is needed at these various geographical levels.

Following this line of reasoning one can also imagine that for heavily indebted poor countries (HIPC), the amount of debt relieved would be linked to the future path of these nations' social indices. The point is that those getting unconditional funds tend to lose their motivation. On many occasions, the best remedy against poverty is not charity, but credit. There is no doubt that social action should be centred on the poorest. Nevertheless, those who strive towards economic independence should be rewarded. The emphasis should be on rewarding future success instead of compensating for past failures.

The social credit mechanisms discussed here can also be perceived as a process of converting social debt into financial wealth. Think of social debt as being equivalent to the amount of resources lacking in a given society for a given period of time to come, say t years.[4] Such a society would be entitled to a given cash flow that would be a function of the evolution of its social debt. One of the few advantages of being poor is the ability to improve. For example, if only 50 per cent of the children attend school, one may ultimately double this initial figure, while in a situation where 97 per cent of the children attend school there is not much room for improvement. It is therefore possible for social credit equity and efficiency to walk hand-in-hand.

The main problem of social targets concerns the short run, given the presence of shocks. The results obtained by the social protagonist depend on factors that are often beyond his reach, as the outcome does not depend only on his efforts or skills, hence the importance of using relative evaluation schemes. The building of a database allowing international comparisons will place each country within the international norm. The system of incentives should be announced a priori and the relative performance should be evaluated a posteriori. Everything functions as a system of credit in which the financial debt resulting from social projects can be reduced in view of social advancements. The advantage of the social credit apparatus is that, if it is well designed, it will attract better social actors and induce them to undertake the best practices.

Many social programmes are based upon the transfer of funds from the federal government to the poorer regions. Obviously, the expenditure of money in these regions improves the living conditions of the local population. One may, however, wonder whether the final result reached could have been better.

It is impossible for the federal government to know the specific needs of each locality in the country. In a region where the HDI is low, the federal government would rarely have more information than the local government.[5] It is the local administration that better understands the region's intricacies and knows who the poor are and what is the best way to help them. For this reason, it is only natural that the local government should be responsible for determining what must be done. The task of the federal government should be to establish a partnership with the municipalities, via target contracts, and monitor how funds are being spent and which are the goals being achieved.

In what follows, we will assume that the mechanisms linking the amount of funds to be received by a given administrative entity to the fulfillment of social targets is pre-established in a contract. The question is what the optimum level of governmental transfers, for example from the federal government to municipalities, is.

In the system proposed, there will be contracts containing clauses fixing the targets and the amount of money to be forwarded from the federal government to the local one, once these goals are reached. The idea is that if the municipality does not reach the established targets, it will not receive the funds, or will receive only an amount proportional to what has been achieved. This kind of contract between the federal and local governments is thus similar to a hiring contract, in which the federal government hires the municipality to run a social service. It is naturally more realistic to assume that for the targets to be reached, the municipality must first receive the funds, and only afterwards will one check whether the targets have been reached. We can then consider the funds received by the local government as an advanced payment – called Social Credit – enabling the municipality to carry out a specific service pre-determined in the contract. If the targets are not reached, the municipality will have a debt towards the federal government because it did not reach an agreed upon target. The debt will be equal to the difference between the advanced payment and the payment the municipality should receive upon obtaining results.

The main problems in this type of model concern the determination of the targets and how to reward the fulfillment of goals. This chapter applies a standard principal–agent model to the previously described relationship between the federal government and local governments. It is organized as follows. Section 12.2 presents the basic framework of analysis. The first part of section 12.3 examines the implications of a static model with perfect information under various scenarios, namely: (1) autarchy; (2) unconditional transfers from the federal government to the municipality; (3) perverse incentives, where the poorest municipalities get more resources; (4) social targets, where the greater the improvement in relevant social indicators, the more resources each municipality would receive. The final part of section 12.3 analyses the implications of the introduction of imperfect information in the static model with two types and a continuum of types of agents.

12.2   The basic model

It is a standard principal–agent model where the federal government (F) is regarded as the principal while the agents are the municipal governments (M), henceforth referred to as municipalities. Aside from the federal and municipal governments, we have the poor (P) for whom the social targets are determined in a contract between the government and the municipality.

A basic hypothesis of the model is that the federal and local governments seek to improve the living conditions of the poor because this would increase the probability of re-election of the federal and local politicians. In the model, the level of income of the poor will be the basis for measuring any improvement in their living conditions. This is equivalent to assuming that the social target is an increase in the average income of the poor.[6]

The key issue when discussing the issue of poverty reduction is to know who will pay the bill. On the one hand, a reduction in poverty brings electoral benefits. On the other hand, for this to occur, it is necessary to invest in income transfer programmes and this reduces the budget available for other types of investments.

Any local government would love to see the federal government making large social investments in its region, especially if such expenses do not include any requirement from the municipality. Such a situation would be similar to a 'free lunch'. The federal government would spend part of its budget and the municipality would obtain political gains. The same analysis is valid in the opposite direction.

Like Besley (1997), Gelbach and Pritchett (1997), and Azam and Laffont (2001), we assume that the federal and local governments have an aversion to poverty, which may be modelled through a utility function, in which the income of the poor is seen as a positive externality for the federal government as well as for the local government. For simplicity, we assume that the government's and the municipality's utility functions are quasi-linear in the available budget, and strictly concave in the income of the poor. The government and the municipality are thus concerned with absolute and not with relative poverty. The desire to help the poor does not depend, however, on the total budget, but only on the income level of the poor.

The utility functions for the federal government, U_F, and for the municipality, U_M, are then respectively given by:

$$U_F = G_F + N_P \cdot v(Y_P) \tag{12.1}$$

$$U_M = G_M + N_P\theta \cdot v(Y_P) \tag{12.2}$$

with $v(0) = 0$, $v'(Y_P) > 0$, $v''(YP) < 0$, $\lim\limits_{v_p \to 0} v'(Y_P) = +\infty$ and $\lim\limits_{v_p \to +\infty} v'(Y_P) = 0$,

where, G_F is the budget available to the federal government. It is assumed that the government has a total budget of Y_F. Part of this budget may be transferred, T, to income programmes directed towards the poor. The difference being $Y_F - T = G_F$. This is the budget the government has for all other necessary expenses. Obviously, the greater the available budget, the larger will be the government's utility.

G_M is the budget available to the municipality. Like the government, the municipality also has its own budget, Y_M. The available budget, G_M, is what is left after the transfers from the municipality to the poor.

θ is the parameter expressing the aversion to poverty of a local government. Different mayors may present different degrees of aversion to poverty. The parameter θ does not appear in the government's utility function because of a normalization that assumes that the government has a parameter θ equal to 1. And N_P is the number of poor in a municipality.

We will assume that the local government is better aware of the local reality, and therefore more capable than the federal government of identifying who really are the poor within the region. The local government has also better ways of managing and implementing an income transfer program to its locality. All government transfers will thus be directly made to the municipality, which will be responsible for allocating them to the poor.

As far as the utility of the poor, U_P, is concerned we will assume that it grows with income: $U_P'(Y_P) \geq 0$. As income increases, there is an improvement for the poor. In what follows we will sometimes refer to the federal government as the principal and to the local government as the agent.

12.3 The basic model

This section is divided into two parts. The first one analyses the case of complete information, when the principal knows the type θ of the agent. Then, in a second part, we assume information asymmetry, implying that the type of agent is unknown to the principal. Such an asymmetry allows some agents to receive informational income, which can be seen as a counterpart that the agent charges for revealing its true type.

Complete information

In this case, the government knows the mayor's (municipality's) aversion to poverty. It is an ideal situation, as it is difficult to know this type of information. However, the study in this case is important for some reasons. One of them is that it allows us to compare the differences in the results of social policies when the government does not know the type of municipality. Besides this, we can obtain some interesting intuitions, which are the key factors in determining the result of social policies.

Autarchy (A)

The basic situation is that in which the government does not carry out any transfer to the municipality. In this case, the municipality's incentive to transfer income to the poor is exclusively due to the positive externality that an improvement in the living conditions of the poor has on the local government. In this situation, the municipality solves the following problem:

$$\text{Max}_{Y_P} \ G_M + N_P \cdot \theta \cdot v(Y_P) \tag{12.3}$$

$$\text{s.t. } G_M + N_P \cdot Y_P \leq Y_M \tag{12.4}$$

The first order condition (FOC) of the above problem is:

$$v'(Y_P^A) = \frac{1}{\theta} \tag{12.5}$$

such that $\theta_1 > \theta_2 \Rightarrow Y_{P_1} > Y_{P_2}$

However, the income of the poor under autarchy, Y_P^A, is determined by the coefficient of the local government's aversion to poverty. The larger this coefficient, the larger will be the income of the poor. Governments more concerned with the social situation of the poor implement better income transfer policies. It is observed that the income of the poor does not depend upon the number of poor nor on the municipality's budget. This is a result of the quasi-linear utility function chosen for the local government.

For the municipality of type θ, the utility after the transfer is:

$$U(\theta) = U_M^A = Y_M - N_P \cdot Y_P^A + N_P \cdot \theta \cdot v(Y_P^A) \tag{12.6}$$

Note that in what follows this equation will refer to the minimum utility that the municipality will require before accepting a contract with the federal government.

Unconditional transfer (T^I)

Suppose the federal government decides to invest in a specific place, transferring funds to the municipality so that it can invest in a social area. As previously mentioned, we assume that the local government is the one in charge of implementing social policies. Suppose the government does not fix any condition (i.e. social target). It transfers unconditionally a fixed amount T^I. The municipality then solves the problem

$$\text{Max}_{Y_P} \ G_M + N_P \cdot \theta \cdot v(Y_P) \tag{12.7}$$

$$\text{s.t. } G_M + N_P \cdot Y_P \leq Y_M + T^I \tag{12.8}$$

Solving the problem, the first order condition obtained is:

$$v'(Y_P^I) = \frac{1}{\theta} \Rightarrow Y_P^I = Y_P^A \tag{12.9}$$

In other words, the income of the poor under autarchy is the same as that under unconditional transfers.

Proposition 12.1: If the federal government makes unconditional transfers to local governments, the situation of the poor does not change.

$$U_M^I = Y_M + T^I - N_P \cdot Y_P^I + N_P \cdot \theta \cdot v(Y_P^I) \overset{Y_P^I = Y_P^A}{=} Y_M + T^I - N_P \cdot Y_P^A + N_P \cdot \theta \cdot v(Y_P^A) \tag{12.10}$$

$$U_M^I = U_M^A + T^I \rightarrow U_M^I > U_M^A \tag{12.11}$$

and

$$U_F^I = U_F^A - T^I \Rightarrow U_F^I > U_F^A \tag{12.12}$$

Defining the funds destined, by the municipality, to the social programme as being T_M, we get

$$T_M^I = N_P \cdot Y_P^I = N_P \cdot Y_P^A = T_M^A \tag{12.13}$$

What is observed in this type of transfer is that the local government does not use the funds transferred to improve the situation of the poor, but starts to include it in its available budget. Another interpretation is to consider that the local government really directs the funds received towards the social programs. There is, however, a crowding out effect in so far as the local government will stop directing part of its own budget to the social area.

In this way, the local government's utility increases, for the poor will be as well off as they would under autarchy, but the available budget increases. The central government, on the other hand, will be worse off, for the well-being of the poor will not have improved while the available budget will be smaller.

Perverse incentive (PI)

Suppose the government decides to concentrate its transfers towards the municipalities where the poor are poorer, so that the smaller the income of the poor, the greater the per capita transfer carried out by the government to the municipality. Assume the government transfers an amount equal to the difference between Y_P and a threshold value, K. The total transfer that a municipality is entitled to is then:

$$T = (K - Y_P) \cdot N_P \qquad (12.14)$$

The municipality, knowing that it will be entitled to this transfer, solves then the problem of determining how much it will invest in the social area. The better the situation of the poor, the less the municipality will receive from the government, but on the other hand, the greater the externality created by the situation of the poor. The municipality's problem can be described as

$$\underset{Y_P}{\text{Max}} \; G_M + N_P \cdot \theta \cdot v(Y_P) \qquad (12.15)$$

$$\text{s.t. } G_M + N_P \cdot Y_P \leq Y_M + (K - Y_P) \cdot N_P \qquad (12.16)$$

Solving for this, we have:

$$v'(Y_P^{IA}) = \frac{2}{\theta} \qquad (12.17)$$

such that, $Y_P^{PI} < Y_P^A$

   Clearly such a system where the greater the poverty, the greater the federal government's investment in the region, creates perverse incentives because it induces the municipal government to reduce its social investments in order to receive more transfers. The final investment ends up being in fact smaller than in the case of autarchy.

Transfer conditional on the fulfillment of social targets (T^C)

We have hitherto studied cases in which the government either undertakes no social transfer or does it without determining any type of social target that could serve as a condition for the municipality to receive funds. Let us now see why the determination of social targets can increase efficiency in the use of public money.

   Suppose the principal offers a contract to the agent under which a transfer is conditioned upon the achievement of a pre-determined income social target. The principal's problem is to define a contract $(T^C(\theta), Y_P(\theta))$, under which an agreement with the agent's type θ is concluded with a target, Y_P, and the transfer, T^C, guarantees that the target will be reached. We have naturally to assume that, in accepting the contract, the agent will obtain at least the same utility it would have under autarchy. This is the well-known Restriction of Participation (RP). The principal's problem is therefore

$$\underset{Y_P, T^C}{\text{Max}} \; Y_F - T^C(Y_P) + N_P \cdot v(Y_P) \qquad (12.18)$$

$$\text{s.t. } (Y_M + T^C(Y_P) - N_P \cdot Y_P) + N_P \cdot \theta \cdot v(Y_P) \geq U(\theta) \quad (RP) \qquad (12.19)$$

From RP we have that:

$$T^C(Y_P) = U(\theta) - Y_M + N_P \cdot Y_P - N_P \cdot \theta \cdot v(Y_P) \qquad (12.20)$$

so that the government's problem may be expressed as

$$\underset{Y_P}{\text{Max}} \ Y_F - \left(U(\theta) - Y_M + N_P \cdot Y_P - N_P \cdot \theta \cdot v(Y_P)\right) + N_P \cdot v(Y_P) \qquad (12.21)$$

A first order condition is that:

$$v'(Y_P^C) = \frac{1}{1+\theta} \Rightarrow Y_P^C > Y_P^A \qquad (12.22)$$

In other words, if the transfer of funds from the federal government to the municipality is conditioned upon the attainment of a specific social target (in our case, the target being an increase in the income of the poor) the final income of the poor will be greater than it would have been had there been no target. As we saw previously, when there are no targets the municipality ends up investing the same value with or without the government's social transfers because the municipality decreases the resources devoted to social goals by an amount equivalent to the transfers of the federal government. We therefore have the following proposition.

Proposition 12.2: The determination of social targets increases the efficiency in the use of the public funds transferred to the municipalities and a higher level of achievements is reached in the social area.
    Note also that

$$\begin{aligned}
U_M^{TC} &= U_M^A \\
\Rightarrow G_M^{TC} + N_P \cdot \theta \cdot v(Y_P^{TC}) &= G_M^A + N_P \cdot \theta \cdot v(Y_P^A) \\
\Rightarrow G_M^{TC} &= G_M^A - N_P \cdot \theta \cdot \left[v(Y_P^{TC}) - v(Y_P^A)\right] \\
\Rightarrow G_M^{TC} &> G_M^A
\end{aligned} \qquad (12.23)$$

Therefore, when a contract stipulates social targets, the municipality, in addition to directing the resources received from government to the social area, will also increase the volume of resources devoted to social goals that it normally would spend had there be no contract with the government.
    In conclusion, the municipality loses utility from having a smaller amount of funds available for 'non-social' expenses, but it gains from the externality resulting from the improvement in the well-being of the poorest, an achievement linked to

the investments made with the federal and municipal funds. Note that Adam and O'Connell (1999) derived a similar result.

A contract with social targets is therefore capable of raising social investments. While in a contract with no targets, the volume of resources reaching the poor remains the same whether there are transfers or not, with social targets the resources reaching the poor are greater than the sum of the funds transferred by the central government and those allocated by the municipality when there are no targets.

It is also possible to derive conclusions concerning the degree of improvement in well-being that the social targets can bring to the poor. Remember that we normalized the government's aversion to poverty as being equal to one ($\theta_F = 1$) so that in the equation $v'(Y_P^{TC}) = 1/(1 + \theta)$ previously derived the number 1 in the denominator is the government's θ_F. Had we written the government's utility function as

$$U_F = G_F + N_P \cdot \theta_F \cdot v(Y_P) \tag{12.24}$$

we would have found as a first order condition:

$$v'(Y_P^{TC}) = \frac{1}{\theta_F + \theta} \tag{12.25}$$

where θ is the degree of local aversion to poverty.

Linear contract

One way of inducing the municipality to reach the projected targets is to offer a contract of the type:

$$T(Y_P) = a + b \cdot Y_P \tag{12.26}$$

In such a contract, the municipality has a guaranteed fixed value. It is worth observing that this value may be positive as well as negative, implying in this last case that there is a penalty to be paid by the municipality when the level of achievements of the social goals is very low. We also have a variable part. The higher is the income of the poor, the greater the transfer. The greater the value of the coefficient b, the greater is the municipality's incentive to reach a higher level of achievements in the social area.

Proposition 12.3: With a linear contract of social targets we derive that

$$a = T(Y_P^{TC}) - b \cdot Y_P^{TC}, \text{ where } T(Y_P^{TC}) = N_P \cdot \left[\left(Y_P^{TC} - Y_P^A \right) - \theta \cdot \left(v(Y_P^{TC}) - v(Y_P^A) \right) \right]$$

$$b = \frac{1}{1+\theta} \tag{12.27}$$

For a proof, see Appendix 12.1 at the end of this chapter.

Incomplete information

The model with complete information is useful as a reference parameter, as it describes the optimum solution to the problem (first-best). However, in reality the type of agent is private information and it is thus unknown to the principal. This is equivalent to saying that the federal government does not know what the local government's degree of aversion to poverty is. It only knows that historically there exists a specific distribution of types reflecting the fact that municipalities have variable degrees of concern with social issues.

We first analyze the case where there are only two types of agents. Then we assume that there is a specific density function of types. In what follows we just give the general direction of this extended analysis. Details are provided in Appendix 12.2.

Two types of agents

The following proposition is proven in Appendix 12.2.

Proposition 12.4: With incomplete information, if the government is averse to poverty the poor will be as well off as they would be with complete information. If, however, the government is less concerned with social issues the poor will be in a worse situation.

Type intervals

Let us now consider the situation in which the municipality is of the type $\theta \in [\theta, \overline{\theta}]$. The municipality's type is private information, but the function $f(\theta)$ is known to everybody.

The government would like to establish a contract with the municipality where the transfer value, T, depends on the accomplishment of certain predetermined social targets, that is, a contract of the type $T = T(Y_P)$, assuming we are dealing with income targets, for example.

Such a contract should fix differentiated targets depending on the type of municipality. As this is unknown information to the government, it is up to the government to establish contracts $(Y_P, T(Y_P))$, and wait for the municipality's choice. This is equivalent to a revelation mechanism associating to each type announced by the municipality, a transfer $T(\hat{\theta})$ for the income target $Y_P(\hat{\theta})$. Several restrictions have to be taken into account.

The first restriction states that municipalities will only agree to a contract with the government if the utility derived from the contract is greater than or equal to the utility which they would obtain had there not been any contract (that is under autarchy).

The second restriction guarantees the municipality the utility obtained when revealing its true type θ is greater than that the one it would obtain if it had identified itself as being of another type $\hat{\theta}$. This is the well-known Incentive Compatibility Restriction of type θ.

The third and final restriction is that the government can identify with which municipalities it is worth to establish a contract. It guarantees that the government's utility in carrying out the contract will be greater than when there are no contracts.

Nothing guarantees, however, that it will be worth for the government to establish a contract with all the municipalities (assuming an infinite number of types). It may then not be worth for the government to contract with municipalities with a low degree of aversion to poverty because such municipalities would invest a small amount in social programmes. The type θ^* corresponds to a threshold which determines whether the government will transfer resources or not. The following proposition may then be proven (see Appendix 12.3).

Proposition 12.5: Municipalities where poverty is more intense because local governments have a low degree of aversion to poverty can be impeded form signing contracts with social targets and thus from receiving government funds.

This is a controversial result since the government is actually expected to intervene in places where it should pass on the responsibility. What happens is that in these municipalities the transfers of the government to the municipalities almost do not change the situation of the poor because municipalities tend to reduce their own allocation to social goals by an amount almost equivalent to that received from the government.[7]

12.4   Conclusions

This chapter discussed the economic rationality of a system of social targets based on Millennium Development Goals (MDGs), as a way for the federal government to increase the efficiency in using the social budget that is transferred to municipalities. The chapter extended a standard principal–agent framework in various directions. The results of the static models show that the use of the focalization criteria where the poorest municipalities get more resources may lead to adverse incentives to poverty eradication. We also show that unconditional transfers from the federal government totally crowd out local social expenditures. The chapter argues in favour of using contracts where the greater the improvement in relevant social indicators, the more resources each municipality would receive. The introduction of imperfect information basically generates a penalty to the poor segments in areas where local governments are less averse to poverty.

An extension of the framework is to show that one advantage of this type of contract is also to reduce the problem of political favouritism when certain social groups receive greater, or smaller, attention from specific governments. With the establishment of social targets it becomes possible to generate proper incentives so that social spending is distributed more equitably between groups.

Notes

1. The authors would like to thank Luisa Carvalhaes Coutinho de Mello and Helen Harris for their general support and research assistance.
2. Marcelo Côrtes Neri is Director of the Center for Social Policies at the Instituto Brasileiro de Economia and Assistant Professor at the Escola de Pós-Graduação de Economia, both from the Fundação Getulio Vargas.

3. Marcelo Casal de Xerez is an Analyst at the Banco Central do Brasil.
4. Perhaps the simplest example to visualize this is to assume that it is equal to the present value of the average income gap (P1) times the population size discounted over T periods.
5. The HDI (Human Development Index) is an index composed of health, education and income indicators where each one of these three components has the same weight.
6. An identical analysis can however be made with other social indicators or even with an average of them, such as the Human Development Index – HDI – or the Life Conditions Index – LCI (Índice de Condições de Vida – ICV). The sole purpose of selecting income as the target is to make the model more intuitive.
7. In practice, this problem is not as critical because part of the investments in the social area (education, health, social services, etc) have a minimum percentage linked to the local budget – refer to the Fiscal Responsibility Law and the Federal Constitution. This way, when the budget increases, the municipality is forced to increase its total expenses in these areas and cannot simply use the federal funds and reduce the local ones by an equivalent amount.

References

Adam, C.S. and S.A. O'Connell (1999) 'Aid, Taxation and Development, in Sub-Saharan Africa', *Economics and Politics*, 11, 225–53.
Azam, J.P. and J.J. Laffont (2001) 'Contracting for aid'. Mimeo. Université de Toulouse.
Besley, T. (1997) 'Political Economy of Alleviating Poverty: Theory and Institutions', *Annual World Bank Conference on Development Economics 1996*. Washington, DC: World Bank.
Dewatripont, M. (1989) 'Renegotiation and Information Revelation over Time: The Case of Optimal Labor Contracts', *Quarterly Journal of Economics*, 104, 589–619.
Gelbach, J.B. and L.H. Pritchett (1997) 'More for the Poor is Less for the Poor'. Policy Research Working Paper 1799. Washington, DC: World Bank.
Hart, O. and J. Tirole (1988) 'Contract Renegotiation and Coasian Dynamics', *Review of Economic Studies*, 55, 509–40.
Hoffmann, R. (1998) *Distribuição de Renda: Medidas de Desigualdade e Pobreza*. São Paulo: EDUSP.
Laffont, J.J. and J. Tirole (1987) 'Comparative Statistics of the Optimal Dynamic Incentives Contract.' *European Economic Review* 31: 901–26.
Laffont, J.J. and J. Tirole (1988) 'The Dynamics of Incentive Contracts'. *Econometrica*, 156(5), 1153–75.
Laffont, J.J. and J. Tirole (1990) 'Adverse Selection and Renegotiation in Procurement', *Review of Economic Studies*, 75, 597–626.
Laffont, J.J. and J. Tirole (1993) *A Theory of Incentives in Procurement and Regulation*. Cambridge: MIT Press.
Laffont, J.J. and J. Tirole (1998) 'The Dynamics of Incentive Contracts', *Econometrica*, 56, 1153–73.
Mas-Colell, A., M.D. Whinston, and J.R. Green (1995) *Microeconomic Theory*. New York: Oxford University Press.
Meyer, M.A. and J. Vickers (1997) 'Performance Comparisons and Dynamic Incentives', *Journal of Political Economy*, 105(3), 547–81.
Neri, M.C. *et al.* (1999) 'Gasto Público en Servicios Sociales Básicos en América Latina y el Caribe: Análisis desde la perspectiva de la Iniciativa 20/20.' October. UNDP, ECLAC and UNICEF. Organized by Enrique Ganuza, Arturo Leon and Pablo Sauma. Santiago, Chile.
Neri, M.C. (2000) 'Metas sociais, para tirar a miséria do país.' *Revista Conjuntura Econômica*, Maio.
Neri, M.C. and M.C. Xerez (2003) 'Desenho de Um Sistema de Metas Sociais', *Ensaios Econômicos*, 519, December. Rio de Janeiro: EPGE/FGV.
Neri, M.C. and M. C. Xerez (2003) 'Aspectos Dinâmicos de um Sistema de Metas Sociais', *Ensaios Econômicos*, 563, December. Rio de Janeiro: EPGE/FGV.

PNUD (1998) *Desenvolvimento Humano e Condições de Vida: Indicadores Brasileiros*. Brasilia: PNUD.
Salanié, B. (1997) *The Economics of Contracts*. Cambridge: MIT Press.

Appendix 12.1:   Proof of Proposition 12.3

In order to have an increase of one unit in income, the municipality must spend $N_P \cdot 1$ in the social project. According to the contract, for each unit of increase in the income of the poor the government will transfer an amount $b \cdot N_P$ to the municipality. The impact on the variation in the budget available locally will hence be

$$\frac{\Delta G_M}{\Delta Y_P} = b \cdot N_P - N_P \qquad (12.28)$$

The government's utility function is expressed as

$$U_F = Y_F - T^C(Y_P) + N_P \cdot v(Y_P) \qquad (12.29)$$

From the municipality's budgetary restriction (BR), we derive that

$$Y_M + T^C(Y_P) = G_M + N_P \cdot Y_P \qquad (12.30)$$

Isolating $T^C(Y_P)$ in the BR and substituting the government's utility function, we get

$$G_M = (Y_F - U_F + Y_M) - N_P \cdot Y_P + N_P \cdot v(Y_P) \qquad (12.31)$$

and hence end up with

$$\frac{dG_M}{dY_P} = -N_P + N_P \cdot v'(Y_P^{TC}) \quad \text{where } v'(Y_P^{TC}) = \frac{1}{1+\theta} \qquad (12.32)$$

Thus,

$$\frac{dG_M}{dY_P} = -N_P + N_P \cdot \frac{1}{1+\theta} \qquad (12.33)$$

From (12.28) and (12.32) we get

$$b \cdot N_P - N_P = -N_P + N_P \cdot \frac{1}{1+\theta} \Rightarrow b = \frac{1}{1+\theta} \qquad (12.34)$$

As far as the coefficient a is concerned we may write that

$$T(Y_P^{TC}) = a + b \cdot Y_P^{TC} \qquad (12.35)$$

so that

$$a = T(Y_P^{TC}) - b \cdot Y_P^{TC} \qquad (12.36)$$

with

$$b = \frac{1}{1+\theta}, \; v'(Y_P^{TC}) = \frac{1}{1+\theta}, \; T(Y_P^{TC}) = N_P \cdot \left[\left(Y_P^{TC} - Y_P^A\right) - \theta \cdot \left(v(Y_P^{TC}) - v(Y_P^A)\right)\right] \qquad (12.37)$$

Appendix 12.2 The Case of Incomplete Information with Two Types of Agents

Suppose that $\theta \in [\underline{\theta}, \overline{\theta}]$ and that the probability of the municipality being a type $\overline{\theta}$ is π. For the municipality to accept a contract determining targets to be accomplished, the contract must guarantee at least the same utility obtained when there are no social targets. This is the Participation Restriction (PR).

As is traditional in problems of adverse selection, the principal must offer a menu of contracts, that is, a contract for each type of agent. The contracts must also have been chosen in a way that an agent of a specific type does not try to pretend to be of another type. This is the Incentive Compatibility Restriction (ICR).

The principal then has to solve the following problem:

$$\underset{\overline{Y}_P, \overline{T}, \underline{Y}_P, \underline{T}}{\text{Max}} \; \pi \left[Y_F - \overline{T} + N_P \cdot v(\overline{Y}_P)\right] + (1 - \pi)\left[Y_F - \underline{T} + N_P \cdot v(\overline{Y}_P)\right] \qquad (12.38)$$

$$\text{s.t. } (Y_M + \underline{T} - N_P \cdot \underline{Y}_P) + N_P \cdot \underline{\theta} \cdot v(\underline{Y}_P) \geq U^A \qquad \text{(PR}\underline{\theta}\text{)}$$

$$(Y_M + \overline{T} - N_P \cdot \overline{Y}_P) + N_P \cdot \overline{\theta} \cdot v(\overline{Y}_P) \geq (Y_M + \underline{T} - N_P \cdot \underline{Y}_P)$$
$$+ N_P \cdot \underline{\theta} \cdot v(\underline{Y}_P) \qquad \text{(ICR}\overline{\theta}\text{)} \qquad (12.39)$$

As is commonly done, we assume that the participation restriction of type θ and the incentive compatibility restriction of type $\overline{\theta}$ are effective.
(PR$\underline{\theta}$):

$$\underline{T} = U^A - Y_M + N_P \cdot \underline{Y}_P - N_P \cdot \underline{\theta} \cdot v(\underline{Y}_P) \qquad (12.40)$$

(12.40) in (ICR$\overline{\theta}$):

$$\overline{T} = (U^A - Y_M) + N_P \cdot v(\underline{Y}_P) \cdot \left[\overline{\theta} - \underline{\theta}\right] + N_P \cdot \overline{Y}_P - N_P \cdot \overline{\theta} \cdot v(\overline{Y}_P) \qquad (12.41)$$

Substituting (12.40) and (12.41) in (12.38) we have:

$$\underset{\overline{Y}_P, \underline{Y}_P}{\text{Max}} \; \pi \left\|Y_F - \left[(U^A - Y_M) + N_P \cdot v(\underline{Y}_P) \cdot \left[\overline{\theta} - \underline{\theta}\right] + N_P \cdot \overline{Y}_P - N_P \cdot \overline{\theta} \cdot v(\overline{Y}_P)\right]\right.$$
$$+ N_P \cdot v(\overline{Y}_P)\right] + (1 - \pi) \cdot \left[Y_F - \left[U^A - Y_M + N_P \cdot \underline{Y}_P - N_P \cdot \underline{\theta} \cdot v(\underline{Y}_P)\right]\right. \qquad (12.42)$$
$$+ N_P \cdot v(\underline{Y}_P)\right]$$

The first order conditions are:

$$v'(\overline{Y}_P) = \frac{1}{1+\theta}, \quad \text{and} \quad (1+\underline{\theta}) \cdot v'(\underline{Y}_P) = 1 + \frac{\pi}{1+\pi}\left[(\overline{\theta} - \underline{\theta}) \cdot v'(\underline{Y}_P)\right] \tag{12.43}$$

Remember that in the case with complete information, we had:

$$v'(\overline{Y}_P^*) = \frac{1}{1+\theta} \quad \text{and} \quad (1+\underline{\theta}) \cdot v'(Y_P^*) = 1 \tag{12.44}$$

Appendix 12.3:   Case of Incomplete Information with Type Intervals

The government's problem is to determine $T(\theta)$ and $Y_P(\theta)$, for each type θ, so as to maximize its utility, taking into consideration a distribution of types given by $f(\theta)$.

$$\underset{Y_P(.),T(.)}{\text{Max}} \int_{\underline{\theta}*}^{\overline{\theta}} \left[G_F + N_P \cdot v(Y_P(\theta))\right] dF(\theta) \tag{12.45}$$

s.t. $G_M(\theta) + N_P \cdot \theta \cdot v(Y_P(\theta)) \geq U(\theta) \quad \forall \, \theta \in \left[\underline{\theta}, \overline{\theta}\right]$ (PRθ)

$\quad G_M(\theta) + N_P \cdot \theta \cdot v(Y_P(\theta)) \geq G_M(\hat{\theta}) + N_P \cdot \theta \cdot v(Y_P(\hat{\theta})) \quad \forall \, \theta \neq \hat{\theta}$ (ICRθ)   (12.46)

$\quad Y_F - T(\theta) + N_P \cdot v(Y_P(\theta)) \geq Y_F + N_P \cdot v(Y_P^A(\theta))$ (PR Government)

Taking into consideration the definitions of G_F, G_M, and $U(\theta)$ we can express the problem as:

$$\underset{Y_P(.),T(.)}{\text{Max}} \int_{\theta*}^{\overline{\theta}} \left[Y_F - T(\theta) + N_P \cdot v(Y_P(\theta)\right] dF(\theta) \tag{12.47}$$

s.t. $\left[Y_M + T(\theta) - N_P \cdot Y_P(\theta)\right] + N_P \cdot \theta \cdot v(Y_P(\theta)) \geq \left[Y_M - N_P \cdot Y_P^A(\theta)\right] + N_P \cdot \theta \cdot v(Y_P^A(\theta))$

$\quad \left[Y_M + T(\theta) - N_P \cdot Y_P(\theta)\right] + N_P \cdot \theta \cdot v(Y_P(\theta)) \geq \left[Y_M + T(\hat{\theta}) - N_P \cdot Y_P(\hat{\theta})\right] + N_P \cdot \theta \cdot v(Y_P(\hat{\theta}))$

$$Y_F - T(\theta) + N_P \cdot v(Y_P(\theta)) \geq Y_F + N_P \cdot v(Y_P^A(\theta)) \tag{12.48}$$

Calling $\hat{\theta}$ the municipality's type of utility after revealing itself and selecting a contract $(Y_P(\hat{\theta}), T(\hat{\theta}))$ as $V(\theta, \hat{\theta})$ we have

$$V(\theta, \hat{\theta}) = \left[Y_M - N_P \cdot Y_P(\hat{\theta}) + T(\hat{\theta})\right] + N_P \cdot \theta \cdot v(Y_P(\hat{\theta})) \tag{12.49}$$

If we now define $V(\theta)$ as the utility from revealing its true type we may write:

$$V(\theta) = V(\theta,\theta) = \left[Y_M - N_P \cdot Y_P(\theta) + T(\theta)\right] + N_P \cdot \theta \cdot v(Y_P(\theta)) \tag{12.50}$$

This way, we can redefine the government's problem as:

$$\underset{Y_P(.),\, V(.)}{\text{Max}} \int_{\theta^*}^{\bar{\theta}} \left\{ \left[Y_F - V(\theta) + Y_M - N_P \cdot Y_P(\theta) + N_P \cdot \theta \cdot v(Y_P(\theta))\right] + N_P \cdot v(Y_P(\theta)) \right\} dF(\theta)$$

$$\tag{12.51}$$

$$\text{s.t. } V(\theta) \geq U(\theta) \quad \forall\, \theta \in [\underline{\theta}, \bar{\theta}] \quad (PR\theta)$$

$$V(\theta,\theta) \geq V(\theta,\hat{\theta}) \quad \forall\, \theta \neq \hat{\theta} \quad (ICR\theta)$$

$$Y_F - \left[V(\theta) - Y_M + N_P \cdot Y_P(\theta) - N_P \cdot \theta \cdot v(Y_P(\theta))\right]$$

$$+ N_P \cdot v(Y_P(\theta)) \geq Y_F + N_P \cdot v(Y_P^A(\theta)) \tag{12.52}$$

Solving the following equation, we derive the following proposition.

Proposition 12.6: The optimum contract to be established between the government and a municipality of type $\theta \geq \theta^*$, given that $\dfrac{d}{dx}\left(\dfrac{1 - F(\theta)}{f(\theta)}\right) \leq 0$, may be characterized by:

$$\left[(1 + \theta) - \frac{1 - F(\theta)}{f(\theta)}\right] \cdot v'(Y_P(\theta)) = 1 \tag{12.53}$$

and

$$T(\theta) = V(\theta) - Y_M + N_P \cdot Y_P(\theta) - N_P \cdot \theta \cdot v(Y_P(\theta)) \quad \forall\, \theta \in \left[\theta^*, \hat{\theta}\right]$$

$$\text{where } V(\theta) = \int_{\theta^*}^{\bar{\theta}} N_P \cdot v(Y_P(\theta)) \cdot d\theta + U(\theta^*) \tag{12.54}$$

and the coefficient θ^*'s value is determined by the government's Participation Restriction.

Proof:
As mentioned previously the government's problem is:

$$\underset{Y_P(.),\, V(.)}{\text{Max}} \int_{\theta^*}^{\bar{\theta}} \left\{ \left[Y_F - V(\theta) + Y_M - N_P \cdot Y_P(\theta) + N_P \cdot \theta \cdot v(Y_P(\theta))\right] + N_P \cdot v(Y_P(\theta)) \right\} dF(\theta)$$

$$\tag{12.55}$$

$$\text{s.t. } V(\theta) \geq U(\theta) \quad \forall\, \theta \in [\underline{\theta}, \overline{\theta}] \quad (\text{PR}\theta)$$

$$V(\theta,\theta) \geq V(\theta,\hat{\theta}) \quad \forall\, \theta \neq \hat{\theta} \quad (\text{ICR}\theta)$$

$$Y_F - [V(\theta) - Y_M + N_P \cdot Y_P(\theta) - N_P \cdot \theta \cdot v(Y_P(\theta))] \tag{12.56}$$

$$+ N_P \cdot v(Y_P(\theta)) \geq Y_F + N_P \geq v(Y_P^A(\theta))$$

Analysing the incentive compatibility restriction, we see that for the local utility to be at a maximum when revealing its true type, it is necessary that:

$$\left. \frac{\partial V(\theta,\hat{\theta})}{\partial \hat{\theta}} \right|_{\hat{\theta}=\theta} = 0 \quad \text{and} \quad \left. \frac{\partial^2 V(\theta,\hat{\theta})}{\partial \hat{\theta}^2} \right|_{\hat{\theta}=\theta} \leq 0 \tag{12.57}$$

Considering that:

$$V(\theta,\hat{\theta}) = [Y_M - N_P \cdot Y_P(\hat{\theta}) + T(\hat{\theta})] + N_P \cdot \theta \cdot v(Y_P(\hat{\theta})) \tag{12.58}$$

$$\frac{\partial V(\theta,\hat{\theta})}{\partial \hat{\theta}} = -N_P \cdot Y_P'(\hat{\theta}) + T'(\hat{\theta}) + N_P \cdot \theta \cdot v'(Y_P(\hat{\theta})) \cdot Y_P'(\hat{\theta}) \tag{12.59}$$

$$\frac{\partial^2 V(\theta,\hat{\theta})}{\partial \hat{\theta}^2} = -N_P \cdot Y_P''(\hat{\theta}) + T''(\hat{\theta}) + N_P \cdot \theta \cdot [v''(Y_P(\hat{\theta})) \cdot Y_P'(\hat{\theta}) \cdot Y_P'(\hat{\theta})$$

$$+ v'(Y_P(\hat{\theta})) \cdot Y_P''(\hat{\theta})] \tag{12.60}$$

Therefore,

$$\left. \frac{\partial V(\theta,\hat{\theta})}{\partial \hat{\theta}} \right|_{\hat{\theta}=\theta} = 0 \Rightarrow T'(\theta) = N_P \cdot Y_P'(\theta) - N_P \cdot \theta \cdot v'(Y_P(\theta)) \cdot Y_P'(\theta) \tag{12.61}$$

and

$$\left. \frac{\partial^2 V(\theta,\hat{\theta})}{\partial \hat{\theta}^2} \right|_{\hat{\theta}=\theta} \leq 0 \Rightarrow T''(\theta) \leq N_P \cdot Y_P''(\theta) - N_P \cdot \theta \cdot [v''(Y_P(\theta)) \cdot (Y_P'(\theta))^2$$

$$+ v'(Y_P(\theta)) \cdot Y_P''(\theta)] \tag{12.62}$$

Deriving (12.61) with respect to θ we obtain

$$T''(\theta) = \underbrace{\left[N_P \cdot Y_P''(\theta) - N_P \cdot \theta \cdot [v''(Y_P(\theta)) \cdot (Y_P'(\theta))^2 + v'(Y_P(\theta)) \cdot Y_P''(\theta)] \right.}_{\text{equation (12.62)}}$$

$$\left. - N_P \cdot v'(Y_P'(\theta)) \cdot Y_P'(\theta) \right] \tag{12.63}$$

Substituting (12.63) in (12.62) we get

$$T''(\theta) \le T''(\theta) + N_P \cdot v'(Y_P(\theta)) \cdot Y_P'(\theta) \Rightarrow v'(Y_P(\theta)) \cdot Y_P'(\theta) \ge 0 \qquad (12.64)$$

Given that $v'(Y_P(\theta)) \ge 0$ and thus

$$Y_P(\theta) \ge 0 \qquad (12.65)$$

since

$$V(\theta) = [Y_M - N_P \cdot Y_P(\theta) + T(\theta)] + N_P \cdot \theta \cdot v(Y_P(\theta)) \qquad (12.66)$$

we derive that

$$V'(\theta) = -N_P \cdot Y_P'(\theta) + T'(\theta) + N_P \cdot v(Y_P(\theta)) + N_P \cdot \theta \cdot v'(Y_P(\theta)) \cdot Y_P(\theta) \Rightarrow$$
$$T'(\theta) = V'(\theta) \quad N_F \cdot v(Y_P(0)) + \underbrace{N_P \cdot Y_P'(\theta) - N_P \cdot \theta \cdot v'(Y_P(\theta)) \cdot Y_P(\theta)}_{\text{equation } 12.61} \qquad (12.67)$$

Substituting (12.67) in (12.61) we get

$$V'(\theta) = N_P \cdot v(Y_P(\theta)) \qquad (12.68)$$

The government's problem with the new restrictions becomes

$$\operatorname*{Max}_{Y_P(.),V(.)} \int_{\theta^*}^{\bar{\theta}} \{[Y_F - V(\theta) + Y_M + -N_P \cdot Y_P(\theta) + N_P \cdot \theta \cdot v(Y_P(\theta))]$$
$$+ N_P \cdot v(Y_P(\theta))\} dF(\theta) \qquad (12.69)$$

$$\text{s.t. } V(\theta) \ge U(\theta) \quad \forall\, \theta \in [\theta, \bar{\theta}] \quad (\text{PR}\theta)$$
$$Y_P'(\theta) \ge 0$$
$$V'(\theta) = N_P \cdot v(Y_P(\theta)) \qquad (12.70)$$
$$Y_F - [V(\theta) - Y_M + N_P \cdot Y_P(\theta) - N_P \cdot \theta \cdot v(Y_P(\theta))] + N_P \cdot v(Y_P(\theta)) \ge$$
$$Y_F + N_P \cdot v(Y_P^A(\theta))$$

The equation's Hamiltonian is given by:

$$H = [Y_F - V(\theta) + Y_M + -N_P \cdot Y_P(\theta) + N_P \cdot \theta \cdot v(Y_P(\theta))]$$
$$+ N_P \cdot v(Y_P(\theta))] \cdot f(\theta) + \mu(\theta) \cdot N_P \cdot v(Y_P(\theta)) \qquad (12.71)$$

$$\frac{\partial H}{\partial V} = -\mu'(\theta) \Rightarrow f(\theta) = \mu'(\theta) \Rightarrow \int_\theta^{\bar{\theta}} \mu(u) \cdot du = \int_\theta^{\bar{\theta}} f(u) \cdot du$$

$$\Rightarrow \mu(\bar{\theta}) - \mu(\theta) = F(\bar{\theta}) - F(\theta)$$

(12.72)

Considering that for $\bar{\theta}$ the restriction is inactive, $\mu(\bar{\theta}) = 0$, and thus

$$\mu(\theta) = -(1 - F(\theta))$$

(12.73)

$$\frac{\partial H}{\partial Y_P} = 0 \Rightarrow [-N_P + N_P \cdot \theta \cdot v'(Y_P(\theta))] + N_P \cdot v'(Y_P(\theta))] \cdot f(\theta)$$

$$+ \mu(\theta) \cdot N_P \cdot v'(Y_P(\theta)) = 0$$

(12.74)

$$\Rightarrow v'(Y_P(\theta)) \cdot [(1 + \theta) \cdot f(\theta) + \mu(\theta)] = f(\theta)$$

Substituting (12.73) in (12.74) we get

$$v'(Y_P(\theta)) \cdot \left[(1 + \theta) - \frac{1 - F(\theta)}{f(\theta)} \right] = 1$$

(12.75)

The equation for the value to be transferred from the government to the municipality is obtained from the definition of $V(\theta)$:

$$V(\theta) = [Y_M - N_P \cdot Y_P(\theta) + T(\theta)] + N_P \cdot \theta \cdot v(Y_P(\theta)) \Rightarrow$$

$$T(\theta) = V(\theta) - Y_M + N_P \cdot Y_P(\theta) - N_P \cdot \theta \cdot v(Y_P(\theta))$$

(12.76)

To obtain $V(\theta)$ take the integral of (12.68):

$$\int_\theta^\theta V'(u) \cdot du = \int_{\theta^*}^\theta N_P \cdot v(Y_P(u)) \cdot du \Rightarrow$$

$$V(\theta) - V(\theta^*) = \int_{\theta^*}^\theta N_P \cdot v(Y_P(u)) \cdot du \Rightarrow$$

$$/ V(\theta^*) = U(\theta^*) / \Rightarrow$$

$$V(\theta) = \int_\theta^{\theta^*} N_P \cdot v(Y_P(\theta)) \cdot du + U(\theta^*)$$

(12.77)

13

On Assessing Pro-Poorness of Government Programmes: International Comparisons*

*Nanak Kakwani and Hyun H. Son**

13.1 Introduction

Governments in developing countries are increasingly considering introducing safety net programmes that provide income for the poor or for those who face a probable risk of falling into poverty, in the absence of the cash or in-kind transfers provided by such programmes. In designing such programmes, governments in developing countries are often faced with the choice between cash and in-kind transfers. Economic theory would lead us to believe that cash transfers are the preferred means of assistance. A range of economic as well as administrative considerations influence this choice (Grosh 1994; Jimenez 1993; Tabor 2002).

Whether the transfer programmes are cash or in-kind, it is obvious that if our objective is to reduce poverty, the transfer programmes should be designed in such a way that they lead to the maximum reduction in poverty under given resource constraints. To achieve this objective, perfect targeting will be an ideal solution when: (i) only the poor get all the benefits; and (ii) benefits given to the poor are proportional to their income shortfall in relation to the poverty line. To implement such a programme, however, we will need to have detailed information on people's incomes or consumption: 'Such detailed information, and the administrative ability to use it is not present in most developing countries' (Haddad and Kanbur 1991). We generally resort to a proxy targeting, which makes the transfers based on easily observable socioeconomic characteristics of households. The proxy targeting can never achieve 100 per cent targeting efficiency. It is, therefore, important to know how good the proxy targeting is compared to perfect targeting. In this chapter, we provide a methodology to assess the targeting efficiency of government programmes, which can be cash or in-kind.

A government programme may be defined as pro-poor if it provides greater absolute benefits to the poor compared to the non-poor. Obviously, with a given fixed cost,

* We would like to acknowledge helpful comments received from Professor Stephan Klasen, which led to a considerable improvement in the paper. We would also like acknowledge comments recived from the participants of the international conference on the 'Many dimensions of Poverty' held by the International Poverty Centre in Brasilia.
** Email address for correspondence: hhson@adb.org.

a pro-poor programme will lead to greater poverty reduction than a non-pro-poor programme. Suppose there are two programmes, *A* and *B*, incurring the same cost, then *A* will be more pro-poor than *B* if it leads to a greater poverty reduction than *B*. Utilizing this definition, the chapter develops a new index called the 'Pro-Poor Policy (PPP)' index, which measures the pro-poorness of government programmes, as well as basic service delivery in education, health, and infrastructure.

The PPP index is defined as the ratio of actual proportional poverty reduction from a government programme, to the proportional poverty reduction that would have been achieved in a counterfactual situation when every individual in society had received exactly the same benefits from the programme. The value of the PPP index, framed in the realm of perfect targeting, provides a means to assess the targeting efficiency of government programmes. In addition, this chapter shows that the Relative Operating Characteristic (ROC) curve – which is a non-parametric technique to evaluate the performance of various targeting indicators – is a particular case of the PPP index.

From the policy point of view, it is important to know how the targeting efficiency of government programmes varies across various socioeconomic groups. To answer this question, the chapter develops two types of PPP indices by socioeconomic groups, which are within-group and total-group PPP indices. While the within-group PPP index measures the pro-poorness of a programme within the group, the total-group PPP index captures the impact of operating a programme in the group on its pro-poorness at national level. The within-group PPP index captures how well targeted a programme is within a group. On the other hand, if our objective is to maximize poverty reduction at the national level, the targeting efficiency of particular group should be judged on the basis of total-group PPP index.

Using micro unit-record data on household surveys from Thailand, Russia, Vietnam, and 15 African countries, the chapter evaluates a wide range of government programmes and services.

The chapter is organized in the following manner: section 13.2 describes poverty measures. Section 13.3 is devoted to the derivation of the Pro-Poor Policy (PPP) index to measure the pro-poorness of governments' welfare programmes and utilization of basic services. Section 13.4 discusses targeting efficiency. In this section, we derive that the ROC curve is a particular case of the PPP index. Section 13.5 formulates the values of the PPP index attainable under perfect targeting and section 13.6 proposes the PPP index by socioeconomic groups. Section 13.7 presents empirical results applied to Thailand, Russia, and Vietnam, and, finally, section 13.8 provides an empirical analysis of 15 African countries. The final section summarizes the major findings emerging from the study.

13.2   Poverty measures

We calculate the pro-poorness of a government policy by measuring its impact on poverty. If there are two policies, *A* and *B*, then policy *A* is more (less) pro-poor than policy *B* if it achieves a greater (smaller) reduction in aggregate poverty for a given cost. Aggregate poverty can be measured in a variety of ways. In this paper, we will focus on a class of additively separable poverty measures that can be written as

$$\theta = \int_0^z P(z,x)f(x)dx \qquad (13.1)$$

where x is the income of an individual, which is a random variable with a density function $f(x)$. An individual is identified as poor if his/her income is less than the poverty line z. $P(z, x)$ may be interpreted as the deprivation suffered by an individual with income x and is a homogenous function of degree zero in z and x, which satisfies the restrictions:

$$P(z, x) = 0 \quad if \geq x \geq z$$

$$\frac{\partial P(z,x)}{\partial x} < 0 \quad and \quad \frac{\partial^2 P(z,x)}{\partial x^2} > 0$$

Individuals do not suffer any deprivation when their income or consumption can meet their basic minimum standard of living defined by the poverty line. θ in (13.1) measures the average deprivation suffered by the society due to the existence of poverty.

Foster, Greer and Thorbecke (1984), for example, proposed a class of poverty measures that is obtained by substituting

$$P(z, x) = \left(\frac{z - x}{z}\right)^\alpha \qquad (13.2)$$

in (13.1), where α is the parameter of inequality aversion. When $\alpha = 0$, 1 and 2, the poverty measure is a headcount ratio, poverty gap ratio and severity of poverty index, respectively.

To formulate a poverty reduction policy, we need to make a choice of poverty measures. For instance, the headcount ratio will require different policies than poverty gap and severity of poverty. The headcount ratio is a crude measure of poverty because it completely ignores the gap in incomes from the poverty line and the distribution of income among the poor. The severity of the poverty index has all the desirable properties.

13.3 Pro-poor policy index

Suppose there is a welfare transfer from the government, which leads to an increase in the recipients' income or consumption expenditure. Accordingly, there will be a reduction in poverty incurred from the increase in income. Suppose x is the income of a person before transfer and $b(x)$ is the benefit received by the person with income x, the percentage change in poverty (because of this benefit) can be written as:

$$\frac{d\theta}{\theta} = \frac{1}{\theta}\int_0^z \frac{\partial P}{\partial x}b(x)f(x)dx \qquad (13.3)$$

We define a government programme to be pro-poor if the poor receive greater absolute benefits than the non-poor. This means that the pro-poor government programme should achieve greater poverty reduction compared to a counterfactual situation where everyone receives exactly the same benefit from the programme.

Suppose that the average benefit generated from the government programme is denoted by $\bar{b}$. The percentage change in aggregate poverty, when the amount of $\bar{b}$ is given to everyone, can be written as:

$$\frac{d\theta}{\theta} = \frac{\bar{b}}{\theta} \int_0^z \frac{\partial P}{\partial x} f(x)dx \qquad (13.4)$$

We define the pro-poor policy (PPP) index as the ratio of actual proportional poverty reduction from the programme as given in (13.3), to the proportional poverty reduction that would have been achieved if every individual in society had received exactly the same benefits (equal to the average benefit from the programme) as given in (13.4). Thus, the pro-poor policy index can be expressed as

$$\lambda = \frac{1}{\bar{b}\eta\theta} \int_0^z \frac{\partial P}{\partial x} b(x)f(x)dx \qquad (13.5)$$

where

$$\eta = \frac{1}{\theta} \int_0^z \frac{\partial P}{\partial x} f(x)dx \qquad (13.6)$$

is the absolute elasticity of poverty: if everyone receives one unit of currency, then poverty will change by $100 \times \eta$ per cent. A programme will be called pro-poor (anti-poor) when $\lambda > 1$ (< 1). The larger the value of λ, the greater will be the degree of pro-poorness of the programme.

Note that the value of λ does not depend on the size of the programme in terms of its budget. This suggests that λ alone cannot estimate the poverty impacts of different programmes with different budgets. However, the poverty impact of the programme can be fully captured by using the product of λ with the size of the programme, which is measured by $\bar{b}$.

Substituting (13.2) into (13.5) gives a general formula for calculating the PPP index for the entire class of FGT poverty measures as

$$\lambda_\alpha = \frac{\bar{b}_\alpha}{\bar{b}} \qquad (13.7)$$

where $\bar{b}_\alpha$ given by

$$\bar{b}_\alpha = \frac{\int_0^z \frac{1}{z}\left(\frac{z-x}{z}\right)^{\alpha-1} b(x)f(x)dx}{\int_0^z \frac{1}{z}\left(\frac{z-x}{z}\right)^{\alpha-1} f(x)dx} \qquad (13.8)$$

is the weighted average of the benefits received by different income levels. Weights decline monotonically with income when $\alpha > 1$: the poorer the individual, the greater will be the weight given to his or her benefits received. When $\alpha = 1$ and the poverty line (z) is the same for all individuals, $\bar{b}_\alpha$ is equal to the average benefits received by the poor, in which case λ is equal to the ratio of the average benefits received by the poor to the average benefits received by the entire population. Thus, the programme will be pro-poor if the average benefits received by the poor are greater than the average benefits received by the whole population.

To calculate λ, the programme does not have be in cash transfers. In fact, a large number of government programmes take the form of providing services in the areas of education, health and other social services. Although these services do not provide a direct form of cash to individuals, they do make important contributions to people's standard of living. Hence, it is reasonable to assume that if an individual utilizes a service provided by the government, he or she receives some notional cash. If all individuals utilizing a government service are assumed to receive exactly the same benefits in the form of notional cash, then we can easily calculate the pro-poor policy index λ, by defining $b(x) = 1$, if a person utilizes a service and 0 otherwise.

13.4 Targeting efficiency

Targeting efficiency is related to the selection of beneficiaries in the programme. The efficient targeting may refer to the targeting that selects the maximum proportion of beneficiaries among the poor. In the process of selecting beneficiaries, there is always the danger of committing two types of errors. Type I errors occur when someone who deserves the benefits is denied them, and type II errors occur when benefits are paid to someone who does not deserve them. Often, these two types of errors do not move in the same direction: attempts to reduce type II errors lead to increased commitment of type I errors. How can we overcome this hurdle?

To tackle this problem, it is often suggested that we use the Relative Operating Characteristic (ROC) curve to evaluate the performance of various targeting indicators.[1] The ROC curve measures the relationship between the probability of selecting a poor person as a beneficiary ($1 - \alpha$, where α is the type I error) and the probability of selecting a non-poor person as a beneficiary (β, the type II error). We may say that a programme is pro-poor if the probability of selecting a poor in the programme is greater than the probability of selecting a non-poor in the programme. In the ROC curve, the vertical axis is the probability of selecting a poor in the programme and the horizontal axis is the probability of selecting a non-poor in the programme.

The pro-poorness can also be defined when the probability of selecting a poor person in the programme is greater than the probability of selecting a person from the entire population in the programme. This suggests that we can have a simplified ROC curve which describes the relationship between the percentage of beneficiaries among the poor and the percentage of beneficiaries in the population as a whole. In our proposed simplified ROC curve, while the probability of selecting a poor person in the programme is in the vertical axis, the probability of selecting a beneficiary is in the horizontal axis. The higher the curve, the greater will be the pro-poorness of the programme.

The simplified ROC curve is intuitively easier to interpret. It is intuitive to assume that the proportion of population covered by the programme is an exogenous variable, which can be determined as a *priori* by the government. Then the simplified ROC curves can tell us which programme, for a given coverage of population, will lead to the highest probability of selecting a poor in the programme.

If it is assumed that all beneficiaries receive exactly the same benefits from the programme, then the PPP index defined in (13.7) should be able to capture the targeting efficiency of the programme. In this case, the only information we require relates to whether or not the individual is a beneficiary. When the person is beneficiary, $b(x)$ takes a value of 1, and otherwise zero. Substituting binary values for $b(x)$ into (13.7), we can define the PPP index for the poverty gap ratio as the ratio of the percentage of beneficiaries among the poor to the percentage of beneficiaries in the total population. This is the simplified ROC curve. Hence, the ROC curve, which measures the targeting efficiency, is a particular case of the PPP index. We can show that the PPP index is the sum of the targeting efficiency and the redistributive efficiency of transfers among the poor.[2] The redistributive efficiency measures the pro-poorness of the distribution of the benefits from the programme among poor beneficiaries. Therefore, the analysis based on the PPP index is more general than the ROC curve in the sense that the PPP index takes account of not only how beneficiaries are selected but also how benefits are distributed among the beneficiaries.

13.5   Perfect targeting

The PPP index has the lowest value – zero – if the government programme does not reduce poverty at all. This can occur when all the benefits of the programme go to the non-poor. This situation can be described as:

$$b(x) = 0 \quad if\, x < z$$

$$b(x) \geq 0 \quad if\, x \geq z$$

(13.9)

Substituting (13.9) into (13.5) gives $\lambda = 0$. This is the extreme situation of imperfect targeting.

Perfect targeting may be defined as a situation where (i) only the poor receive all the benefits, and (ii) benefits given to the poor are proportional to the income shortfall from the poverty line. This situation may be described as:

$$b(x) = k(z - x) \quad if\, x < z$$

$$b(x) = 0 \quad if\, x \geq z$$

(13.10)

When $k = 1$, poverty is completely eliminated. k should be less than 1 in order to avoid the adverse effects on the labour supply that may arise from providing transfer payments.

Experience in the industrialized economies suggests that cash transfer programmes can put upward pressure on wages, bias consumption toward leisure instead of labour, stimulate shirking behavior, discourage job searches, encourage early retirement, introduce rigidities into the labour market, and ultimately raise the long-term unemployment rate (Kanbur, Keen and Tuomala 1994; Karni 1999).

Per capita cost of such a programme, which excludes administrative costs, is given by

$$\bar{b} = k\int_0^z (z - x)f(x)dx$$

λ, in this situation, is derived from (13.5) as

$$\lambda_m = \frac{1}{\bar{b}\eta\theta}\int_0^z \frac{\partial P}{\partial x}(z - x)f(x)dx \tag{13.11}$$

where λ_m is the value of PPP index obtainable in the case of perfect targeting. Note that in the computation of λ_m, we do not need to assume one single poverty line for all households. Every household can have different poverty lines depending on the household composition and the regional prices faced by the households. In our empirical study of Thailand, the official poverty line varies with households, but in the case of Vietnam, the poverty line is fixed for all households. If we assume that all households have the same per capita poverty line, then by substitutions it is easy to demonstrate that the value of λ_m for the poverty gap ratio is equal to the inverse of the headcount index H (i.e. $1/H$). Similarly, it can be easily proved that λ_m for the severity of poverty index is equal to s/g^2, where g is the poverty gap ratio and s is the severity of poverty index.[3]

Thus, we have obtained the values of λ attainable under the situation of perfect targeting. In practice, it is not possible to attain perfect targeting because it is difficult to obtain accurate data concerning people's income or consumption. We generally resort to proxy targeting such as by geographical regions or by other socioeconomic characteristics of households. Since the value of λ_m can be easily calculated from (13.11), we can then judge the target efficiency of a programme by comparing it with its value attainable under perfect targeting.

13.6 PPP index by socioeconomic groups

Suppose that there are K mutually exclusive socioeconomic groups in the population, then the PPP index for the kth group can be obtained from equation (13.5) as:

$$\lambda_k = \frac{1}{\bar{b}_k\eta_k\theta_k}\int_0^z \frac{\partial P}{\partial x} b(x)f_k(x)dx \tag{13.12}$$

where $\bar{b}_k$ is the mean benefit of the programme in the kth group, θ_k is the poverty measure in the kth group, $f_k(x)$ is the density function of the kth group and η_k is the absolute elasticity of the poverty of the kth group, which can be written as:

$$\eta_k = \frac{1}{\theta_k} \int_0^z \frac{\partial P}{\partial x} f_k(x) dx \tag{13.13}$$

which is the proportional change in poverty within the kth group when everyone in the kth group receives one unit of currency.

If a_k is the population share of the kth group, such that $\sum_{k=1}^K a_k = 1$, then

$$f(x) = \sum_{k=1}^K a_k f_k(x) \tag{13.14}$$

Utilizing (13.5), (13.12), (13.13) and (13.14) easily gives us

$$\lambda = \frac{1}{\bar{b}\eta\theta} \sum_{k=1}^K \bar{b}_k \eta_k \theta_k a_k \lambda_k \tag{13.15}$$

which shows that the PPP index for the whole country is the weighted sum of the PPP indices for the individual groups.

λ_k measures the degree of pro-poorness of a programme within the kth group. Although this within-group PPP index is useful in knowing how well targeted a programme is within a group, it does not tell us whether targeting the kth group will necessarily lead to a pro-poor outcome at national level. Since our objective is to achieve the maximum reduction in poverty at the national level, we need to see the impact of targeting the kth group on national poverty. To capture this effect, we derive below a total-group PPP index for the kth group.

Since the poverty measures given in (13.1) are additively decomposable, we can express the total poverty in country as the weighted average of poverty in individual groups with weights proportional to their population shares:

$$\theta = \sum_{k=1}^K a_k \theta_k \tag{13.16}$$

where a_k is the population share of the kth group such that $\sum_{k=1}^K a_k = 1$ and θ_k is the poverty measure in the kth group. Differentiating both sides of (13.16) gives

$$\frac{d\theta}{\theta} = \sum_{k=1}^K \left(\frac{a_k \theta_k}{\theta} \right) \left(\frac{d\theta_k}{\theta_k} \right) \tag{13.17}$$

Suppose a programme $b(x)$ operates only in the kth group, then the proportional change in poverty in the kth group will be given by

$$\frac{d\theta_k}{\theta_k} = \frac{1}{\theta_k} \int_0^z \frac{\partial P}{\partial x} b(x) f_k(x) dx \tag{13.18}$$

where $f_k(x)$ is the density function of the kth group. Utilizing (13.18) into (13.17), we obtain the proportional change in national poverty, when the government programme operates only in the kth group, as:

$$\left(\frac{d\theta}{\theta}\right)_k = \frac{a_k}{\theta}\int_0^z \frac{\partial P}{\partial x}b(x)f_k(x)dx \tag{13.19}$$

Suppose $\bar{b}_k$ is the mean benefit of the programme in the kth group. Thus, the total cost per person (in the whole population) for operating the programme in the kth group is given by $a_k\bar{b}_k$. If we had considered a scenario of universal targeting for the whole population of providing every individual with the benefit equal to $a_k\bar{b}_k$, then the proportional reduction in national poverty would have been $a_k\bar{b}_k\eta$. Obviously then, operating a programme in the kth group will be pro-poor if the magnitude of poverty reduction in (13.19) is greater than the poverty reduction obtained from a universal targeting, while both incur the same costs. Hence, we define the total-group PPP index for the kth group as:

$$\lambda_k^* = \frac{1}{\bar{b}_k\eta\theta}\int_0^z \frac{\partial P}{\partial x}b(x)f_k(x)dx \tag{13.20}$$

Operating the government programme $b(x)$ in the kth group is pro-poor (anti-poor) if λ_k^* is greater (less) than 1. Note that λ_k^* measures the pro-poorness of the programme in the kth group with respect to the whole population and not with respect to the population within the kth group.

Utilizing (13.5), (13.14) and (13.20) easily gives us the following formula:

$$\lambda = \frac{1}{h}\sum_{k-1}^K \bar{b}_k a_k \lambda_k^* \tag{13.21}$$

which shows that the PPP for the whole country is simply the weighted average of the total-group PPP indices for the individual groups, with the weight proportional to shares of benefits received by each group.

Equation (13.21) demonstrates that to reduce poverty at national level, operating the government programme in some groups will be more efficient than in other groups. This efficiency can be captured by the value of λ_k^*: the larger the value of λ_k^*, the more efficient will be the kth group in reducing the national poverty. On the whole, the methodology presented in this section can help us to identify the socioeconomic groups that should be targeted in order to achieve the maximum reduction in national poverty.

13.7 Case Studies I: Thailand, Russia and Vietnam

In this section we apply our methodology proposed in sections 13.3 to 13.6 to studies of three countries: Thailand, Russia and Vietnam. While the pro-poor policy (PPP) index is applied to Thailand and Russia to capture the extent to which the governments' welfare schemes benefit the poor, the PPP index is applied to

Vietnam to estimate the degree of effectiveness of basic services – including education and health – utilized by the population.

For all three countries, we utilized nationwide household surveys covering the periods of 2000, 2002, and 1997–98 for Thailand, Russia and Vietnam, respectively. Poverty lines are country-specific. While a single average national poverty line is used for Vietnam, Thai and Russian poverty lines differ across households because they take into account different needs of household members by gender and age, as well as spatial costs of living across regions and areas in both Thailand and Russia.[4]

13.7.1   Welfare programmes in Thailand and Russia

Thailand

In recent years, the Thai government has implemented a series of social welfare programmes, including social pensions for the elderly, low-income medical cards, health insurance cards, and free school lunch programmes. These are means-tested and designed specifically to target the low-income group. In this section we examine whether these welfare programmes have indeed benefited poor people in the society by means of our proposed PPP index.

Table 13.1 presents the Pro-Poor Policy (PPP) index for Thailand's social welfare programmes. As can be seen from the table, for all four welfare programmes the value of the PPP index is greater than 1. On this account, we may conclude that all the four welfare programmes benefit the poor more than the non-poor. Overall, the poor have greater access to government welfare programmes than the non-poor.

It is interesting to note that the welfare programmes – low-income medical cards and free school lunches – have higher values of the PPP index for the severity of poverty measure. Since the severity of poverty measure gives greater weight to the ultra-poor, the absolute benefits of low-income medical cards and free school lunch programmes flow to the ultra-poor more than the moderately poor.

We have also calculated the PPP index in the hypothetical case of a universal pension system. Suppose that every elderly person over 65 years of age receives a pension from the government. Is this scenario more pro-poor than the actual pension system? The PPP index indicates that although a universal pension scheme for the elderly is pro-poor and is even more beneficial to the ultra-poor, the present pension system is far more pro-poor than the universal one. This implies that the

Table 13.1   Pro-Poor Policy index for welfare programmes in Thailand: 2000

Welfare schemes	Poverty gap ratio	Severity of poverty
Social pension for the elderly	1.68	1.54
Low-income medical cards	2.02	2.12
Health insurance cards	1.29	1.25
Free school lunches	2.02	2.06
Perfect targeting	*6.77*	*10.31*
Universal social pensions *(for elderly over 65 years of age)*	*1.21*	*1.24*

current means-tested pension system provides more benefits to the poor than the universal pension system for people of 65 years of age and over. In this analysis, we have not taken into account administrative costs involved in providing means-tested pensions.

Perfect targeting is the ideal policy for poverty reduction. In practice, it is not feasible to operate such a policy because: (i) the administrative cost is very high; and (ii) it is difficult to obtain accurately details of individuals' income or consumption particularly in the countries, where the informal sector might be very large. If the government in Thailand had succeeded in implementing perfect targeting, the PPP index would have been 6.77 for the poverty gap and 10.31 for the severity of poverty measure. Thus, the Thai welfare programmes, although pro-poor, have much lower values on the PPP index than the values that would have been obtained with perfect targeting. This suggests that there is scope for improving the targeting efficiency of the Thai welfare programmes.

In section 13.6, we derived two types of PPP indicates for groups λ_k and λ_k^*. The former may be called within-group PPP index as it measures the pro-poorness of a programme within the kth group. The latter may be referred to as total-group PPP index because it captures the impact of operating a programme in the kth group on its pro-poorness at the national level. The results are presented in Table 13.2. The total-group PPP index shown in the table reveals that the welfare programmes are more pro-poor in the rural areas than in the urban areas. Welfare schemes such as the health-care cards and free school lunches are not pro-poor in the urban areas. This suggests that the government expenditures made on these programmes in the urban areas did not benefit the poor more than the non-poor.

It is, however, interesting to note that the within-group PPP index shows that all programmes are more pro-poor in the urban areas than in the rural areas. Thus, the two types of indices (total-group and within-group) present opposite results. The main

Table 13.2 Pro-Poor Policy index by urban and rural areas in Thailand, 2000

Welfare schemes	Total-group PPP index		Within-group PPP index	
	Urban	Rural	Urban	Rural
	Poverty gap ratio			
Social pension for the elderly	1.13	1.76	4.41	1.31
Low-income medical cards	1.44	2.10	5.60	1.56
Health insurance cards	0.70	1.39	2.72	1.03
Free school lunches	0.81	2.21	3.15	1.64
	Severity of poverty			
Social pension for the elderly	1.18	1.60	5.42	1.17
Low-income medical cards	1.34	2.23	6.18	1.63
Health insurance cards	0.61	1.36	2.83	0.99
Free school lunches	0.73	2.27	3.37	1.66

reason for this is that welfare programmes in Thailand are better targeted in urban than rural areas. Since the concentration of poor is higher in the rural areas, the impact of targeting the rural areas turns out to be more pro-poor at the national level. It is worth stressing that the targeting efficiency of particular group should be judged on the basis of total-group PPP index.

Russia

Russia has a well developed social benefits system, of which pensions constitute the largest component. Table 13.3 gives the population in millions receiving some kind of benefits. There are some persons, who receive more than one benefit at the same time but numbers of such people are so small that we have ignored them.

From Table 13.3, it can be seen that out of the total population of 143.32 million, 53.62 million are receiving some kind of government benefit, which means that 37.41 per cent of the total population depends on government benefits. This shows that the Russian social benefits system is very large.

The old-age pension is the largest welfare programme, benefiting about 26.32 million people. The second largest programme is the children allowance, benefiting 17.42 million children. The disability pension is given to 3.19 million people.

The Russian government spends 46.79 billion Rubles per month on welfare programmes (without the administrative costs) of which 38.74 billion Rubles go towards the payment of pensions. The expenditure on children's allowance is only 1.45 billion Rubles, which means that the children's allowance per beneficiary is only 83.1 Rubles per month. Given the fact that the incidence of poverty among children is very severe, the children's allowance is too small to have a significant impact on poverty among children.

The government pays average benefits equal to Rubles 326.5 per person per month. Our average lower poverty line for Russia is Rubles 1055.9 per person per month, which means that the government pays benefits equal to one third of the poverty line.

Table 13.3 Russian welfare systems in 2002

Welfare benefits	Beneficiaries in million	Percentage share	Per month cost in billion (Rubles)	Percentage share
Old-age pension	26.32	49.08	38.74	82.79
Disability pension	3.19	5.96	3.61	7.71
Loss of breadwinner pension	1.64	3.05	1.27	2.72
Social pension	0.27	0.5	0.26	0.56
Care for children under 18 months	0.84	1.57	0.41	0.88
Children allowance	17.42	32.49	1.45	3.09
Unemployment benefits	0.45	0.84	0.31	0.65
Other benefits	0.95	1.77	0.2	0.42
Scholarship	2.55	4.76	0.55	1.17
All benefits	*53.63*	*100*	*46.79*	*100*

To what extent do the government benefits go to the poor compared to the non-poor in the Russian Federation? This question is answered through our proposed PPP index. Table 13.4 gives the empirical estimates of the pro-poorness of each of government welfare programmes that are currently implemented in Russia.

As can be seen from Table 13.4, the benefits as a whole have the value of the PPP index far greater than 1. From this, we may conclude that the welfare system in Russia tends to benefit the poor more than the non-poor. More importantly, the absolute benefits of the welfare system do indeed flow more to the ultra-poor than to the poor as suggested by the value of PPP index for the severity of poverty measure, equal to 3.90. Note that the PPP index of all benefits is the weighted average of the PPP indices of all nine welfare programmes, with the weight proportional to the share of each programme presented in the third column of Table 13.3.

Table 13.4 also reveals that if the government of the Russian Federation had implemented perfect targeting, the PPP index would have been 3.02 and 5.71 for the poverty gap and the severity of poverty, respectively. This suggests that although Russian welfare programmes are not perfectly targeted at the poor, their deviation from perfect targeting is not large.

It is important to note that welfare programmes, such as the children's allowance given to those aged below 16 years and scholarships, are not pro-poor, particularly in relation to the severity of poverty index. This is evident from the result that the PPP indices of these two programmes for the severity of poverty measure fall far below unity. This suggests that the absolute benefits of these programmes do not flow to the ultra-poor. This further suggests that these programmes may require better targeting than the current system in a way that favours the ultra-poor living far below the poverty threshold.

13.7.2 Health services in Vietnam

Over the past decade or so, Vietnam has enjoyed a significant improvement in standard of living with its impressive performance in growth and poverty reduction.

Table 13.4 PPP indices for Russian welfare system in 2002

Types of government benefits	Poverty gap ratio	Severity of poverty
Old-age pension	2.20	4.13
Disability pension	2.18	4.16
Loss-of-breadwinner pension	2.09	2.40
Social pension	2.22	2.80
Care for children under 18 months	1.78	1.87
Children (under 16 years) allowance	1.19	0.79
Unemployment benefits	2.22	3.80
Other benefits	1.74	2.75
Scholarship	0.90	0.62
All benefits	*2.14*	*3.90*
Perfect targeting	*3.02*	*5.71*

More importantly, its growth process has been pro-poor in a way that growth benefits the poor proportionally more than the non-poor (Kakwani and Son, 2004). In
this context, it will be interesting to see whether, along with a rising standard of
living and its pro-poor growth, poor people benefit from the utilization of current
health services in Vietnam. Table 13.5 presents the PPP index for the utilization of
various health facilities in Vietnam.

As the results in Table 13.5 reveal, only commune health centres display an index
value greater than 1. This suggests that the poor utilize commune health centres more
than the non-poor. Unfortunately, commune health centres do not provide quality
health services because they are generally poorly staffed and not well equipped. Thus,
the poor in Vietnam are generally not receiving the best quality health services.

Public hospitals in Vietnam provide higher-quality care and are mainly utilized
by individuals with health insurance. It can be noted that the utilization of government hospitals is shown to have a value of PPP index far less than 1, implying
that public hospitals in Vietnam provide greater benefits to the non-poor than the
poor. As such, the poor are unable to access quality health services that are provided by public hospitals.

Nevertheless, it is not surprising to see that the utilization of health insurance is not
pro-poor because in Vietnam, those who are covered by health insurance have access
to government hospitals. Moreover, insurance coverage under the health insurance
programme is more extensive for relatively better-off individuals. As such, having
health insurance is positively correlated with individual income: while the insurance
coverage rate is 9.2 per cent in the bottom income quartile, 24.5 per cent in the top
income quartile have health insurance.

Our results presented in Table 13.5 indicate that pharmacy utilization is close to
being pro-poor (0.96) when calculated for the poverty gap ratio. It is reasonable to
assume that more highly educated individuals, and hence presumably those better
aware of the risks of self-medication, avoid pharmacy visits. As such, pharmacy
utilization appears to be an inferior good for the high-income group since rich

Table 13.5   Pro-Poor Policy index for health services in Vietnam: 1997–98, poverty gap ratio

Health facilities	Vietnam	Total-group PPP index		Within-group PPP index	
		Urban	Rural	Urban	Rural
		Poverty gap ratio			
Government hospitals	0.62	0.07	0.91	0.34	0.74
Commune health centres	1.17	0.27	1.23	1.38	1.00
Regional polyclinics	0.84	0.42	0.98	2.14	0.79
Eastern medicine facilities	0.96	0.04	1.15	0.21	0.94
Pharmacies	0.96	0.26	1.16	1.29	0.94
Private doctors	0.79	0.12	0.98	0.59	0.80
Health insurance	0.50	0.08	0.79	0.40	0.64
Perfect targeting	2.86				

individuals go to public hospitals for their health care. On the other hand, pharmacy visits are a normal good for poor households.

Table 13.5 also reveals that, as indicated by the total-group PPP index, the utilization of three health facilities is more pro-poor in the rural areas than in the urban areas. These facilities include commune health centres, pharmacies, and eastern medicine facilities. This suggests that government subsidies of these health services in rural areas do benefit poor people more than non-poor people. In addition, the within-group PPP index indicates that within the urban sector, sick and injured individuals from poor households receive fewer benefits from utilization of health care services such as government hospitals and eastern medicine facilities. By comparison, the poor in rural settlements have greater benefits from utilizing facilities such as commune health centres, eastern medicine facilities, and pharmacies.

13.7.3 Educational services in Vietnam

In this subsection, we apply our proposed PPP index methodology to assess educational services in Vietnam. Our prime objective is to find out to what extent public education at primary and secondary levels is pro-poor. We also seek answering whether free universal education will benefit the poor more than the non-poor.

Table 13.6 reveals that public primary education benefits the poor more than the non-poor. Benefits provided by public primary education are even more pro-poor for the ultra-poor in Vietnam. This is supported by the fact that net enrolments in primary school increased from 87 to 91 per cent over the period 1993–98 (Nguyen, 2002). Coupled with substantial improvement in primary school enrolment rates, changes in the allocation of public spending on education in the 1990s could have further favoured lower levels of education. The share of public spending on education going to the poor increased from 16.5 per cent in 1993 to 18.1 per cent in 1998 (Nguyen, 2002). Although public schools at the primary education level are found to be pro-poor, other types of schools at the same level are highly anti-poor. In other words, primary schools, which are semi-public or sponsored by the private sector, benefit better-off children more than poor ones. This suggests that educational

Table 13.6 Pro-Poor Policy index for education service in Vietnam, 1997–98

School types	Primary	Lower secondary	Upper secondary
		Poverty gap ratio	
Public	1.29	0.79	0.37
Semi-public	0.55	0.15	0.23
Sponsored	0.63	0.51	0.00
		Severity of poverty	
Public	1.31	0.65	0.23
Semi-public	0.19	0.08	0.09
Sponsored	0.14	0.26	0.00

Table 13.7   Pro-Poor Policy index if universal education is provided in Vietnam

	Poverty gap ratio	Severity of poverty
Primary	1.28	1.33
Lower secondary	1.08	1.06
Upper secondary	0.91	0.85

subsidies given to these types of schools are likely to benefit the non-poor more than the poor.

As shown in Table 13.6, lower secondary education in Vietnam is not pro-poor as indicated by the PPP index. This finding emerges consistently irrespective of school types. At the lower secondary level, net enrolment rates more than doubled in Vietnam between 1993 and 1998, to 30 per cent and 62 per cent, respectively. However, for the population as a whole, 38 per cent of children aged 11-14 years were not enrolled in lower secondary school, and 66 per cent of the poorest children in this age range were not enrolled in primary school. The disparity in the enrolments rates between the richest and poorest quintiles is highly distinctive over the years.

As would be expected, the PPP index signals that upper secondary schools strongly favour children from the better-off households. This is consistent with all types of schools at this level. Note that there are no children from poor households enrolled in the upper secondary level schools sponsored by the private sector. Over the period 1993–98, children from the poorest quintile experienced an increase in enrolment in upper secondary schools from 1 to 5 per cent as compared to an increase from 21 to 64 per cent for the richest quintile (Nguyen, 2002). On the whole, much still needs to be done to achieve universal primary and secondary education in Vietnam. Having said that, we follow up with the question of whether universal education can really deliver educational outcomes that are pro-poor. The PPP index under a system of universal education is compared to that under the current education system.

Table 13.7 shows that universal education at primary and lower secondary levels will provide more benefits to the poor children than to non-poor ones. The degree of pro-poorness of universal access to primary education among six-to ten-year-old children is almost as high as that actually obtained from the current education system in Vietnam. Similarly, if lower secondary education is made universal for children aged between 11 and 14 years, it will provide pro-poor outcomes. This is in contrast with the result obtained from the actual situation as indicated by the PPP index: the index is 0.79 in the current lower secondary education, whereas it is 1.08 when lower secondary education is universal. At higher levels, its universal provision is not likely to deliver pro-poor outcomes. The PPP index for upper secondary is shown to be less than unity. In short, universal education at higher levels will not be pro-poor, but will provide greater opportunities to poor individuals aged between 15 and 17 at the upper secondary level to have greater access to higher education compared to the current situation in Vietnam.

Table 13.8 Pro-Poor Policy index for basic infrastructure service in Vietnam, 1997–98

Access to basic infrastructure services	Poverty gap ratio	Severity of poverty
Electricity	0.80	0.71
Piped and tap water	0.86	0.81
Collected waste	0.10	0.07
Sanitary toilets	0.10	0.05

13.7.4 Basic infrastructure services in Vietnam

Basic infrastructure services make significant contributions to people's well-being. Basic services such as piped water and sanitation (for example, sewerage systems, flushing toilets, etc.) have direct impacts on people's health status and overall well-being. Having access to other services like electricity and telephones helps households to increase their productivity for income generation. A number of studies reveal that a household's access to basic services is highly and significantly correlated with a lower probability of being poor.

As shown in Table 13.8, in Vietnam the benefits generated from all types of basic services go to the non-poor more than the poor. Poor households in general have much greater access to piped water and electricity than sanitary systems: the PPP index for water and electricity are 0.86 and 0.80, respectively, when measured by the poverty gap ratio, whereas the indices for the other services are just 0.10 for sanitary facilities. As suggested in Table 13.8, benefits generated from sanitary services (collected waste and flushing toilets in this case) are highly skewed in favour of the non-poor. The benefits of all types of basic services are lower for the severity of poverty measure. This suggests that the ultra-poor have even lower access to the basic infrastructure services than the poor.

13.8 Case Studies II: 15 African countries

The study utilizes the unit-record household data sets from 15 African countries. These data sets were obtained from the African Household Survey Data Bank of the World Bank. The countries and year of the survey include: Burundi in 1998, Burkina Faso in 1998, Ivory Coast in 1998, Cameroon in 1996, Ethiopia in 2000, Ghana in 1998, Guinea in 1994, Gambia in 1998, Kenya in 1997, Madagascar in 2001, Mozambique in 1996, Malawi in 1997, Nigeria in 1996, Uganda in 1999, and Zambia in 1998.

The study uses the national poverty lines for the 15 countries, which have been obtained from various poverty assessment reports. These poverty lines were originally very crude, and did not take into account different needs of household members by age and gender. What is more, these poverty lines were not adjusted for the economies of scale which exist in large households. To overcome these shortcomings stemming from the official poverty lines, Kakwani and Subbarao (2005) made some modifications to the national poverty lines taking into account different needs of household members and economies of scale.

13.8.1   Targeting children: targeting vs universal

According to Coady, Grosh, and Hoddinott (2002), more than a quarter of targeted programmes in developing countries overall had regressive benefit incidence. For instance, they found that the poorest 40 per cent of the income distribution was receiving less than 40 per cent of poverty alleviation budgets. Such ineffective targeting of poor households suggests that the overall impact on poverty is much smaller than that it would have been if well targeted. Moreover, administrative costs involved in implementing any targeted programmes are very high. Much of the budget is spent on simply getting the resources to poor families. Consequently, the cost per unit of income transferred can be substantially large. Transfer programmes seem to be administratively complex as they require resources to undertake targeting of transfers and to monitor the recipients' actions. In this context, one might argue for a scenario of universal transfers.

In this section, we estimate the PPP indices under a universal transfer programme for the children aged between 5 and 16 years old. Under this programme, every child in this age group is assumed to receive a certain amount of transfer, irrespective of their poverty status. The results are presented in both Figure 13.1 and Table 13.9.

From Figures 13.1 and 13.2, it is important to note that the value of PPP index with perfect targeting is quite small compared to the index values shown for Thailand, Russia, and Vietnam. In fact, the PPP indices under perfect targeting show a small difference from the indices resulted from universal transfers. This suggests that perfect

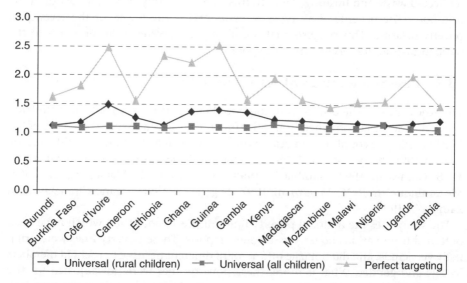

Figure 13.1   Pro-Poor Policy indices under universal transfers and perfect targeting (poverty gap ratio)

targeting may not be necessary in cases like these 15 African countries, where the rate of poverty is extremely high.

Table 13.9 carries two important messages. First, the results indicate that universal transfers will provide more absolute benefits to children from poor families than to those from non-poor families. Secondly, a universal-transfer scheme is likely to

Table 13.9 Pro-Poor Policy index for universal transfers to rural and urban areas

Country	Poverty gap ratio				Severity of poverty			
	Universal targeting			Perfect targeting	Universal targeting			Perfect targeting
	Rural	Urban	Total		Rural	Urban	Total	
Burundi	1.12	0.28	1.09	1.59	1.16	0.23	1.12	2.11
Burkina Faso	1.18	0.43	1.07	1.81	1.21	0.38	1.08	2.53
Côte d'Ivoire	1.51	0.60	1.10	2.51	1.63	0.45	1.09	3.63
Cameroon	1.28	0.60	1.09	1.54	1.32	0.50	1.08	2.05
Ethiopia	1.13	0.73	1.07	2.37	1.14	0.74	1.09	3.42
Ghana	1.39	0.54	1.09	2.24	1.47	0.42	1.10	3.03
Guinea	1.42	0.37	1.08	2.56	1.47	0.31	1.10	3.40
Gambia	1.37	0.65	1.08	1.56	1.56	0.39	1.08	2.00
Kenya	1.25	0.29	1.14	1.95	1.27	0.18	1.16	2.53
Madagascar	1.22	0.65	1.09	1.57	1.29	0.57	1.13	1.95
Mozambique	1.19	0.62	1.07	1.42	1.24	0.59	1.11	1.77
Malawi	1.17	0.18	1.07	1.52	1.21	0.09	1.09	1.93
Nigeria	1.14	1.13	1.14	1.54	1.12	1.21	1.16	1.91
Uganda	1.17	0.25	1.06	2.00	1.20	0.19	1.08	2.75
Zambia	1.23	0.76	1.05	1.45	1.34	0.57	1.06	1.80

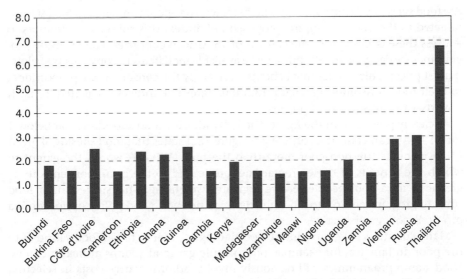

Figure 13.2 PPP indices under perfect targeting for 18 countries (poverty gap ratio)

bring an even more pro-poor outcome if it is implemented in the rural areas where most of poor children are. One exception is Nigeria. This occurs because poverty in Nigeria is widespread over both the urban and rural areas, whereas in the other countries it is predominant in rural areas.

One criticism of this methodology is that we do not have an actual scenario that can compare targeted transfers with universal transfers. Nevertheless, the main implication emerging from the PPP index is that if a transfer is given to every child of between 5 and 16 years of age, it is likely to provide more absolute benefits to poor children, particularly in rural areas. Furthermore, this analysis suggests that universal targeting of children may not be a bad policy option in rural areas in particular. This may be more cost effective as targeting only a small subgroup of children may involve large administrative costs in identifying the poor ones.

13.8.2   Food subsidies

Food subsidy programmes are under increasing scrutiny in many developing countries because their contributions to government budget deficits are generally large. According to critics, food subsidies pose both an unnecessary burden on the public budget and are economically inefficient as their benefits do not often accrue to the poor. These critics argue that due to improper targeting, a large part of food subsidies is leaked to better-off people in society.

Proponents of food subsidies argue, however, that such programmes are necessary to guarantee the supply of basic foods to the poor. Proponents claim that food subsidies are needed to protect the welfare and nutritional status of the economically disadvantaged because poor people spend higher proportions of their income on food than do rich ones.

Do food subsidy programmes benefit the poor or needy groups? Are the benefits of these programmes leaked to non-needy groups, such as high-income households? Are food subsidies to the population more (or less) pro-poor compared to food stamps targeted to the poor? Using the proposed PPP index, this subsection attempts to address these issues within the context of 15 African countries. Food subsidy programmes are designed to sell and/or make available food items to consumers at below-market prices. This implies that benefits received by the consumers are proportional to their food consumption. Figure 13.3 illustrates PPP indices calculated for both poverty gap and severity of poverty.

As clearly presented in the figure, the PPP index for food subsidies is far below 1 for all 15 African countries considered. Figure 13.3 states that food subsidy, if given to all, benefits the non-poor more than the poor. What is worse, the extent to which the benefits of these programmes are leaked to the non-poor tends to be greater if ultra-poor people receive a greater weighting. This suggests that food subsidy programmes in African countries may not be a good policy option from a pro-poor policy perspective.

Many countries have introduced food stamps in order to target food subsidies to the poor. In Jamaica, for example, poor people get food stamps at health clinics. Food stamp programmes will obviously involve administrative costs in selecting their beneficiaries. Given the administrative costs, we have calculated the degree

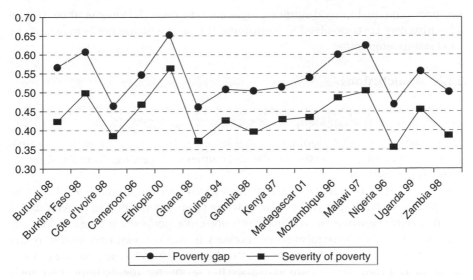

Figure 13.3 PPP indices for a food subsidy programme

Table 13.10 PPP index for giving food stamps to poor

	PPP index		Maximum value	
	Poverty gap ratio	*Severity of poverty*	*Poverty gap ratio*	*Severity of poverty*
Burundi 98	1.59	1.19	1.63	2.11
Burkina Faso 98	1.85	1.51	1.90	2.53
Côte d'Ivoire 98	2.56	2.13	2.72	3.63
Cameroon 96	1.54	1.32	1.64	2.05
Ethiopia 00	2.39	2.06	2.45	3.42
Ghana 98	2.22	1.77	2.30	3.03
Guinea 94	2.56	2.14	2.63	3.40
Gambia 98	1.53	1.21	1.61	2.00
Kenya 97	1.95	1.63	2.01	2.53
Madagascar 01	1.56	1.25	1.61	1.95
Mozambique 96	1.40	1.13	1.45	1.77
Malawi 97	1.52	1.22	1.56	1.93
Nigeria 96	1.48	1.12	1.58	1.91
Uganda 99	2.02	1.65	2.08	2.75
Zambia 98	1.45	1.12	1.50	1.80

of pro-poorness for food stamps targeting the poor. The results are presented in Table 13.10.

According to Table 13.10, food stamps given to the poor will bring about a highly pro-poor outcome. This is true for all 15 countries. This suggests that if food stamps are provided and targeted to the poor, their benefits will be received by the poor much more than the non-poor. All in all, food stamps given to the poor are much more pro-poor compared to food subsidy programmes in general. However, there will be administrative costs involved in identifying the poor who are the beneficiaries of food stamp programme.

13.9   Conclusions

This chapter has proposed a new index called the Pro-Poor Policy (PPP) index. This index measures the pro-poorness of government welfare programmes and basic service delivery in education, health and infrastructure. It is an attempt to introduce a methodology in assessing the techniques of targeting, to make it better suited for evaluation.

If our objective is to reduce poverty, then social transfer programmes should be designed in such a way that they lead to the maximum reduction in poverty under given resource constraints. To achieve this objective, perfect targeting would be an ideal solution. Two prerequisites are necessary in this context: first, that only the poor get all the benefits and, secondly, that benefits given to the poor are proportional to their income shortfalls in relation to the poverty line. To implement such a programme, we will need to have detailed information about people's incomes or their consumption expenditure. Such detailed information and the administrative abilities to use it are, of course, not present in most developing countries. So the policy makers have to resort to a form of proxy targeting which makes the transfers based on easily absorbable socioeconomic characteristics of the household. The proxy targeting can never achieve complete targeting success. In this respect, this study is an important methodological attempt to assess the targeting efficiency of government programmes by trying to find out how good the proxy targeting is, as compared to perfect targeting. In addition, the ROC curve that is generally used to measure targeting efficiency is proved to be a particular case of the proposed PPP index.

Using micro unit-record household surveys, the proposed methodology was applied to 18 countries, including Thailand, Russia, Vietnam, and 15 African countries. Major conclusions emerging from our empirical analysis can be synthesized as follows:

First, all the four welfare programmes implemented recently by the Thai government – that is, social pensions for the elderly, low income medical cards, health insurance cards and free school lunches were found to be pro-poor. In particular, welfare programmes designed to help the very poor – including low-income medical cards and free school lunches – were shown to be highly pro-poor, benefiting the ultra-poor more than the poor. In addition, our study has shown that the universal pension for those over 65 years of age is likely to be less pro-poor than the present old-age pension system. This suggests that the Thai government should continue with its present old-age pension scheme.

Secondly, the study found that the welfare system in Russia tends to benefit the poor more than the non-poor. Moreover, the absolute benefits of the welfare system do indeed flow more to the ultra-poor than to the poor, as suggested by a higher value of PPP index for the severity of poverty than the index value for the poverty gap. Furthermore, the study found that the overall Russian welfare programmes are reasonably well targeted. This was evident from the finding that the values of PPP indices of welfare programmes are quite close to (but still lower than) the expected value of index under perfect targeting. The study also found that welfare programmes – such as child allowances given to those aged below 16 years and also scholarships – are not pro-poor for the ultra-poor in particular. This suggests that these programmes may require a better targeting than the current system in a way that favours the ultra-poor living far below the poverty threshold.

Thirdly, basic services – health and education – in Vietnam were found to be mostly not pro-poor. From the health perspective, although government hospitals provide the highest quality of health care, the poor are unlikely to utilize them. This is, however, not true for commune health centres which appear to provide more services to individuals from poor households. Unfortunately, commune health centres do not provide high-quality health services because they are in general poorly staffed and equipped. On the whole, the poor in Vietnam have less access to quality health care. However, public primary schools in Vietnam were found to be pro-poor. This was due partly to the increase in public spending on education for the poor in the 1990s. In contrast, secondary education in Vietnam was found to be not pro-poor. What is more, the Vietnamese study has indicated that universal education at primary and lower secondary levels can provide more benefits to students from poor households, but this cannot be said for higher levels of education.

Fourthly, the study discussed *ex-ante* simulations of universal cash transfers to school-aged children in the 15 African countries. The results indicated that universal transfers will provide more absolute benefits to children from poor families than to those from non-poor families. In addition, the study found that all universal-transfer scheme is likely to produce an even more pro-poor outcome if it is implemented in the rural areas where most poor children reside. This finding was true for all the countries except for Nigeria, where poverty is widespread over both the urban and rural areas, while poverty is acute mainly in rural areas in the other countries.

Fifthly, the study found that in the 15 African countries, the value of PPP index with perfect targeting was quite small compared to the index values estimated for Thailand, Russia and Vietnam. The index value of perfect targeting for Thailand was far greater than that of perfect targeting for countries like Russia and Vietnam. In fact, in the case of the African countries the PPP indices under perfect targeting showed a small difference from the indices resulting from universal targeting of the children. Therefore, we may conclude that perfect targeting is not necessary for cases like these 15 African countries, where poverty is extremely high.

Finally, the study found that if food subsidy programmes are implemented through selling and/or making available food items to consumers at below-market prices, their absolute benefits are likely to go to rich people more than to poor ones within the context of the 15 African countries. Our finding suggests that food subsidies may not be a good policy option in the sense that their benefits are not received by the poor. Nevertheless, the study found that food stamps targeted to the poor are highly pro-poor.

Notes

1. Targeting indicators are generally based on the individual or family characteristics that are highly correlated with poverty but are readily observable. The elderly, the disabled, orphans, homeless, unemployed, family size, single-parent families are some of the examples of targeting indicators. Wodon (1997) has provided a thorough analysis of ROC curves to identify targeting indicators for Bangladesh.
2. The idea of redistributive efficiency has been taken from Coady and Skoufias (2004).
3. It must be pointed out that λ_m is not an upper bound of λ. Suppose we give a fixed amount of transfer only to the poor, then $b(x) = b$ (if $x < z$) and 0 otherwise. From this, it can be easily seen that $\lambda = 1/H$ for the entire class of additive and separable poverty measures as defined in (13.1). In some cases, this programme may offer larger values of λ compared to the case of perfect targeting.
4. For a detailed discussion on Thailand and Russian poverty lines, see Kakwani (2000, 2004).

References

Coady, D., M. Grosh and J. Hoddinott (2002) 'The Targeting of Transfers in Developing Countries: Review of Experiences and Lessons', Social Safety Net Primer Series. Washington, DC: World Bank.

Coady, D. and E. Skoufias (2004) 'On the Targeting and Redistribution Efficiencies of Alternative Transfer Instruments', *Review of Income and Wealth*, Series 50, No. 1.

Foster, J., J. Greer and E. Thorbecke (1984) 'A Class of Decomposable Poverty Measures', *Econometrica* 52(3), 761–6.

Grosh, M. (1994) 'Administering Targeted Social Programmes in Latin America: From Platitudes to Practice', World Bank Regional and Sectoral Studies. Washington, DC: World Bank.

Haddad, L. J. and R. Kanbur (1991) 'Intra-household Inequality and the Theory of Targeting', Policy, Research, and External Affairs Working Paper. Washington, DC: World Bank.

Jimenez, E. (1993) 'Cash versus In-kind Transfers', Lecture Notes, EDI seminar on Labor Market and the Social Safety Net in the Former Soviet Union/CIS countries. Washington, DC: World Bank.

Kakwani, N. (2000) 'Issues in Setting Absolute Poverty Lines', Poverty and Social Development Paper No. 4. Manila: Asian Development Bank.

Kakwani, N. and Z. Sajaia (2004) 'New Poverty Thresholds for Russia', unpublished mimeo. Washington, DC: World Bank.

Kakwani, N. and H. H. Son (2004) 'Pro-Poor Growth: Asian Experience', Working paper No. 1. Brazil: International Poverty Centre.

Kakwani, N. and K. Subbarao (2005) 'Ageing and Poverty in Africa and the Role of Social Pensions', Working Paper No. 6. Brazil: International Poverty Centre.

Kanbur, R., M. Keen and M. Tuomala (1994) 'Labour Supply and Targeting in Poverty Alleviation Programs' *The World Bank Economic Review*, 8, 191–211.

Karni, E. (1999) 'Optimal Unemployment Insurance: A Guide to the Literature', Social Protection Discussion Paper No. 9906. Washington, DC: World Bank.

Nguyen N. N. (2002) 'Trends in the Education Sector from 1993–1998', World Bank Policy Research Working Paper. Washington DC: World Bank.

Rodriguez, A. and C. A. Herran, (2000) *Secondary Education in Brazil*. Washington, DC: Inter-American Development Bank.

Tabor, S. R. (2002) 'Assisting the Poor with Cash: Design and Implementation of Social Transfer Programmes', Social Protection Discussion Paper. Washington, DC: World Bank.

Trivedi, P. (2002) 'Patterns of Health Care Utilization in Vietnam', World Bank Policy Research Working Paper. Washington, D.C: World Bank.

Wodon, Q. (1997) 'Targeting the Poor using ROC Curves', *World Development*, 25(12), 2083–92.

Index